"To say Buckley is merely an entertainer is to do him gross injustice. His thoughts and epithets crackle from the page; he engages himself squarely in all the issues of the day, and his gadfly stings often draw blood. Buckley is a man of character and conviction."

—*New York Times*

WILLIAM F. BUCKLEY, Jr.

Buckley at his biting brilliant best. The man liberals love to hate takes on John Lindsay, Lyndon Johnson, Joe Namath, Richard Nixon, Eugene McCarthy, The Beatles; talks of Yale and Harvard, pot, sex and sailing; savages Gore Vidal.

"In our time, free minds are desperately rare and precious, and in Buckley I detect one."

—Malcolm Muggeridge, *Esquire*

"There is no one in the world I would rather take lessons on superciliousness from than Mr. Buckley."

—Arthur Schlesinger, 'Jr.

BY THE SAME AUTHOR

THE JEWELER'S EYE

For Old Lady (Marjorie Otis Gifford)

—with love and gratitude

ACKNOWLEDGMENTS

My thanks to the proprietors of the *New York Times Almanac*, the *Atlantic Monthly*, *Esquire*, *Life*, *Look*, *National Review*, *The New Guard*, the New York *Times*, *Rudder*, the *Saturday Evening Post*, and the Washington Star Syndicate, for whom I originally wrote the material in this book. My special thanks to Miss Agatha Schmidt, without whose help I could not possibly have managed this book. In fact, I cannot imagine how anybody manages a book without Aggie.

CONTENTS

INTRODUCTION

The Jeweler's Eye, published in 1968, was well received critically and sold well. I like to think that it was for *both* reasons that Mr. Walter Minton of Putnam's asked me to bring together another collection, but I do not know him well enough to ask. In any event, I am grateful to him for his prodding, and happy that some of my material is thought to be worth reading a while after it is composed.

But then I am sounding coy, and that simply will not do. *The Jeweler's Eye* was subtitled "A Book of Irresistible Political Reflections," a defi that went strangely unresented by the critical press: indeed, I don't think I received a single note of protest even from a reader. I have upped the ante with the subtitle to this book. I don't believe I'd have dared to use it ten years ago, away back when so many people believed that some things *are* Revealed. Nowadays, a "revelation" is taken by most of the reading public as metaphor, which is certainly the way in which I use it, because I do not like blasphemy and attempt not to be blasphemous and hope that if anyone deploys that word against me, it will be understood that he is using a metaphor.

I was much struck by the passage in the Bible from which I wrested the title to this book. It will be found only in the King James Version, succeeding translations having gone to great lengths to find ways of rendering whatever the Greek original was, away from "whithersoever the governor listeth," on over in the direction of "wherever the pilot desires." A lot of semantical commotion; whereas I desire only to make the unobtrusive point that indeed, as St. James points out, the tongue is a mighty instrument, that it can indeed exert great influence on human affairs, that that influence should be exerted in the direction that the individual who uses his tongue consciously desires: that mine is at the service of people and ideas I venerate; that I do not understand myself, most of the time, to be at play, but rather, hoping to effect events and to affect people. Whether I succeed is a question to debate—those who care to do so—and, according as they are disposed, to be glad or sorry over. The point of it is that this governor does greatly desire to influence, along the lines he most ardently listeth. There is no other reason for living by the word.

W. F. B.

Stamford, Connecticut
January 3, 1970

In many things we offend all. If any man offend not in word, the same is a perfect man, and able also to bridle the whole body. Behold, we put bits in the horses' mouths, that they may obey us; and we turn about their whole body. Behold also the ships, which though they be so great, and are driven of fierce winds, yet are turned about with a very small helm, whithersoever the governor listeth. Even so the tongue is a little member, and boasteth great things. Behold, how great a matter a little fire kindleth!

JAMES 3

THE GOVERNOR LISTETH

A Book of Inspired Political Revelations

I. POLITICS

1968

REFLECTIONS ON THE ASSASSINATION
OF MARTIN LUTHER KING

April 19, 1968

Address to the American Society of Newspaper Editors

Ladies and gentlemen. Although I was carefully coached by my devoted friend Harry Elmlark, I did neglect to ask him what is perhaps the critical question, namely: Am I supposed to make a good impression on *you;* or are *you* supposed to make a good impression on me? As a conservative, I suppose that I should adopt the prudent alternative. And in my case, to do so would seem to be congruent with the national posture of the moment: We seek to please. The President of the United States implores the President of North Vietnam to accept the earnest of his American sincerity. The pastor of an

ethically uptight suburban community church begs Stokely
Carmichael to believe that our intentions are godly. It is
thought to be cantankerous to behave otherwise toward
our critics. It has been a long, long time since William
Butler Yeats, upon hearing criticisms of the Lord Mayor
of Dublin for not having done anything recently to
commend himself to the people of Dublin, asked what had
the people of Dublin recently done to commend
themselves to the Lord Mayor? But, of course, when in
doubt, try servility. We column writers are, I am led to
believe, the original Toms. Murray Kempton recently
observed that the Communist *Worker,* on announcing its
intentions last January of becoming a daily publication,
could get all the favorable publicity it needed merely by
announcing that it was in the market for daily columnists.
Mr. Kempton, although in some respects he is innocent
beyond the imagination of Walt Disney, is as a columnist
the noblest of us all: "Columnists," Mr. Kempton
reminisced, "have attacked Albert Schweitzer, the Pope in
Rome, Mrs. Roosevelt, and even J. Edgar Hoover, but I
can think of only one who ever attacked his publisher.
That, of course, was Westbrook Pegler, who disappeared.
A more typical case"—Mr. Kempton continues—"is that
of Joseph Alsop, a man whose pride towers at least as
high as Pegler's ever did. I remember when we trailed into
Indianapolis with Eisenhower in 1952 and Joe Alsop said
he was going to dinner with Eugene Pulliam, publisher of
the Indianapolis *Star.* Now Alsop is a man I would expect
to be unable to look at Indianapolis without returning to
his hotel room with the sheets over his face; he has been
known to send the Hollandaise sauce back at Maxim's; he
would not normally endure twaddle at dinner from Dean
Acheson. From what I know of Eugene Pulliam's
generosity, he was probably paying Joe twenty dollars a
week for the column; from what I know of Pulliam's
charm, I would sooner dine with Senator Hruska; I know
nothing of his table, which must be unimaginable. Yet Joe
Alsop spoke of the prospect of dinner with Pulliam not

with alarm but with delight. If Malcolm X had been a columnist, he would have Tommed to D. Tennant Bryan of the Richmond *News-Leader*."

Now of course Mr. Kempton, in order to make his point, is saying a lot of unjust things about some very nice people, a technique any editor will understand, if not sympathize with.

But it never *has* been all that clear what are the ideal relations between the columnist and the editor. I think of Conrad's notions about the proper relations between the sailor and the sea. The sea, Conrad observes—and he is not lightly dismissed by any philosopher of the sea—is the enemy. But it is the irresistible enemy. The sea is the creature which, at the margin, can drown the sailor. But however tempestuous, however arbitrary, however sullen the sea can be—however much like an editor—the sea maintains its basic integrity; and if the sailor observes the rules, if he maintains his guard, if he propitiates the elements, he is permitted to survive, and the experience is sublime. Imagine the thrill of negotiating successfully a passage across the editorial page of the New York *Post!* I feel a kinship with Sir Francis Chichester. I am certain that, upon approaching the Horn, he asked himself agonizingly, "What, what is Dolly preparing for me?"

I had a curious experience, which I presume to mention to you only because you are, visibly, on your best behavior. I wrote a syndicated column for eighteen months before meeting a single editor or publisher of any of the newspapers that carried my column. At first I thought this healthy, in a perverse sort of way—a way of proving something about the essential integrity of the whole process. But two unruly thoughts stalked that romantic notion. One was that many of my generous patrons were probably patronizing not me, but the undeniable Harry Elmlark; the other was that, in fact, I was feeling a little lonely. I yearned—I still do —occasionally to begin a column by saying: "Hi! Say, Boston, how do you like Teddy's latest nomination to the federal judiciary? Pretty offputting, no? How's the weather in Boston, by the way? Good for a little weekend rioting? Good morning, Mr. Manchester, and what do you propose to do *now* about the state of New Hampshire? Offer it to the Vietcong as a part of a general settlement? Look here, L.A., if you think that by cutting my last three pro-Reagan columns, you are succeeding in telling me something, you are absolutely correct." But no, the conventions always seem to close in on us, don't they? The same conventions that keep us from telling a man to his face what we are willing—indeed anxious—to say about him when he is gone, and we are writing his obituary or speaking his eulogy. As you can see, I do not know what is, finally, the way in which the columnist and the editor can approach each other to their mutual advantage. I know only that here I am, and there you are, and it would be nice if we managed to touch each other.

I prefer, as you might expect, to ponder the delinquencies of editors, over against the delinquencies of columnists. Perhaps you will understand my yielding to this temptation, purely in human terms. After all, the editor can discharge the unsatisfactory columnist, but the columnist has no way of discharging the unsatisfactory editor—assuming such a creature existed. Mr. Howard K. Smith recently resigned from our profession, complaining that editors are irresponsibly attracted to the reporting of irresponsible people. I understand his point of view, in particular in an age that appears to be dominated by the pseudoevent. I remember being in Africa a few years ago and picking up an English-language newspaper whose headline read: AMERICAN NEGROES TO BE DEPORTED TO AFRICA IN 1972. That, I thought, was certainly a scoop, if ever I saw one. I read on, and the story, datelined Arlington, said: "George Lincoln Rockwell, commander of the American Nazi Party, announced today that he expected to win the governorship of Virginia in 1970, and the Presidency in 1972, and that he would instantly undertake to remove all American

Negroes to Africa." That of course is parody, the kind of news story Mr. Herblock most easily festoons. But the thought sticks with me that the decision of the editor of that newspaper in Liberia to give such prominence to such a story is not so easily explained by suggesting that he is an agent of the Communist Party of Monrovia, or that he was educated in America and was refused admission into Delta Kappa Upsilon at the University of Pennsylvania. What caused that headline, the sensationalism aside, was at least one part a disposition to think ill of America; is related to the general disposition—certainly journalistic; but also, I think, intellectual—to think ill of America. I find that certainly this theme, so evident abroad, is reflected *mutatis mutandis* in American journalism.

I grant two contributing factors. One of them is neurotic. The theologians of yore identified the sin of scrupulosity, that heresy from which people suffer who believe that they are necessarily unclean and, therefore, undeserving. The other factor is virtuous, altogether noble, reflecting that simple, eternal concern with one's shortcomings which one associates with the dogged discomposure of the saints. But I do believe that some of the featured reactions a fortnight ago to the slaughter of Dr. Martin Luther King reflected the first rather than the second disposition. The Christian idea is the acknowledgment that all of us—those who are dead, those who are alive, and those who are yet unborn—conspired to make necessary the sacrifice of Christ. But that metaphysical communion in sin, which may bind us in our looser complicity with evil, hardly commits us—or does it?—in the murder of Martin Luther King. I found myself, twenty-four hours after the tragedy of Memphis, Tennessee, debating on the subject of civil rights, before an audience of 6,000 against Mr. Julian Bond—in Nashville, Tennessee. I shall not soon forget the solicitude of the chancellor of Vanderbilt University, who brought Mr. Bond and me together at the corner of the cafeteria

moments before the debate and whispered to us: "My
men went over every square inch of the gymnasium late
this afternoon"—he beamed triumphantly—"and we
didn't find a *thing*." Mr. Bond and I registered our
gratitude—what other response is appropriate?—and the
chancellor continued, still *sotto voce:* "And in addition, I
want you to know that I have distributed ninety-five
plainclothesmen throughout the audience." That is
Southern hospitality.

Mr. Bond, who began the evening's discussion,
punctuated his manifesto against America with the heroic
trope: *"All of this was killed last night at Memphis."* By
"all of this" he meant—indeed he said that he meant—all
that which America has ever claimed for itself. Any
pretensions that we have to justice. Any that we have for
the rule of law. Any that we have for equality,
compassion, mutual esteem, love. The audience cheered
him. That young audience thus sought to atone for the
crime against Martin Luther King by offering its body,
prostrate—once again for reasons both pathological and
sublime—in expiation. Its own innocent—virginal—body,
unflexed, to the scourges of Julian Bond. There is a sense
in which that was a chivalrous reaction, young and
generous. But I do not understand that as an adequate
explanation for the more considered reaction of older
America. *Time* magazine is able to orchestrate whatever
response it desires to project to any American crisis, and
the editors choose in the current issue to feature letters
which raise doubts about the "worthwhileness" of the
American republic. The lead letter, from California, says:
"Martin Luther King was murdered because he was our
uncomfortable conscience. I am filled with shame and
loathing for our race." The correspondent here betrayed
genocidal convictions of the kind Dr. King fought
against—never mind. Again: "When statesmen look to
give aid to the uncivilized and underdeveloped countries
of the world, please let ours be first on their list"—a
moving letter from a lady in New Jersey who, perhaps

understandably, does not go on to list the countries so
manifestly qualified to instruct us in the ways of
civilization. . . . And a gentleman from Arizona says:
"The land of the free and the home of the brave—and
probably the only civilized nation on earth where a winner
of the Nobel Peace Prize, holding no political office, can
be assassinated while serving on his mission"—an
objurgation so vastly confused and confusing as to require
hours to unravel, recalling the limitations of analysis, the
unhappy prospects of any disavowal that would begin
patiently with the observation that, for instance, Mr.
Pasternak was not even permitted to accept the Nobel
Prize, that the subsequent moral assassination of
Pasternak was a collective undertaking, coolly executed by
a killer state. But no, the mood is—hate America. That
isn't, needless to say, the mood of the majority of the
editors of American periodicals: Their attitude is not one
of complicity with the general *Weltschmerz;* it is
something altogether different, having to do—as I
understand it—with a general sense of shared responsibility.

I judge this reaction, even when the intention is to
harness it to ends that we approve of, to be
philosophically dangerous. Blood guilt is the matrix of
genocide. I asked the audience of 6,000 people at
Vanderbilt University whether they were representative of
America. Were there rich men in the audience? Poor men?
Old, young? Southerners, Easterners, Westerners, Middle
Westerners? Catholic? Protestant? Jewish? College graduates? High-school dropouts? Yes—yes—yes—yes— All
right, then, raise your hands, those of you who consider
yourselves implicated in the assassination of Martin Luther
King.

"I am filled with shame and loathing for my race," says
the featured correspondent of *Time* magazine. Why?
There, at Nashville, not one person could be got to profess
satisfaction from the great perversion at Memphis. Who is
it that we Americans are so busily engaged in blaming?

Not when you come down to asking individuals about it, when you pose the question directly to 6,000 members of the community at Nashville, Tennessee—not them; not, one may be sure, the editors of *Time* magazine—they are surely blameless. It is always . . . those other people—those people whose ranks yield forth the John Wilkes Booths and the Lee Harvey Oswalds, those few who roam about the country, seeking the destruction not only of individual souls, but of the soul of America.

Me, I say this: that more significant by far than the ghastly executions of John Kennedy and Martin Luther King—acts committed by isolatable and isolated men—more significant by far is the spontaneous, universal grief of a community which in fact considers itself aggrieved. That is the salient datum in America, not that we bred the aberrant executioners of John Kennedy and Martin Luther King, but that we generated the most widely shared and the most intensely felt sense of grief: such grief over the loss of Mr. Kennedy and Mr. King as is felt over the loss of one's brothers.

That is what I judge to be a newsworthy datum; a point I stress not because I feel the need to flatter the United States of America, but because I feel the need to reassure the United States of America, which is the land where I was born and choose to live; which is the land where you were born and choose to live; which land, I feel increasingly, needs us all as her devoted bodyguards, even as Messrs. Kennedy and King needed more bodyguards at the crucial moment in *their* histories. She needs us, however quarrelsome; however disparate our views; however pronounced our separations. I feel that we should be grateful, whatever our differences, to be facing the sea—this sea; this enemy—in this bark. I do believe that the time is overdue to profess our continuing faith in this country and in its institutions—including its press.

THE AGONY OF MR. NIXON

December 19, 1967

A year ago Mr. Richard Nixon, reminiscing with a visitor, confessed that he had come by a maxim rather late in life which seems to be obvious; namely, that a Republican cannot win with the support of the right wing only, but that neither can he win without the support of his right wing. In 1960 Nixon needed a mere handful of extra votes, whether left or right, to win the election. It wasn't that loss that hurt him professionally—it isn't bad for anyone's prestige to miss being President of the United States by one-tenth of 1 percent of the vote. What he is even now reeling from is the California election, and what he did there, in 1962, was to neglect the conservatives. They beat him. And he knows that.

And now he is up against the same problem, how at once to commend himself to conservatives and liberals alike. Mostly, of course, politicians accomplish that kind of thing by a melodious swivel-hipping—who, for instance, except the most practiced historian, can remember where General Eisenhower stood on matters in general that separated the right from the left? But every now and again there is no way out, as when, a week ago, Richard Nixon found himself all alone, in front of a microphone, the spotlight fixed remorselessly on him, at a testimonial dinner to, of all people, Jacob Javits, senior Senator from New York, the man about whom the late George Sokolsky once remarked that he has about as much business in the Republican Party as Leon Trotsky.

What did Nixon do? Examine the range of choices. To begin with, there he was—he had accepted the invitation.

What to do now? Well, he might have fainted. But there are dangers in that, too—the voters might reason that a President Nixon might face a crisis as serious in the course of his stay in the White House as finding something pleasant to say about Senator Javits, and it would hardly do to faint when such crises occur. Well, the next alternative would have been to say something more or less neutral about the state of the world and sit down. But that would have offended the liberals. They wanted a little unction. The third alternative was to give it to them, which Mr. Nixon did. He spoke favorably of Senator Javits in a general sort of a way. And then he added a specific piece of information, most dreadfully upsetting to New York's conservatives, that if a primary fight developed, he would support Mr. Javits. "CONSERVATIVES 'STARTLED' BY NIXON'S BACKING JAVITS" was the headline in the New York *Times*.

In fairness to Mr. Nixon, it should be observed that although indeed the tradition is for senior party members to stay out of primary fights, New York's Conservative Party, which is the main philanthropic force behind the forthcoming challenge to Mr. Javits from within the Republican Party, is not itself intending to play by the rules which it desires Mr. Nixon to play by. Because the conservatives intend not merely to throw their support behind the man who challenges Mr. Javits in the Republican primary. They intend to continue to support that man even after he is beaten by Mr. Javits, if indeed he is, which of course is likely. It is one thing to say to Mr. Nixon: Look, stay out of a contest, and we'll see who wins; if Javits wins, we'll step aside. The conservatives have no intention whatever of stepping aside, and indeed there is no reason why the conservatives should, it being their function to present the voters with a choice at election time; and there is no choice at all when it comes to Javits against a typical New York Democrat.

On the other hand, Mr. Nixon needn't really have got into the matter of the primary. Perhaps Mr. Javits, or friends of Mr. Javits, approached Nixon ahead of time, reasoning that he could do more than any other New Yorker to derail the conservatives. It seems more likely that Mr. Nixon was directly asked to make that observation than that he preferred it spontaneously. Because he has indeed hurt himself with the conservatives. And the contest in New York State may very well be crucial during the 1968 elections. Indeed the *Civil Service Leader* ("America's largest weekly for public employees," November 28) points out that the conservatives have already acquired the balance of power in many districts and makes a startling prediction: "The party's roots are now so deep that it could very well be the deciding factor in which column the state's forty-three electoral votes are cast in 1968." At this point Mr. Nixon needs liberal support more than he needs conservative support; but to quote a seasoned politician who learned the lesson late, he needs conservative support, too.

THE GOOD SENATOR McCARTHY

November 18, 1967

It looks as though Senator Eugene McCarthy of Minnesota is the chosen instrument through which left-leaning Democrats will commit damage on President Lyndon Johnson, and of course Senator McCarthy is splendidly qualified. On the one hand, he is meticulously liberal—never ever has he erred in the direction of common sense when the alternative was to vote liberal. On the other hand, he has managed not to get himself so far out on the left limb as to fall down and go kook, like Henry Wallace. When Mr. Wallace was fired from the Cabinet by President Harry Truman, it was generally accepted that he had become an ideological weirdo, as indeed he proved to be. History certifies that Mr. Wallace's third-party movement was dominated by the Communist Party of the United States, which means dominated by Joseph Stalin. Eugene McCarthy is not a type so easily taken over.

Now the difficulties. They are several. In case you didn't know it, Senator Eugene McCarthy is not a fan of Senator Robert Kennedy. Those who demand proof of that assertion cannot be satisfied. There is no proof, at least none of the kind you could discount with your local banker. It is generally remembered that at Los Angeles, at the Democratic Convention in 1960, the single most impassioned speech was by Eugene McCarthy—in favor of Adlai Stevenson. The Kennedy forces looked on, unamused. Not that they were afraid that Senator McCarthy, whose oratorical cadenza was dazzling in its beauty, could succeed in changing the prescribed outcome of the Los Angeles Convention, which was clearly Kennedy. But they did fear that Senator McCarthy's extraordinarily effective oratory might have the effect, on certain critically situated people, of suggesting to them that the nomination of John F. Kennedy had nothing whatever to do with democratic idealism, that, in fact, John Kennedy got himself the nomination by wresting it from the truly qualified dauphin of democratic idealism, Adlai Stevenson.

But then Mr. Kennedy was not only nominated, but also elected; and—which is important in purely political discussions—martyrized. It was well known that Senator Eugene McCarthy wanted most anxiously to be nominated as Vice President in 1964, back when it was not known, until the very last minute, just whom Lyndon Johnson would designate as Vice President. Mr. Johnson, exercising his pathological concern for secrecy, invited Hubert Humphrey, Thomas Dodd, and Eugene McCarthy to Atlantic City, suggesting to each in turn that the question was unsettled in his mind which of the three he would finally designate.

If Lyndon Johnson actually had made up his mind, he certainly succeeded in concealing the fact from the three postulants. I was there, at Atlantic City, when Senator Eugene McCarthy called a press conference, twenty-four hours before the designation of the Vice President, at which press conference Senator McCarthy, who arrived thirty-five minutes late—always the sign of the successful, or at least optimistic politician—flirted oo-la-la with the press, suggesting that he was in a position positively to demonstrate his relative desirability as a Vice Presidential candidate.

How far, now, it has gone! Lyndon Johnson took himself another bride. Eugene McCarthy, who had held out against John Kennedy at Los Angeles, found himself spurned by someone who, one might have thought, was at least an ally of convenience. Now Eugene McCarthy is offering himself to dissatisfied Democrats as the alternative to Lyndon Johnson. The instinctive assumption of professional observers is that Senator McCarthy is part of Senator Bobby Kennedy's far-flung operations. In fact, this appears to be unlikely—Senator McCarthy retains healthy disrespect for Senator Kennedy.

On the other hand, there is no doubting that Senator McCarthy's campaign is most likely to benefit Senator Kennedy. If Mr. McCarthy succeeds in draining a considerable vote away from President Johnson, then the chances of a Republican's succeeding to the White House are obviously augmented. And if the Republicans win in 1968, the influence of Lyndon Johnson and Hubert Humphrey at the Democratic Convention in 1972 will be, to search exactly for the right word, nugatory. The nominee would be, all things being otherwise equal, Kennedy.

Which is why, although the two gentlemen, Messrs. Kennedy and McCarthy, do not work together in tandem, nevertheless there is a pro-Kennedy symbiosis in the script viewed whole. Eugene McCarthy may well (a) sink Johnson in '68; and (b) elect Kennedy in '72. That is rather a lot for a dreamy Stevensonian to accomplish, wouldn't you agree?

THE STATE OF THE UNION

January 23, 1968

The President, it is said, handwrote the version of the State of the Union Address we all heard, and the credibility gap notwithstanding, it is altogether plausible that it is so. It was a pretty awful speech, awful in every sense. In concept, it was utterly unimaginative. In style, totally, relentlessly lacking in distinction. Mr. Johnson's delivery—surely?—is the worst in history. My own memory goes back only as far as FDR, who was supreme, and they say that President Buchanan was pretty bad, but sight unseen, I'd listen to James Buchanan read through the entire encyclopedia, rather than the incumbent recite one poem by Edgar Guest.

The principal deficiencies of the speech have been fully remarked—the failure to integrate the Vietnam War to our foreign policy; the failure to explore the root causes of the restlessness to which he fleetingly alluded; the encyclopedia enumeration of all the blessings he has conferred upon us (the President even found time to mention his program for the redwood trees in California, at which point Mr. Arthur Schlesinger leaned over to me and whispered, "Better redwoods than deadwoods," whereupon I granted him a plenary indulgence for all his past sins); etc. etc. etc. But besides all that, the speech was peppered with irritating phrases of little moment except insofar as they suggest the profile of the President's thought.

What are we to make, for instance, of the sentence "Tonight our nation is accomplishing more for its people than has ever been accomplished before"? A moment's concentration on that sentence leads one to the brink of total dismay. Consider, to begin with, the syntax. What does he mean, "tonight"? Apparently, a synonym—more technically, a synecdoche—for "at this point." But the clumsiness is distracting. And then again, on the point of syntax, if one learns English good like a President should, you don't change from the active voice ("our nation is accomplishing") to the passive voice (". . . than has ever been accomplished") unless required to by a great national depression or a world war. And finally, what is this about "the nation" accomplishing something for "its people"? The nation *is* its people. If he meant to say that the people of America are accomplishing a great deal for the people of America, then that's okay, only hardly worth saying because it is tautological. One cannot refrain from suspecting that what the President had in mind was "the government"—that he meant to say that "the government" is accomplishing more for the people. Whereupon one objects: But *the government* isn't *the nation*. And don't forget that, buddy. And tempted moreover to insist: The people don't belong to the government, so that Johnson should not have referred to the nation's accomplishing more for "its" people.

Let those who will say that this is nitpicking. I write for those who care to ponder the President's thought habits, which, ideally, should be all of the nation's people.

Or consider this: "Surely a nation that can go to the moon can place a decent home within the reach of its families." Once again, a statement which, read fast or heard fast, tends to cross the stage quickly and disappear into the wings of platitude. But it is a very foolish thought. In the first place, it is the government that decides whether to go to the moon. And the way the government gets to the moon is by taking money from the people which might otherwise have been spent in building more houses. Since the government's decisions are backed by the power of the police, what the government desires, the government gets. In a totalitarian state like Russia's, the government can decide to go to the moon even if it means that in its capital city families have to live two to a room, separated by a curtain. It is relentlessly clear that the government of Russia couldn't possibly go to the moon if it permitted the people the freedom to spend their money as they saw fit. And it is relentlessly clear that the United States will have fewer houses on account of our decision to go to the moon.

And again, what is this business about a nation's "placing" a decent home within the reach of "its" (there we go again) families? The government has practically nothing to do with houses, if you consider government-built or subsidized houses as a percentage of the whole. (Between 1950 and 1960, free enterprise built 18,000,000 housing units, while the government, net, destroyed 100,000.) The people of America come within reach of houses as a result of their own exertions and as a result of the disposition of other people to save. What makes it difficult for people to build their houses is: (a) taxes (taken by the government); (b) inflation (caused by the government); and (c) restrictive labor-union policies (protected by the government). The most useful thing the government could do to place decent homes within the reach of its people is to go away.

And so on. Fortunately, the state of the union is better than the state of its President's mind.

THE PRESSURES MOUNT ON
SENATOR McCARTHY

February 17, 1968

The *Village Voice* is a little New York journal which energetically does its iconoclastic push-ups once a week and sort of looks about—whee!—at its audience, as if to say, Have you *ever* seen anybody as irreverent as us-folks? The editors do it all with considerable panache, and although the readership is confined largely to adolescents who blush with the mischievous delight of seeing four-letter words in print, it also has a readership among bitter-end belletrists who enjoy the abandon of its criticisms, and Carthusian leftists who devour its dogmas even unto the fourth generation. One can dismiss the *Village Voice,* as the critic did Thomas Hardy, commenting that his work was the village atheist talking to the village idiot, a penetration Hardy never survived; but it is not the way to treat the *Voice,* which has working for it here and there talented writers. So that what the *VV* is saying about Bobby Kennedy is worth looking at, worth meditating.

I have in mind a recent article by *VV* columnist Jack Newfield, which really lays it on the line. What he says to Bobby Kennedy is tougher, more relentless, than anything ever ascribed to the Founding Father. He says to Bobby Kennedy: Either run for President, NOW, or lose us, Forever . . . There are those of us who would run nonstop to lose the *Village Voice* forever. But it is a definite part of Robert's constituency, one might say the glamorous part, and therefore it must be assumed that the *VV* and its epigoni are among those voices which are causing Senator Robert that dark night of the soul about which we have been reading.

Mr. Newfield begins by saying that Eugene McCarthy's campaign is—but let me use his language—bowdlerized. "Let the unhappy, brutal truth come out," he begins, even as Cotton Mather might have begun. "Eugene McCarthy's campaign is a disaster. It has been run as if King Constantine was the manager. McCarthy's speeches are dull, vague, and without either — or poetry. He is lazy and vain . . ." Mr. Newfield goes on to say that Senator McCarthy's failure leaves the radicals without an obvious thing to do except:

(1) ". . . to start organizing now for disruption of the Democratic Convention in Chicago next August." Yes, says Mr. Newfield, he knows all the arguments against this type of activity, but truthfully, he is tired of them. "There may be no other way of saying that LBJ is simply not my President, the Democrats are not my party, and Vietnam is not my war."

The obvious comment being, of course: What right does he, then, have to disrupt the Democratic Convention? One surely disrupts, assuming one wishes to disrupt, those conventions that are one's own. If Mr. Johnson is not Mr. Newfield's President, and the Democratic Party is not his party, why then shouldn't Mr. Newfield go about founding another party, which will nominate another candidate? Like Spock, say, or Jules Feiffer? I bet it never *occurred* to him.

And then (2) the second proposal, to draft Kennedy. Here Mr. Newfield gets very rough-tough, as though he were Edward G. Robinson talking to a Mafioso who had conscience twinges about the proposed caper.

"Kennedy," he explains, "is now torn about what to do. The part of him that is the cold, cynical political manager with an instinct for arithmetic majorities thinks he can't win, that even if he wrests the nomination from LBJ, the party would be so split he could never win in November. This is the 'Bad Bobby' . . . conventional, safe, ambitious. And if it finally comes to dominate the rest of Kennedy, and kill off the other, subterranean [exactly the right word] Kennedy, our hopes for him will turn to ashes."

But, says Newfield chiliastically, "there is another Kennedy. It is the Kennedy who sounds like Fidel Castro . . . Kennedy's best quality is his ability to be himself, to be authentic in the existential sense. This is the quality the young identify with so instinctively in Kennedy. And it is this quality Kennedy will lose if he doesn't make his stand now against Johnson. He will become a robot mouthing dishonest rhetoric like all other politicians. To everything there is a time, to everything there is a season."

Had enough? So undeniably, has poor Robert had enough. Whether to strike out with Freak House, or stay within the Democratic Party. And poor Eugene McCarthy. He dissents from Vietnam but refuses—so far—to be carried away into irresponsibility; declines the way of Henry Wallace. One confronts the dreadful possibility of having to vote, next November, for a Presidential candidate unauthorized by the *Village Voice*. That would certainly prove that American democracy is without — or poetry.

L—ND—N J—HNS—N

April 2, 1968

The left was not content merely to abominate the policies of Lyndon Johnson; they went further and chose to abominate the man. Now they are going one step further—the final step, which is to justify their hatred intellectually. Dr. Benjamin Spock, the great humanitarian, can say, as he recently did, that he did not know it was possible to "despise a man the way I despise Lyndon Johnson." One passes off such comment as one would the man who despises a personal allergy ("I can't stand garlic!"). But we are being invited to despise not merely Johnson's policies, not merely Johnson's style, but Johnson's person. And to feel proud of ourselves for doing so. In the name of humanity, you understand.

It is an old saw that professional tolerance teachers, almost all of them, harbor foxes in their bosoms that eat anyone who disagrees. Show me the most adamantly liberal professor at any university, and I will show you the likeliest candidate for dean of illiberal arts and letters. The critics of Lyndon Johnson who specialize in Johnson's inhumanity are beginning to display toward him what can only be described as attitudes such as are prerequisite to the kind of barbarism they are imputing to him.

Leaf through a little book cravenly entitled *LBJ Lampooned*, which does to Johnson what Bosch would have hesitated to do to adulterous Popes. Now this is not accidental vituperation. A long introduction by my friend Mr. Jules Feiffer, about whom it could be said that he apparently hates Johnson because Johnson is incapable of hating as intensely as Feiffer, solemnly records and ardently applauds the progress in anti-Johnsonism from vigorous dissent to personal loathing. "There are charitable ways of describing Lyndon Johnson. They will not be found in this volume . . . to be fair is to be cruel." The "secret ingredient" of truly successful cartooning, explains Professor Feiffer, is "hate. Not personal hate"—here is a ritual relapse into convention, which he instantly gets over—"but professional hate: the intensity of conviction that comes to a craftsman's work when he has made the decision to kill; a commitment to shun all political and behavioral complexities, so that the subject becomes, for example, not an overburdened leader struggling tragically with the agony of power, but purely and simply, a demon."

He explains rather shamefacedly why the liberals used to be pro-Johnson, the idea being that the public is entitled to know why the liberals were ever in favor of a demon. You see, Johnson was, for a while, a winner.

"Winning is the personality trait that first recommended him to our favor: If we were to love Johnson at all, it had to be for his winning. There is nothing else to admire him for: Joe McCarthy had more charm, Richard Nixon, as much sincerity, and Thomas E. Dewey, equal warmth. Or, as Joseph Alsop puts it: 'The fact has to be faced that President Johnson has an uninspiring perhaps even a downright bad moral style.' We can suffer a bad moral style in victory only," Mr. Feiffer moralizes. ". . . When civil-rights legislation was passed, when the War on Poverty was organized, when Medicare went through, the Johnson style was discussed either defensively or affirmatively, and all good liberals hoped that the Bobby Baker case would quietly go away. What we wouldn't give to have it back with us today."

What we wouldn't give for a little bit more of the honesty with which Mr. Feiffer and other contributors to this volume bare their moral pathology. I do not like Mr. Johnson, but I do not believe him capable of any intentional cruelty in Vietnam. But the spirit of some of his critics is the spirit of the VC. And come to think of it, they too have their justifiers.

THE UNSEATING OF MR. JOHNSON

April 6, 1968

The withdrawal of Mr. Johnson is among other things technically interesting. The adage that an incumbent President can effect his own renomination appears to be mortally wounded. The objection will be raised that Lyndon Johnson didn't after all fail to effect his renomination, that he simply didn't try. But it is likely that he didn't try because he was uncertain that he would succeed. Those who lived through the year 1948 thought it a pretty boisterous year, what with the Wallace movement, the civil rights walkout, and the staggering upset by Harry Truman. But even though Harry Truman was despised by his own people, the Democratic Party was never in any serious sense refractory. When Harry Truman went to Philadelphia, he was in command of the convention, and no one doubted it. Lyndon Johnson did doubt whether, in the age of television, in this moment of high emotional volatility, he could command the movements of the delegates.

That is an important datum in American history. Some will hail it as evidence that The People are in better command of their own affairs. Others, conservatives for the most part, will wonder whether it is all a cause for rejoicing. The conservative fears plebiscitary government, for the very same reasons given by Burke and Adams. Instant guidance by the people of the government means instability, and instability is subversive of 'freedom. If Lyndon Johnson has to step down because 45 percent of the Democrats in New Hampshire, half of them unable to reply accurately to the question whether Senator McCarthy was for or against the Vietnam War, voted for McCarthy, and because tens of thousands of college students moo over Bobby Kennedy who has delusions of being Ringo Starr, there is something somehow unsettling about it all.

It isn't, of course, that a solid case against Johnson had not been developed. Encyclopedias have been written detailing his shortcomings, and those of his policies, by men deeply moved in their opposition to him. But Johnson was more the victim of something closer to a seizure in American public opinion than of a thoughtful and strategical judgment voted against him or his policies. And that is an unfortunate development in American politics.

Who, now, will benefit from the cultivation of the mass approach? Bobby Kennedy, inasmuch as it is his technique to egg on hysterical adulation (could you imagine him saying to one of those audiences, "Oh, cut it out and stop behaving like silly children"?). Senator McCarthy is by contrast in the tradition of. Adlai Stevenson and Woodrow Wilson, and one fears that for precisely that reason, he is going to lose. (He should lose for other reasons.) Have you noticed how disappointed some of his followers betrayed themselves as being in Senator Eugene McCarthy? And for the most interesting reason; namely, the senator's adamant sense of responsibility.

It is an ironic masterstroke that Senator McCarthy's name is the same as Bad Joe's. Whose behavior his critics wept tears of rage over. Whose behavior they now not-so-secretly wish Senator Eugene were just a little bit more capable of. . . . "He [Eugene] called us to Armageddon, and then located it in Scarsdale, New York—or perhaps Pasadena, California [writes Dwight Macdonald in *Esquire*]. His campaign has been muted to the point of silence [how that other wicked McCarthy would have grabbed the headlines this virtuous one hasn't]. Well-bred to the point of boredom, he may put us to sleep, but he'll never, no, never be vulgar . . . Why doesn't he give the works to his President? It's been done before in American politics." To be sure, that was written before New Hampshire, but McCarthy's style hasn't changed since before New Hampshire. Yet it would appear to be plain that however encouraging McCarthy's performance in New Hampshire and Wisconsin, he is bound to lose up against the demagogic juggernaut from New York.

It is interesting to meditate the role of enthusiasm in politics. Obviously there is room for it. But somewhere along the line enthusiasm subtly deteriorates into unreason and such conscious rejection of standards and restraints as sustained Mussolini and Perón. The morale is high, but it is, as Albert Jay Nock used to point out, "the morale of an army on the march." Such is the morale of the forces that have unseated Lyndon Johnson.

ENTER ROCKEFELLER

April 13, 1968

The question conservatives have been asking themselves during the past year or so is: What can we
expect from Nelson Rockefeller by way of a foreign
policy? Traditionally, Mr. Rockefeller has lined up with
the anti-Communist community. I remember a few years
ago, when the governor was alternating between militarism
in our foreign policy and Barnum and Bailey welfarism at
home, a history-minded observer remarking that he was in
the tradition of the old Roman emperors who, in order to
keep their legions full and happy, needed a lot of bread
and a lot of circuses.

Then, suddenly, silence. The assumption was that the
governor was preparing for the crucial battle of 1966 and
did not want to distract attention from the problems of his
unruly state. Every now and then he would say a word or
two in support of the Vietnam effort, but nothing like the
cataract of pronouncements to which he had been given
over the years.

Came then the election, which he won, and the period
immediately after it during which the governor remained
more or less silent. The excuse then was that inasmuch as
Governor Romney was the anointed instrument of
Republican moderation, Rockefeller should stay out of the
way, lest he utter thoughts on foreign policy that would
compete with Romney's, as indeed any thoughts would
have. But then Romney quit, and still there was silence,
although a front-page story in the New York *Times*
reported that Governor Rockefeller had been "rethinking"
his foreign policy; and so the anti-Communist community
went on biting its fingernails.

Now it has happened. Mr. Rockefeller in a most conspicuous gesture has named Emmet John Hughes as his principal campaign adviser. Now Mr. Hughes is not the kind of man who knows whom to call in order to deliver the Tenth Ward in Chicago or the New Mexican delegation. Thus, although he is listed in the news as the campaign director of Mr. Rockefeller, he is really Mr. Rockefeller's speech writer and policy adviser; and a knowledge of his work is central to understanding the thought of the new Rockefeller.

Alas, Emmet John Hughes has not been silent on foreign policy during the past years. He was a dove before Picasso. He has challenged the central contentions of our anti-Communist foreign policy for years, insistently, with diminishing patience for those who disagree with him. He is an absolutely resolute man on the matter of getting out of Vietnam and pursuing convergence with the Soviet Union. In a gesture that recalls Franklin Roosevelt's dealings with his subordinates, Mr. Rockefeller also appointed Professor Henry Kissinger, who is the anti-Communist at Harvard, as a member of his staff. That will be a happy office.

Obviously Mr. Rockefeller is, as they say, strung out on Mr. Hughes, because not only do the bulk of the Republicans object to his analysis of our foreign policy, but one particular Republican does not permit the mention of Mr. Hughes's name in his presence. "Hi ya, fella"—I can hear Mr. Rockefeller saying to General Eisenhower at Miami—"you remember Emmet Hughes?" There goes Mr. Eisenhower's vote, which is not available to anyone who makes an association with the former aide who violated all those confidences in his book on the Eisenhower administration.

Mr. Hughes's appointment at a considerable personal sacrifice (he had to resign a job with *Newsweek* which was wonderfully lucrative and gloriously unexacting) can mean only that Mr. Rockefeller is in this business for a long haul. If he contrives to win the nomination and then the Presidency, that will certainly keep Mr. Hughes occupied on into the future. If he loses the nomination, then Mr. Hughes will have to, well, write another book, which is what we people do when life peters out for us. But meanwhile, we must brace ourselves for the extension of Mr. Hughes's voice in the Rockefeller edition of *Newsweek*.

KENNEDY HAS A SECRET

April 16, 1968

At a major Midwestern university one day recently, two of its brightest students found themselves planning for an impending visit by Senator Robert Kennedy. Both are highly practiced in making arrangements for visiting dignitaries, having served as heads of the student speakers' series, so that although they worked diligently to make certain that everything would be just right, they felt no stage fright at producing an appearance by a Presidential candidate, not even by the Presidential candidate they ardently favor, for they have been, ever since Kennedy's entry into the race, president and vice president of the state Youth for Kennedy.

Twenty-four hours before the visitation, an incredible ten (10) advance men pile out of an airplane and begin issuing orders at the rate of approximately ten per minute, for a period of about ten hours, totally rearranging, not to say convulsing, the well-laid plans of the two college students. For one thing, the appearance will not be in the field house, but in the gymnasium. Why? the student ask. The field house holds 10,000, the gym 3,000; surely it is better to talk to 10,000 than to 3,000? The chief advance man smiles. Look, he says, in the first place, how are you going to be sure that 10,000 people will come to fill up the field house? There are only 150,000 people in this whole town, and a lot of them just aren't interested. Sure, Charlie will try to get the school board to declare a holiday so the kids can come. But maybe he'll succeed, maybe he won't. Meanwhile, we can be sure to fill the gym, and what matters is that TV shows SRO. Better a full room of 100 people than the Hollywood Bowl with 100 empty seats.

The technique, a professional carefully explains, is at the one hand obvious, but even so, effective. Mr. Kennedy's appeal is to the youth, and he is as aware as anyone that they do not vote. But never mind, they are the instruments through which he intends to communicate an enthusiasm for his candidacy to older people, and by one simple means: the six o'clock and the eleven o'clock news every day. Every day at that time, when the television networks give their reports on the day's news, there will be shots of a mass student audience at a gymnasium somewhere, having been carefully deployed by the advance men, responding like snake dancers to the directions of the high priest. The idea is that the viewer will come soon to believe that this is *force majeure*. That is when the delegates will begin to feel—or so it is programmed by Mr. Kennedy's strategists—that an irresistible force is moving through the land. And in politics what you do about irresistible forces is lie down and enjoy them.

The two students, awaiting the arrival of the Senator, are amused by it all. They are of a rather different breed from the typical Kennedymaniacs who treat him as they would a visit by Our Lady of Lourdes, exposing all their infirmities to him for instant curing. For one thing, they have no particular respect for Mr. Kennedy's mind, and none at all for what he is saying. They can agree that he is most fearfully demagogic, that one can never tell what he really believes, that a line pursuing his disjointed statements on Johnson and Vietnam would touch every point of any graph; that the revivalist aspect of the public meetings is the result of intensive planning, of exquisitely orchestrated emotions and programming. . . .

Still, what matters, as one of them puts it, is: "Kennedy is in motion." There. There is the excitement of Kennedy. They don't like it where they are, and Kennedy will move things in another direction. What direction? It seems to matter only that it should be in a direction other than the inertial direction. In that sense we are sitting on top of the North Pole, and wherever we go, we are going south. The Kennedy watchers must grasp this element. It is the key to his success.

There is no other key. What, just what, has he said in the month he has been campaigning that would stick in the mind of anyone? Nothing, nothing at all. What about his delivery, his general appearance? For all his efforts to look like the boy-king, he manages, in the words of Murray Kempton, to look "more like early Sal Mineo than late James Dean."

But he knows how to give the impression of fluidity, of that magic motion one hankers after when one is convinced that, as a society, we are stranded in the middle of the road, with great world forces careening by us in every direction.

MYSTIFIER

April 23, 1968

It must be very discouraging to be a politician. Here is the governor of the most influential state of the Union, running hard for the Presidential nomination of his party, richer even than Bobby Kennedy, abetted by one of the two or three most expensive speech writers in the English-speaking world, addressing the editors of just about every newspaper in America, delivering a much-heralded speech in which he managed to spend 150 billion American dollars—and you know what the headline is the next morning? In one of the nation's most liberal newspapers, devoting voluminous attention to national and world affairs? "ROCKEFELLER SPEECH/ HEARD IN SILENCE."

Surely Mr. Rockefeller envisioned other headlines? "ROCKEFELLER SOLVES/PROBLEMS OF CITY" might have been one. Or "ROCKEFELLER MAG-NETISM/WOWS EDITORS" would have been satisfactory. Or even "ROCKEFELLER SPEECH/BRINGS GOP RAVES." But the reporter (Mr. David Broder, one of the nation's best) was as uninspired as the general audience, as uninterested in what Mr. Rockefeller ended up saying as the editors who heard him. A total of two sentences from the massive speech was reproduced in the morning paper—way off, toward the end of the first-page story which began: "Governor Nelson A. Rockefeller of New York made his long-heralded debut as a 'non-candidate' yesterday, delivering a thirty-minute speech on urban problems, uninterrupted by applause, to the luncheon meeting of the American Society of Newspaper Editors at the Shoreham Hotel."

What happened?

Well, to begin with, the speech was so heavy with rhetorical pomposity that it would have required a Saturn IV booster to launch it. Would you like a taste? "Our time of testing now follows—like a twin heritage of challenge—from both these earlier ages [Lincoln's and Roosevelt's]. The signs of peril—and the chances for leadership—rise as high on both fronts: from within—and from without—our nation. For we are not only struggling to build peace in the world. We are also striving to live at peace with ourselves."

If you believe that I selected the single worst passage, I give you the peroration which, I have a paralyzing suspicion, somebody at Rockefeller's shop actually thought was eloquent. . . .

"I believe deeply in such a new government, such a new leadership, and such a new America.

"We as a people, have—right now—a choice to make.

"We must choose between new division or new dedication.

"We can live together as bullies—or as brothers.

"We can practice retribution or reconciliation.

"We can choose a life of the jungle or a life of justice.

"We cannot have both.

"We cannot live for long with parts and pieces of both.

"We must choose."

We must cut the crap.

Really, we must. And it is an objective indication that such emptinesses are boring, that they bored the audience, and bored the reporters, and permanently traumatized the Muses. "The audience reaction," says the account in the Washington *Post*, "was noted with concern by some Rockefeller for President sponsors in the room. One of them said afterward, 'I hope this convinces Emmet Hughes (the Rockefeller adviser and writer whose stylistic touches were evident in the text) that it will take more than the power of his words to nominate Rockefeller.'"

A pity, really. Because Mr. Rockefeller is a very able man. His delivery is first-rate. He has great facility for extempore talk, and his ideas, if one excavates them from all that lard, are worth pondering. For instance, the recognitions that the private sector is five times more resourceful than the public sector, and that if the cities are to be saved, it will have to be largely by private enterprise. For instance, his observation that we are spending five times as much money subsidizing our rich farms as our poor cities. But it takes men of archaeological passion to find Mr. Rockefeller's ideas in Mr. Rockefeller's current prose. Next time, he should furnish his audience with a trot.

THE REPUBLICAN TEAM

August 13, 1968

The selection of Governor Agnew was, as we all know, a surprise, but it didn't take long for the delegates to get over it. Instant research into the history of the relatively obscure lawyer, who a few months ago was clamoring for the nomination of Mr. Nixon's archantagonist Nelson Rockefeller, fails to betray any serious weakness the Democrats are likely to profit from. He rescued Maryland, in 1966, from the leadership of a Democrat committed to segregationism and did so only two years after George Wallace, running in a Presidential primary, had demonstrated how greatly disposed Maryland was to the old allure of segregation. Indeed, the candidacy of Agnew was endorsed by the Washington *Post,* and the Baltimore *Sun;* so much for a Wassermann test, pre-1968.

But then Governor Agnew, in the spring of this year, took certain measures and made certain statements which distinguished him from the school of men that bravely justifies any civil disorder at all on the grounds that 400 years ago slaves were brought into this country by our forefathers. Governor Agnew answered a sit-down seizure of a local college by arresting a couple of hundred students, no less. He then read a lecture to local Negro leaders instructing them that their own interests, to say nothing of those of the community of Baltimore, lay in a firm repudiation of such as Rap Brown and Stokely Carmichael. He went on to deplore—and for such penetration and courage he should have riveted national attention—the Kerner Commission report, wherein we were instructed that the reason why we have had riots and disorders is that white Americans are racist.

Governor Agnew's position is that such an analysis is at best incomplete, and at worst misleading. No doubt it was his stand on that report, combined with his stand against riots and disorder in general, that drew him to the attention of Southern leaders as out of the ordinary among civil rights governors. And then, having earlier resigned himself, with no apparent trauma, to Nelson Rockefeller's unavailability to make the race for the Presidency, Governor Agnew popped up in support of Richard Nixon. His doing so attracted a great deal of attention, and in due course what do you know, he was singled out by the Presidential nominee, Mr. Nixon, as his running mate.

There was considerable confusion in Miami Beach when the announcement was made. For one thing, it is generally supposed—it having been stressed over recent years that he is a cunning, crafty man—that Mr. Nixon was being permitted to get away with something. Had he put something over on somebody? There was a lot of murmuring. Little mutinous blips showed up on the screen, and indeed Governor Romney permitted a few zealous supporters to put up his own name as an alternative. But the opposition was anarchic and diffuse. Moreover, it was impossible to sustain it by moral arguments. A moral case against Governor Agnew was simply not available.

Such a case against him as was attempted was to the effect that his nomination was done "in order to appease the South." By some people, this charge is deployed as a dreadnought. There are those, however, who pause to recall that the South, like other sections of the country, is inhabited by Americans, and until we hear otherwise from the Supreme Court, they too are entitled to political consideration.

It is hardly as though Mr. Nixon had nominated George Wallace for Vice President. His nomination of a Southerner whose reputation arose from his defense of civil rights is hardly in the order of an affront, but rather in the order of giving encouragement to civil rights Southerners who, however, draw a line between the exercise of civil rights and of civil disorder. It is ironic that the principal opponents of the choice of Agnew, most of them advocates of the nomination of John Lindsay, were using arguments in Lindsay's behalf which were most readily translatable as suggesting the imperative need of appeasing the North and the cities.

Mr. Agnew, to judge from his acceptance speech, is unlikely to emerge as a great magnetic field. It will be Nixon's campaign, all the way, even as it was Eisenhower's campaign in 1952, when Richard Nixon tagged along as Vice President. But the presence of Agnew there should reassure not only Southerners, but also liberals who believe that it is, if anything, overdue for the Republican Party to put forward public officials who are attempting a reconciliation between civil rights for a minority, and civil rights for the majority.

SHERLOCK BUCKLEY RIDES AGAIN

September 10, 1968

The trouble with any attempt to elevate standards in politics is that yesterday's infamy is of no interest today. Still, there is some sort of duty, I guess, to file away juicy incidents as they occur. For the record, as they say, and just in case St. Peter overlooked them.

I have a beauty. During the Miami Beach Convention of the Republican Party, the Miami *Herald* carried a monstrous big ad entitled: "Memorandum To: Delegates to the Republican National Convention/ From: Black America/ Subject: The Presidential Nomination." The advertisement instructed the delegates to vote for

Rockefeller or else. "We take this opportunity to advise you that candidates with records such as Richard Nixon and Ronald Reagan are not acceptable to black Americans."

The chairman of the list of seventy-six Negro signers was Mr. Louis Lomax, the Los Angeles writer, and among the seventy-six were names of very prominent Negroes; for instance, Charles Evers, Marian Anderson, Louis Armstrong, Cab Calloway, and Lionel Hampton, who are not given to lightly implying that other Americans are racist, that being the clear implication of this advertisement concerning Nixon and Reagan. I was asked, at a public situation in Miami, to comment on the advertisement. I said that it was reprehensible from every point of view, and that it was clearly, on the face of it, a Rockefeller operation undoubtedly paid for by Rockefeller headquarters. A foreign journalist, over-hearing me, challenged Governor Rockefeller at a press conference that afternoon. "Governor Rockefeller, this morning Mr. Buckley charged that the advertisement sponsored by Citizens of Black America was a Rockefeller operation. Is that true?"

"No," said the governor. "It isn't true." Whereupon he added genially, "You have to understand that Mr. Buckley fell off a boat a couple of days ago." Everybody laughed, myself included when I saw it on television, but as my laughter died down I beamed at the set. "You'll be sorry, Governor." But he didn't hear me.

A week or two later, my office telephones the Miami *Herald*. We are put on to Mr. Bob Govin who handled the Citizens of Black America ad. He advises us that at the very last minute, a woman named Evelyne Cunningham had come to the offices of the *Herald,* cash in hand, with copy of the Black America ad, which the *Herald* routinely accepted.

But he was very sorry he had done so.

Why, we asked?

Because, he said, he had received somewhere between

thirty and fifty letters from people whose names had been listed as signers, protesting that they had never given their permission to appear on the advertisement. Who, for instance, we asked? Well, he couldn't remember them all, but he could offhand remember that he had heard from Charles Evers, Lionel Hampton, Marian Anderson, and Louis Armstrong who had emphatically disavowed the ad.

Who was Miss Cunningham, we persevered?

Don't know, he said. All he got from her by way of address was Hotel Lucerne, Miami Beach, and her permanent address was 4919 Sixteenth Street, N.W., Washington, D.C.

We found that address listed in the Washington phone book as belonging to one Barrington D. Parker who—what do you know—turned out to be one of the three delegates from D.C. pledged to Rockefeller. On a hunch, we then called Rockefeller for President headquarters, which was winding up its affairs, and brashly asked to speak to Evelyne Cunningham. The answer came that Miss Cunningham could be reached at—Rockefeller's New York gubernatorial office.

At this point, chivalry sets in, and we promise not to tax Miss Cunningham.

Incidentally, there is no more reason to infer that Nelson Rockefeller is untruthful than there is to infer that Richard Nixon is a racist. The chances are overwhelming that he was personally unaware of what his staff was up to. One of the signers was Jackie Robinson, whose favorite sport, now that he has retired from baseball, is imputing racism to anyone he disagrees with. How it probably went was that Robinson called Lomax, in order to give the ad a West Coast feel, so as to keep it from sounding too obviously like a New York Rockefeller operation. How they got the names heaven only knows; presumably, somebody just made up a list of prominent Negroes. Then, to attend to the mechanics of the ad, it was arranged for an efficient young lady to deliver the cash (whose cash? Anybody out there willing to guess, who hasn't recently fallen off a boat?) to the Miami *Herald*.

Simple.

But you can't fool old Sherlock Buckley.

THE REPORTER AND THE POLITICIAN

August 31, 1968

Late, very late at night, while the orators droned on about this or that triumph or ignominy or the credentials committee, a CBS reporter on the prowl spotted Richard Daley of Chicago and thought to while away a minute or two by questioning him. Ho, ho, ho, he said; and how are you, Mayor Daley?

Grunt.

Mr. Mayor, would you tell us why it is that you covered up some of the city's eyesores just for the sake of the Convention?

(Testily) Why didn't you people ask 'em that in Miami?

(A moment's pause. Politicians don't hardly speak that way to CBS.) Well, er, Mr. Mayor, I wasn't talking about Miami. I was talking about here, Chicago.

Silence.

(Gamely) Well, tell me this, Mr. Mayor, could you answer some of the criticisms that have been made about security precautions here?

At this point, Mayor Daley engages someone else in conversation, as though—can you imagine?—CBS didn't exist. Mercifully, Walter Cronkite pans himself in, smiles urbanely, and says something about how he guesses the mayor is in an irritated mood tonight, and maybe he hasn't appreciated all the criticism the visitors here have made of him.

The episode throws light on several aspects of the convention in Chicago, some of them applicable to other conventions and, indeed, other situations.

There is the matter of the reporter with microphone in hand. There you are, minding your own, or even the public's business, and suddenly a microphone is thrust two inches away from your mouth, a question is asked of you, and you are unhappily aware that 50,000,000 people are listening for your answer. There are several appropriate responses. If you are, say, Harold Stassen, you grab the mike and embark on a speech on anything at all until—and it will be very soon—Walter Cronkite gently vaporizes you from the screen.

Then there is the gentleman who doesn't want to say anything at this point to anybody, let alone to 50,000,000 people; but he is genial by nature and perhaps wary of antagonizing the media (as we are called), so he answers the questions, evasively and cheerfully, exchanging a little repartee. By the way—very important—he must call the reporter by his first name, else he'll be thought aloof (bad) or so unimportant as not to have been sufficiently interesting to the press in the past as to have got onto first-name terms (very sad).

Then there are those politicians who feel either that they are ex officio big enough to write their own rules concerning press conferences (Mayor Daley), or those lesser ones who believe that they have that right irrespective of how big they are (Gene McCarthy). They run grave risks, but they cause at least this heart to flutter with pride at occasional assertions of privacy. Nothing is better calculated to destroy a carefully constructed impression than careless submissions to redundant interrogation. Richard Nixon delivered, at Miami Beach, a grandiloquent oration—that is exactly how to describe it—and immediately upon finishing it, instead of disappearing and permitting the impression he had successfully created to sink in—would you believe it?—consented on the way out to pause fifteen or twenty minutes to chitchat with reporters on matters of utter triviality.

That is the stylistic problem. Another problem is the impossibility of dealing captiously with certain kinds of questions. "Now, Mr. Buckley," I was asked on statewide TV at the end of a political campaign, "we have exactly twenty seconds. Would you give us your views on rent control?" I blurted out: "I cannot give my views on rent control in twenty seconds." I say I blurted not because that is not precisely the correct answer to give intellectually, but because it is a politically unsatisfactory answer to give. The proper answer would have been something like: "I believe that all Americans should have a decent place to live in at a price they can afford to pay, and I deplore and have deplored for years the people who profit from human misery." Hubert Humphrey could have improved on that. Which is why he is the Democratic candidate.

REFORM THE CONVENTIONS?

August 17, 1968

In the blissful interval between the two conventions, survivors of the first, particularly those who are bound for the second, have been ruminating on the institution, and asking themselves what might be done to improve it.

Surely some reforms are obvious. Favorite sons should be nominated on the morning of Wednesday. I see no particular reason why the speeches in nomination, or those that second the nominations, should be limited, under the circumstances. No one will be listening anyway, not even, one suspects, first cousins of the favorite son. The television networks would be free to cover the speeches or not, as they choose. The listening public would be relieved of the mischievous effect of night nominations, which is to delay the balloting for President until early in the morning, ruining one's subsequent working day.

Rather this, I should think, than a serious attempt to abolish the idea of the favorite son. That idea should be preserved, not only because on the unusual occasion a favorite son may command attention, but because it is a genial way for a state, under special circumstances, to pay special tribute to—a favorite son. It is a pity, of course, that the practice has been so greatly abused.

And it is testimony to the eternal vanity of man that even such cool numeros as Clifford Case of New Jersey permit these cloying oblations. It is one thing to see a Harold Stassen nominated: His eccentric conceit and utter humorless narcissism put him beyond the line of vexatiousness—one merely feels sorry for him, as, say, for Senator Morse. But a Clifford Case, all cool and book-weathered and high-minded—why doesn't he say to the boys, Look, boys, sure I'll hold the delegation together, but when the times comes actually to nominate me for President, just say, "I nominate Clifford Case," and let the seconders say, "I second the nomination of Clifford Case."

One way to cut down on the number of favorite sons would be to decree that the one with the fewest votes at the end of the first ballot would be publicly executed. That might, however, strike some of the smaller states as too drastic. So why not leave it that they can go at a time of day when nothing else is happening? Such a simple reform; so easy to effect mechanically.

Then there is the matter of polling the delegation. That happens, you will recall, at almost exactly the moment that you least want it to happen, *i.e.*, when great excitement has built up. It is the exact equivalent of the

television commercial that comes in just when the hero
has been pinned to the wall by George Raft. Surely
convention officials could arrange for polling to be
conducted in private, with the old lady tabulator
instructed to accept the chairman's count until and unless
the individual balloting finds it false. So that it would go
as follows:

Delegate: Mr. Chairman, the California delegation
requests that it be polled. Chairman: Request granted.
COLORADO.

After all, it is a little unseemly to suggest that the
chairman of a delegation deliberately miscounted the
votes. Rather like a teller rising at an examiner's meeting
and requesting that the bank president's figures be
reexamined. If we need a compromise between accepting
as presumptively correct the word of the chairman, and
testing that word there and then against the individually
stated votes of every member of the delegation, why not
wire in all state chairmen to a lie-detecting device, so that
when the chairman says twenty votes for Rockefeller and
twenty-two votes for Nixon, a great big blip will go up on
a screen if the chairman is lying? *Then* you can poll the
delegation.

And, finally, on the matter of the demonstrations, I
myself do not mind them. Granted, I do not look at them;
but I do not even mind other people looking at them.
There are those who deem them undignified. Quite so, and
therefore they are perfectly appropriate to politics. I
cannot imagine why anyone who is prepared to
countenance the systematic dissimulations of great big
President-aspiring politicians should bother to criticize
rotarian exhibitions of enthusiasm expressed by mere
balloons and confetti.

Senator Morton—who looked straight into the
television camera 100 times at Miami Beach and swore
that Nixon would not be nominated on the first ballot,
that Rockefeller would come in along about the second or
third—calmly confessed, after it was all over, that he

knew perfectly well, ten days before the convention, that Nixon would get it on the first. And people resent the humbuggery of the demonstrations!

THE DOUBTS ABOUT AGNEW

October 22, 1968

Spiro Agnew has become the gravamen of the anti-Nixonites' case these days, what with the exemplary performance of Mr. Nixon, with which they are finding it difficult to take plausible exception. So that the case against Agnew is being diligently pursued, with heaviest emphasis on his so-called bloopers, which are on the order of calling an old and apparently obese reporter friend of his a "fat Jap," minutes before—or was it after?—a jovial reference to the "Polack" vote.

For these acts of genocide Mr. Agnew was made to eat crow, although he managed somewhere in his recantation to wonder out loud whether the United States was losing its sense of humor (it isn't), whereas he should have wondered whether the critics of Mr. Nixon aren't simply on the prowl to make a heavy case against Mr. Nixon's associate, Spiro Agnew.

What is the quality of his public performance, leaving aside his ethnic diction? His most recent nationwide appearance was on "Face the Nation," where he was bearded by three toughies who went after him with zest. The best Agnew could do on the eternal question of why-doesn't-Nixon-debate-with-Humphrey was so's your old man. A not ineffective answer publicly, though of course at root it is evasive, since it is obvious that Mr. Nixon does not want to debate with Mr. Humphrey, plain and simple.

Agnew scored by pointing to Democratic behavior in analogous circumstances. "Let's go back to sixty-four, when the Democratic candidate didn't want to debate the Republican because he was so far ahead." To drive the point nearer to home, Agnew wondered why Humphrey, believing as firmly as he apparently does in debates, refused Senator McCarthy and Senator McGovern when they pleaded with him to debate before the Chicago Convention.

And then he was asked, did he believe "that the civil rights revolution has gone too fast in the last five years and that it is time for something of a pause?"

He came back fast. "You know, that is a very interesting phrase you used, when you said 'civil rights revolution. . . .' I don't think the civil rights movement has gone too far, but I think the civil rights revolution went too far the day the revolution began, and by that I mean the lawbreaking that has been hooked up and rationalized and excused and condoned to some extent by my Vice Presidential opponent [as for instance when the media reported him as saying that] it is all right to break the law as long as you are willing to pay the penalty."

Why, if he is so good on civil rights, did the NAACP vote no confidence in him? Simple, said Agnew: The NAACP is practically 100 percent Democrat. Well, was he qualified for the highest office? Agnew cited his extensive background in state government, adding, "President Johnson appointed me to the Advisory Commission on Intergovernmental Relations, so he must have had some confidence in my ability." And oh, yes, "I have taught law school for seven years."

Well, but what about foreign policy? Ask me about it, he said. Go ahead: Ask me. Hmmm. Bombing pause? Not unless the enemy makes a conciliatory movement, absolutely not. Well, then, doesn't he back Johnson, in this respect, even more than Humphrey backs Johnson? "Well," said the governor, "that is not what the Vice President says. He says he defends it [Johnson's Vietnam policy] wholeheartedly because, after all, it is his record, too."

Q: "He is also saying he is going to move in new directions, if he is elected."

Agnew: "He is moving in every direction."

Let's face it, Mr. Agnew is the only spontaneous thing in town, and I like that. His instincts are gloriously unprogrammed, and I like that, too. There are those who believe that Mr. Nixon appointed Mr. Agnew as a sort of personal life insurance. No one, they reason, will pop off President Nixon while Vice President Agnew is around. There is a view, and I share it, that in Mr. Agnew, Nixon found a high deposit of some of the best American ore lying around: toughness, sincerity, decent-mindedness, decisiveness—much of what, after a fair amount of exposure, went into making Harry Truman a relatively happy national memory.

A LOOK AT GEORGE WALLACE*

October 29, 1968

When early this year *Human Events* released its poll on George Wallace, conservative watchers were astonished. The poll had been shrewdly conceived and reported not on the views of the general reader but on those of 220 conservative writers, politicians, and organization heads—"most of the leading names in American conservatism." *"Do you believe Mr. Wallace to be a fiscal conservative?"* No, 51 percent (yes, 30 percent). *"Will Mr. Wallace's candidacy help or hurt the election of conservatives running for the House and Senate?"* Hurt, 69 percent (help, 14 percent). *"Will the effect of Mr.*

* Reprinted by permission of *Look* magazine.

Wallace's candidacy be to strengthen or to hurt the conservative movement in America?" Hurt, 74 percent (strengthen, 16 percent). *"How would you vote in the 1968 general election given the following possibilities?"* Nixon, 79 percent; Johnson, 5 percent; Wallace, 8 percent (Rockefeller, 43 percent, Johnson, 12 percent; Wallace, 23 percent). *"Do you believe Mr. Wallace is knowingly conducting a campaign that is calculated to appeal to racial prejudice?"* Yes, 68 percent (no, 25 percent).

The figures greatly surprised those who believed (many still do) that Wallace is the answer to conservative prayers; who wondered, therefore, at the apparent ingratitude of conservative leaders. Or was it that their opposition is purely tactical? Is it because conservatives, though they do not really object to George Wallace, far from it, do object (the thinking members among them) to the *effect* his candidacy is likely to have on the candidacy of Richard Nixon, who is the closest thing to a conservative running for President who also has a chance to make it?

The questions are worth asking and answering, not merely in order to understand George Wallace, but to understand the political metabolism of the country. Researchers so inclined can carefully study Wallace's personal and political background for clues to the question: Do we have here a sure-enough "conservative"? The findings are at least confusing. Twenty years ago, George Wallace refused to join Strom Thurmond's famous defection from the Democratic Convention, in protest against Hubert Humphrey's civil rights plank. During that period and for a while after that, Wallace was a self-avowed "Folsomite," *i.e.,* a backer of the enormous pretensions of Kissing Jim Folsom, the Alabama governor who thought himself Presidential material and served as a *Henry* Wallace delegate at the 1944 Democratic Convention and had taken the governorship of Alabama—in the words of the London *Economist*—"on the most liberal platform ever offered in Alabama."

Wallace broke with Folsom, for reasons irrelevant to this narrative; but he was still down as a strong believer in federal welfare programs. He backed John Kennedy in 1956 and 1960, and, as governor, he tripled Alabama's bonded indebtedness. Then, of course, came the famous encounter of 1963 where it all officially began.

On the other hand, other public officials publicly resented the use of force as an instrument of integration before Wallace and after him; and yet we are concerned nowadays with Wallace. What happened, after the federal marshals forced Governor Wallace to step aside to make way for a Negro boy and a Negro girl who were thereupon registered as students at the University of Alabama, was that history and George Wallace embarked upon an elaborate courtship, to which each contributed about equally, so that now they have quite a thing going. For his part, Wallace began diligently to cultivate a race-free rhetoric. "I have never said anything unkind about the Negro anywhere," Wallace has said, like Mark Antony addressing the Romans on his devotion to Brutus. He then went on to perfect analytical and rhetorical techniques which (a) stimulate discontents where discontents are scarce; (b) aggravate them where they are already there; and (c) galvanize his listeners into a hot desire to hurl their bodies (never ever their minds) in the path of the federal juggernaut.

For its part history gave us Lyndon Johnson and his enormous appetite to dominate the affairs of America at every level. And gave us, too, the paralysis of action that grew out of Johnson's failure to reckon on the relative weakness of his own resources (the conservatives would put it that way) or on the relative strength of other people's inertia (as the liberals would prefer). Thus, the war in Vietnam stalled and, at home, the war against poverty and the urban ghetto.

Now listen to George Wallace: *"I respect the right of dissent all right"*—note that the formality, what one might call the liberal amenities, has been complied with (I don't have anything against niggers)—*"but anybody who undertakes to give aid to the Vietcong is engaged in treason"*—note that treason is (as indeed it ought to be) a devil word; and note how useful it is rhetorically, handled thus gravely—*"That's the way I see it"*—a touch of modesty; but shrewdly programmed, to suggest the, er, triumph of innocence in a sick-slick world. *"I'd order the Justice Department to proceed against"*—now watch how the tone changes, so as to introduce true American Resolution—*"those bastards, indict 'em, try 'em. And if any judges tried to say it isn't legally treason because we aren't formally at war, I'd get some new judges. They wouldn't be judges like Earl Warren, either, who sits there and applauds the President—applauds him while he talks about bills the court will have to pass on!"* A wee bit complicated. But the point is not unsound. Warren has shown visible pleasure at the description of legislation the constitutionality of which is due to be challenged by members of the legislature. . . .

There it is. American conservatives are the most distressed of all, not so much because they despise what Wallace says as because they despise what they know to be his venture in political profiteering on grave mutual concerns: even as the responsible Left, in the thirties, wept tears over the exploitation of their genuine concerns by such as Huey Long. What's more, even the veneer breaks down at the organizational level. Wallace admits, among his official electors, such as Gerald L. K. Smith, the consecrated anti-Semite, and Leander Perez, the devoted anti-Negro. Nobody knows how exactly he will distribute his hurt. During the primaries in 1964 Wallace made his big points among Democrats. But then he was running only among Democrats in the primaries. In November, he will hurt the Republicans most in the South, where they will lose electoral votes to him; but in the North, the Humphrey Democrats will lose, who might otherwise have counted on votes that now will go to a man whose mode reflects frustrations readily intellectualizable by other Americans, who know that something is wrong and arrive, by careful and morally responsible reasoning, at conclusions similar to Wallace's.

His mode is crude, but hardly unique. He said once, about a federal judge who was his classmate at college but now found himself an adversary in one of those endless legal brawls Wallace is always caught up in, that the judge was "an integrating, carpetbagging, scalawagging, race-mixing, bald-faced liar." That is the kind of assault, if you change the political coordinates and wipe it up a little, that some thoroughbred liberals—*e.g.,* Emanuel Celler and Martin Luther King, Jr. and George Meany—were making on Goldwater in 1964, when they saw him as somehow in the tradition of Adolf Hitler.

What are we left with? The coarsening of distinctions, certainly. Polarization, just as certainly. But also the disintegrating penetration of Big Daddy Government, accelerated by the thumping dissent of the backwoods heckler. Those conservatives who take sly pleasure from Wallace's techniques should reflect that that kind of thing is do-able against anybody at all; do-able for instance by the Folsomite Wallace of yesteryear, who roared his approval of his candidate's attack on the "Wall Street Gotrocks," "the damned decency crowd," and "them Hoover Republicans." Those who see in Wallace the end of the world should reflect on the great political movements of the past twenty years. Strom Thurmond, in 1948, led the movement against civil rights. Today, firmly incorporated into a Republican Party that is pledged to defend civil rights, he leads, in effect, the fight against Wallace, who has taken Thurmond's old position, in the South.

That, and reflect also on this: The Wallace candidacy is among other things a great national reaction against the ravenous appetites of an overweening federal government to craft for us a great society, never mind the disposition of those who are to benefit from it. Not inconceivably, we will be better off for the irruption. Wallace is to one position what Eugene McCarthy is to another. The country rejected (quite wisely) Eugene McCarthy, but the Democrats learned from him. The country will reject (quite wisely) George Wallace; but Democrats and Republicans alike stand to learn from the experience.

CAMPAIGN NOTES

October 29, 1968

The heat is on. And, as one would expect, it is mostly on Richard Nixon. Not because he is the front-runner, but because he is the conservative alternative.

Arthur Schlesinger, Jr., has weighed in with an endorsement of Hubert Humphrey. One would think that, after a while, Mr. Schlesinger's endorsements would depreciate, so numerous are they becoming. First he was for Senator McCarthy. But then when Senator Kennedy announced, Mr. Schlesinger simply abandoned McCarthy in favor of the Jacobite Restoration. Then when tragedy struck Kennedy down, Schlesinger went—not back home to McCarthy as one would have supposed, but to Senator McGovern.

During that period Mr. Schlesinger made a number of cracks about Mr. Humphrey's disqualifications, based on his support of the Vietnam War, but now he says that "people change their minds," and concerning no one else is it more eagerly hoped he will continue to change his mind. Mr. Humphrey, says Mr. Schlesinger, has personally reassured him that if he is elected, he will drastically alter our Vietnam position.

And anyway, said Mr. Schlesinger the historian, Mr. Nixon's campaign is "an intellectual and moral disgrace, to such a point that no one knows what he would do about anything as President." Therefore, Mr. Schlesinger concludes, "he cannot make a good President of the United States." Students of logic will recognize the enthymematic problem here. If it isn't known what Mr. Nixon will do as President, how is it predictable that he will make a poor President?

Suppose he named Arthur Schlesinger as Secretary of State, John Kenneth Galbraith as Secretary of Commerce, and Benjamin Spock as Secretary of Defense? Wouldn't he make a marvelous President then? And how does Mr. Schlesinger know that that isn't exactly what old Tricky Dick has in mind, if Mr. Schlesinger says that he doesn't in fact know just what he does have in mind?

And we hear from James Reston, the Duns Scotus of the world of journalism. He goes through an entire column criticizing Richard Nixon for declining to debate with Humphrey, drawing verbose moral conclusions concerning the bad character of Mr. Nixon—without once mentioning, not even in the late city editions, that Mr. Hubert Humphrey was in the forefront of the movement four years ago to prevent a debate between Barry Goldwater and Lyndon Johnson.

Now it is one thing to point out, simply, that Mr. Nixon's switched position on debates did not embellish his prestige, but it is altogether something else to draw from that decision, which was obviously a tactical decision, dark invidious inferences concerning his character. Unless he had been willing to draw similar decisions concerning Mr. Humphrey, on account of his own switcheroo. Never mind, the partisans are riding their horses nowadays at full gallop, and reason is a detour.

And while we are in search of political hygiene, how about the extraordinary exemptions that are being granted to Senator Jacob Javits? The polls in New York State show that Mr. Nixon is leading by a bare 2 percent. Mr. Javits conspired two months ago to prevent the Conservative Party from endorsing Mr. Nixon, with the altogether possible result that Mr. Nixon will for that reason alone lose the state of New York and possibly the national election. Mr. Javits took the position, as one would expect, as a matter of principle—his principled opposition to third parties. However, that principle did not prevent him from accepting the designation of the Liberal Party, and in the past few days, huge newspaper ads have been appearing urging the voters to go for Humphrey and Javits.

Very confusing to New York State Republicans; on the other hand they thrive on confusion, as witness the perpetuation of the myth of Mr. Javits' Republicanism, which myth the voters have certified year after year. Talking of debates, the most competent, the most exciting, the most tense that could possibly be staged, is one between Mr. Javits when speaking downstate and Mr. Javits when speaking upstate. I cannot imagine which of them would win. Perhaps, as someone predicted about a previous Presidential election, they would both surely lose.

DEMOCRATIC GALA

November 19, 1968

It was billed as a "Halloween Gala." The egregious sponsors were the Americans for Democratic Action, the New Coalition for Humphrey-Muskie, and the Students' Coalition for Humphrey-Muskie. The auditorium was the vast Manhattan Center, capacity 4,000. The speakers were the authors of approximately one quarter of the Current Books section of the New York Public Library, an easy quorum of the Establishment left: Arthur Schlesinger, Jr., Michael Harrington, Daniel Patrick Moynihan, Ted Sorensen, William Fitts Ryan, Joseph

Rauh, Jr., James Farmer, Norman Cousins. It was quite an evening.

Shelley Winters, the master of ceremonies, came in, between the speeches, with ideological chitchat which, with that background of poets and professors, gave something of the impression of Mother Bloor lecturing to the faculty of the Lenin Institute. Her principal complaint was that as an actress she lives in California, and back when Ronald Reagan was head of her union, the actors wanted something, and Reagan settled for 2 percent, and in later years, he spent two "zillion" dollars on something else, vote for Humphrey.

The genial Mr. Moynihan opened by observing my presence at the press table and remarking that the Church "has always made provision for late vocations." Whereupon Mr. Moynihan announced that the cessation of the bombing was a vindication of the young people. That assumes that the young protesters so touched Ho Chi Minh or Lyndon Johnson that they decided on a stop-bombing agreement as a sort of Halloween present to the kids. Another explanation, of course, is that the young people in South Vietnam, who have been fighting there for what some people consider idealistic reasons, had something to do with bringing about the pressures that may lead to peace. And of course, there is the third explanation, which is that the stop-bombing agreement is a vindication of what the kids have been saying about Lyndon Johnson's cynicism.

Marietta Tree, the queenly consort of Adlai Stevenson, said that over in the United Nations, everybody is praying that Humphrey will win. The last part was supererogatory. It was quite reassuring enough to learn that everyone over at the United Nations is praying. Shelley Winters was so overcome by this news that she volunteered the knowledge that she always knew that there was something terribly spiritual about India, and this confirmed it.

William vanden Heuvel said that all of this was in the memory of Robert Kennedy, and that he knew that

Nelson Rockefeller in his heart of hearts regretted that the
Republican Party had been taken over by the
reactionaries. Whereupon Shelley Winters volunteered
that she felt a special sense of obligation to liberal politics
because when she was a five-year-old girl, the New Deal
"gave me a hot lunch, even though Herbert Hoover hat-
ed me." Really, Mr. Hoover was a man of quite
extraordinary vision.

Norman Cousins said that nothing had changed in
twenty-three years and proved it by giving a speech I first
heard him give twenty-three years ago. Arthur Schlesinger
said that Nixon and Agnew would usher in the end of—I
didn't quite catch the word, but it was something quite
awful, like "America," or "the world," or something.

But the best was yet to be. Galbraith was introduced,
and a line straight as a superhighway was quickly
constructed by the introducer between Aristotle, Erasmus,
Locke, Adam Smith, John Maynard Keynes—and your
next speaker. At which point, opening his mouth to speak,
the tall, austere Scotsman, for the first time since he was
four and one-half years old, froze.

A lovely young couple had dashed up to the
proscenium, and there shed their raincoats revealing, well,
revealing absolutely everything. Eve was rather quickly
detained, and the raincoat put back on her shoulders. But
Adam bounced up on stage and, holding a pig's head in
hand, danced like a leprechaun around the silent, not to
say awestruck, Professor Galbraith. Out came the fuzz
from the wings (police brutality—everywhere you go,
police brutality), and Galbraith finally turned to his
speech, but alas, not many people were really listening
and, to show how upset he was, he forgot to blame Adam
and Eve on Richard Nixon.

THE PRESSURE ON NIXON

November 23, 1968

Mr. James Murray, the sports columnist (who is surely one of the funniest men in the world), remarked the other day at a public occasion that "already Mr. Murray Kempton has classified Richard Nixon as one of the five worst Presidents in American history." A few days later Drew Pearson revealed that Mr. Nixon had taken treatment from a psychiatrist during the fifties. It transpired that the psychiatrist wasn't practicing psychiatry at the time that Mr. Nixon visited him in search of extrakooky ministrations, but that didn't stop the gang, oh, no. Miss Harriet Van Horne smiled sweetly and said that really it was very courageous of Mr. Nixon to visit a psychiatrist, I mean, if you're nuts, isn't it the very best thing to do to go to a guy who tries to make you sane? Miss Van Horne is so understanding.

New York City is, of course, the capital of the anti-Nixon world, and it does not tire in its vocation of disparagement. A few days after the election, Mr. James Wechsler, editor of the New York *Post,* confessed that even after years and years of thunderous anti-Nixonism, he had reached now the conclusion, "rather offhandedly," that "his administration was [is] more likely to be dull than dangerous, more mediocre than menacing." Wechsler had *tried* to understand Nixon, has read everything there is to read about him, but the portraits are "invariably unsatisfying and barren. . . . The temptation is to conclude that he is a man at once informed and shallow, persevering and hollow, who will seek in his own fashion to restore peace and quiet to a turbulent country rather than confound his conservative constituency."

But the Big Bertha was fired by our old friend Arthur Schlesinger, Jr., in, appropriately, the *New York Times Magazine*. Mr. Schlesinger's interest in Nixon dates from way back. Indeed Professor Schlesinger wrote an entire book about Nixon in something like thirteen hours, during the 1960 campaign. It was called *Kennedy or Nixon—Does It Make a Difference?* and the answer was: Yes, the Difference Between Life and Death. During the recent campaign, Professor Schlesinger (a) announced his retirement from active politics; and (b) proceeded every couple of days to engage in active politics.

The theme of Mr. Schlesinger's criticism of Mr. Nixon is that Mr. Nixon speaks for the "possessing class." Now, the possessing class appears to be everybody who has exerted himself so as to acquire some education, some property, some skills, and a family; and I would think it altogether appropriate to speak for the possessing class, in a society which seeks, as our own does, constantly to expand that class, by inviting others to join it. Still, it sounds grubby to be a spokesman for the "possessing class"—does it not? It does. And that is why Mr. Schlesinger so refers to Mr. Nixon.

He faults Mr. Nixon on many other grounds. Faults him for his "admiration for generals as well as for Lewis Strauss and nuclear scientists of the Teller-Libby persuasion." Mr. Nixon, says Schlesinger, isn't all bad, and it doesn't really matter anymore what he said about Helen Gahagan Douglas in 1950.

In fact, says Mr. Schlesinger, it isn't even fair to say that Mr. Nixon is a warmonger. It's just that "Mr. Nixon has never shown much concern about nuclear war—not that for one moment he would wish such a war, but rather that, unlike Kennedy, Macmillan, and Khrushchev, he seems unable to conceive imaginatively how horrible a nuclear holocaust would be." If only Richard Nixon could understand these things as Khrushchev understands them! Nixon or Khrushchev—Is There a Difference?

And on and on. At quite incontinent length. Mr. Schlesinger goes so far as to disdain Mr. Nixon's predilection for tax incentives by arguing, in effect, that the incentives are a way to increase the national deficit. "Tax revenues transferred in advance to private business are just as clearly government spending and increase the budget deficit just as much as tax revenues directly received and used by the government." But, of course, Mr. Nixon's point has been that the lightening of the tax load would have the effect of intensifying social effort.

Poor Mr. Nixon. If only he would cease, forever and ever, trying to please these gentry. How he, and the country, would profit from it!

EMK

November 14, 1968

Morningafterwise, what would you have thought if the mail had brought you a lapel button that read simply, "EMK"? My reaction would have been that my name had got on the mailing list of a Greek terrorist organization, and I'd have tossed the thing away.

But that is a sign of what sociologists might call Deficient Kennedy Awareness. Because—you guessed it—"EMK" stands for Edward Moore Kennedy; the button I speak of exists and was sent out on November 6 to how many thousands of people I do not know; the symbol EMK is obviously intended as this season's totemic replacement of the older manifests of political purity, like the PT 109 tie clips and the FKBLA (For Kennedy Before Los Angeles) buttons.

Really, the dynastic assertiveness of the Kennedys is a wonder of the world. Six years ago latecomers to Camelot were grumbling that Teddy's decision to run for the Senate on the slogan "He Can Do More for Massachusetts" was arrant opportunism such as to embarrass the entire country. Now many of the same people who were saying that are asking us to prepare to name Teddy, not to a seat in the Senate because he is a Kennedy, but to the White House because he is a Kennedy. There are conservatives around who are accused of wanting to put back the clock. But none that I know of who desire to restore the divine right of kings.

Consider, for a moment, how mere non-Kennedys are treated. It is interesting to note how quickly Senator Eugene McCarthy, notwithstanding his abundant qualifications—he is wittier, profounder, more convincingly liberal, better read than any of Kennedys—is being discarded. Even after the assassination of Robert Kennedy, the court refused to turn to him. They gave as the reasons Mr. McCarthy's temperamental disqualifications. But similar disqualifications did not prevent the same group from being captivated by Adlai Stevenson, back Before Los Angeles.

No, the sin of Eugene McCarthy, one suspects, is insufficient servility to the Kennedy myth and to the Kennedy court. Notice how after the convention he was being not-so-gently bad-mouthed. Arthur Schlesinger, Jr., said about him, a few weeks before the election, that he was an unlikely leader for the new America, because his following consisted of a "semiprecious fraternity of college graduates" (quite true, quite true; but nonetheless a provocative thing for one left Democrat to say about another).

And then Mr. Allard Lowenstein, who began the Draft McCarthy movement, has now announced coolly that Senator McCarthy is not the designated new leader of American liberalism, that the young people who supported him in New Hampshire and elsewhere were supporting not him, but his ideas. And the suggestion, of course, was that a more suitable vehicle could be found for carrying

Senator McCarthy's ideals. Such as who? Why, such as Senator Kennedy.

Now it isn't going to be absolutely open and shut—disgraceful, the way our country forces Kennedys to fight for their throne. There are quite a lot of people around who are fiercely impressed by Senator Muskie. If Muskie were an ambitious man, who knows, he might prove to be an able contender, though he would probably be treated like Hamlet's stepfather. And then, too, there is a slight problem involving John Lindsay. Mr. Lindsay's plans were severely affected by Mr. Nixon's victory.

Friends of Mr. Lindsay hoped for the following sequence of events. Mr. Nixon would lose. And his loss would be generally attributed to his deficient personality and excessive conservatism. Who then would rise as representing exactly the opposite features? John Lindsay, needless to say. Now, suddenly, bereft of his automatic standing as heir apparent, Mr. Lindsay faces a number of political problems, among them the accelerating disintegration of the city he promised to lead to paradise.

On the other hand, no doubt there are dreams that Nixon will prove as unpopular as Lyndon Johnson, and perhaps Lindsay would then emerge as 1972's Republican Eugene McCarthy. And if he won and was pitted against Teddy Kennedy, wouldn't that sort of spoil things for Kennedy? Not to say for the country?

LBJ PACKS UP

December 12, 1968

We read these days about Lyndon Johnson's staggered goodbyes to his many staffs. The other day it was the gardeners at the White House, then the secret service men, then the telephone operators, and so on. Truly he is sorry to go and desires to extract as much ceremony as he can out of the painful act of separation, like John McCormack, who made something like six world tours in order adequately to bid his fans adieu.

It is more than punctilio that moves the President. Nor is he by nature given to preoccupation with those little attentions to which an altogether different kind of man is given. Lyndon Johnson's favors are conceived on a far grander scale, and it is no doubt supremely galling to him that he leaves office lonely, unloved, and discredited, after giving us the Great Society, which he defined in a speech in 1964 as a society concerned more for the quality of its goals than for the quality of its goods.

There never was a man, never in all of history, who conferred such prodigious favors on his subjects. I beg you to be patient as I catalog the programs passed during Mr. Johnson's reign, because although like any list it is tedious, still, it is hard to grasp the appetite of the government under Mr. Johnson to look after us unless one plows through it. The whole of it is costing $25 billion per year, which is two and one-half times as much as Ike was spending at the end there, and more than twice as much as JFK was spending.

Under LBJ we got anti-poverty programs, mass transportation bills, model cities help, rent supplements, crime control, antisegregation acts, voting acts, housing acts, a communication relations act, acts on water and air pollution, on waste, roads, recreation, and parks, on meat and poultry and fabrics and firm prices, on truth in lending, on fair packaging, on electronic radiation, on traffic; aid for elementary schools, for higher education, for teacher corps, aid to the poor, adult education, job opportunity training, the job corps, business aid, aid for Appalachia, an increase in the minimum wage, Medicare for the elderly, Medicaid for the nonelderly, doctors' training, nurses' training, mental health, immunization, health centers, and child health.

A few questions suggest themselves:

(1) How is it that the people are so dissatisfied? I mean those among the people who are critical of the government for not spending more? Is it as easy as this, that if one can find a single poor family, or a derelict building, or a contaminated creek, or an illiterate child, the government has not spent as much money as it ought to have spent?

(2) Why is it that so many observers of government have chosen this moment to disavow government spending as an efficacious means of bringing about a socially desirable end, such as the diminution of poverty? Was it Johnson's handling of the money; or is the problem inherent in government spending?

And (3) Do the people feel as much better off—as much more secure—as one would expect that they should, as beneficiaries of goods and services valued at approximately $1,250 per family? Granted, the wiser among them realize that the money Johnson gave them was the same money Johnson took away from them; still, were there enough people who calculated that after all is said and done, they managed not only to get their own back, but also a little of their neighbor's?

If not, (4) Could it be that under Johnson we came finally to the end of the period exultantly memorialized by Harry Hopkins who thought he had the perpetual key to political success when he announced: Tax and tax, spend and spend, elect and elect?

All of which, in Mr. Johnson's case, reduced him, at the prime of his life, to ceremonial leavetakings at the White House, whose staff probably value more highly the little bauble the President left them, than all these splendors of the Great Society which left America cold.

Crime and Punishment

THE POLITICS OF ASSASSINATION*

October, 1968

Robert F. Kennedy had a way of saying things loosely, and it may be that that is among the reasons why so many people invested so much idealism in him, it being in the idealistic (as distinguished from the analytical) mode to make large and good-sounding generalities, like the generality he spoke on April 5, after the assassination of Martin Luther King, two months exactly before his own assassination. *"What has violence ever accomplished?"* he asked—as if, one broods in retrospect, he were pleading with the assassin whose name neither he nor anyone else knew, but whose existence he had frequently conjectured—*"What has it ever created? No martyr's cause has ever been stilled by his assassin's bullet."* A martyr being someone who sacrifices his life, station, or what is of great value for the sake of principle or to sustain a cause, it is readily seen (a) that not every assassin's victim can lay claim to martyrdom; violence is in fact frequently inflicted against persons qua persons, rather than against persons as representative of causes or principles; and (b) that some "causes" *have* in fact been stilled by assassins' bullets, it being, however, important to note that "causes" are not necessarily noble causes. The

* First published in *Esquire* magazine.

assassination of George Lincoln Rockwell put an end to the American Nazi Party, which was most clearly a "cause." The assassination of Imre Nagy and his followers certainly settled *that* problem. The assassination of Malcolm X accomplished the liquidation of the competition to Elijah Muhammad's hegemony. The assassination of Huey Long accomplished the termination of a political threat to President Franklin Roosevelt which he greatly feared. The assassination of Trotsky accomplished the disorganization of the only significant dissident faction then operating within the Communist movement. The assassination of Trujillo accomplished the reintroduction of democracy to the Dominican Republic. The assassination of Faisal brought republicanism, if that is the word for it, to Iraq. The assassination of King Carlos and Crown Prince Luis Felipe instantly resulted in the resignation of the Dictator Franco and ultimately caused the dissolution of the Portuguese monarchy. The assassination of McKinley brought on Theodore Roosevelt and a brand-new life-style for the American Presidency. The civil-rights assassinations in the South, beginning with William Moore the mailman in 1963 and ending (ending?) with the death of Martin Luther King five years later, incontestably created an encyclopedia of civil-rights legislation. The assassination of President John F. Kennedy, it is widely believed, introduced a rigidity to America's Far Eastern policy from which, it is widely believed, the whole world is suffering, most of all the United States. The assassination of Robert Kennedy all but assured the nomination of Hubert H. Humphrey by the Democratic Party.

Indeed, assassinations more often than not *do* accomplish something—I think offhand only of the exception of Hendrik Verwoerd and maybe Diem in recent times. It is not surprising that they should, inasmuch as every man is unique, exactly irreplaceable. "Why do they want to kill you?" somebody asked Malcolm X. "Because I'm me," he answered. That is why one is driven to consider, as we are redundantly urged to do, not merely the morals of assassination—assassination is in almost all cases indefensible—but the politics of assassination; because, in an age of totalism, assassination is—an instrument of policy. It is no less so because some assassinations bring about consequences different from those desired by the assassins. The wretched young anarchist who killed McKinley could not have known that McKinley's successor would enormously increase the powers and prestige of the chief magistracy against which the anarchists railed. But it was the politics of anarchy, or more accurately of one school of anarchy, to kill important people, and kill an important person Leon Czolgosz most certainly did. Only psychological simpletons would have supposed that the killing of Southern Negro school children or Northern civil-rights workers would serve the cause of segregation, but psychological simpletons make politics, too, and sometimes succeed. And in any case, once there is certitude concerning the consequence, what about the politics of the political sophisticate? Such a man as reasons, as Truman Capote did after the killing of Dr. King, that he was most probably killed by the left for reasons involuted yet after all obvious (*cui bono?* the death, at the hands of a white assassin, of Martin Luther King?). The assassination of Senator Kennedy certainly will not affect U.S.-Israel relations; but it is widely believed that this, for many people, was the marginal assassination, that a number of private decisions have been reached which will be of considerable political consequence. It is observed that there are at this writing twelve fatherless Kennedy children, and that this is a point Mrs. Edward Kennedy is trenchantly stressing to her husband, even as it would be strange if Mrs. John Lindsay sleeps untroubled by the vision of a sniper drawing a bead on her peripatetic husband. Governor Nelson Rockefeller rejects the suggestion that the latest Kennedy assassination should decree an end to person-to-person politicking in the streets, insisting that any such change, let alone the introduction of a President-selected-by-the-Cabinet, would change American democracy. Just so. It may be that the politics of assassination will end up doing exactly that, changing American democracy.

It was long ago ordained, by thinkers in closer conscious communion with Providence than contemporary moral authorities, that it is unwise to count on wickedness being punished and virtue rewarded even in the especially scrutinized world of the mighty. "Servius Tullius," St. Augustine observed, "was foully murdered by his son-in-law Tarquinius Superbus, who succeeded him on the throne. Nor did so flagrant a parricide committed against Rome's best king drive from their altars and shrines those gods who were said to have been moved by Paris' adultery to treat poor Troy in this style, and abandon it to the fire and sword of the Greeks. Nay," said sadly but didactically the principal author of the distinction between the city of God and the city of man, "the very Tarquin who had murdered was allowed to succeed his father-in-law."

Not even the volatile and interventionist gods of Roman mythology, was Augustine's point, were moved to the rectification of injustices committed upon reigning princes. Do not expect, he was saying, that the Christian God, whose kingdom is not of this world, will necessarily intervene to punish the parricide.

That intuition became central to the political thought of the Christian West, expressed even in the pagan agony of King Lear and Coriolanus. Montaigne reflected on the undependability of Providence. But he also considered the correlative problem which is even now the daily problem of the President of the United States, of the Secret Service, and of the FBI: How elaborately must a chief of state protect himself? J. Edgar Hoover, wounded by emanations from the Warren Commission to the effect that the FBI should have picked up Oswald and sequestered him for as long as President Kennedy was within shooting range of Dallas, replied that if the FBI

impounded everyone of the same degree of unreliability as
Oswald in every city the President of the United States
visited, there would result a most fearful—and most
justified—public uproar. It is reported that President
Johnson agreed with Hoover and that a compromise was
struck, that the FBI and the Secret Service would keep
track of more subversives and kinkies than they had been
in the practice of keeping their eyes on, but that the
President, in his turn, would disguise his movements, so as
to inconvenience fixed-position ambushers. The trouble is,
Lyndon Johnson stressed—and then proceeded during the
campaign of 1964 to disregard his own commitments to
personal security (which, as his unpopularity grew in size
and in quality, he would later renew)—that the President
who yields totally to the demands of personal security is
(a) making a concession to potential assassins which
recognizes their relative sovereignty over the freedom of
movement of the President; and (b) affronting, in effect,
the whole of the citizenry, who suffer from the implied
guilt by association with the unknown, and even
unknowable, assassin.

Montaigne mused on the dilemma, which he sharpened
by citing the situation of Caesar Augustus on uncovering
yet another plot on his life. He scheduled the usual
exemplary public execution. But having done so, he was
seized by doubts, suddenly become jaded by the thought
of all those whom he had put out of the way in order to
insure the emperor's survival. "Why livest thou,"
Montaigne reconstructs the soliloquy, "if it be for the
good of so many that thou shouldst die?" In other words,
if there are *that* many people who desire the death
of—Lyndon Johnson, let us say—ought he to go to such
extraordinary pains to prevent that death? "Must there be
no end of thy revenges and cruelties?" he asks himself. "Is
thy life of so great value that so many mischiefs must be
done to preserve it?"

He is fortunate to have handy his wife "Livia [who],
seeing him in this perplexity [asks], 'Will you take a

woman's counsel? Do as the physicians do, who, when the ordinary recipes will do no good, make trial of the contrary. By severity you have hitherto prevailed nothing; Lepidus has followed Salvidienus; Murena, Lepidus; Caepio, Murena; Egnatius, Caepio. Begin now, and try how sweetness and clemency will succeed. Cinna' "—the plotter—" 'is convict; forgive him, he will never henceforth have the heart to hurt thee, and it will be an act to thy glory.'

"Augustus," Montaigne reports, "was well pleased that he had met with an advocate of his own humor"—and proceeds to forgive Cinna but only after delivering a two-hour homily which stands up as a sort of précis of what Hubert Humphrey would deliver under the circumstances. The reader is left feeling wonderfully mellow and fortified in his faith in the beauty of unabashed appeals to reason and good nature. Montaigne does not disappoint you. . . . "Now, from the time of this [incident] which befell Augustus in the fortieth year of his age, he never had any conspiracy or attempt against him, and so reaped the due reward of this his so generous clemency."

But then we brought sharply to earth, without even a new paragraph to brake the fall. "But it did not so happen with *our* prince,"—Montaigne is now talking about a ruler of more recent period, who also forgave his plotter—"his moderation and mercy not so securing him, but that he afterward fell into the toils of the like treason, so vain and futile a thing is human prudence throughout all our projects, counsels, and precautions." And then Montaigne's summation: "Fortune will still be mistress of events."

John Kennedy told a friend that any plotter who was prepared to give his own life in exchange could bring him down. It cannot be otherwise. Dionysius of Syracuse required everyone, including his own son (it is said), to undress and submit to search before entering into the royal presence. Such precautions even *mutatis mutandis* (could you imagine telling Dean Rusk to strip before entering the Oval Room?) are presumably intolerable. But nothing short of them is reliable. There is no scientific table. Assassination is still unusual enough to leave us without such an accumulation as scientists and security experts could pore over and come up with a graph suggesting the correspondence between the degree of exposure and the degree of risk. Fortune is mistress of events. Assassins and assassins *manqués* have aimed their guns at Presidents Andrew Jackson, Abraham Lincoln, James Garfield, William McKinley, Franklin Roosevelt, Harry Truman, and John Kennedy. Three misses and four hits. As many attempts, exactly, were made on the life of Queen Victoria, a beamier target during most of the years she was shot at. Charles de Gaulle was shot at four times during the first six years of the Fifth Republic, but a well-dressed fortune was mistress of the events. (He has since then released from prison army officers implicated in at least one of those attempted assassinations—without the two-hour homily, and not exactly driven by impulses of sweetness and clemency.) But the general meanwhile continues to guard against an alienated fortune. He travels within the folds of bulletproof glass, at eighty miles per hour, helicopters hovering overhead, the hospitals en route well-stocked with physicians and supplies of vintage blood. He continues in his occasional encounters with the multitudes. They are flash meetings, rather like the later Lyndon Johnson's, but they go a long way toward maintaining the impression that the President of France, like the President of the United States, is free and safe to roam about in the company of his subjects. The point is of enormous psychic and political importance. It is remarked somewhere that the emergence of Nikita Khrushchev in the streets of Moscow, halfway through his reign, in such sharp contrast to the Dionysius-type behavior of Stalin, had the profoundest political effect on the Russian public, as though here were *a posteriori* evidence that Khrushchev was their elected chief of state.

Not a shot rang out, not even from the throats of the same people who had produced the Narodniki.

They never exactly flourished, but they existed, in Russia, toward the end of the days of the czars. Although their techniques didn't affect the doctrine of the major ideologies (which continued formally to denounce assassination), their personal heroism made lasting impressions on many revolutionists.

"I came to communism," Whittaker Chambers wrote a friend, ". . . above all under the influence of the Narodniki. It has been deliberately forgotten, but, in those days, Lenin urged us to revere the Narodniki—'those who went with bomb or revolver against this or that individual monster.'

"I remember how Ulrich, my first commander in the Fourth Section, once mentioned Vera Zasulich and added: 'I suppose you never heard that name,' I said: 'Zasulich shot General Trepov for flogging the student, Bogomolsky, in the Paviak prison.'

"Like Ulrich, I may presume in supposing that the name of Ragozinikova is unknown to you. But the facts are these. In 1907, the Russian government instituted a policy of systematically beating its political prisoners. One night, a fashionably dressed young woman called at the Central Prison in Petersburg and asked to speak with the commandant, Maximovsky. This was Ragozinikova, who had come to protest the government's policy. Inside the bodice of her dress were sewed thirteen pounds of dynamite and a detonator. When Maximovsky appeared, she shot him with her revolver and killed him. The dynamite was for another purpose. After the murder of Maximovsky, Ragozinikova asked the police to interrogate her at headquarters of the Okhrana. She meant to blow it up together with herself: She had not known any other way to penetrate it. But she was searched and the dynamite discovered. She was sentenced to be hanged.

Awaiting execution, she wrote her family: 'Death itself is nothing. . . . Frightful only is the thought of dying without having achieved what I could have done.' When she was hanged, Ragozinikova was twenty years old."

The scholars tell us that political assassination prospers when there is a loosening of the repressive traditional regime, which indeed was happening at the turn of the century in Russia; and when ethnic and religious conflicts are in full force. The most galvanizing assassination of the century—at Sarajevo—was the distillate of the two conditions. Political assassination as a systematic instrument of revolutionary doctrine is relatively recent. It was adumbrated in Algeria and Cuba and reached assembly-line perfection in South Vietnam, where any little man who accepts the least position of responsibility in the hierarchy of the opposition (*e.g.*, schoolmaster) becomes ex officio a target for assassination.

The trend, then, appears to be not so much toward an increase in casual assassination (there was much more of that kind of thing in almost any century than this one) as in (a) the increased appreciation of the political possibilities of assassination as a clinical discipline, whether carried on pointillistically on a terrorist scale (as by Castro against Batista), or on a total, greedy scale (as by the Vietcong); and (b) the evolution of assassination as the logical next step for those plungers who are on the march toward a new order of whatever specifications and do not know any of the arguments against escalation. Locke's reassuring proscription against regicide (". . . the person of the prince by the law is sacred, and so whatever he commands or does, his person is still free from all question or violence, not liable to force, or any judicial censure or condemnation") is still a hazy part of the spiritual-political patrimony of the West, but more and more on the order of the proscription against fornication with a member of the royal family (really, it's nice if you don't). Queen Elizabeth observed the regicide of King Faisal by attending the races at Ascot. It is, rather than the sense of outrage against the natural order, the potentially disastrous consequences of assassination, especially involving one of the two great powers, that for instance accounted for the breath-catching horror with which the assassination of President Kennedy was universally met among the professional ruling class. There were some, and they spoke with especial candor in Europe, who feared Dallas might actually bring on a nuclear war. In that respect, everyone was involved in the end of Camelot; and as it was of yore, one grieves to face the truth of it, that when they wept, they wept, many of them, not so much for the fallen prince as for fear that they too would be victimized by the circumstances of his leave-taking. What one might call the Lancaster Vote. Mr. J. C. Lancaster, a white salesman in Mississippi, commented on the assassination of Medgar Evers: "If they don't get the guy who killed him, nobody's safe. Not my wife nor my family. They could even come after me."

It was the harrowing duty of Arthur Schlesinger, Jr., later in the same morning that Robert Kennedy was shot, to deliver a commencement address, and although it is perhaps not quite right under the circumstances to hold him accountable for the words he uttered, still the words were his and as much a projection of his thought, however deranged at the moment, as the pistol shots which we all are bent upon analyzing were a projection of the dislocated emotions of Sirhan Sirhan earlier that day. Moreover, Mr. Schlesinger's words are not in disharmony with those spoken before June 6 and after by American intellectuals who were never emotionally involved with the Kennedy family. Mr. Schlesinger said: "The world today is asking"—not, actually, having had the opportunity to consult the world today on what it was asking—"a terrible question which every citizen of this republic should be putting to himself: What sort of people are we, we Americans? And the answer"—having invented the question, Professor Schlesinger was uniquely equipped to

supply the answer—"which much of the world is bound to
return is that we are today the most frightening people on
this planet. We are a frightening people because for three
years we have been devastating a small country on the
other side of the world in a war which bears no rational
relationship to our national security or our national
interest." A curious statement, even under the emotional
stress, when one reflects that that devastation was
administered over the years by Robert McNamara in his
capacity as principal interpreter of the needs of the
national security, appointed to that post by John F.
Kennedy and confirmed in that post by Lyndon Johnson,
right through the progressive escalation of the war which
McNamara, who played so prominent a role at Robert
Kennedy's funeral, administered without apparent scruple.
If the war was so obviously outrageous to reason or to the
national security, surely its principal executor should have
been repudiated by Robert Kennedy? Or vice versa? "We
are a frightening people because we have already in this
decade murdered the two of our citizens who stood
preeminently before the world as the embodiments of
American idealism—and because last night we tried to
murder a third. . . . The ghastly things we do to other
people—these must at last compel us to look searchingly
at ourselves and our society before hatred and violence
rush us on to more evil and finally tear our nation apart.
. . ."

That proved too much for most people, and the world
soon *was* asking whether Professor Schlesinger hadn't
finally gone too far, from the Washington *Post* "(Arthur
Schlesinger, Jr., sometimes forgets that he is a historian
and a son of a historian and seems to imagine that he is a
prophet and a son of a prophet") to *National Review*
("Arthur Schlesinger***"). He had, of course, gone too
far; but he was scarcely alone. Erich Fromm told us that
ours was "one of the most materialistic cultures that exist.
As a result . . . we are getting more and more
dehumanized," etc. Harriet Van Horne was so choked up

with disgust for "this bloody land" that she satisfied herself to quote the London *Times,* which had written about America more in anger than lucidity, that "the continuing stupidity over gun laws is only part of the larger system [*sic*] under which the United States has been governed so long. It is no more a cause for amazement than the brutal fact that the wealthiest country in the world permits millions of Americans to starve [*sic*]." And all of this, and of course much, much more, against a relentless background that had been building for years, during which Susan Sontag at one point announced her finding that "the white race is the cancer of history," making altogether clear and logical the (FIGHT CANCER) legend on H. Rap Brown's banner, "How many white folks you killed today?"

There is a sense other than that intended by Mr. Schlesinger in which the United States may indeed have become the most frightening country in the world. Ccertainly it is the case if it is true, as is widely believed, that the United States is both primarily responsible for maintaining international order and peace and is incapable of maintaining her own internal order and peace.

The recent assassinations are or are not a sign of a recently evolved national addition to violence. Which was the salient datum? The killing of Dr. King and Senator Kennedy? Or the universal reaction against their killing? "It proceedeth," Hobbes wrote in *Leviathan,* "that men give different names to one and the same thing from the difference of their own passions: as they that approve a private opinion call it opinion; but they that mislike it, heresy: and yet heresy signifies no more than private opinion, but has only a greater tincture of choler. From the same also it proceedeth that men cannot distinguish, without study and great understanding, between one action of many men and many actions of one multitude; as for example, between the one action of all the senators of Rome in killing Catiline, and the many actions of a number of senators in killing Caesar; and therefore are disposed to take for the action of the people that which is a multitude of actions done by a multitude of men, led perhaps by the persuasion of one."

What is more, not even "many men" have been involved. In the case of President Kennedy, the investigation was sufficient to satisfy his brother, the then-Attorney General, that a single man was involved, and an aberrant at that. In the case of Dr. King it would appear that more men than one were involved, but surely not even a multitude of men, let alone "the people." And once again, in the case of Robert Kennedy, the assailant was far removed from John Doe. He was neither *de jure* nor *de facto* American. He was legally a Jordanian citizen. His loyalties were clearly to Jordan. His motivation to kill was entirely un-American. Americans are not given to killing as a means of protesting American foreign policy in the Mideast or, for that matter, so far, anywhere else.

Professor Will Herberg isolates the two principal categories of political assassination: the Continental type, which is done in behalf of a cause—a tradition which is alien to a country whose habits are anti-ideological; and the American type, which is the take-the-law-into-your-own-hands (Jack Ruby), the tradition of frontier justice which however is disappearing along with the frontier, and which in any case never attained to the status of an American ethos, having been steadfastly rejected by most of the most populated states of the Union.

What is happening nowadays, as we pause to wonder how our institutions will fare at the turn of the century, is of course that remote quarrels are conducted in America because America, as an imperial power, disposes of, for instance, the critical say in the Mideast situation. That is not altogether a new cross. It was from America, Professor Herberg reminds us, that the Irish fought the English on the diplomatic front. The construction of the state of Israel was largely an American effort, and the state of Czechoslovakia was promulgated in Pittsburgh.

"We *need* not have any more political assassinations"—Professor Herberg observes—"although we not
unprobably will; we will have to look to our security and
police arrangements for that. But the tensions out of which
political assassinations come are bound to grow and
multiply."

It is, I fear, worse than probable that we shall have
more political assassinations for the reasons Dr. Herberg
gives. Assassination is, as we all tire of repeating, politics
à outrance; and we are well entered into a politics of
totalism. The distance between a student's attending
college and a student's revolutionary occupation of a
college building is a psychological quantum jump on a
scale suggestive of the distance between passionate but
self-disciplined political dissidence and assassination.
Political assassinations such as that against Robert
Kennedy are "unimaginable," we keep reassuring
ourselves. But so also, in another frame of reference, is
the occupation of the office of the president of Columbia
University unimaginable, not to mention defecating in his
wastebasket, scribbling obscenities over his family
pictures, or destroying ten years' research material in an
adjacent scholar's office. While Americans in general,
those who are routinely blamed for the deaths of Martin
Luther King and the Kennedy brothers, appear to be
making progress in the crystallization of a national
resolution against political violence, the same cannot be
said about the young academic community. Political
lynchings have all but disappeared. There was no
equivalent, in 1963 or 1968, to the noisy and public
celebration among anarchists in Paterson, New Jersey,
when the news came down that President McKinley had
been shot in Buffalo. No newspaper, in 1967, welcomed
the assassination of George Lincoln Rockwell with the
openness with which the New York *Daily News* welcomed
the assassination of Huey Long (". . . he invited some
excitable opponent of his to snatch up and use the last
weapon available against tyrants—assassination. . . . Too

bad all this could not have been accomplished by ballots instead of bullets. But Long had with full intent of the will made the ballot a joke in Louisiana. He paid the price"). Nothing like the same progress can be reported among the highly educated. "The reason we didn't move against the occupants of Hamilton Hall," a member of the Columbia administration patiently explained to a reporter, "is that we were quite certain that if we did, they would burn it to the ground."

The toleration of student violence. It is *their* violence, not that of the police who ultimately eject them, that figures; though the allocation of blame to the law enforcers rather than the lawbreakers is a part of the prevailing disingenuousness, as though the maxim of John Stuart Mill ("If any mischief come in such cases, it is not to be charged upon him who defends his own right, but on him that invades his neighbor's") were impenetrable. The toleration the students get from their mentors can be compared to the toleration of the Ku Klux Klan over the years by some of the best people in the South.

Professor John Kenneth Galbraith, speaking at Commencement, 1968, digs in not against the violence and disorder which were the most significant phenomena of the academic year, but against those who deplore them—"They are the men who see the absence of violence as the opportunity for inaction," he jeers. It is immaterial that there are no readily discernible objectives of the new left, that the students of Columbia are, in Professor Jeffrey Hart's phrase, driven by esoteric furies. It is significant enough that the practitioners of that frenzy intend to disrupt and to take effective control if only to dispose of a veto power; and that they have not reasoned, any more than the thoroughbreds of civil disobedience like Drs. Spock and Coffin have done, about the apocalyptic consequences of private licentiousness when justified by idealism, which is many times worse than private licentiousness justified by an appetite for the good life. Better Bonnie and Clyde than Evita and Juan Perón.

Professor Dan Boorstin of the University of Chicago calls for universal ostracism as the only civilized means of dealing with those who strike out in civil disobedience. He insists on the increasing difficulty in distinguishing "violence and so-called non-violence. This," he explains, "is a result of what I'd call a rise of 'flow technology.' It used to be that if you wanted to hurt somebody, you had to hit him. But nowadays when everything is in motion, all you have to do is stop. If you are on a super-highway, all you have to do is drive slower. The result is that other people then seem to do the damage. This makes it easy for people to obscure the fact that they are hurting other people when all they are doing is interrupting the flow of society. The result is that people are able to take the halo of St. Francis when what they really want is the crown of Napoleon. This would be true of the Stokely Carmichaels, the 'student power' leaders, and all the other idealizers of power in our society. There is a great increase both in the need and temptation to be violent, and in the opportunity to get the prestige of the meek and the gentle—when one is really interested in bollixing up the works or in getting power. In recent years there has been a tendency to condone the use of violence if it travels under the false passport of nonviolence, and to condone out-and-out violence because it is in a 'good cause.' "

Such analysis, introducing the concept of a flow technology, is the highest justification of social science at the disposal of old axioms. As to the old axioms, they continue relevant. *The Federalist* promised that the resources of the government would be sufficient "to those partial commotions and insurrections which sometimes disquiet society," or "from sudden or occasional ill humors"—provided they "do not infect the great body of the community."

But against "those mortal feuds which, in certain conjunctures, spread a conflagration through a whole nation, or through a very large proportion of it, proceeding either from weighty causes of discontent given by the government or from the contagion of some violent popular paroxysm, they do not fall within any ordinary rules of calculation. When they happen, they commonly amount to revolution and dismemberments of empire. No form of government can always either avoid or control them." Political assassinations being the antithesis of effective government, they can be expected to increase as effective government decreases.

REFLECTIONS ON THE SIRHAN TRIAL

February 25, 1969

It is not to be in contempt of court to muse about the ludicrous aspects of the Sirhan trial, carefully withholding any (necessarily) uninformed opinion on the question of whether Sirhan was sane or insane when he killed Robert Kennedy. Even that much we are permitted by legal protocol to say only because Sirhan's lawyer has recited the ritual lines: "There is no doubt . . . that [Sirhan] did, in fact, fire the shot that killed Senator Kennedy." From Emile Zola Berman, that is a considerable concession, and he must have made it sound like Bertrand Russell grandly conceding the divinity of Christ. Because, of course, the next step is to persuade that jury that Sirhan's responsibility for firing that shot is no greater than, say, yours or mine. All of which prompts a few reflections:

1. Isn't the whole thing approaching farce? On September 6, 1901, Leon Czolgosz shot President William McKinley. Less than two months later Czolgosz died in the electric chair. I am not here arguing for capital punishment, but reflecting that Leon Czolgosz would very likely still be alive if our courts were operating then as

they operate today; and, conversely, if they operated today as they operated then, more than six months would have gone by since the execution of Sirhan Sirhan for the crime of killing a human being.

2. An aspect of what we are now permitting is not merely the almost infinite elongation between the time of the murder and the execution of the sentence, but something very like a special kind of legal sanctuary for the killer of the very big man—for the magnicide, as he is sometimes called. You may be young, and impoverished, and lacking altogether in influence, but if you will slaughter somebody extremely important—a Kennedy or a Martin Luther King—you will be defended by the very best people around. Suggesting an interesting phenomenon: the Law of Inverse Hazard for the Killing of Important People.

3. Capital punishment, let us face it, is a dead letter. If tomorrow the Supreme Court abolished it on the grounds that it has become unusual punishment, not even the John Birch Society could fault the Court's reasoning. There were no executions last year, only one the year before, and a half dozen the year before that, notwithstanding that the population of the death houses is at an all-time high. The Sirhan trial, under existing law, requires the authorities of the State of California to insist that Sirhan premeditated the death of Senator Kennedy and that, therefore, he earned the death penalty, as prescribed by California law. But even if the prosecution convinces the jury, what would happen? Would Sirhan go to the gas chamber? Not a chance. Because:

4. The techniques of gluing up the mechanisms of justice are so highly refined that almost everybody gets into the act, conspiring to make the killer's approach to the chair an asymptotic curve. Consider, for instance, the case of Sirhan. The trial, it is estimated, will last three months. Imagine the length of the trial record. Imagine the time that reviewing courts will have to put in to mastering it sufficiently to rule on the cascade of objections which

would be filed by the defense. And to what purpose?

Even if, in Sirhan's senility, the last judge on earth, plus the World Court at The Hague, approved the sentence, what would the governor of California do? Would he permit himself to send Kennedy's killer to the gas chamber, when he hasn't sent John Doe's killer to the chair? That would be undemocratic, he would reason—as indeed it would be, even if we cautiously observe that to be undemocratic is not necessarily the supreme offense (Israel was altogether undemocratic, and altogether justified, in suspending its anticapital punishment law in order to hang Mr. Eichmann).

5. Certain reforms can only be made by conservatives, others only by liberals. Only liberals, for instance, are likely to succeed in, say, decreasing taxes for the very rich. Only conservatives are likely to succeed in reforming the penal code to the apparent advantage of the killer, *i.e.,* by abolishing capital punishment.

To abolish capital punishment, incidentally, is not necessarily to come out in theoretical opposition to capital punishment. It is altogether consistent to approve of capital punishment conceived as the all but automatic punishment for anyone who kills somebody else, and at the same time advocate the repeal of existing capital punishment laws on the grounds that their formalistic survival is a net disadvantage to the processes of justice.

THE NEGLECTED NOTEBOOKS OF SIRHAN SIRHAN

May 24, 1969

The newsletter *Combat* has performed a signal service by publishing three pages from the notebooks of Sirhan Sirhan, most of which were ignored by the press at the time of the trial. They are nevertheless instructive for those who desire to understand the crime of Sirhan Sirhan which, it transpires, was more than merely a homicidal paroxysm of a young man deranged.

Last fall I wrote in *Esquire* magazine that Sirhan was "neither *de jure* nor *de facto* American." Legally, I observed, he was "a Jordanian citizen, [whose] loyalties were clearly to Jordan." Shortly before his trial, in an interview with a writer for *Life* magazine, Sirhan angrily quoted this observation: " 'What does he mean?' asks Sirhan, his eyes blazing. 'Not American?' Later he told me [the *Life* reporter continues], 'I feel like an American. If I went back to Jordan, I would be a foreigner.' "

If we can assume that Sirhan's rage was sincere (certainly it has proved unsafe to get in the way of that rage), it repays one's attention, in the context of his deed, to reflect on his belief that he was, in fact, an American; that he shot Senator Kennedy not in his capacity as a Jordanian, seeking to remove a prominent political figure who was siding with Israel, but as an American seeking to adjust American policy into other directions. What other directions? Besides revising our Mideastern policies?

The opinion makers have been as reluctant to draw conclusions based on Sirhan's ideological inclinations as they would have been anxious to draw such conclusions if it had proved that Sirhan was, say, a member of the John Birch Society. Thus also it was with Oswald, whose objection to President Kennedy had no ideological foundation whatever except for the obvious one; namely, that Oswald was a Communist, and President Kennedy was the leader of the great anti-Communist world power. But for every line reflecting on the possible nexus between Oswald's pro-Communism and Oswald's deed, twenty have been written probing illusory byways leading to the CIA, or the oil interests, or the Fascist subculture of Dallas, or just about anything at all, rather than the reality: an amply documented history of relentless pro-Sovietism.

And now listen to Sirhan Sirhan writing in his notebook: "I advocate the overthrow of the current president of the [obscenity] United States of America. The U.S. says that life in Russia is bad. *Why?* [underlined three times] Supposedly no average American has ever lived in a slavic society so how can he tell if it is good or bad—isn't his gov't putting words in his mouth?"

And finally, the Sirhan Manifesto: "I firmly support the Communist cause and its people—whether [*sic*] Russian, Chinese, Albanian, Hungarian or whoever—Workers of the world unite, You have nothing to loose [*sic*] but your chains, and a world to win."

The temptation to dismiss these passages as illiterate rubbish, the rantings of a madman, was specifically rejected by the jury asked to consider them. Notwithstanding the sloppiness of syntax, the thought is neither incoherent, nor the writing illiterate. One page later Sirhan wrote a line which does not issue from illiterates. "My line of thought in this presentation is not steady in flow—due to the multiplicity of grievances and charged emotions that generate within me."

One concludes that Sirhan understood himself to be acting not merely as an anti-Zionist, a Pasadena-based fedayee, but as an American, aroused by, God save us, the rhetoric of the Communist manifesto to strike down a prominent American bound for the Presidency. It is a mistake to suppose that Kennedy alone was his target. Kennedy was a target of opportunity. "Sirhan Sirhan," he wrote in his notebook, "must begin to work on upholding solving the problems and difficulties of assassinating the 36th president of the glorious United States." The thirty-sixth President was Lyndon Johnson. The moral is that the thirty-fifth President and the man who might have been the thirty-seventh President were removed from this world by men indoctrinated in Communism. Even though George Kennan no longer knows what Communism is, some people do who also know how to aim firearms.

JAMES EARL RAY

July 4, 1968

There are strange and interesting elements in the unfolding story of James Earl Ray. It is reported that in London, where extradition proceedings were instituted on the grounds that he had murdered Dr. Martin Luther King, he slumped down and sighed, "Oh my God, I feel trapped." But Ray's demoralization was only temporary, and it soon transpired that he had hired a prominent Birmingham attorney to go to London, and that said attorney was the very same man who managed the successful defense of the KKK types who were accused of killing Mrs. Liuzzo.

Although this is the land of John Birch and Mark Lane and highly inflamed political imaginations, it cannot be imagined by the average American how gleefully Europeans leap to conclusions of Florentine complexity whenever political assassinations are involved. A fortnight ago, Prince Rainier of Monaco asked a visitor whether he had meditated on the first initial of the last name of the three great recent American victims of assassination —K(ennedy), K(ing), K(ennedy). The visitor confessed that he had not reflected on the three initials' significance and forbore going on to say that no American who knows anything at all about anything at all would invest any meaning in the coincidental K's.

The Ku Klux Klan is as capable of organizing the killing of a President of the United States, the most prominent Negro in the world, and the most prominent liberal politician in the world as Monaco is of deposing De Gaulle. It is hard for a people whose history is watered with organized and even incestuous connivings for power to imagine individualistic assassination.

Having said all of which, there is something about the James Earl Ray case which does suggest that if indeed it was he who fired the shot, he did not work alone in the tradition of Leon Czolgosz and Lee Harvey Oswald. Too much is known about Ray, and he is more readily imaginable as a hired killer than as a lusting fanatic. He has been small-time always, a nonideologue, uninterested in politics, untroubled by racial differences. Moreover, the escape from Memphis suggested the cooperation of at least one ally. Assuming Ray was the assassin, the escape required a kind of cosmopolitan sophistication one does not learn at Midwest penitentiaries. The ample supply of cash isn't particularly surprising, inasmuch as the professional training of James Earl Ray is in acquiring fairly large amounts of cash on short, stick-em-up notice. But the exhaustive research necessary, for instance, to appear halfway plausible when applying for foreign passports was more likely supplied by someone other than himself.

Mr. Truman Capote ventured early during the mystery that the killer was a paid assassin and was in all likelihood dead. If the FBI's contentions are validated, then Ray is the killer and is most certainly not dead, nor will he die, except many years from now—from arteriosclerosis or whatever—Tennessee having abolished the death penalty. But as long as he is alive, he of course jeopardizes his silent partners, and it is supremely in the interest of the state to establish who they are, and to discover what was the motivation for the killing of Dr. King.

Mr. Capote reasoned inferentially when he guessed that the man or men who planned the killing were leftists: that the intention was to bring on the kind of disunity and convulsion which typically help not conservative Americans, but hard leftists who know how to profiteer from any general distress. If the idea of killing Martin Luther King was that of the KKK, or some local white supremacist group, then in the light of the experience with the Birmingham church, the three civil-rights workers in Mississippi, Mrs. Liuzzo, and the others—the killing of whom consolidated national sentiment in favor of more and more civil-rights legislation—then the KKK is even more stupid than it is supposed to be, which is an extraordinary achievement. Such stupidity does not go hand in hand with the super-sophisticated provisions made for the assassin's escape: does not explain the easy success that he had in eluding the greatest manhunt in the history of the world (yes, in the history of the world) until, by committing a foolish mistake of the kind that catches up the suspect in second-rate detective stories, the accused as good as turned himself in.

Up until now, Ray has kept his mouth shut. And no doubt the Birmingham lawyer will counsel him to continue to do so. But Ray is not the type to suffer in order to sustain the underworld's code. If he is the assassin, he is likelier to crack up when he realizes fully that he is indeed trapped—perhaps in the years ahead?

The Labor Unions

MR. GALBRAITH AT THE PICKET LINE

April 13, 1967

AFTRA, you have noticed, struck the networks. Even the casual television viewer was aware of it, if only because he was treated to news broadcasts conducted by network executives who, in the sprightly observation of an editor of *Time,* had regaled us with news of "Veet Nom," "Cheeze Juftif Warren," "cloddy skies," and "mosterly easterly winds."

The big strike news was the defection of Mr. Chet Huntley, who crossed his own union's picket line in protest against membership by newscasters in the American Federation of Television and Radio Artists (his point is that newsmen aren't artists, really).

Less widely known and discussed were the causes of the strike, the first in the history of the union. The dispute was over the wages of 100 network newsmen. They wanted $18,200 per year plus 50 percent of the sponsors' fees, whereas the television networks wanted to give them only $16,900 per year and 25 percent of the sponsors' fees.

My own hope is for a constitutional amendment guaranteeing to all newsmen, including newspaper columnists, a minimum of $100,000 per year. But pending that, it did not seem to me that the newsmen captured the emotional imagination of the public in the way that, say, John Steinbeck succeeded in doing for the fruit pickers of California in *The Grapes of Wrath.*

What AFTRA succeeded in catalyzing is, of course, the old superstitions, which flowed most copiously from that flowering cactus of late middle-aged liberalism, Professor John Kenneth Galbraith. The gentleman hastened from his inaugural address as president of Americans for Democratic Action, in which he pledged himself to renewed liberalism, on over to the building from which he was scheduled to broadcast on "Meet the Press," merely to give himself the satisfaction of refusing to cross the picket line.

The author of *The Affluent Society* presumably wants us all to concert to deny the right of anyone to pay anybody less than $18,200 per year, which no doubt will be advanced as the desirable minimum wage in Mr. Galbraith's next book; and indeed, in the kind of society Mr. Galbraith would manage, it would not be long before $18,000 was a starvation wage.

It was a nostalgic demonstration of an old faith, rather as if Marlene Dietrich, emulating the Victorian ladies of yesteryear, were to faint upon overhearing an obscenity. Liberalism, which has been spotted in the past advancing itself as a national political faith, asks people automatically to take sides—against management and in favor of the union, irrespective of the merits of the issue (there are some who call that prejudice).

Mrs. Eleanor Roosevelt once said that she would not cross a picket line "under any circumstance." Giving rise to the most ineluctably rationalist reply I have ever known, namely the call—it having been ascertained that she was in residence—for volunteers to picket round the clock all the exits from Hyde Park.

Several prominent newscasters and television celebrities have said that although they disagree with the demands of the newsmen and the strike call of the union, they honored the strike "as a matter of principle." Their principle being that they are bound to observe the union's directives. Even if we accept the principle that a union can control the activities of its members in the sense even that no modern church could hope to do (imagine a church "ordering" its members not to patronize, say, a particular movie house!), what about the principle of those members of AFTRA who are members not out of choice, but because they have been forced into membership?

Me, for instance.

It would be jolly to observe Mr. Galbraith, en route to address the union, finding himself face-to-face with a picket line outside AFTRA headquarters, manned by American democrats striking for the right to resign from the union and be permitted to work. The outcome? Professor Galbraith would catch cold and be ordered to bed by his doctor, whence he could issue his weekly lamentations upon the inadequacies of South Vietnamese democracy.

IS THERE A LAST STRAW?

February 6, 1968

It is increasingly difficult to work up public indignation over outrage, as long as it is committed by a labor union. In the past few years in New York City labor unions have closed down newspapers and killed off three of them. Labor unions have shut down the ships at sea, closing off passenger and freight traffic. Labor unions have grounded the airlines, or most of them, leaving passengers the option of flying either to Toronto or to Detroit, but nowhere else. The labor unions have shut down the schools, all the schools, in violation of the laws which it is the supposed purpose of the schools to preach obedience to. The labor unions have shut down public transportation, causing something very like a closing of the entire city. The labor unions struck the taxis, and violence was inflicted on the independent operators who declined to join in the strike. New York's severest retaliation against these strikes, some of them illegal, others merely convulsive, economically, socially, and culturally, was fifteen days in jail during the Christmas holidays for Mr. Albert Shanker, the leader of the teachers' union, during which he is said to have run out of tea and crumpets on the third day, resulting in a loss of weight of three and one-half ounces.

I remember three years ago arriving at a television station and meeting at the elevator Professor John Kenneth Galbraith, all six feet five of that eminent intelligence, who always gives the impression that he is on very temporary leave of absence from Olympus, where he holds classes on the maintenance of divine standards. We rode up the elevator and met Billy Rose, the impresario, rich, famous, a little cranky, and (if my memory serves) Dick Gregory, the amiable but extremely touchy Negro comedian. It was opening night for a new talk show hosted by David Susskind, and the gimmick was a Sony-sized television, set on a swivel, which would face whichever member of the panel the questioner, who spoke from a half mile away at Grand Central Station, was addressing his question to.

"Now, gentlemen," Mr. Susskind explained, "there has been a jurisdictional question between the unions here as to which union has the responsibility for turning the knob at the control booth which swivels the television set toward the guest being questioned. So when a question is asked, the person the question is directed to should get up from his chair and run quickly toward the chair opposite the television, exchanging places with whoever was sitting there."

To this day I cannot believe it. We all received our instructions as dutifully as if we had met at the rim of Mount Sinai to receive there from our transfigured Maker eternal commandments concerning our future behavior. I dimly remember an evening spent jumping up from my chair and passing Mr. Galbraith running at sprint speed from his chair to occupy mine, diving into the empty chair, panting, and attempting a suave answer to the lady or the gentleman from Grand Central Station who little knew what heroic physical exertions were involved in situating the guest in front of the little screen.

I do solemnly believe that if the Queen of England had asked Mr. Galbraith or Mr. Rose or Mr. Gregory or myself to make such asses of ourselves in order to indulge her imperial pleasure, we'd every one of us have said, "Madam, go jump in the royal lake." But not so the labor unions. You treat them as fatalistically as a fog, a drought, a hurricane.

The other day a colleague of mine, a lady of bright disposition and middle years, went to her garage to fetch her car—only to find the garage doors closed and her car interred inside. A strike. She asked the doorman of the apartment building to raise the garage door, but he informed her that the striking garage attendants removed the sparkplugs from the machine that hoists the doors, so that there is no feasible way to lift them. I speak of "her garage" intending to be precise. She *owns* her apartment and, accordingly, a part of the garage, which is a part of the building. So that *her* car is being detained in *her* garage against *her* will, and if you think that big brave courageous law-abiding people-loving John Lindsay is going to utter one word of reproach to the labor unions, let alone dispatch a unit of policemen to wrench open that garage door and restore a citizen's rights, you are a romantic, and a patriot, and out, out of this crazy world.

II. IDEAS, CONVICTIONS, IDEOLOGY

NOTES FOR THE PLATFORM COMMITTEE

May 16, 1968

In due course the policymakers will thrash out their platforms. They will be high on rhetoric and low on content, if their predecessors are any guide. Herewith an attempt to suggest a few conservative insights into public problems, in the vainglorious hope that they will catch the eye, if not of the platform writers, perhaps of the incidental voter and opinion-maker whom the platform writers are supposed to please.

Vietnam. The great effort there has been worthwhile. The GOP pledges not to panic. Disavow any agreement reached in Paris which commits South Vietnam to effective rule by the Vietcong, although, of course, any succeeding GOP administration will be pledged to carry out the terms of any treaty executed during the summer. Existing situation too fluid to permit specific recommendations. What is needed is general reaffirmation of the strategic analysis that warranted our helping South Vietnam in the first instance.

World Communism. It continues to exist. The ongoing fragmentation is welcome but isn't of the kind that warrants rethinking of our worldview. There is an effective alliance among the Communist powers vis-à-vis the United States and her allies. That is the dominant power consideration on the basis of which policy should be written in the immediate future.

Red China. It is dangerous to assume that the great convulsions within Red China will forever dissipate or deflect her imperialist ambitions. It is necessary under the circumstances to encourage a counterpower in Asia, capable of staring down a nuclear-armed, missile-developed China. Negotiations should begin with Japan to revise the peace treaty so as to permit her to develop a defensive nuclear arsenal.

Europe. Reaffirm our willingness to help in the defense of Europe, but stress diminishing need for heavy U.S. troop concentrations. Re France, the United States pledges to outlive De Gaulle. And Gaullism.

Mideast. Bring pressure on Arab countries to recognize pre-1967 Israel boundaries if Israel withdraws to those boundaries. Pressure on Israel to make reparations to Palestinian refugees. Encourage international authority under UN Secretariat to lease from Egypt at substantial annual fee right to use Suez Canal, which will then be open to all shipping. Similar arrangement for Panama Canal should be considered.

Africa. United States renounces any intention of interfering in African affairs, though its good offices are at the disposal of any country desiring technical aid or diplomatic assistance. Repeal embargoes on Rhodesia and South Africa. Permit commerce with all African nations.

Latin America. Stress desirability of increasing commercial relations; keep lowering tariff barriers; draft legislation providing guarantees against confiscation by foreign governments, financed by regular, tax deductible payments.

UN. Pledge cooperation with the Secretariat. But

announce a policy henceforward of participating fully in all the debates of the General Assembly, but declining to vote. By so doing, we announce symbolically that we cannot pledge ourselves to abide by the decisions of the majority. We look upon them purely as advisory. Instruct our ambassador to the UN to raise the question of the East European countries whenever the subject of colonialism or neocolonialism is raised.

Balance of payments. The evidence grows that fixed exchange rates are an anachronism. It is a matter of coincidence when a nation finishes a year having exported goods exactly equal to the value of goods imported and dollars spent abroad. The existing system is ultimately based not only on our maintaining such a coincidence over a period of years, but on an unending series of such coincidences, a failure in which gives rise to a strain on our economic credibility. The answer (to which, according to Professor Paul Samuelson, the majority of United States economists now subscribe): flexible exchange rates. The advantages are manifest: The dollar is worth whatever buyers are willing to pay for it. If the dollar diminishes in value, that exactly indicates the settled estimate of its worth. It is the means by which automatic disciplinary pressures are brought to bear on (1) internal inflation) (2) increases in the cost of production; (3) inefficiency. If flexible exchange rates are adopted, and the United States discontinues its purchase of gold, then profligate spending abroad breeds its own *pro tanto* punishment.

Domestic taxation. Think big. Tax reform is urgently needed. The more intensively the subject is studied, the clearer it becomes that government is very poor at trying to make justice through discriminatory taxation. The heaviest burden is, relatively, on the shoulders of the lower middle class. Upward mobility becomes progressively difficult. Inflation heightens the graduated feature of the tax. The very rich have special privileges, loopholes. The very poor are strangled by bureaucracy, inflation. Proposal: Adopt the Friedman Plan: (1) Eliminate all personal deductions; (2) double the exemption rate from the existing $600 to $1,200, an acknowledgment of inflationary reality; (3) set a uniform rate of around 20 percent on all income. The resulting revenue would equal existing revenue from income taxes.* Meanwhile, consciously explore the advisability of a:

Negative income tax. Pledge a thorough examination of the negative income tax but only on the condition that it replace all federal welfare programs. If supplementary welfare is desired, that becomes the business of the individual states. If the negative income tax is instituted, the rates should clearly point up the relative advantage of working as against not working, *i.e.*, every dollar earned should be net remunerative to the dollar earner. If the negative income tax were adopted along the lines proposed by Professor Friedman, a single unemployed worker earning at the rate of zero, would receive from the government at the rate of $1,500 per year. If he is earning at the rate of $2,000 per year, he would receive welfare at the rate of $500 per year.

Poverty programs. If the negative income tax is established, the formal problem of poverty ends. But the psychological problem remains. The maintenance of life and health is insufficient. But the government is ill-equipped to supervise the problem of the disorganized poor, *i.e.*, those who are poor not because of temporary economic circumstances, but because they are utterly lacking in self-discipline. It is estimated that in New York City, one half of the chronically poor are disorganized poor, who cannot be persuaded even to flush their own toilets. These are the most urgent domestic problems in America, and they must be sought out with evangelical zeal by the nation's public-spirited community. Special inducements should be offered to families and small

* See page 116 ("On Fiscal Reform") for an expanded treatment of this plan.

businessmen who are willing to take one or more members of the disorganized poor and oversee their education into usefulness. The government has the responsibility to declare hopelessly irresponsible parents unqualified to bring up children, who should then be turned over to charitable organizations to bring up. The axiom that bad parents are better than no parents at all is a bad axiom, which is worse than no axiom at all.

The government can be useful by repealing the minimum wage laws which have drastically adverse effects on the marginally employed (*e.g.*, the rise in the minimum wage rates in the past ten years is apparently responsible for tripling the rate of Negro teen-age unemployment during the same period).

Labor unions. It may well be too late, but before the country goes down, a major political party should call for removing from any one labor union the right to tie down the entire country or an entire community, as various of the unions have recently done. Needed: extension of the antitrust principle to the labor movement, plus a bill of rights for management, exactly specifying the rights of management against the exercise of which strikes are unlawful as conspiracies to deny civil rights. Also needed: laws that prohibit compulsory unionism. The labor union itself should be reviewed in terms of public policy. Research establishes that the unions are a means of increasing the wages for the better off (approximately 10-15 percent of the labor force) by 10-15 percent at the expense of the less well off (85-90 percent) by 4 percent. It is accepted public policy that the government should enforce the country's antimonopoly policies, the result of which removes the urgent necessity for labor unions, so many of which now serve purely extortionist functions which liberals look increasingly clumsy defending.

Housing. The public housing program and the urban renewal programs suffer from advanced bureaucratism, and from a failure to appreciate the reserves of the private sector. In 1940, 49 percent of American living units were judged below standard. In 1950, 37 percent. In 1960, 19 percent. By 1970, the number will be down to 7.7 percent. During the period 1950-1960, when nearly 18.5 million new dwelling units were being constructed, urban renewal supplied only 28,000 units, less than one-fifth of 1 percent of the whole. And during the period that the federal government built these, it tore down 126,000 units; so that the government during that period was a net destroyer of nearly 100,000 units of living quarters in which the poor had lived. The case grows for taking the government out of the housing business altogether, and permitting the poor to find their own quarters and pay for them, if necessary, out of funds that come in from general federal and state welfare subsidies.

Race. The Negro community must be encouraged to exert itself in every field of endeavor. Subject to minimum standards of civility, this means that the white community should acquiesce even in impulses to separatism, such as the Brownsville experiment in New York City. For instance, the continuing exclusion of Negroes by the prosperous and oligopolistic construction trades unions should be met by encouraging the formation of Negro unions. Negro-dominated schools, where there is community pressure for them, should be encouraged as tactical experiments leading to a strategic integration of the kind that tends to occur between people of similar economic and intellectual achievement. Such emphases as Judge Skelly Wright of Washington, D.C. has put on checkerboard integration are exercises in abstractionist lunacy. Granted the danger of autarky, it is a significant statistic that in their respective New York communities forty times more Chinese than Negroes had traditionally patronized businesses operated by members of their own race. Deflate the rhetoric of racial utopianism. It is worse than useless; it is mischievous and frustrating. We shall not overcome tomorrow, or the day after. Hold out realistic hope; tranquilize; bring calm. Emphasize order.

Civil disobedience. Wage a national campaign against it, irrespective of race, color, creed, or age groups. Raise penalties for infractions. Instruct prosecutors to give top priority to the prosecution of civil disobedience.

Education. The new thing in education is the encouragement of privately sponsored, privately administered pedagogical techniques; *e.g.,* "I'll teach your children to read for seventy-five dollars apiece." An extension of this innovative approach to education is the gradual loosening of the superstitions that publicly administered education is the most desirable kind of education for everyone. Parents who want them should receive vouchers, exchangeable at private schools of one's choosing. The social purpose would be to permit pluralism, individuation, and the adaptation of schools to the special needs of those who have special needs.

Social Security. Remove the limits on the amount that can be earned without penalty by recipients of Social Security payments. The present rules are rightly resented by all elder citizens as a bureaucratic brake on initiative and a mockery of the insurance principle. They are, besides, a costly administrative monstrosity.

ON "WORKABLE" PROPOSALS

April 19, 1969

Mr. Nixon was apparently pressed to adumbrate his proposals for domestic reform ahead of schedule, and he was good-humoredly annoyed. He wanted to take his time, one gathers. So that, in his press conference, he chided some of his pursuers by observing that reforms are very easily proposed by those who have merely to tap them out on their typewriters; but that what he strove after was "workable" reforms.

Now a "workable" reform can mean one of several things, and Mr. Nixon was careful not to specify which he had in mind. By "workable" he might mean (a) a reform that he might hope to pass through a Congress which, after all, is organized by Democrats. Or he might mean by "workable" (b) a reform which the public would tolerate, the public and the Congress not being, on all matters, agreed. Or he might mean (c) workable in the sense that it would work, *i.e.,* that things would actually improve, by almost everybody's reckoning, upon the passage of such a reform.

Consider a few examples. Lowering taxes, at this particular moment, could probably get through (a) and (b) but not (c)—the threat of inflation being as it is. Lowering the oil depletion allowance substantially might get past (b) and (c) but not (a). Eliminating the draft and substituting a volunteer military would probably make it through tests (a) and (c) but not, Gallup tells us, (b).

It is in such quandaries as these that one sees especially the necessity for the leader who concerns himself primarily with what is workable in fact and then mobilizes public opinion and Congress to go along. The politicians' temptation is usually in the other direction: to consult first what a Congress led by the opposition party will likely consent to go along with—keeping a weather eye on public opinion—and to ignore even a fight for what it is that should be done and which a morally and empirically alert public might be persuaded to sanction if the case for it were cogently made.

Mr. Peter Drucker has written an essay which, really, Mr. Nixon and his advisers should closely read. It is a part of his book *The Age of Discontinuity,* and it is called the "Sickness of Government."

Government, Mr. Drucker said, is precisely not a "doer." Its role is to focus on that which, in behalf of people, needs publicly to be accomplished. But the moment the government seeks to do what needs doing by itself, it almost guarantees poor results. Mr. Drucker goes so far as to observe that if the government had done absolutely nothing at all in the big cities, said cities would probably be better off today than they are now. And he gives examples in other parts of the world which lend credence to his gruesome conclusions.

One of the reasons why government is not a doer, he stresses, is that it proves almost impossible to get governments out of a bad engagement. He cites, among others, the farm subsidy program, which goes on and on and on, because the elimination of it would be blocked by (a). The virtue of private business is perhaps what it can accomplish. But its principal virtue, viewed as a coordinate institution of government, is that it is capable of going broke. There is, always, some relation between the goal of a business and the survival of a business. Henry Ford I was forced to retire his Model T, and Henry Ford III was forced to retire his Edsel. If the Fords had been the government, the Model T would still be chugging along. Could we not gear all government enterprises to performance, providing for their automatic elimination when they cease to provide what services they are set up to achieve?

Mr. Drucker's thesis, as elaborated by him, is above all exciting because it is eminently workable according to standard (c). The notion, for instance, of turning over the Post Office to some sort of public corporation was proposed even by a Democratic postmaster, Mr. O'Brien. If Mr. Nixon were to strike out audaciously, in pursuit of a new relationship between government and executives of government policy, he might, just might, win the approval of a dumbfounded Congress. Certainly he could attract the excitement of the public. Granted there would be many casualties: precisely those expensive accretions (the Brooklyn Navy Yard multiplied by 1,000), which we need to do away with in order to get government back to the business of governing, rather than doing or administering.

ON FISCAL REFORM

March 22, 1969

We are told that one of Mr. Nixon's commissions is hard at work on the revision of the tax laws, and that is reassuring. They should certainly be revised. They groan under the weight of inequity and asymmetry, but by that I do not mean oil depletion allowances—that incarnation of evil without the existence of which *The Nation* magazine would simply have to fold.

I have always thought that the oil depletion allowance is positively the easiest thing around to handle: If the Department of Commerce reasons that there is overproduction in oil (there is, by the way), well, let the department recommend that oil discovered after January 1, 1970, shall not be subject to depletion benefits. Where the typical liberal errs is in lusting for retroactive penalties. Although he is all the time talking about justice, he somehow reasons that it is just (a) to encourage drilling for oil by offering the reward of a depletion allowance; and then (b) to eliminate that allowance after a prospector has risked his money and struck the oil. It is as if Governor Rockefeller, after plying his lottery tickets and offering $10,000 to the winner of the lucky ticket, should on the day of the drawing announce that on second thought, $5,000 for the winner is quite enough.

Then there is the bugaboo about the man with the $1,000,000 income in 1968 who paid zero taxes. Sounds bad, but it bears examination. What if in 1967 he lost $1,000,000? I note that my brother writers were unanimous a few years ago in asking that rewards for successful books should be applied over a period of five years, *i.e.*, to compensate for the lean years. What we desire for ourselves in measuring our exiguous income should presumably apply to others, even if they are rich. Every now and then it pays to remind ourselves that it is not a sin to be rich, yea, neither is it antisocial to be rich.

One fears that Mr. Nixon's reforms will be jerry-built. Raise this tax, lower that one, increase that exemption, reduce the other one, up the sickness allowance, down the cocktail deduction; that kind of thing. And never mind that it has been proved again and again and again that every single effort to make justice by tax laws results in the making of new injustices; and, always, the tax form becomes longer, the tax law more complicated, and always, always, human ingenuity manages to exploit the loopholes so that in eliminating this one, you merely create that one.

If only Mr. Nixon would advocate truly radical reform. Professor Milton Friedman has pointed out that if the federal government (a) eliminated all personal deductions; and (b) doubled all dependent exemptions, the government could (c) raise as much money as it now raises by laying down a flat tax of 20 percent on all income. Any attempt to strain that proposal through the usual injustice-collecting filters leaves us a little confused. Obviously the poor would greatly benefit from doubling the exemption—which, obviously, should be doubled if it is to remain a serious effort to judge the cost of rearing and maintaining a child. Obviously the rich would be hurt from the removing of deductions, tax deductibles having become perforce a way of life for so many of them. And on top of it all to abandon finally the progressive feature of the income tax!—that socialist accretion of the twenties and thirties, so relatively useless as a revenue raiser (less than 2 percent of the government's revenue comes from the—over $50,000 per year—rich), so obviously punitive.

Then let the individual states write their own tax codes—including progressive rates, as the individual

state sees fit. And let the facilities of the federal
government be available to the states, so that, for instance,
a resident of Illinois earning $15,000 per year would pay
the 20 percent to Washington and—after looking at the
Illinois chart under $15,000—an additional 5 percent,
which will be remitted by Washington to Illinois. The
simplicity, the reorientation of economic effort away from
tax advantage toward true economic advantage staggers
the imagination. Alas, not unlikely it will stagger the
imagination of Mr. Nixon's tax advisers who will be afraid
to reach out for true reform, fearing the demagogic furies.
But who knows, maybe Mr. Nixon has a surprise for us. It
is about time.

SHELL GAME

January 10, 1970

The national attention given to the rise of the subway
fares in New York City is instructive, as also the
suggestion, published in the Washington *Post,* that after
all, why shouldn't the subways be free, like public schools
and (adds the author) free private hospitals?

Instructive because it suggests how far away we have
got from what would appear to be a rudimentary
understanding of how things work. There are two reasons
why the subway fares in New York City rose. The
secondary reason is that the Transport Workers Union is
utterly unafraid of breaking the no-strike laws of the State
of New York, particularly in an election year, so that it
disposes of the effective power to blackmail the city
administration.

But the primary reason is that New York City subway
workers weren't making enough money and needed a

raise. And the reason they weren't making enough money is because the government is spending too much money. One way to put it is this: that the cost of riding the subway will rise because the American people are receiving so many things free of charge. That would appear to be a paradox. It is the beginning of economic wisdom to recognize that it is not a paradox.

Inasmuch as it is predictable that before these words appear in print, Mayor John Lindsay will have blamed the rise in the fares equally on Nelson Rockefeller and the Vietnam War, it is appropriate to point out that during the Johnson administration money spent on defense rose by 50 percent, while money spent on welfare rose by 100 percent.

As for the argument that Nelson Rockefeller is responsible, the counterargument that comes most readily to mind is also the best argument; namely, that there is simply no obvious reason why Cayuga County apple pickers need to be taxed in order to subsidize the 5,000,000 New Yorkers who regularly ride the subways. And if they were taxed (to quote myself ten years ago) a reciprocal obligation would be implicitly lodged, by the terms of which, very soon, the subway riders in New York City would be taxed in order to help the apple pickers of Cayuga County; and before you know it, the sky is blackened by criss-crossing dollars, and one contemplates, yet again, the mysterious axiom of contemporary liberalism, that one should continually elongate the distance between where a dollar is collected and where a dollar is spent.

John Lindsay would be happy if Albany were to subsidize New York subway riders, happier still if Washington were to do so, and presumably elated if the United Nations were to do it.

What the raise means, to most people, is one dollar extra per week. Since getting to work is a necessary expense, that dollar will either shrink the individual's disposable income; or, in due course, he will wrest that dollar from his employer, who in turn will charge more for his product, and back we go again.

But the assumption that the way to handle the matter is to subsidize the subways is of course ludicrous, not merely because arguments at least as cogent could then be made for providing free food (in order to work you have to eat) and free shoes (in order to get from the subway to the offices you have to use shoe leather), but because after you reach a certain point, it is all but impossible to effect a subsidy.

That point is easily reached by the 5,000,000 subway riders of New York City. That bloc of people is so numerous as to belong solidly in the economic bloodstream of the country. Among them are income tax payers, property tax payers, excise tax payers, and sales tax payers; so that the idea of subsidizing them from funds into which they are not already contributing, and into which they will need to contribute more if the "subsidy" were enacted, is, well, a political shell game. It is our old friend the Economics of Hallucination without which, one might add, most of the people who are elected to office could not have got there.

A CANARD BITES THE DUST

March 16, 1967

About five years ago a public-spirited civic group set out to make a dramatic demonstration of the cupidity of the slum landlord. The slum landlord is instantly recognizable as the villain who profits from the misery of the poor who come to the cities and pay exorbitant sums of money in order to huddle together in grimy quarters in company with the rats and cold and dirt.

Why not, thought the Citizens Housing and Planning Council, buy a slum of our own, renovate it, and show all the world how it can be operated at a perfectly decent profit charging perfectly reasonable rents. Such a demonstration would put the spotlight on the landlords and force, through the pressure of public opinion, a reform in their habits.

So the good Citizens went out and persuaded Mr. Laurence Rockefeller to put up a quarter of a million dollars with which they bought themselves two wonderful stinking slums. They called in the repair people, dressed up the slums by no means luxuriously, but sufficiently to meet bare standards of cleanliness and convenience. On top of the free capital, they enjoyed, as a nonprofit corporation, a tax abatement. And to finance the repairs they managed to wheedle interest from a bank at a very low rate. And the Citizens Housing and Planning Council's slums were open for business.

Business came, all right. One of the astonishing discoveries of the Citizens was that the turnover in one of their slums was an astonishing 80 percent. Moreover, the Citizens found that costs were such as to require increasing the rents over the old rate—indeed, rents were tripled by the new, philanthropic landlords, from the old rate of $23 per month charged by the slumlords, to a new rate of $65, with the result that many old tenants moved out.

But did they then make their handsome profit? Instead of turning in the predicted profit of 8 percent, the Citizens turned in a loss of 3 percent. And that, as the saying goes, blew it. The experiment was officially hailed as a bust. "After four years as the owners of two tenements on the Lower East Side," the New York *Times* solemnly introduced the story, "a leading civic group has decided that it is virtually impossible for a landlord to maintain decent living conditions in a slum area and make a fair profit." "It soon became clear," said the chief Citizen Mr. Roger Starr, "that you couldn't make any profit at all. It simply costs more money to keep up your property than you collect from rents at this level of the economic system."

So what have we here, other than an exoneration of the slum landlord? (Incidentally, one wonders whether all those picketing ministers organized by Mr. Saul Alinsky will reexamine the rhetoric on their placards.) What else was learned?

For one thing, according to the Citizens, that the cost of vandalism is very high. They did not put a figure on it, but perhaps the final report will estimate it. For another, we learn the obvious: that there is a "high cost of maintenance and materials." The Citizens' conclusions are that it will prove impossible to relieve the housing situation by attracting private investment into the slums. You just can't make a profit, they say, at the rates you have to pay, and in dealing with the kind of people you have to deal with.

What kind of people? People who move in and out of tenements at a great rate and leave the quarters they inhabit in very bad condition; who fail to do their own elementary maintenance; and who vandalize at a prodigious rate. The answer, the Citizens say, is—you guessed it—public housing.

Senator Charles Percy has been advocating a plan which would permit slum residents to buy their own apartments, the idea being that by actually acquiring ownership, they would look after their quarters lovingly and with pride. Not feasible, say the Citizens. It is simply too complicated to maintain a building, and the kind of people who live in slums have not acquired the necessary experience or sense of responsibility. Moreover, they would not think of an apartment as truly their own unless they made a substantial down payment—and how is that to be contriived?

Problems enough to drive the average Citizen into the hands of the federal government. The unaverage citizen is liable to ask: Wasn't the Citizens Housing and Planning Council the federal government in miniature? And don't we therefore have something to learn from its failure?

THEY ARE GOING TO DO IT

November 6, 1969

It is the supreme irony of the Court's decision that some white families will now emigrate from the South in order to place their children in segregated schools. I have in mind a specific example, a Southerner from Greenville, Mississippi, whose salary is $11,000 and who believes that integration of the schools will diminish the quality of public education for his children. At $11,000, he cannot afford private schools; so he will go north, where the movement to integrate the schools started, and he will find no difficulty in establishing himself in an area where *de facto* segregation survives unruffled by Supreme Court decisions.

On the other hand, the mood of the South is not by any means mutinous. They saw it coming, with the inexorability which a people come to experience who know deceit and adversity. As a political matter, it is not likely that the Supreme Court's decision will drive the bitter-enders into the arms of Wallace. The reason is that they know that President Nixon, and Mr. Finch, and the Attorney General, all of them counseled and sought out a little more time. The Supreme Court said no brusquely, quite unambiguously. So, what would President Wallace have done? Impeach Warren Burger?

The South has been to Appomattox before and knows the name of the game and isn't disposed to believe that it has been victimized by a grand stratagem of Tricky Dick. The unanimous decision of the Warren Court in 1954 may well have been, as some of us believe, bad law and bad sociology. But it was always inconceivable that so fundamental a finding could be eroded by judicial temporizing. When the Court said that the dual school system should be terminated with all deliberate speed, it was inevitable that the stress would sooner or later move away from the modifier "deliberate."

The political repercussions are not, then, likely to be pronounced, inasmuch as the South recognizes that the Supreme Court has moved at its own deliberate speed, independently of a new President who in fact had just recently designated a new Chief Justice. The repercussions will be of another nature. The ideal would be the serendipitous discovery that integrated education is altogether desirable. Some communities, forced to taste it, will find it less bitter than supposed. Much of the South which feared the consequences of the public accommodations law sees it now as pretty much unobjectionable.

The school system, integrated, may benefit in part from the benevolent consequences of the public accommodations law: It won't be so bad as many expect it. But there are differences. Commerce is a great regulator, the sublimest instrument of egalitarianism. The motel owner who had grudgingly to accept Negro patronage found himself enjoying the dollars, and his motel unaffected by the presence of a few Negroes. The school situation is tougher. In Greenville, Mississippi, for instance, there is very little organized black pressure for integrated schools. The old battle cry has lost its resonance, confused by the more modern-sounding calls for black power, black pride, black unity. And then, too, the Negro teachers wonder about their security in an integrated school system. Won't the school boards prefer white over against black teachers?

What of the 5-10 percent of the affluent whites who

will either leave town or set up private schools? What will that do to the standing of the public schools? There are areas, small areas in America, where the affluent as a matter of course send their children to private schools. But these are rare. Even so, the private school population is growing. Washington, D.C. has always served as the Rose Bowl of hypocrisy, the place where integration became an institutionalized national goal, even as its own schools became *pari passu* segregated, as the entire white population moved its children out, wave after wave of them, after each civil rights bill passed triumphantly through Congress.

It is a pity, perhaps even a tragedy, that the great reconciliations which the early integrators foresaw as the inevitable result of social integration are unlikely. The South will have to let matters take their course. And the best elements of the South will bear in mind that no hardship visited on it by Northern egalitarians or judicial ideologues warrants retaliation against Negro school-children. The specter of New Orleans a few years ago, where the *tricoteuses* expressed themselves against the Supreme Court by spitting on Negro schoolgirls, will haunt the American memory for generations after the sins of Earl Warren are finally bleached by time.

WHAT MAKES BUCKLEY RUN? (A SELF-INTERVIEW)*

April, 1968

Q. Mr. Buckley, last October you suddenly announced your candidacy for membership in the Yale Corporation,

* Reprinted by permission of the *Atlantic Monthly*.

and the story broke into the front page of the New York *Times*. Tell us, please, why (a) you decided to run; and why (b) the New York *Times* should give your decision such heroic attention.

A. The New York *Times* will always remain inscrutable, but perhaps its attention was drawn by the knowledge that in the past I have been critical of Yale, and therefore that the announcement of my intention to run for the corporation is in the nature of an announcement of a projected beachhead on enemy territory.

Q. You haven't said why you decided to run for the Yale Corporation.

A. In fact, the idea wasn't my own, but that of a good friend who is also my lawyer and *National Review*'s. He is an alumnus of Yale of great distinction, Mr. C. Dickerman Williams, BA 1922, LLB 1924, former editor of the *Yale Law Journal*, who clerked under Chief Justice William Howard Taft. I mentioned that once to Groucho Marx, in some connection or other, and he was greatly impressed. Overimpressed. It turned out he was under the impression that Mr. Williams had been President Taft's Attorney General.

Q. Our interest in the historical circumstances that moved you to run is limited. All right, so it wasn't you who thought to run. (a) Why not? and (b) What was it that your genius lawyer-friend said to you that prompted you to run?

A. It didn't occur to me to run because the reaction among Yale alumni to my book *God and Man at Yale* (1951) was unbelieving, not to say hostile, and it had not occurred to me that in the seventeen years that have gone by, the alumni might either have reconsidered that book or gone on to assume that those parts of it which they found most objectionable most likely were no longer a part of my general program, for Yale or for any other college. What shook me up was Mr. Williams' extraordinary contention that I might just possibly win election to the Yale Corporation. He reasons that many alumni are dissatisfied with various policies at Yale, and that although many of them do not agree with all of my own positions, they do agree that such positions as I tend to take are not vigorously enough defended within the Yale Corporation.

Q. Do you mean to say that some, or even many, alumni will be voting for you who wouldn't be doing so if they thought that your views would prevail?

A. Alas, yes.

Q. Isn't that a little unreasonable?

A. No. It is reasonable to desire that someone within the council of the mighty should put forward the merits of a conservative case, even without committing oneself finally to the merits of that case. A conservative becomes a presence in the room. This doesn't mean that he overwhelms the majority but does mean that the majority have a better opportunity to test their own views. You might even go so far as to say that minority representation is an aspect of academic freedom.

Q. Are you suggesting that if you were elected, yours would be the only conservative voice in the Yale Corporation?

A. No. There are undoubtedly other conservatives among the eighteen regular members of the Yale Corporation. But there isn't anyone else who is identified as a sort of public defender of conservative points of view.

Q. Won't it be rather a bore for the corporation to have you there at every meeting, nagging, and tattling, and filibustering?

A. I shouldn't think they would find me any more boring than I would find them. Actually, I have every reason to believe that they are very nice people and, therefore, that I would find myself among people like myself. As for nagging, I don't believe in it, am temperamentally incapable of it. Tattling? I would, of course, respect the privacy of that organization, even as I have respected the privacy of others I have belonged to. However, I would not go so far as to deprive myself of freedoms I now have, to criticize Yale's policies as they are publicly discernible. As for filibustering, I assume that the bylaws of the corporation provide for limiting the time given over to discussion of pending proposals. If there is no such bylaw, I shall propose one.

Q. Has there been public discussion of your candidacy?

A. Most of it has been conversational. Newspapers throughout the country remarked my candidacy, some of them even commenting editorially on it, but Yale has been publicly silent, at least so far. The *Yale Alumni Magazine,* for instance, has, at least as of the moment I write, exhibited a most exemplary *sangfroid.* Not a mention of my candidacy, even in issues which report the social and political doings of the university's white mice. I am very grateful.

Q. You mean there has been no public discussion at Yale of your candidacy?

A. No, I don't mean that. Within a fortnight of my announcement, the student body canvassed its members in two different polls. The first was an open discussion before the Yale Political Union, at which a dozen student speakers arose, some of them to espouse, others to denounce, my candicacy. At the end of the speeches the union voted—in favor of electing me. I attach no significance whatever to this, though it is, of course, interesting to me that a favorable vote should have followed upon a public *debate* over my candidacy. I like that.

Q. How could the students have known what your views are?

A. Some of them have known my views from my writings. One or two of them called me over the telephone, while preparing for the debate, and elicited answers to several supersensitive questions.

Q. And the other student canvass?

A. Went against me. That was a poll of the entire student body, conducted by the Yale Political Union.

Against me were 52 percent of those polled. For me, 36 percent. Don't know, 12 percent.

Q. What was your reaction to that vote?

A. Magnificently political. An editor of the *Yale Daily News* telephoned me before the afternoon of the day the results would be tabulated to ask whether I could be reached for comment at 10 o'clock that night, at which point it would be known whether I had won or lost. I replied that unfortunately I could not be reached at 10 P.M. that particular night, but that—such is my recent education in politics—I was even now prepared to give two statements, one of them suitable for the contingency of my winning, the other suitable if I lost. If the students voted for me, I should be quoted as saying that I had anticipated their *cri de coeur* and was coming fast to the rescue. If the vote was against me, I should be quoted as observing that here was proof (a) of how greatly the students needed my guidance; and (b) of how wise Yale's policy is that students are not permitted to vote for corporation members, or even alumni, until they have been out of college for five years; the presumption being that after five years, they will grow wiser. Wise enough to vote for me.

Q. Why—would you say—did the majority of the student body vote against you?

A. In part because it's fashionable to vote against a conservative (ask Goldwater). In part because the publicity given to my candidacy focused on my views on Yale's admissions policy. These views were strenuously misrepresented in the New York *Times*, enough to convince the Yale student who is a graduate of a public high school that were my views to prevail, a graduate of a public high school stands little chance of getting into Yale.

Q. What, specifically, did the New York *Times* say, and how did what it said misrepresent your position?

A. The *Times* quoted me as saying, "The son of an alumnus, who goes to a private preparatory school, now has less of a chance of getting in than some boy from PS 109 somewhere. There should be a presumption in favor of those who are supporting the university—the alumni."

Q. How does that misrepresent your position?

A. Triumphantly. A few days before announcing my candidacy, I had published a column insisting that the distinction ought to be plain that a positive bias in favor of sons of Yale alumni is not the same thing as a positive bias against graduates of the public schools. My position has been that *all other qualifications being equal,* the son of the Yale alumnus should have preference over the son of a nonalumnus; no matter what school the respective candidates have been attending. In other words, the son of a Yale alumnus who graduates from PS 109 should receive favorable consideration over the son of a nonalumnus who graduates from Groton, *assuming*—as I have said and will not, incidentally, say one more time for fear of pandering to egalitarian greed—that the two boys are otherwise equally qualified, by which I mean that the two boys achieved roughly equal grades on the college scoring tests, got comparably enthusiastic recommendations from the headmaster and principal, showed equal zeal for extra-academic pursuits, etc.

Q. But, in fact, you must acknowledge the likelihood that in such a case as you mention, it would be the Grotonian who is typically the son of the Yale alumnus, rather than the boy from PS 109.

A. Yes, I do, but you mustn't jump to conclusions which would betray an inverse snobbism. I believe that there shouldn't be a positive bias against any boy merely because his father sends him to Groton. Yet I do believe that something of the sort has got itself spliced in the thinking of some of those who have fashioned Yale's admission policies. I grant that my conclusions are impressionistic, but to the extent that it is feasible to substantiate them, let me cite three incidents:

1. The headmaster of a prominent Eastern preparatory school told me a year ago, in commenting on Yale's

admissions policy, that if he were approached by a superbly qualified student who above all earthly things desired to go on to Yale, he would counsel the student to withdraw from his school and enroll in a public school, whence he could more safely count on attracting the favorable attention of Yale's gathering system.

2. The headmaster of another famous private school reported to class agents his concern over Yale's positive bias against graduates of the preparatory schools and sons of alumni but, on being asked to make public his criticisms, was manifestly afraid to do so—one must assume for fear of incurring the retaliatory displeasure of Yale's Admissions Office.

3. The figures. In the Class of 1940 the percentage of the entering class at Yale whose fathers were alumni was 29 percent. In the Class of 1950, the percentage was 24 percent. In 1960, 22 percent; in 1966, 20 percent; in 1969, 18 percent; in 1971, 14 percent. Now, there are two explanations for the diminishing percentage of Yale undergraduates whose fathers were Yale alumni: One —and it raises an interesting intellectual question—is that the academic standards for admission to Yale have been rising at a rate beyond the capacity of the typical son of the typical Yale graduate to keep up with, in which case it is time to ask how come the sons of Yale are failing *their* sons? The other explanation is that sons of Yale alumni are being discriminated against for social reasons, giving rise to the equally interesting question, namely, why does Yale disdain the sons of men who were taught the social values of Yale University?

Q. What do you consider the desirable standard for admission to Yale?

A. The desirable standard is the standard that was explicitly adopted by Princeton University—after the Second World War, or at least specifically acknowledged at that time—a standard from which, by the way, Princeton now appears to have retreated, under the pressures of atmospheric egalitarianism. What a spokesman for Princeton said as recently as in 1958 was very simply this: We reserve the right to set academic standards for the freshman class as high as we like. However, having set them at the level we desire to set them, we shall admit into the freshman class the son of any alumnus of Princeton whose academic record and achievement tests indicate that he would graduate with his class, provided he is also qualified on the basis of the normal extra-academic considerations.

Q. Isn't it so that such policies would tend to make the great private universities sort of endogamous, class-conscious havens for the privileged?

A. Yes and no. Yes to that much of what you allege which is desirable and also, by the way, realistic; no to that much which is undesirable and unrealistic. Neither Yale nor Princeton nor Harvard nor Stanford—not any university, no matter how fecund its graduates—can procreate, one wife at a time, fast enough to make for freshmen classes composed entirely of alumni sons, so that there is bound to be a biological watering of the freshman class with sons of fathers who were not alumni. When Princeton was meticulously observing the policy of granting preference to Princeton sons provided they could graduate with their class (I promised earlier in this article that I wouldn't make that qualification again, but I have mellowed since I began writing it), only about 20 percent of Princeton's entering class were Princeton sons. The entire freshman class at Yale would consist of sons of Yalemen only if (a) every Yale graduate married (which is conceivable, and also desirable); (b) every Yale graduate, upon marrying, instantly impregnated his wife (which is conceivable, and presumably desirable, provided somewhere along the line the process came to a seemly halt); (c) the fruit of said union was a son (neither conceivable—the iron laws of genetics being as they are; nor desirable—for so long as the survival of the other sex is held to be desirable); and (d) the sons of the Yale fathers were every one of them to qualify academically, temperamentally, and socially to achieve membership in the freshman class (not conceivable though most desirable).

I deduce from the figures of the Admissions Committee that if every single alumnus' son who applied for admission to the Class of 1970 had been admitted, even then the freshman class would have been only 55 percent sons of alumni. Suppose that had happened? One has only to imagine the high esteem of the first-rank university whose pedagogy proved so durable and so animating that the majority of the sons of its graduates succeeded in establishing their competitive parity with the best sons of the best parents from all quarters of American society.

In other words, the fear that a private university that favors the sons of its alumni subject-to-etc. will become incestuous and fetid breaks down under scrutiny. It need only be added that such is the diversity even among Yale graduates that if one assumed that the firstborn of each one of them had a preemptive right to admission, which is a travesty on what I am recommending, it would not necessarily follow that the cultural or educational effect upon the university would be suffocating. There are as many differences among sons of Yale alumni—cultural, biological, glandular, intellectual—as there are among the sons, if not of any random sample group of American citizens, then of at least a random sample group of such parents as in fact constitute the parents of existing freshman classes.

Q. You have elaborated what you consider to be the desirable admissions policy. Suppose you answer the question: Why *should* a college favor the sons of its alumni? For purely mercenary reasons?

A. No, not for *purely* mercenary reasons, though "purely mercenary reasons" can be transmuted by the lightest rhetorical legerdemain into "purely altruistic reasons." There are several reasons. Probably the easiest to dispose of is also the most vulgar—which is also the most frequently raised, to wit, your leering question about the mercenary consideration.

Permit me to answer it by asking you a question. Why *should* an alumnus contribute to his alma mater? I recognize one answer to that as pretty much convincing. It is this: that every graduate of every college that paid out more toward his education than the graduate paid in tuition fees ought to feel psychologically indebted at least for the difference. Suppose that it cost Yale $12,000 to cope with me, and that as an undergraduate I paid Yale $6,000. There is a debt of honor there, by my figuring, of $6,000. Not, to be sure, a debt to which anyone can lay formal claim. But a debt of considerable moral cogency.

All right. Now, to whom is this debt payable? The automatic answer (to your alma mater) is, upon reflection, unconvincing. At least, it is unconvincing under the existing philanthropical rubric, which is that your subsidy is utterly unrelated to your being a member, so to speak, of the Yale (read Princeton, Harvard, Columbia, what-have-you) family. If your education by Yale was a benefaction which records nothing more than Yale's generic interest in higher education, then the debt that you incurred is repayable to the Cause of Higher Education wherever you spot that cause as marginally most efficient. Indeed, if we measure our debt to our alma mater in the coin of a reciprocated devotion to the cause of education, then we quite reasonably observe the criteria of our own university in distributing our largesse: Don't give to the privileged few; give to others. Don't give to Yale; give to Tuskegee. Now, I know very well, and indeed am about to dilate upon, the case for multiplying the advantages of the few. But the acceptance of the case for the few requires corollary suppositions which existing admissions standards are reluctant to acknowledge, suppositions the disavowal of which requires the conscientious alumnus to ask: Why, then, give money to Yale, at a time when the College of the Ozarks is also wanting? Yale has got itself a gymnasium the cost of the yearly maintenance of which is more than Ozark pays all its liberal arts faculty. Doesn't it then follow that an appeal by Yale for funds, to the extent that its appeal is based on reminding us that we were the beneficiaries of higher education, is an appeal which we can most plausibly respond to—in the context of its existing admissions policy—by addressing our contributions to the College of the Ozarks?

Q. Are you suggesting that contributions to your alma mater should be based on self-interest?

A. You have a faculty for vulgarizing. I am leading up to the point that self-interest isn't necessarily antisocial, no more in education than in commerce. Permit me to illustrate. A few years ago Yale University, ardently pursuing a distinguished professor of American history, lured a renowned scholar from Johns Hopkins to Yale. The transaction was, by university standards, gaudy, and I shall not divulge the terms of it beyond remarking that the inducement to that particular professor (and please bear in mind that there is nothing here that is intended to disparage the professor, whom I would no more disparage in this context than I would the Hope Diamond—both are expensive and ought to be) was equal to about ten times the contributions to Yale of the entire graduating class of that year. Now I raise the question: What was accomplished by the alumni of Yale who in effect put up the money in order to lure Professor Jones from Baltimore to New Haven? New Haven and Baltimore are not at war, so that we must dismiss that explanation. Well, then? Shall we ventilate the suspicion about which gentility teaches us to keep silent, namely, that only in New Haven can the cause of education fully exploit Mr. Jones? But that explanation must be resisted. Because the academic standards at Johns Hopkins are very high, and indeed we can produce students who were accepted by Yale and turned down by Johns Hopkins, as well as vice versa, even as we can document the high intellectual attainments of many of the faculty of Johns Hopkins. Well, then, shall we assume that Professor Jones has the opportunity at Yale, which he did not have at Johns Hopkins, to write more books? That is altogether possible, because it is true that some universities absorb more of the time of their professors than others do. But then if *that* is the criterion the donor should observe, the alumni should be prepared to put up even more money to lure Professor Jones away from Yale, where he does after all have some teaching duties, to, say, the staff of the Carnegie Foundation or whatever, where he could devote all, instead of merely a part of, his time to writing books.

One senses the difficulty. That difficulty—for the benefit of those who are not sons of graduates of logic courses—is that there isn't really any reason at all for asking sons of Eli to put up money to lure Professor Jones away from Baltimore to New Haven if one invokes merely Higher Education. Indeed, the more you try to make the case, the less you make it: assuming the demonstration was makable that Johns Hopkins is intellectually inferior to Yale; then perhaps disinterested philanthropy should go toward enticing a few Yale professors to migrate to Johns Hopkins. . . .

The perspiring alumni agent has two arguments left to use. The first is the agitated response of those who are taught to reply to reason by a barrage of fatuity. It is the argument that the accumulation of excellence in one place is in itself an excellent cause. The answer, of course, is that yes, it is, assuming that the argument calls for rescuing Albert Einstein from the University of the Ozarks, Samuel Eliot Morison from Kalamazoo, and Edward Teller from Middletown, so as to unite them at a place where they can meet together at the same refectory and pool their knowledge of man's plight. But—once again, of course—the whole thing is phony. If we get Einstein to Yale, we take him away not from the Ozarks but from Princeton. If we get Sam Morison, we take him away from Harvard. If we get Teller, what does that leave

Berkeley? If our preoccupation with a single campus is such that we care nothing about the deprivations of other campuses that ensue upon our predatory academic recruiting, we need to ask ourselves: *Why* that preoccupation?

Q. I assume you are about to say for selfish reasons . . .

A. By your apparent standards, reasons are either (a) "social" or (b) "selfish." Very well, then. If "good" reasons are "social" reasons, then I say flatly, there are no "social" reasons for giving money to any one top-flight university. The best reasons for giving support to a university *are* "selfish." Such reasons as that you desire a particular university to maintain the highest standards because (a) it is a university which is committed to taking on your son, assuming he qualifies to study in that community; and/or—brace yourself—because (b) that university fulfills a particular function, the fulfilling of which endows the nation in which you live with citizens whose attitudes toward their country are such as indirectly to endow that country, and hence you and your progeny, with the benefit of their education and dedication.

Q. Do you then conceive of Yale and other front-rank private universities as educational watering places for a governing class?

A. I am, of course, aware that you are not permitted to use the phrase "governing class" in America. What makes the term invidious is its association with the class system, or even the caste system, in such societies as England's or India's. Curiously, there is no opprobrium attached in America to the concept of individual families being associated over the course of generations with public service, loosely viewed. We are proud of the Adams family, of the Lodges, of the Rockefellers, of the Roosevelts. We should also be proud of institutions an exposure to which sets the mind to thinking in terms of a general sense of obligation to society. Instead, we denounce them as havens for the privileged, summon the spirit of Andy Jackson, and reach for our democratic leveling guns.

There are those who so overstate the imperatives of the democratic tradition that they find themselves, in effect, hard at work attempting to fracture the elite. That spirit is, of course, codified in the progressive income tax that rises, or did until recently, to levels of 91 percent. It is a robust and thoroughly commendable American tradition that there should be instant access to the top for everyone who qualifies, and that there should be ample opportunities to qualify. But recent admissions policies of the large private colleges seem to argue that it is equally important to fracture coalescing classes of governors. The effect of such policies is in part to absorb new members into the governing class, in part to demote others even if they have done nothing to earn that demotion. "You will laugh," I wrote a while ago, and some people did laugh, "but it is true that a Mexican-American from El Paso High with identical scores on the achievement tests and identically ardent recommendations from their headmasters has a better chance of being admitted to Yale than Jonathan Edwards XVI from St. Paul's School."

Any college that wishes to serve within the American tradition should guard against exclusivity for the sake of it. It should never exclude the talented in order to give preferences to its own grossly untalented. But it should not decline to include its own simply in order to multiply opportunity. We should bear in mind that there must emerge a *reason* for the private college if the private college is going to survive. If Yale has no sense of obligation to its alumni, no sense of adherence to any special traditions, why should it be private? I have no doubt that the State of Connecticut would gratefully accept the gift of the plant, facilities, and faculty contracts of Yale University, which gift would (a) provide the final solution to the problem of financing Yale; and (b) forever allay any suspicion that Yale is undemocratic.

Q. Are you then predicting that the private colleges will disappear—or that they will adopt your approach?

A. The private colleges, as nobody tires of saying, are in crisis. They need more money. Paradoxically, the crisis appears to deepen even as the people become more affluent. By today's standards, America was very, very poor in 1891, and the rhetoric of academic extortion was accordingly genteel. Consider President Timothy Dwight (the younger) in 1891, dressing down the alumni who complained of incessant fund raising: "There are perhaps some who object that Yale always wants funds. But is not this the proof of her progress and life? When she ceases to have wants . . . she will no longer be worthy of her past history or of our present devotion."

Consider Whitney Griswold in 1956, reporting that we were in "one of the worse crises in the history of American education." At that time I wrote in *National Review:* "No one paid much attention to Mr. Griswold because yesterday's Worst Crisis is fresh in everyone's mind, and most of us are willing to give odds that when the annual reports came in from the other college presidents, tomorrow, next year, a decade hence (1967), we will find ourselves in yet-the-worst crisis."

1967: "AP, New York. McGeorge Bundy, president of the Ford Foundation, announced today that the nation's private colleges face 'imminent bankruptcy.' The solution, he said, is a drastic increase in government support."

A decade ago the emphasis had already begun to move from support by individuals to support by corporations. There had been an important test case in 1951 when a stockholder objected to the A. P. Smith Company's giving money to Princeton. The judge ended up authorizing the philanthropy, although on grounds most embarrassing to university officials. The gift was legal, said the judge, because "Princeton emphasizes by precept and indoctrination the principles which are vital to the preservation of our own democratic system of business and government." It being a clear violation of currently understood standards of academic freedom for a college to emphasize anything by precept or indoctrination, the language of the decision was avoided like a litany from a Black Mass. Even so, the universities interpreted the decision as carte blanche for corporations to give large sums of money to colleges and universities. Accordingly, in the spring of 1956, the presidents of the large private colleges issued a set of "Guiding Principles for Industrial Gifts." The preamble to the Guiding Principles began by remarking such things as that "colleges and universities have a deep obligation to society" and then hurried on to discuss "the form of corporate giving most useful to the college or university [cash]." Delicately, the presidents warned colleges and universities against permitting "their names to be used in any related advertising" of their corporation donors but hastened to grant that "corporations obviously deserve the goodwill that is the natural and appropriate dividend of genuine philanthropy." (The distinction for which they were groping is not altogether clear. Presumably, it is all right to establish a Colgate Chair of Political Economy, but not a Colgate "It Cleans Your Breath While It Cleans Your Teeth" Chair of anything at all.) Accordingly, such things as the plain and simple Socony Mobil Professorship of Nuclear Engineering (Princeton) started to crop up.

But we see now, ten years later, that the corporations couldn't, or at any rate didn't, give enough. So that McGeorge Bundy, who was educated at Yale when Charles Seymour was its president—a gentleman of progressive inclination and humane disposition who warned repeatedly against incurring any dependency on the federal government—now calls for "a drastic increase in government support." Yale has not, then, ceased to have wants. But is she no longer worthy of her past history? Or of the sometime devotion of her alumni? Why?

Q. Well, why? Purely because of this positive bias you speak of against sons of alumni?

A. I think it goes beyond that. There is the sense of mission, clumsily formulated by the judge in the A. P. Smith case who, unwittingly and in a single sentence, challenged root and branch the central presumptions, not to say vanities, of that special kind of academic freedom which is nihilistic in its implications. The conventional argument against Yale, made by its critics, myself included, has been along conservative-liberal lines: the charge, for instance, that not only is Yale in practice distinctly and observably hostile to one point of view (the conservative point of view), and therefore living outside the bounds of true impartiality; but that such partiality as Yale does exercise is intellectually and politically faddish and very dimly related to the higher ambitions of a great university.

Q. Do you have in mind, specifically, the activities of such conspicuous Yalemen as Staughton Lynd and William Sloane Coffin, Jr.?

A. Former Yaleman Staughton Lynd (Yale is not powerless suavely to excommunicate, when the will is finally mustered). Concerning Dr. Coffin, it is true that he is conspicuous, and that although he has a great deal of support among the students and faculty of Yale (which support is of his political opinions and activities, one has to acknowledge, rather than of the Christian fires that rage within his breast), he is not an *official* spokesman for Yale. But the argument that Dr. Coffin's activities are not to be confused with the mind-set of Yale University is not altogether convincing. It was only a very few years ago that official Yale conferred a doctor of laws on Martin Luther King, who more clearly qualifies as a doctor of lawbreaking. It seems to me that even if you accept totally unexamined the most fanatical statements on academic freedom, for instance, those in Professor Robert MacIver's book, then you definitely need, for the sake of balance, for the sake of intellectual excitement, for the sake of its survival as a private university, a conservative revival at Yale.

Q. What are you doing to try to encourage such a revival?

A. Running for the corporation.

THE END OF THE PUBLIC SCHOOLS

January 13, 1968

There is in the air a sense of great excitement among American conservatives who have reason to believe that their time is coming. In the past few years any number of ideas developed in the garrets of conservative scriveners and roundly dismissed as radical and irrelevant have suddenly begun to appear in the classiest political shopwindows. Four years ago they laughed themselves silly at Barry Goldwater's proposal that they sell the TVA. Now the Democratic Postmaster General proposes selling off the Post Office (to a public corporation).

Twenty years ago Lord Keynes' fiscal policies were written into the economics textbooks as holy writ; and now the monetary policies of Milton Friedman are beginning to displace the obsession with fiscal policy. There are other examples, the sudden perception of the metaphysical limitations of government action, the slow understanding of the derivative limitations of poverty and urban renewal programs. But the most exciting of the lot is the emergence from the fever swamps of the idea of private schools—in preference to public schools.

Seventeen years ago Mr. James Conant, then president of Harvard University, delivered a speech in which he called for the formal abolition of the private schools. Formal because in any case the private schools had diminished to a mere 5 percent of the whole. But Mr.

Conant's brief against them was that they were "divisive," his reasoning, which I do believe that he would at this point gracefully repudiate, being that all Americans should have a shared experience, and that the place to have that is at school.

Now the private schools are proliferating. It is generally supposed that the reason why is the racist prejudices of so many white people. That answer is superficial. The reason why is because an increasing number of parents believe that their children can be better educated in private schools, removed from the political pressures of overwrought communities which are at least as much concerned with making agreeable politics as with producing literate children; and because there is increasing dissatisfaction, among rich and poor, among white and black, with the whole idea of a central school authority specifying textbooks, curricula, standards, and the rest of it—a dissatisfaction mirrored in the Bundy Report presented to Mayor Lindsay of New York a couple of months ago, calling for virtually autonomous school districts.

No one now doubts that what maintains the majority of American students in the public schools in the major cities is economic pressure. Let us admit that if the state were to give each child a voucher, on the order of what is given to veterans under the GI Bill of Rights, cashable for sum X at any accredited school, there would be massive redeployments of children in all the major centers of the United States. And not only the children of the upper middle class. Also poor Negro children, for instance—to private schools especially designed to give special assistance to meet special needs.

Once admit that such movements would occur, and the mind focuses on the coercive nature of existing arrangements. Libertarian philosophers have been interested in the question for years. But now it isn't merely a matter of the liberty of the parents to select their

own schools: America isn't given to the pursuit of
abstractionist freedoms at the expense of politically
profitable egalitarian principles.

It is the dawning realization that everybody would be
better off under a mixed system in which public schools
remained—for those who chose to patronize them. It is
even suggested now by pedagogues of great reputation that
it might be sound for the public schools to employ private
contractors to teach the art of reading to individual
students aged four and five and six. Indeed, the day may
not be far away when it becomes possible—one is
breathless at the prospect—to advocate the voucher
system and take education away from the bureaucrats and
the egalitarians and the politicians and return it to the
teachers and to the parents.

There are many first-rate public schools in America.
But most of these have the characteristics of the private
school. They are mostly in exurban areas and are
supervised by committees of teachers and parents,
reflecting ambitious community standards. The students
are well disciplined, academic standards are high. The
preternatural advantages that inure to them are the
ultimate affront on democracy. So that even people whose
primary interest is in what they call democracy are
beginning to understand the relevance of the idea of the
private school.

SOME CONSERVATIVES AND
THE REAL WORLD*

April, 1969

Mr. David Friedman has written (*The New Guard*, April, 1969) an essay entitled, "Is William F. Buckley a Contagious Disease?" His reasoning did not surprise me, having heard it a year or so earlier from Mr. Friedman's famous father as we chatted in a television studio.

I think it fair to paraphrase the argument of father and son as follows, namely, that the term "contagious" must not be used metaphorically, and that this is what I did when, on recommending a public policy for drug addicts, I wrote a paper in 1965 under the title, "Narcotics Is a Plague." "Do you see what's wrong with that argument?" Professor Milton smiled at me, that smile which has destroyed a thousand collectivist dogmas. His question turns out to be rhetorical. "Don't you see, what's to keep me from saying, 'Conservatism is a contagious disease'?" There isn't time, in those fleeting encounters, for extended analysis, so that characteristically one attempts quick-shot arguments by analogy. I asked Professor Milton, "Is it your position that, assuming the community decided to license the whores, it would be wrong to insist that they check in at regular intervals for health certificates?" Yes, he thought that would be wrong—"After all, if the customer contracts a venereal disease, the prostitute having warranted that she was clean, he has available a tort action against her."

"Buckley's analogy," intones David Friedman, "—(He calls narcotics addiction a contagious disease because

* Reprinted by permission of *The New Guard*.

most addicts acquire the habit from other addicts)
—denies free will. Catching a disease requires no
cooperation on the part of the victim. . . . The victim must
[after all] CHOOSE TO TAKE THE DRUG. Mr.
Buckley, associating with a dozen addicts, would be in no
danger of addiction. . . . Narcotics addiction is a
contagious disease only in the same sense as conservatism
and Catholicism. Like narcotics addiction, both are
patterns of belief and addiction which many people regard
as harmful to both the 'addict' and his society. . . .
Certainly the doctor should warn the addict of the effect
of overlarge doses. If, knowing this, the addict is willing to
trade his health, or his life, for a few years, or months, or
minutes, of drug-induced ecstasy, that is his affair. Part of
freedom is the right of each of us to go to hell in his own
fashion. It sounds brutal to say that an addict should be
allowed to kill himself with drugs. Consider the alternative
to which Mr. Buckley is driven. Out of a benevolent
regard for the addict's health, we limit his consumption of
drugs. Because of his desire for more drugs, the addict
becomes a danger to us, his benevolent protectors. So we
put him in jail and, so far as I can tell from Mr. Buckley's
statements, throw away the key. After all, as Mr. Buckley
says: 'It is practically impossible to "cure" a narcotics
addict who does not desire to be cured.' "

I invite Messrs. Friedman to take a look at the real
world. I quote from *Manchild in the Promised Land,* by
Claude Brown:

> Most of the time, I would go up to Harlem on the
> weekends, because this was the only place I knew to go
> when I wanted some fun. It seemed that if I stayed
> away two weeks, Harlem had changed a lot. I wasn't
> certain about how it was changing or what was
> happening, but I knew it had a lot to do with duji,
> heroin.
> Heroin had just about taken over Harlem. It seemed

to be a kind of plague. Every time I went uptown, somebody else was hooked, somebody else was strung out. People talked about them as if they were dead. You'd ask about an old friend, and they'd say, "Oh, well, he's strung out." It wasn't just a comment or an answer to a question. It was a eulogy for someone. He was just dead, through.

At that time, I didn't know anybody who had kicked it. Heroin had been the thing in Harlem for about five years, and I don't think anybody knew anyone who had kicked it. They knew a lot of guys who were going away, getting cures, and coming back, but never kicking it. Cats were even going into the Army or to jail, coming back, and getting strung out again. I guess this was why everybody felt that when somebody was strung out on drugs, he was through. It was almost the same as saying he was dying. And a lot of cats were dying. . . .

Drugs were killing just about everybody off in one way or another. It had taken over the neighborhood, the entire community. I didn't know of one family in Harlem with three or more kids between the ages of fourteen and nineteen in which at least one of them wasn't on drugs. This was just how it was.

It was like a plague, and the plague usually afflicted the eldest child of every family, like the one of the firstborn with Pharaoh's people in the Bible. Sometimes it was even worse than the biblical plague. In Danny Rogers' family, it had everybody. There were four boys, and it had all of them. It was a disheartening thing for a mother and father to see all their sons strung out on drugs at the same time. It was as though drugs were a ghost, a big ghost, haunting the community.

People were more afraid than they'd ever been before. Everybody was afraid of this drug thing, even the older people who would never use it. They were afraid to go out of their houses with just one lock on the door. They had two, three and four locks. People had guns in their houses because of the junkies. The junkies were committing almost all the crimes in Harlem. They were snatching pocketbooks. A truck couldn't come into the community to unload anything anymore. Even if it was toilet paper or soap powder, the junkies would clean it out if the driver left it for a second. . . .

Fathers were picking up guns and saying, "Now, look, if you f—— with that rent money, I'm going to kill you," and they meant it. Cats were taking butcher knives and going at their fathers because they had to have money to get drugs. . . .

If the plague didn't hit you directly, it hit you indirectly. It seemed as though nobody could really get away from it. There were a lot of guys trying to get young girls started on drugs so that they could put them on the corner. When a chick's habit came down on her, she'd usually end up down in the "marketplace," 125th Street between Third Avenue and St. Nicholas. . . . If a young girl got strung out on drugs, she wouldn't go around trying to steal. Most girls were afraid they might get caught. Most girls would start selling body. So if a cat was strung out, if there was a young girl he knew who had eyes for him, he would cut her into some drugs to try to get her strung out, too. Then he could get the chick to sell—[herself]—for him and get enough money to keep them both high. . . .

It was a plague. You couldn't close all the doors and all the windows and keep everything out. It was getting to everybody. . . .

There was never a time that I could remember in Harlem when there were young girls who looked so bad as after the s—— plague hit. You'd find strung-out fifteen-, sixteen-, seventeen-year-old girls who didn't look too bad at first. But they got so bad that even cats with long collars would get tired of s—— these cold junkie b——. . . . It was a plague.

Whittaker Chambers once wrote that the conservatism that could not make way for the machine was not even a twitch, it had become a literary whimsy. As much, I fear, is to be said about a theory which holds that if the people of Harlem (or of wherever) choose to torture themselves to death, they have every "right" to do so. If the alternatives are to spare Harlem and by extension the whole of New York City—and who knows, the whole of the republic—or to spare the integrity of a Pure Theory, I would not hesitate.

In fact I do not believe that the proper theory and practice exclude one another. The powers of the state are conceded in the matter of quarantine. It is rather an exertion of the imagination, than a travesty of the truth, to say that narcotics is a plague. I did not read Mr. Brown's book until several years after electing, by coincidence, to use the word he used to describe the situation in Harlem. Is it a metaphor? Is it clinically establishable that those who become addicts do so of their own free will? Is there no relevant recourse to what we know of psychology? Is it the assumption of libertarians that those who of their own free will decide to live in a slave state may do so, notwithstanding the impact of their decision not only upon themselves but upon others? Is there a libertarian around who, knowing what we know about the Communist system, would elect to permit a society to vote itself into Communism rather than back, by force if necessary, the minority which sought the preservation of freedom? Is it paternalism to take advantage of such knowledge as, in fact, you have? Does our willingness to tolerate self-destruction through obesity commit us to toleration of self-destruction through drugs? Does our enthusiasm for libertarian principle require of us such sociological blindness as prevents us from understanding that an individual who determines to destroy himself through drugs brings down a part of society with him—his sisters, brothers, parents, community, *vide* the descriptions of Mr. Brown?

One can only smile at some aspects of Mr. Friedman's (*père*) extension of libertarian thought, concerning which there is truly reason to smile. Presumably, libertarian theory assumes that encounters between a gentleman and a lady of pleasure will be consummated only after attorneys representing both parties have negotiated a warranty concerning the lady's wholesomeness, physical if not moral (an interesting point: How does libertarian theory, pursued à outrance, handle moral problems, other than by denying their existence?)—which warranty becomes Exhibit A at the civil trial of John Doe versus Suzy A. See? Simple.

Simple like what makes libertarianism sound simple to worldly people, when it graduates into dogmatic theology. I love and adore Milton Friedman, and no man living has done more to reestablish the relevance of the free market in intricate economic affairs, but when he talks this kind of thing, he can only be smiled at in return, a smile with a trace of irony in it because on the particular matter of narcotics there is a great deal at stake, like human life; and because a posteriori, there is so very much damage to be done this-away to the wholesome major contentions of libertarian theory. To fanaticize is to discredit, even as Oliver Wendell Holmes warned that the logic of the contention that to the homeowner belongs the airspace above his home is damaged by the extension of that claim as entitling him to a shaft of space reaching up in a straight line from the center of the earth through his roof on up into infinity—such as would require astronauts to receive permission from each one of us before gamboling about unlicensed in our private territory. The articulation of libertarian theory to such lengths as Mr. Friedman is able to take it ought to be understood to be a form of intellectual sport. As such, it is fun, and rewarding in the same kind of way that medieval theologians found it rewarding to speculate on such mélanges de genre as the engagements of spiritual essences with corporeal objects—a form of fun, like scrabble, only more so. But it is terribly important not to take that kind of thing seriously.

THE NEW CONSERVATISM *

April, 1969

The question is asked, What is the new conservatism? because it is supposed (correctly) that it is in some respects at least different from the "old" conservatism. Let me see, ten years ago? Conservatives in America rallied in their disapproval of the invitation to Nikita Khrushchev to visit the United States, attaching to that visit a symbolic significance which, indeed, it had, notwithstanding the violent reversals in United States-Soviet relations during the next three years, in which Khrushchev successively (1) withdrew his reciprocal invitation to Eisenhower, on the grounds that the U-2 so greatly offended him; (2) constructed the Berlin Wall; and (3) sent missiles to Cuba with which to threaten us. But the trend had set in, and when, in June, 1967, Kosygin came over to the UN and popped down to New Jersey to visit with President Johnson, there wasn't a picketer in sight.

The incident is revealing not only for reteaching us what is after all obvious, that that which arouses public protest can quickly become routine, and routinely accepted. It teaches us that some issues are forever snapped by merely turning the symbolic switch. What appeared so very wrong to some people was the notion of a state visit by the active leader of the most highly organized totalitarian force in history. But the moment that visit was consummated, it would become all but impossible to restore the *status quo ante;* so that the

* © 1969 by The New York Times Company. Reprinted by permission.

return to chastity became, in a way, pointless: once
deflowered, that is it; one moves on. And conservatives,
who continue to be, loosely speaking, the most orthodox
anti-Communists in America, look for new forms through
which to express themselves. The Soviet Union does not
let too much time go by without giving them cause, though
every time it becomes a little tougher, on account of the
general attrition of anti-Communism and the great
symbolic rupture of 1959. Thus when the invasion of
Czechoslovakia took place, the editorial chastisements
were just a little perfunctory, rather like what one would
write about Belsen a year after beholding Buchenwald. *Sub
specie* they are equally horrifying: the rape of Hungary, as
we used to call it, and that of Czechoslovakia. But
somewhere along the line the word had gone out, and its
force on conservatives was not lost, that it had become
vulgar to raise one's voice against the Communists. So
that when we did so in the summer of 1968, it was like an
unscripted cadenza, the climax of which was Richard
Nixon's suggestion that perhaps this was not the ideal
climate in which to vest our confidence in an
antiproliferation treaty. Six months later President Nixon
routinely sent the treaty on through for ratification, with
an explanation as to why things were different now from
what they were in August, which nobody could quite
recall.

What does all of this do to the new conservatives? It
drives them back, even as domestic developments drive
them back, toward different, if not exactly more basic,
positions.

The next major battle was over ABM. Leave alone the
scientific dispute which, after all, is neatly consigned to
irrelevance by the observation that after all if the one
group of scientists is correct, we have lost $5 billion; if
the other is correct, we might lose 30,000,000 lives. The
anti-Communism of the old conservatives was one part
evangelistic. It held that we had an obligation of sorts to
help those who could not help themselves, to fend off the

juggernaut. There was talk, even, of rolling back the Iron Curtain—the liberation rhetoric of the early fifties. But the principal strength of anti-Communism was less evangelistic than self-affirmative. Anti-Communism was not only a means of saying that we disliked Stalin, but that we liked the opposite of Stalin: represented, roughly speaking, by—us.

The debate on ABM joined, at one level, the true conservatives and the true—call them what you will—doubters, perhaps, is the least provocative designation. The new conservatives are reduced to insisting that the defense of their country is worth it at any cost—and we speak now not of the lousy $5 billion, but of 1,000 hydrogen bombs aimed at the enemy that finally threatens our survival. This was at the heart of the debate. During the four or five years preceding it, doubts had been cast about America which raised questions never raised before outside the camps of armed ideology. Who, let us say, listening to every public utterance during that period made by the Reverend William Sloane Coffin or Dr. Benjamin Spock—not to say the typical contributor to the *New York Review of Books*—could conclude that in order to save what we have, we are justified in slaughtering 10,000,000 Russians? What we have is (ask the Kerner Commission) a country deeply and passionately committed to racism; a country (ask Seymour Melman) altogether dominated by the military-industrial complex; the world's principal agent of violence and savagery (ask Martin Luther King); the apogee of materialism and hypocrisy (Marcuse). Why would anyone go to such lengths as conceivably might be required to defend such a nation as that? A velleity to survive is one thing. An atomic war is another.

I see it as the historical role of the new conservatives not to abandon their traditional concerns, but to accept the necessity of gut affirmations respecting America's way of doing things, some of which were traditionally espoused by the liberals and the progressives, whose contemporary uncertainty about them (Messrs. Wicker and Reston of the New York *Times* have several times, for instance, shown themselves sympathetic to the use of force by Negro militants) imposes special burdens on the conservatives. For instance:

1. The democratic process. This was never considered by the conservatives as a principal responsibility of theirs. There were enough bards of democracy floating about, even ideologists of democracy, even imperialists of democracy. So that for years conservatives thought it better to ask questions about what it was that democracy had ushered in, rather than join in the chorus that made of the democratic process itself the venerable thing.

It is a little different now; because order has been challenged, and the conservatives have always believed in the blessings of order. It was (primarily) the conservatives who observed that Lyndon Johnson had been elected President by the democratic process, and that under the circumstances, pending his repudiation, he had rights which were his to exercise. The new conservatives have had to stress the democratic process at other levels. It is not exactly a democracy which designates who will be the president and the governors of Harvard University, but there is a feel of democracy there. Some of the governors are directly elected by the relevant constituency—the alumni of Harvard. Those who are not so elected, but are designated by the incumbents, cannot in fact be so offensive to the alumni body as to cause it to mutiny—Harvard is rich but not that rich. So that conservatives find themselves defending the rights of the authorities of Harvard, over against the mobocratic demands of students and faculty who wish to leapfrog the authorities so as to have their way, instantly.

2. And due process, the meticulous cousin of the democratic process. Due process was looked at cynically by many conservatives as a means, along with the Constitution's commerce clause, by which the federal government managed whatever intervention in human

affairs appealed to it at the time. This due process was used by the Court to revolutionize criminal prosecutions, even as the courts had used the commerce clause to defend Congress' right, via its authority over interstate commerce, to set the rate of pay of elevator operators. The abuse of due process was rampant; but how valuable due process becomes, up against Marcusean furies. Thus the new conservatives, though perhaps historically bitter at what due process can be made to do at the hands of abstractionists and ideological profiteers, find themselves fighting especially hard for its survival. The guillotine is sharpened for many victims. Not alone those who have been raised over us by the exercise of democratic authority—the Lyndon Johnsons, the Mayor Daleys, the Nathan Puseys—but the prosperous owners of Dow Chemical (merchants of death; take away what they have) and the little Jewish delicatessen owner in Harlem (racist exploiter; vandalize him out of existence).

3. Upward mobility. Over the years the social democrats were thought of as the principal enthusiasts for it because of their social programs which were essentially egalitarian, redistributionist. The conservatives insisted (quite rightly) that upward mobility was precisely what the free-market system most generously contributed to, and they had the figures to prove it. But having said as much, the conservatives left it (quite naturally) to human resources, up against the system, to take advantage of the opportunities to rise. Many, many millions did so. But now the need for that mobility is more acute than ever, so much so that the new conservatives are giving the free marketplace something of a hand—for instance, by preferential hiring of Negroes. That is helpful. More helpful, I think most of them would agree, is a concerted assault on institutional barriers to the rise of the depressed, to the victimization of the poor. So? Repeal of minimum wage laws. Destroy antiblack discrimination in the labor unions. Ease the progressive feature of the income tax. Adopt an altogether different attitude toward what Mr.

Starr so acutely isolates as the "disorganized poor," in contrast to the transient poor.

Here, then, is an order of concerns for the new conservatives, which by no means suggests the abandonment, let alone the theoretical repudiation, of some of our other concerns. (One of these days I'd like to find out just who *did* promote Peress.) But the historical responsibility of the conservatives is altogether clear: It is to defend what is best in America. At all costs. Against any enemy, foreign or domestic.

III. AMERICA AND THE BLACKS

CLEAVER FOR PRESIDENT

San Francisco, November 19, 1968

A little paragraph in the New York *Times* appearing a week or so before the national election revealed how the editorial board of the Columbia University newspaper had resolved to vote for President. The vote was for Eldridge Cleaver.

The gentleman preferred by the students to Richard Nixon is not widely known in the United States, because we are not all of us so well informed or well educated as the young journalists of Columbia University. I spent an hour with Mr. Cleaver here in San Francisco after having read up on him a little bit. His name does not appear in *Who's Who,* but if it did, *Who's Who* would briefly record that he is currently the information minister of the Black Panthers and was the Presidential candidate of the Peace and Freedom Party in 1968; that early on in his life he elected to defy the law, which he began to do as a boy by hustling marijuana, for which he was sent up to a juvenile reformatory, after graduation from which he turned to the serious business of rape, beginning first with black victims but moving on to white women for ideological reasons carefully explained in his best-selling autobiography, *Soul on Ice*.

But upon being caught and sentenced to prison for fourteen years, he undertook his self-education and prevailed upon lawyers generally friendly to iconoclasm to argue for his parole, which parole was granted after nine years in prison, whereupon Mr. Cleaver enrolled as a Panther and rose instantly to a position of prominence.

In due course a rumble ensued at which a young Panther was killed, and the State of California contends that Mr. Cleaver was consorting with such persons as the parole regulations prohibited keeping company with, resulting in (a) his recall to prison) (b) his release from prison by order of the lower courts; (c) which ruling has been overturned by a higher court; (d) whose ruling is under appeal resulting in the protagonist's continued, if temporary, freedom.

Concerning Mr. Cleaver's activities and those of his party, one can suggest only the flavor of his approach. Ronald Reagan, for instance, is, in Mr. Cleaver's language, "a punk, a sissy, and a coward, and I challenge him to a duel to the death or until he says Uncle Eldridge." Those who take a little clandestine pleasure at that kind of thing said about Ronald Reagan might however find a little bit off-putting the *Black Panther Journal* published after the assassination of Bobby Kennedy, which ran a drawing of Mr. Kennedy as a dead pig. Those who find this understandable as campaign oratory may wonder at Mr. Cleaver's treatment of Julian Bond, whom he recently accused of being "a pig [who] might just end up being barbecued with the rest of the pigs."

Well, then, what should we do about it all? "I hope," Mr. Cleaver said recently, "I hope you'll take your guns and shoot judges and police." I asked Mr. Cleaver whether he finds it consistent with his ideology to encourage the assassination of Mr. Richard Nixon, who, after all, is the chief pig-elect, and Mr. Cleaver replied that he would not publicly encourage the assassination of Mr. Nixon because the pigs would come after him if he did, but that privately he would do so, satisfied as he is that Nixon deserves to die, even as did the pig Kennedy.

Had enough? Ah, but your stomachs are not as strong as those of the more educated members of the community, like the faculty members of the University of California who have invited Mr. Cleaver to give a course for credit at the Berkeley campus. Actually they really wouldn't want him for President; they are just getting their kicks without confronting the consequences: a venture in ideological onanism.

I told Mr. Cleaver that the supreme irony of it all is that such support as he has is mostly from the white folks. The blacks are too dignified, too honest, too gentle. It takes middle-class educated white folks to say "Cleaver for President," even as, in eighteenth-century France, it was the sports in the upper class who lionized De Sade. Cleaver is half right to feel such contempt as he feels for those of us who tolerate him and his disciples.

THE NEW FACES OF RACISM

May 17, 1969

For those who keep track of legal and extralegal comings and goings in the practice and theory of racism, here are three interesting incidents.

(1) In Chicago a United States District Court judge counseled a convicted Negro who had participated in a mail fraud scheme and got caught at it to avoid, especially, a career in such crime as, distinctively, the white man is good at. The judge's point, one gathers, is

that there is an expertise in crime, and it takes a good long time for Negroes to become educated in the high Caucasian arts of, *e.g.,* bank robbing, swindling, counterfeiting—that sort of thing.

The judge is on solid grounds, provided he is not assumed to be saying something which is racially invidious. In other words, according to existing canons, it is okay to say to the Negro: Don't try to counterfeit money, because to do so requires skills in engraving and miniaturization which the white man, through exclusionist union and educational policies, has husbanded to his own. But it is not okay to suggest—and of course there is danger that the innocent Negro's mind will stray in that direction—that the Negro has to wait before he can aspire to the high criminal mentality of the white man.

There are those who make just that point explicitly—Elijah Muhammad, for instance, the Black Muslim leader who says that white men are biologically inclined to kill and to exploit. One must assume that the judge meant no such thing, even if one wonders at the questionable prudence of the advice he gave. Surely if a young Negro is disposed to rob a bank, better he should attempt to do so while unskilled enough to fail at it than when skilled enough to succeed.

(2) At Cornell, a few white students were picked up and arrested during the general upheaval that focused on the occupation of a building by Negro militants armed with rifles and shotguns and the interruption of the ROTC. The lawyers—the honkies' lawyers—have come up, in behalf of their clients, with a most interesting complaint, namely that it is a violation of the equal provisions of the law either to prosecute, or to fail to prosecute, by reference to race, color, or creed.

In other words, it is a form of racism—the lawyers are in effect contending—to refuse to prosecute the black militants merely because they are black, while prosecuting whites. Yet another burden for the (manifestly) overburdened Mr. Perkins, the forlorn president of the

University of Anarchy, on the banks of old Cayuga.

And (3), and most interesting of all, the decision of the judge over in Ohio concerning the segregationist policies of the black students at Antioch College. Last winter an irate Roy Wilkins of the National Association for the Advancement of Colored People announced that he would go right back to court to challenge black-inspired compulsory segregation, just as he had tackled white folks in years gone by.

Along comes a judge who authorizes the exclusion of white students from the all-black arrangements at Antioch on the following grounds, all ye sophists take note. You see, says the judge, white people aren't being excluded because they're white—that indeed would be unconstitutional—but because they do not have the relevant background, namely, blackness.

Imagine, for a minute, what a judge would do if a white group excluded blacks not because they are black, for heaven's sake, but because they don't share the background experience of being white. Get it? Well, the chances are that his honor is in for a great big official rebuke from the higher court.

Still, it is interesting how mixed up you get when you harness the law so as to make it do what people aren't inclined to do, black or white. It cannot be long, at this rate, before it becomes a totally mystifying question which is the problack thing to advocate—the racist, or the antiracist, proposal.

WILKINS *v.* INNIS

January 25, 1969

The stand taken a few days ago by Mr. Roy Wilkins, the head of the National Association for the Advancement of Colored People, was in one respect welcome. He denounced black extremism, and there is no denying the need to denounce it. But in the course of doing so, he planted squarely his objections to the evolution of the black movement during the last couple of years, and that is something else again.

Mr. Wilkins made two points, one of them constitutional, the other social. As a matter of law, surely he is correct in suggesting that what white people are not permitted to do to black people, black people surely ought not to be permitted to do to white people. If it is wrong under the Constitution for white people to compel segregation, then it is wrong for black people to compel segregation. Accordingly, said Mr. Wilkins, if it becomes necessary for the National Association for the Advancement of Colored People to go back to the courts and sue black defendants, he is quite prepared to do so.

This declaration has now brought a vigorous denunciation from Mr. Roy Innis, who is the head of the Congress of Racial Equality. Mr. Innis spoke well of Mr. Wilkins' historic role as head of the NAACP but suggested that, really, Mr. Wilkins' retirement is overdue; that he is behind the times, that he does not understand the meaning of the current struggle of the Negroes for self-identification. On the matter of turning back to the courts, Mr. Innis was emphatic: "The latest NAACP outrage is the last straw. If Wilkins can use funds supposedly earmarked for black people to fight against those same people, then CORE will commit resources to defend and safeguard the students in their demands."

Now there is a happy prospect for an innocent judge sitting somewhere—to find himself one day presiding over a lawsuit brought by the NAACP against, say, the administration of Northwestern University, for acceding to Negro student demands that Negro students be given their own living quarters, with CORE defending Northwestern. How to untangle *that* mess. . . .

The key, surely, is whether the new Negro militancy

will permit Negroes so disposed to proceed as they are disposed, toward integration. The stories of black militants booing non-conformists are now legion. They proceed as if they have the rights of union leaders to bully and to intimidate those who do not want to join. How, one wonders for instance, would a Negro student fare at San Francisco State College if he arrived there as a freshman and announced that he did not desire to join the Black Students Union, or to associate exclusively with the black students? To whom would he turn for protection? Would the administration protect him? If not, would he need to turn to the NAACP?

These questions are not idle, because although the machinery against coercion is technically available to any free citizen, in fact it is likely to be useless if the social situation is such as to cause people to submit to demands by black militants in order to achieve just a little serenity. Mr. Wilkins' legal threat, under the circumstances, is valid: The machinery should be kept lubricated. We must not permit ourselves to graduate into the assumption that only whites are capable of intimidating blacks.

But Mr. Wilkins, in his anger, failed to make the proper distinction. As an advocate of integration backed by law (Mr. Wilkins grew up in the integrationist tradition of liberalism), he has indeed failed to give serious enough attention to the role of self-consciousness in improving the Negroes' lot. It is that self-consciousness which many wise Negro leaders appear to be asking for: Negroes helping Negroes, relying upon themselves, helping themselves, organizing themselves, educating themselves. The great psychological question is: Can Negroes achieve this solidarity, this self-consciousness, without—in pursuit of exclusiveness—encouraging the hatred of others? Can one be a proud Negro without being proudly antiwhite?

The answer is clearly in the affirmative, even as one could be a proud Christian without being anti-Semitic. But the dangers are there, witness Elijah Muhammad and his kindergarten racism, of which there are overtones even in the sophisticated writings of James Baldwin and Richard Wright. But the excesses do not condemn the idea, and in this respect Roy Innis scores against Roy Wilkins, not because integration isn't what is ultimately desirable, but because voluntary segregation may be the quickest historical way to achieve it.

THE BROWNSVILLE AFFAIR

December 14, 1968

The other day I showed a member of the admissions committee of a famous Eastern college an article published by the indignant editors of Choate Preparatory School, which is where JFK went to school. Need we say more? The piece was called, "How Can One Tell?" and it gave the academic and extracurricular profiles of a dozen students together with the colleges for which they had applied, and the colleges' response. The point of the exposé was to demonstrate that, in fact, you Cannot Tell. That is to say, that it does not follow from superior grades and superior achievement in extracurricular activities that you will make it into the college of your choice.

The perfect score in verbal aptitude in the college tests is 800, and I spotted one gentleman in the Choate demonstration who had scored a subnormal 475 and was way down in his class but had nevertheless been admitted to Harvard University. Now—I asked the dean's assistant—just how do you account for that? Oh, he replied, almost certainly a Negro.

I raise the point because we have in the past period come slowly to realizing that the old antidiscrimination doctrines are insufficient. It is not a discovery to say that we must in fact encourage a pro-Negro discrimination—Mr. Garry Wills was making that argument as long ago as 1965 in the pages of *National Review;* and quite recently Daniel Patrick Moynihan made the argument in the *Atlantic Monthly.* The point needs to be carefully made and understood primarily for the reason that those who tend to make it tend to be immune from the practical consequences of it.

Garry Wills is a doctored classicist in a major university and a journalist whose talents are rated very high in the free marketplace—he is not going to be edged out of anything. Patrick Moynihan, the indomitable Democrat, has just now been hired by Richard Nixon away from MIT, and that shows how desirable *his* talents are. The demand for my own services is not, on the one hand, exactly inflexible; on the other hand, I am not likely to be summarily replaced by an editor or columnist merely because he is a Negro. What one needs to consider is the individual who stands to suffer. Not only the student at Choate with much the higher verbal score and much higher standing in his class, who, after all, stands to suffer a fate no worse than a college slightly less distinguished than the one he sought access to; but the butcher and the candlestick maker for whom, under tight competitive situations, it means that if they yield their places to a Negro, they lose their jobs.

I suspect that this is behind much of the bitterness in the New York teachers' strike. It is a strike which may go down as the most complicated in history, but certainly one of the causes of it is the feeling by white teachers that Negro teachers are being advanced without regard to the common criteria for advancement.

"Discrimination against teachers by reason of a white skin is no more defensible than discrimination against blacks," writes the eminent Mr. Eugene Lyons, adding, "What's wrong with a teacher's concern for his 'job security'? Particularly in the light of massive violations of teachers' tenure without pretense of due process?"

Mr. Lyons has isolated perhaps the crucial point, which

sheds light not only on the school strike in New York but on the future of the black power movement in America. It is this: The white community must protect those of its members who are dispossessed by black competitors favored precisely because of their race. It may not be an obligation of Harvard or Yale or Columbia to place qualified white applicants who are turned aside in order to favor black applicants—there are opportunities aplenty for these rejects. But in such cases as New York's, it surely was somebody's responsibility to find jobs for the eighty-seven white teachers summarily dismissed at Ocean Hill-Brownsville by the Negro superintendents without just cause. It is one thing to justify the assumption of power by Negro managers, another to be indifferent to the plight of the victims of their arbitrary decisions. It is one thing (and in my judgment, subject to certain safeguards, the right thing) to turn over to black administrators the responsibilities of education in black areas, another to neglect the casualties of their ethnocentric hiring policies.

The first duty of New York City, as of other cities, is to provide for those who are dislocated. Assuming that we approve of discriminatory hiring in favor of blacks (as I do), we must acknowledge the concomitant obligation to protect the whites whose jobs are taken. Are there then no limits that should be imposed on the new black administrators?

Granted that a city encouraging the decentralization of its schools so as to secure black control of black schools should look after teachers who are arbitrarily relieved of their teaching duties. To say as much is to concede that the new black superintendents will dispose of the power to fire whom they like. Should they have the power to hire whom they like? The struggle in New York focuses essentially on that question. It is hard to give a persuasive answer, hard to draw an exactly plausible line. Herewith some thoughts on the matter:

Q. Should Negro administrators be permitted to hire

teachers irrespective of state licensing requirements?

A. Irrespective of some state licensing requirements, yes. Such requirements as specify, for instance, residence at teachers colleges should be waived. Others that require some evidence of proficiency in the subjects to be taught obviously should not. However, the superintendent and the board of the appropriate unit should be given the power to waive any requirement in any individual case.

Q. What if the administrators of a black school hired a teacher who taught hatred for white people, or for white officials, or for policemen?

A. The teaching of race hatred should not be permitted. A useful definition of what ought not to be permitted is embodied in the UN's Genocide Convention. A teacher judged guilty of teaching such doctrines should be suspended for a period of, say, three years.

Q. What about ideological indoctrination? What if the teacher preaches the thought of Mao Tse-tung or advances the principles of Karl Marx? Should that be tolerated?

A. My inclination would be to say yes: Tolerate it, say, over a period of two or three years. Such toleration would be an act of faith in the strategic good sense of the Negro community. During that trial period, arrangements should be made to protect the minority which desires to go to a different school because of the parents' opposition to the other indicated school. If after a few years it becomes manifest that the black community as a whole does not bother to control the schools, that in fact they are conscript to an ideological clique, then the only answer is to move massively to recapture the schools. But until it is so proven, it would appear wise to make the experiment.

Q. How can you talk about "making the experiment" when conceivably it is at the expense of ruining the minds of young children?

A. In the first place, the minds, qua minds, are being ruined anyway, by inadequate education. In the second place, it isn't only in black schools at Ocean Hill-Brownsville that you run the danger of ideological indoctrination. You get i.i. in schools throughout the country. At Princeton University, more members of the faculty registered a preference for Dick Gregory for President than for Richard Nixon for President. It is not as though one were threatening what was heretofore a well-balanced civic situation. In Harlem they have had centrally administered public schools for years, and for years they have had Adam Clayton Powell, Jr.

Q. But aren't you making recommendations which are in a sense racist?

A. Yes, but only in the sense that reverse discrimination is racist. It is apparent that the black community desires the exercise of power. Now in order to exercise power it becomes necessary to permit black people to assume positions for which they are not qualified by conventional standards. That is no different from what the white colleges are doing when they lower their standards in order to admit Negro freshmen ahead of others who are better qualified academically. To appoint a black teacher because he is black is racist, granted. But we have reached a point in race relations where it becomes desirable to act consciously in such a way as to accede to such demands of the Negro community as are in the least way plausible. Negro control over the education of Negro children would appear to be one of these defensible objectives.

Q. Do you then assume that only black teachers would be hired?

A. No. In Brownsville, for instance, the majority of the teachers were white even under the rump regime of Mr. McCoy. What seemed to make the difference was that those particular teachers were hired by the black administrators. It is the authority that they seem to desire: That is the crucial point.

Q. And how can one prevent the minority of fanatical blacks from taking over?

A. How does one prevent the minority of fanatical whites from taking over? By periodic elections, overseen by the courts.

A MEMORIAL FOR DR. KING

October 7, 1969

What to do posthumously about Martin Luther King is
becoming a Cause. One encounters here and there petition
forms to Congress, requesting that his birthday be made a
national holiday, like Lincoln's, or that the day of his
assassination be made a national day of mourning, like
Memorial Day. And then Mrs. Martin Luther King, who
clearly learned from her husband the uses of the press, is
omnipresent; saying, sometimes, useful things. Saying,
other times, most unfortunate things.

A week ago she revealed that she had been in
communication with the administration concerning a
national memorial to her dead husband. So far,
unexceptionable. But she has now said she has abandoned
the negotiations, on the grounds that she has detected an
"indifferent attitude" toward black and poor people. "We
felt that to get federal support for a memorial would have
been a beautiful thing. . . . But President Nixon's attitude,
his lack of real concern, suggests that his administration is
motivated by racist attitudes."

Really, it is enough to drive a politician up a tree. I can
imagine what Mr. Nixon and his lieutenants and the
leaders of Congress are saying privately about Mrs. King's
intemperance, and it isn't good. The notion that "racist
attitudes" motivate Mr. Nixon is paradoxically correct.
Because Mr. Nixon would never have paused to negotiate
with Mrs. King concerning a national memorial to her
husband except for the fact that Dr. King was a Negro,
and some might call this racist, as the word is nowadays
used. If he had been white, the suggestion of raising a

monument to him would have been presumptively
ridiculous, not because a white man carrying the message
of Dr. King on into martyrdom would be less than an
object of national honor, but because there is a long line of
men who are deemed to have been national benefactors
who have not yet been memorialized in concrete, and
some of them have been dead (Andrew Jackson, say) for
more than 100 years.

Mrs. King and the supporters of her plan put a curious
emphasis on the desirability of using federal funds. The
fact of it is that Dr. Martin Luther King was a hero and a
martyr in one respect. In others—one thinks of his
celebration of civil disobedience—he was the spokesman
for a point of view on citizenship which in the opinion of
some—e.g., me—is mortal to civil society.

Dr. King's discovery of the transcendent rights of the
individual conscience is the kind of thing that killed Jim
Crow all right. But it is also the kind of thing that killed
Bobby Kennedy. And there are those who would be
reluctant, for that reason, to be co-opted, as implicitly
they would be, in any national monument constructed by
federal funds, or any holiday which called for the shutting
down of national institutions.

Surely what makes sense here, as so often is the case, is
to encourage people to act in their own behalf, to express
themselves freely. The statue to Franklin Delano
Roosevelt in London was built by the contributions of the
British people, collected on a voluntary basis. When
Senator Robert A. Taft died, his friends, feeling deeply his
loss, instituted a Robert Taft Institute, one purpose of
which was to collect money to construct a carillon on the
park outside the Capitol. True, the government deeded
over a few square feet of sod for the use of the friends of
Robert Taft. And surely it would be a sensible
compromise, in the present impasse, for the government to
do as much for the friends of Martin Luther King. But let
them then raise the money from private sources.

Memorials so constructed may be less grand than the

behemoths undertaken by an act of Congress. But they are in many ways more impressive. And surely it is fitting, under the circumstances, to follow the precedent; even as the friends of Robert Kennedy intend to do.

Above all, Mrs. King should be counseled to stop the racist talk. Because more of that, and she will antagonize those whom there is no purpose in antagonizing. It is time to mute the memory of one Martin Luther King, the advocate of civil disobedience who once likened America's foreign policy to Nazi Germany's; and stress instead the qualities that made him admirable—his courage, his moral strength, his great eloquence. That is not accomplished by attributing racism to the Nixon administration.

A TOUR OF THE GHETTOS

May 27, 1969

Cleveland: *How Does It Go with Hough?*

At Hough, which is the ghetto area of Cleveland that went berserk in the summer of 1966, there are those who are trying to fight despair. I think we—"we" are a dozen journalists touring the nation's slums under the sponsorship of Whitney Young's Urban League—must have met them all, and they are an impressive lot. In their thirties, mostly; strikingly intelligent, resolutely dignified, rather a bit too worldly (except about their own concerns); and here and there a little fiesty.

One gentleman, seated with a half-dozen others who were gathered to explain the work of the Hough Development Corporation, declined to proceed unless each of the journalists rose to give his name and publication, schoolboy fashion. It is wonderfully leveling. "Luce, *Time*." A friend recalls an experience at the Harvard Law School when a classmate on the prowl turned brusquely to a lonely black student eating at the other end of the table, to ask provocatively, "What does *your* father do?" The boy looked up. "He's a king."

The journalists, predominantly white, are thus put gently in their place and are given to know that the Hough Development Corporation is headed, and largely staffed, by "black nationalists." It isn't altogether clear nowadays exactly what that means. It can mean something as specific as Milton Henry's separate black republic, and something as general as local autonomy.

But it isn't racist in the exclusionist sense of a James Forman, who will not nowadays shake the hand of Joseph L. Rauh, Jr., because that hand is white. In that semicircle was a young man just out of the Yale Law School, white as the driven snow, who does the legal work for HDC ("We figure we ought to know what the laws are when we break them," the chairman said cheerily); and a second lanky and grave young man, soon to matriculate at the Harvard Law School, who works as a volunteer, harnessing his not inconsiderable connections as son of the president of the principal bank in Cleveland.

What is it all about? Not, they tell you, "black capitalism." Black capitalism is out in the jargon. Why? For one thing, it is a term that is used approvingly by "the structure." For another, "capitalism" sounds bad in progressive circles. So that the term is not permitted to be used in describing the activities of HDC, which probably would not cause offense to Adam Smith, such are the heresies committed by HDC on capitalist doctrine.

On the other hand, the antipoverty entrepreneurs seem to revel in the swinging vocabulary of capitalism. Their Handyman's Maintenance Project is not only "Incorporated"; it is stipulated (on this arrangement both the graduate of Yale *and* the novitiate at Harvard apparently pooled their organizational expertise) that the handymen themselves would be the only shareholders.

"Does the organization make money?" an unfeeling journalist asked. Well, no. Silence. Well, why the stock hokum? But nobody asked that question. We had already been told by the chairman that handymen cannot take pride unless they are working for themselves, whence the corporation.

How were the handymen recruited? Beautiful. The first twenty-seven men who walked in from the street. "Some of them punched the clock during the training period and then left before classes began. Some of them smoked pot during class hours."

There were occasional difficulties in on-the-spot training (twenty-five of the twenty-seven had criminal records): "One cat out on a job would cop a machine and split with it." But, eventually, half of the matriculators graduated and are now earning $2.25 per hour. They are not numerous; they do not prove or disprove an ideological point.

It is hardly an exercise in capitalism. The program was funded by government money. The per capita cost of rehabilitation is wildly excessive in free-market terms. The rhetoric of the private corporation is phony, and the projected dividends are illusory. But they are, like others who have been set right at Hough, testimony to the practical idealism of the anxious, busy, talkative, ambitious, ingratiating black social entrepreneurs of Cleveland.

San Francisco: *Making It with the BSU*

May 29, 1969

Twelve journalists gather (a little wearily: They had a full day even before crossing two time zones) at the dilapidated (the government has withdrawn its subsidy after the long illegal strike) headquarters of the Black

Students Union and sundry epigoni from San Francisco State College. On the walls are Black Panther posters, sample caption: "The racist dog policemen must withdraw immediately from our community . . ." The students are very uptight (as they say) and are bent on doing their thing (as they say) to The Man (us).

As a matter of fact, it isn't the journalists who are the principal oppressors. "You are no more the cats who run this country than we are," one leader dismissed us. "Who runs this country is the capitalist exploiters." For those who tuned in late, journalists write not what they feel, not what they see, what it is necessary to write in order to make credible the hypocrisies and make secure the power of—The Structure.

Who is The Structure? The only one given by name by these students of higher education is Standard Oil. Why don't the oppressed buy shares of Standard Oil? The question isn't raised: We are there to listen, not to debate.

But very soon we were ticked off one by one and challenged. Did you have anything to do with the story in *The Wall Street Journal* about me? I'd beat you up personally if you did . . . Did you, NBC, have a hand in the broadcasts distorting our positions? You—*Ebony*—go back and tell your slavemaster to cover some of our activities over here. You, *Newsweek*, what do you consider a relevant education? Answer, and don't give us no—.

The lady guide from the Urban League intervened and asked for a little order. She is shouted down as a slut agent of The Structure. *Newsweek* says, no, he doesn't believe education is necessarily relevant at this point—he is interrupted: Make a commitment, and cut out the ——.

Life magazine, what are you doing about racism, which is the necessary companion of capitalism? What am *I* doing? *Life* collapses in indignation. Why, I all but wrote the Kerner Report you just finished praising! No excuses, *Life*—make a commitment. You, New York *Times*, are you willing to make a commitment RIGHT NOW to the

700 students busted at San Francisco? The New York *Times* demurs—he doesn't know all the facts; how can he be expected to make a commitment? Typical Fascist evasion.

The *Christian Science Monitor* leans over and whispers, what the hell, let's get out of here. Not that easy. We are surrounded by revolutionaries. They have several times informed us that they are just about through with us, because they don't want to waste their time ——ing around with us; but prudence suggests that one wait until the king withdraws. Abruptly, the chairman calls the meeting ended, and the journalists peel away, after a few comments with the students individually, rather than *en banc,* at which meetings the inquisitors elide into naturalness, even as the hanging judges were said to do after their official business was done.

The next day, Bobby Seale, chairman of the Black Panthers, and his lieutenants. We arrive dutifully and are met on the sidewalk by a representative of the chairman: "The meeting has been called off. By order of the chairman. You may as well disperse." Well, indeed we may just as well, and off we trudge to the bus, no mention made at this point about discourtesy—you don't notice it if the hangman splits an infinitive. In the bus, a messenger. The chairman is willing to negotiate (the Panthers are mellowing?) a cash price for the privilege of interviewing them. A quick plebiscite. *Life* magazine, who is a natural leader, says: There are three alternatives: (1) individual option; (2) negotiate; (3) cut out. By a vote of 2—3—6, we decide to leave. But the driver's delay in getting off (he had forms to fill, Melville) gave time for a second messenger from the chairman: He would consent to see one of us without pay, and to discuss at the session the price of seeing the balance of us. But the time is gone, and we head out for an engagement with Ron Karenga in Los Angeles, who, it now appears, will be kept waiting as a result of the materialist preoccupations of the chairman of the Black Panthers.

Watts: *Up from Watts*

May 31, 1969

"There are four men," said the short middle-aged
Negro who had lived there for twenty-three years, "who
can decide whether to begin or to terminate a riot in
Watts, and all four of them are in this room." Along with
fifty or sixty other residents of Watts, a dozen journalists
were there to ask questions while eating supper. I asked
one of the four whether the assessment was correct; he
hesitated and said, yes, it was correct. Well, why didn't
you stop the big riot of 1965? Because he didn't want to,
he said; there were injustices to be shriven by fire. Whose
injustices? The usual injustices, but also injustices
administered by black exploiters, whose buildings were
among the first to go down in flames.

As almost everywhere else, the black leaders here are
bright, passionate, a little cynical, greatly talented. One of
them gave up a job as a landscape engineer to join
the Watts development group; another had been an
aeronautical engineer. Proud men, who knew they had
made it in the competitive world, who could accordingly
move in the ghetto world without anyone's suspecting that
they turned to social work because the marketplace had no
room for them.

Oh, how they had desired a victory for Mr. Bradley
over Mr. Yorty! Mr. Yorty, one of them said, had waged
the most vicious campaign in history. Reflect. That isn't
merely black talk. About what election haven't we heard
the same kind of thing? In fact, Bradley's supporters
stressed that he is black, even, as some of Yorty's
supporters stressed that he was white. More whites voted
for Bradley than blacks for Yorty. But the blacks need
their victories, even as the Irish in Boston needed theirs
and the Jews in New York City.

The dawning consciousness of the political way up the

ladder is racing through the ghettos. Strategically it may be dangerous, since the temptation is universal to substitute political for economic means of self-aggrandizement; but tactical rewards in human pride and faith in the political system are considerable. The figures aren't in, and no doubt many Los Angeles blacks didn't bother to vote at all. But the percentage will be higher, much higher than before.

Also in Los Angeles there is Ron Karenga, the head of an organization called US, the meaning of which is kept obscure, even as the meaning of much of what Karenga does is kept obscure. Occasionally, his critics observe, he finds it necessary, in order to establish his seriousness, to have somebody killed. It is formally alleged that his followers are responsible for the killing of two Black Panthers at UCLA a few months ago in the course of a power struggle.

Mr. Karenga, who affects the manners of an Oriental satrap and appears in his tabernacle under circumstances of maximum pomp, preceded by incense and incantation, would smile inscrutably and change the subject. He prefers to speak most genially about his philosophy, which is composed of agglutinations of social clichés, neatly and amusingly strung together. He gets a headmaster's reception. His disciples on either flank laugh adoringly at every witticism, including not a few which are stillborn.

On his right is his extravagantly beautiful wife. On his left a handsome sixteen-year-old in a warrior's stance, his lips fiercely contrived into a permanently menacing mold, who during the whole hour that the saviour speaks moves not a muscle, not a nerve.

Mr. Karenga intersperses his sociopolitical badinage with a Swahili word here and there, even as the greetings are in Swahili. There was one lexicographical revelation of extraordinary interest. Mr. Karenga referred to one of his concepts as *kawaida*. "That," he explained matter-of-factly, "is Swahili for 'neotraditionalism.' " Catch those Swahili reactionaries!

A confidence man? There is much of that, and by no means all the blacks in Los Angeles take him seriously, though they do not disparage one another (it is hard to find a black man in San Francisco who will publicly criticize even the Black Students Union). They feel the sense of community, the sense of common purpose. The Structure—the omnipresent, accursed, obstinate, filthy rich, miserly, racist Structure—is the common enemy. They struggle with it in their own way, some choosing the superstitious neononsense of Ron Karenga, others the hard-headed wiry idealism of Ted Watkins and Henry Talbert and Duane West of Watts. They make one feel, on the whole, terribly glad for the resources of the human spirit, and altogether convinced that they are, many of them, engaged in efforts which distinguish the best that the white men did, under other circumstances, in California 100 and more years ago.

Washington, D.C.: *Tour's End*

June 3, 1969

The end of a tour that took the traveling journalists to Cleveland, Detroit, Chicago, San Francisco, Oakland, Los Angeles, Atlanta, and Washington, D.C. They gathered around Whitney Young to exchange impressions, en route to a debriefing with Patrick Moynihan (who, in the service of Richard Nixon, reminds us that we must always allow for late vocations) and other important officials. As in any human situation, the conclusions drawn by the participants differed.

My own, drastically truncated:

1. Leaders of the Negro community must learn to say no to their own. Not a single black organization disavowed the strike or the tactics of the Black Students Union of San Francisco State. Roy Wilkins and Bayard Rustin have shown a monumental courage by denouncing

the firebrands—they must be encouraged in their temperance. Too many black leaders now feel toward any other black leader the way the Communists felt toward Stalin: His will was theirs. White "understanding" of this phenomenon is a form of condescension; it might even be called racist.

2. There is universal distrust of the police. One grants—must grant—exaggeration: even so, there is an ugly residue. "You see over there"—a black guide in Forest Park in Chicago pointed to a policeman walking away from a ghetto grocery shop laden down with a shopping bag—"it's this simple. The cops don't raid the store, which is also a bookie joint, and they get free groceries." A good free-market arrangement, except that the police are supposed to defend the law.

In San Francisco, a black man-of-all-trades is stopped by a policeman who visibly reacts to his bizarre costume—turtleneck, beads, beard, the works. "Let me see your license." He hands it over. The policeman pockets it. "I said, let me see your license." "I just gave it to you." He is arrested for driving without a license. Paul Goodman has said that it is wrong to have policemen who are agents of an alien value system: that the laws of the ghetto ought to be made by the ghetto and enforced by the ghetto. The impracticality of Goodman's insight oughtn't to distract from its acuity. Major, deep reforms are necessary.

3. The nature of "democratic participation" needs to be refined. It has become a slogan, and every man is permitted, indeed encouraged, to "do his thing," a term which, after hearing it one thousand times, begins to cloy. G. K. Chesterton wrote a half century ago that men should be free to be their own potty little selves. But doing one's thing is too often regarded in the ghetto as the freedom to express oneself at the very direct expense of others.

We did not meet anyone who went so far as to say, for example, that Sirhan Sirhan was merely doing his thing, but the idea of authority, the idea of self-denial, is evanescent in the culture of the ghetto. Another job for black leaders: to restore the prestige of authority, whether defined as political authority or the authority of standards.

4. What is the nature of racism? I do believe that the man was never born who is not a racist under one of the definitions so freely used in the ghetto. A favorite maxim is that "capitalism is racist." Once again, unintentionally imbedded in that phrase is a form of racism: the notion that black entrepreneurs cannot produce a successful mousetrap. Why can't they? The answer is that, of course, they can, and the ancillary superstition that it is exploitative of the people to produce a mousetrap cheaper than the one which people are currently buying is one of those delusions of socialism on which people have wasted their energy and spirit for years. Quick, before it hardens, black leaders should point out that if one is serious about abolishing poverty, one should encourage the preservation of economic institutional arrangements which have graduated more people out of poverty than any other arrangement in the history of the world.

5. The quality and the energy—and the charm—of the black leaders in all of these cities is a major marvel: a quite extraordinary cultural and ethnic achievement. Anyone expecting to hear better speech, better organized ideas, greater enthusiasm in the graduate schools of the Ivy League, has a pleasant surprise coming to him. The black people, graduates of ghetto schools, in some cases graduates of no schools, through their wit and grace, singing their song in a strange land, have made a triumphant entry upon the scene.

A NEGRO FOR PRESIDENT?*

January 13, 1970

When they used to ask Bobby Kennedy about the FBI calling one morning in the predawn hours at the homes of the steel executives his brother the President was harassing, he would say, "I know you won't believe it, but it happens to be true: I simply did not know the calls were being made. I was Attorney General, but I wasn't consulted." I ran for mayor of New York City a few years ago, and the headline in the New York *Herald Tribune* the day after I introduced my running mates was "BUCKLEY HAS A 'BALANCED TICKET':/MARKEY, MRS. GUNNING—ALL IRISH." The professionals rocked with mirth when I subsequently announced that I hadn't known that Mrs. Gunning was Irish and hadn't known even that she was Catholic. I was stung by the criticism of my naïveté and tried to turn it to my advantage later in the campaign by observing that those who sought a religiously balanced ticket or an ethnically balanced ticker were, after all, the ethnically self-conscious and hence the opportunists of discord and of totemic political practices. And I was right—am right—but I am talking out-of-this-world where, ideally, politics has nothing to do. In this world it is different—especially different in my judgment—where the Negro is concerned for reasons which insofar as they are obvious are, for that reason, painful to relate, yet relevant to the objective at hand, which is the election of a Negro (no, not any Negro) as President of the United States in 1980 (or thereabouts).

* Reprinted by permission of *Look* magazine.

High political office in America (and in most other places) tends, after all, to carry social distinction, and it is for this reason that some Americans, who might have been otherwise inclined if purely political considerations had been consulted, voted for John Kennedy in 1960. Not merely Catholics, who desired to see the decertification of the legend that no Catholic could be elected President; but others who also wished to see broken a religious barrier which they believed generically unhealthy and (in some cases) practically inconvenient: for instance, the Jews, some of whom believed that the election of JFK would more easily remove, by collateral action, impediments to the election of a Jewish President, than would a direct assault by a Jewish candidate against Fort Bigotry. It seems to me that this was in fact the case, that the election of Kennedy had this reassuring general effect. And, of course, what happens, when people are reassured, is that they tend to become less ambitious in that particular direction. Thus when Abraham Beame, running for mayor of New York in 1965, was urged on the voters by his friends as potentially the first Jewish mayor of New York, the old ethnocentric juices somehow didn't stir, and the defections among Jewish voters caused the election of a WASP. A grand gesture: The Jewish community had, in effect, transcended race and religion, at least as determinative in a mayoralty election. One senses that the accomplishments of the Jew in America are so pronounced that he disdains now also the Presidency, not because the Presidency is small potatoes, but because the achievement of it is unlikely to add anything to the sense the American Jew now has of being In. Such a certification—election to the Presidency—would now-adays strike most American Jews as a redundant affirmation of their importance, of their qualification to serve. In 1957, breaking all tradition—most markedly Bolshevik tradition—Khrushchev, as head of state, wrote a casual letter to the *New Statesman*. Banner headlines. A few weeks later the unpredictable Khrushchev wrote yet another letter to the *New Statesman,* which of course published it; under the lackadaisical banner, this time, "KHRUSHCHEV WRITES AGAIN."

It isn't so with the American Negro. He has not won a dozen Nobel Prizes or crowded Groton graduates out of Harvard or coached us in the mysteries of atom splitting. The debate will continue on the question of whether his gifts are genetically other than those of the Caucasian or only apparently other for reasons of training or environment. I do not myself believe that the final scientific adjudication of that debate will prove to be particularly important, except perhaps in a narrow pedagogical sense. George Washington was less "intelligent" than Einstein, an obvious way of making a point which is nonetheless subtle. But the American Negro needs the kind of reassurance that Einstein did not need. It is the reassurance that he can move into the reaches of reservations from which he has grown up thinking that Americans whose skins are black are permanently excluded.

There are reasons for urging that final achievement (the black President) which are more important than merely buying the reassurance of American Negroes. They are a form not exactly of white expiation, though I would not dismiss this as a factor in any corporate effort to elect a black President. They are a form of self-assurance. The outstanding charge against America is hypocrisy. It is greatly exaggerated, beyond even the exaggeration that always marks the distance between national practice and national ideal. But where the Negroes are concerned, the practice of inequality directly belies the vision of equality of opportunity, so that the election of Negro public officials (yes, because they are Negro) is a considerable tonic for the white soul.

It helps, though it is not enough, to "encourage" the careers of a Sugar Ray Robinson, a Duke Ellington, a Martin Luther King. But such as they will not need, in the 1970's, any particular help, inasmuch as their talents pull them up as inexorably as an escalator. The area in which the Negro needs helps is increasingly the area in which raw talent is not mechanically measured. It is not necessary to experience the goodwill of a predominantly white community in order to confirm that Joe Louis is a better boxer than Max Schmeling. But it is only the white community that can, *e.g.*, express itself—as an act of faith—that it is preferable to elect Carl Stokes as mayor of Cleveland than Seth Taft.

I have had a brief experience with the black militants, and they are as attractive as I would imagine the Red Guards from Yellowland to be, as attractive as the Aryans who cheered along the drive of Adolf Hitler for racial purity. These militants receive much attention, as indeed they should: They bamboozle a lot of Americans, most typically those Americans who are happiest believing the worst about America. But they remain a very small minority of their people, for reasons that reconfirm the health and sanity of the large body of Negroes for whom they presume to speak. The race of the next decade will be over the question: Who will attract the attention of the majority of the American Negroes? The Rap Browns—the misanthropic bitter enders, whose satisfaction issues out of the politics of implacability; who cherish and fondle the statistics of white intransigence even as Herbert Marcuse is happy only in finding confirmation of the organic corruption which is the center of his social theology (Marcuse, the perfect Calvinist!)—or the civilized Negroes? A great unpublicized phenomenon is the arrival in America of a class of young Negro leaders who work in the ghettos, in economic cooperatives, in straightforward social work, who are arguing that progress is possible within the System. They are harassed by the demagogy of the racists who say that America cannot make way for the Negroes. But they nevertheless survive—and they proliferate. You can find them in Cleveland (some of them will make it a point to be just a little bit rude, just for the record), struggling to do something for Hough; in Detroit, learning the politics of adjustment, throwing their weight around in economic and political maneuvers; in San Francisco, deeply involved in trying to spread an understanding of the role of education as the instrument of liberation; in Los Angeles, calmly (if not openly) countering the witch doctors and practicing a tough-minded idealism (the top people at Watts are brilliant, ingenious, tough, graceful, irresistible).

It is from the ranks of these young men, now thirty, thirty-five, forty years old, that I can imagine someone rising, in the next decade, to national prominence as a Presidential candidate. When it happens, I think that it is quite possible that he will be greeted gladly by those who, having satisfied themselves that the point they are about to make will not be at the expense of the survival of the Republic, will join in a quite general enthusiasm over his election as President of the United States; who will celebrate his achievement of the highest office in the world as a personal celebration, as a celebration of the ideals of a country which by this act alone would reassert its idealism—shrugging off, as is America's way, by practical accomplishment the chains of cynicism and despair which the detractors and the cynics wear so gladly, singing their songs of hopelessness. How shall we sing the Lord's song in a strange land? the prophet asked. Whittaker Chambers wrote twenty years ago of the Negro people that they have been the most man-despised and God-obsessed people in the history of the world, that on coming to this strange land they had struck their tuning fork, and the sorrow songs, the spirituals, were born. But the sorrow songs are of another age, describing another spiritual plight. "Jes' call me Prez-i-dent Jones," they sing now in the Bahamas, where they have elected their own "Prez-i-dent." It will be even better when "President" Jones is elected by others who, seeking to alleviate the sorrow of the few, alleviate the burden of the many.

IV. THE COLD WAR

Muscle

YAF *v.* IBM

March 30, 1968

The Young Americans for Freedom, an organization of the politically sane on the college campuses, has been picketing IBM's offices in protest against its vigorous solicitation of business behind the Iron Curtain. Vigorous, that is, in Eastern Europe. By no means vigorous as advertised in America, because the company's officials are aware that there is public hostility to trade with the Communist bloc. You are not likely, then, to see full-page ads by IBM boasting, "America's Leading Manufacturer of Computers Has Sold Its 1400 Line to Bulgaria, Poland, Czechoslovakia, and Hungary . . . Our newest 360 system has been sold to Yugoslavia and is offered for sale to the other East European states. There is no accuracy like IBM accuracy. With IBM, you can fire a missile 5,000 miles away and hit the town square in Armonk, New York! Put in your order now, while America still lasts."

Mr. Arthur Watson, who is head of the world trade division of IBM, went running for help last October to Secretary of State Dean Rusk who obliged him with a fiery letter of approval, stating that IBM's sale of computers to the East Communist governments was "consistent with the foreign policy of the United States." One would think that Mr. Watson would have suppressed any letter charging IBM with being consistent with the foreign policy of the United States, such foreign policy (love all Communists west of longitude 140 degrees and north of latitude 50 degrees, kill all Communists elsewhere) being one which would overtax even the comprehension of a 360. However, Dean Rusk's letter is being given a wide circulation, though it has not, of course, persuaded the Young Americans for Freedom, perhaps because, although Dean Rusk manages to sound as hickorystickish as a New York *Times* editorial, he ends the letter sweatily, with the imperial observation that foreign policy is for the Chief Executive to make, which is the same thing he has been telling Senator Fulbright, who is as unimpressed as the Young Americans for Freedom.

These young boys and girls of YAF don't deny that Mr. Johnson's State Department has the power to authorize IBM to sell the most sophisticated computing machinery in the world to countries engaged in sustaining the North Vietnamese war effort—they merely assert their right to protest IBM's complicity with that policy. After all, there is no law that requires an American company to deal with the East European Communist countries: The initiative was entirely IBM's. The counterinitiative is YAF's. A most enterprising organization, by the way. At the University of Arizona, they countered a public fast, waged by the local peaceniks, with an eat-in. I like that.

One wonders how history will deal with the leaders of the bridge-building movement. Perhaps kindly—that, at least, is the going assumption of the Establishment, which believes that convergence will follow upon trade, cultural exchange, and the rest of it. Certainly there are wonderfully encouraging developments, most recently the ouster of Novotny of Czechoslovakia by someone demonstrably preferable (anyone would have been demonstrably preferable), and of course the student protests in Poland. However, it isn't by any means obvious that the loosening of the system has been accelerated by East-West trade. It might well have been acceleratd by Draconian boycotts.

In 1936, the Olympic games were held in Berlin, and the government of Adolf Hitler, it is generally conceded, was fortified by the prestige of the games. Now Poland's Communist hierarchy, thrashing out against the rioters, starts pogrom-talking about the Jews, those pathetic few who are left after Hitler's ravages. Two hundred and thirty-five English MP's protest anti-Semitism in the Soviet Union. De Gaulle, Professor Raymond Aron insists, has renewed anti-Semitism on a continental scale. Would Secretary Rusk scold the American Jew who refuses to patronize Air France or to commit his company to trading with Poland or the Soviet Union? Or the Gentile who wishes to support the Jew?

Isn't there a permissible form of private protest? We know about the impermissible forms, the physical obstruction of agents of Dow Chemical, the refusal to permit the other side to be heard . . . But is there nothing between that and direct government action? It seems to me, as it does to younger Americans for Freedom, that there is; and there are reasons to believe that many officials and employees of IBM agree.

DE-BOGEY THE BOMB

February 22, 1968

I begin by saying I do not, repeat do not, believe it was all a Communist plot, but only because the Communists most likely didn't think of it. Certainly the mysterious, anonymous telephone call served their purpose. The anonymous call that reported to the staff of a Senate committee that the Pentagon was considering the use of tactical nuclear weapons in South Vietnam, as witness that Professor Richard L. Garwin of Columbia University, an expert in the subject, was off on a mission to Saigon.

During the ensuing ten days, that became the talk of the world, and the moralizers rushed to their typewriters, their pulpits, and their rostrums, to denounce the United States. Harold Wilson of Great Britan, who was in Washington apparently because he was temporarily out of ideas on how further to mismanage British affairs, contributed his opinion, namely, that the use of such weapons would be "sheer lunacy." Pretty soon the Pentagon and the White House were sputtering their denials, and indeed it transpired that Professor Garwin was in Saigon on business wholly unrelated to the atom; which, as a matter of fact, is a pity.

The pity is that we are saving our tactical nuclear weapons for melodramatic use, for use, presumably, at the apocalypse toward which we may very well be headed in the long term. Take, for instance, the discussion of the use of tactical nuclear weapons in the defense of Khesanh. By this time, so much attention has been given to the plight of Khesanh that to use these weapons, for the first time in military history, in the defense of Khesanh suggests a mood of total desperation, perhaps even of panic. That interpretation feeds on itself, even as a bear market is said to justify itself. Everyone immediately begins to believe that the United States has gotten punch-drunk, and talk veers toward the whole business of third world wars and an intentional exchange of thermonuclear bombs.

The time to introduce the use of tactical nuclear arms was a long time ago, in a perfectly routine way, when there was not a suspicion of immediate crisis, of panic. In 1964, Senator Goldwater was burned in oil not even for advocating the use of low-yield atomic bombs for defoliation, but for reporting that the plan was under consideration by the Pentagon. Everyone got so worked up at the idea that nobody thought to ask the question: Why not? The use of limited atomic bombs for purely military operations is many times easier to defend on the morality scale then one slit throat of a civilian for terrorism's sake; and yet, incredibly, the Vietcong seem to win all the propaganda victories, and the moralizers' inveighing is against us, not against them.

The tactical nuclear bomb is a weapon designed to increase the efficiency of warmaking, and warmaking, when conducted by the good guys, is supposed to be preferred to, let us say, permitting Hitler to kill millions of Jews and conquer Europe; preferred to, let us say, turning Berlin over to the Soviet Union; preferred to ushering in an age of misery and bloodshed in Southeast Asia. We are constantly being reminded about Confucius, or whoever it was, who warned the United States against a land war in Asia, but we are practically never told about how to multiply those advantages that are naturally ours, advantages by which we might stand to offset the enemy's advantages in potential manpower and in ubiquitous ruthlessness. Even as we never dare to talk about economic blockades against the major suppliers of the Vietcong, we are not permitted to talk about the use of tactical nuclear weapons. Not allowed to speculate, even, on whether the careful use of them, years and years ago, might not have saved us and the South Vietnamese—and the North Vietnamese—years and years of misery.

One recalls the last Berlin crisis when Eisenhower was President and Khrushchev was sounding as though he really intended, this time, to seize the city. At his next press conference, President Eisenhower was asked what would be his response to an attempt by force to take Berlin, and he replied that he would defend Berlin by force, "not excluding nuclear force." What do you know, tra-la, that was about the last time Khrushchev ever mentioned Berlin, though he did, in a fit of pique a few months later, initiate President Kennedy in Khrushchevism by building his pique into a great big cement wall.

If that anonymous telephone call had come to me, I'd have answered, "Shh! Don't tell anybody. But it's absolutely true. And they are due to go off around Khesanh tomorrow at seven forty-five, Vietnam Daylight Time." That might have proved a busy morning for the Vietcong around Khesanh.

THE ABC'S OF ABM

April 12, 1969

Although it will be another month before the Senate considers the proposals of Richard Nixon for a modified anti-ballistic missile system, the pressures are hard underway to affect the Congressional decision. The perplexity of many legislators derives from, on the one hand, the general public acquiescence (to which the polls attest) on the necessity to adopt ABM, and on the other hand, the surprising ratio of anti-ABM mail over pro-ABM mail. One Senator advises that the ratio is an extraordinary

15 to 1. Why? The answer, one must assume, is that the anti-Vietnam apparatus has elided easily and naturally into anti-ABM.

Although there is no necessary connection between opposition to the Vietnam War and opposition to the deployment of ABM missiles, in fact the man who is against the former is almost certainly against the latter, for reasons which are less interesting logically than sociologically.

People who oppose ABM do so for very different reasons. But the mass of those who oppose ABM emotionally are directly descended from those who opposed America's development of a hydrogen bomb. Next they joined with others in opposition to nuclear testing. After that they voted (again, with others) in favor of the nuclear test-ban treaty and, most recently, in favor of the antiproliferation treaty.

It is wrong to suggest that those who adopted these positions are forlorn of logic and sophistication. But it is quite correct to suggest that the emotional inertia that drives the majority of the disarmament types has led them from one to the other position. So that those who believe that Vietnam should be abandoned tend to do so because they also believe that the East-West confrontation is a synthetic problem: that the Communists do not represent a genuine threat to the security of the United States.

Under the circumstances they reason that the installation of ABM is a way of saying at very considerable expense that we actually believe in the possibility that the Soviet Union would be capable of initiating a nuclear strike against us. They go on to say that the institutionalization of that suspicion via ABM has the perverse effect of giving that suspicion concrete expression; and that to do that is precisely to encourage the enemy to live up to the worst expectations of him. It is as though Father Spencer Tracy at Boys Town had said to young Johnny, "Johnny, I think you are a wretched little boy." Who, under the circumstances, would expect other than that Johnny would then behave wretchedly?

It sounds naïve and simplistic. But, of course, many human emotions are, most particularly those which vest confidence in the behavior of the Soviet Union. Mr. Joseph Alsop, quoting Senator Robert Kennedy and, through him, President John Kennedy, remarks that even though the odds were overwhelmingly against the Soviet Union during the great confrontation of October, 1962, a significant minority of the Soviet General Staff counseled Khrushchev to call the United States' challenge—to refuse to withdraw their missiles.

Congress has, in the past, proved singularly immune to such sentimentalizations of military problems as are implicit in the anti-ABM talk (or, rather, most of it). But Congress is hungry for support from Americans who, presumably not realizing the pressure that is coming in from the other side, have neglected to make their views known. In other words, your Senator would be grateful for hearing from you that you endorse the call by the Commander-in-Chief to provide the United States with the limited but, in his judgment, essential protection which a limited ABM system would provide. Address: Washington, D.C. The postmaster will take it from there; eventually.

WHY THE TREATY?

February 11, 1969

Mr. Nixon has said that he is prepared to sign the non-proliferation treaty but that actually it would come better as a part of a general settlement. One hopes that the last is a way of saying: Look, what we're up to here is a deal between the Soviet Union and the United States to discourage, if not to prevent, West Germany's getting hold of nuclear bombs. Okay, but what is the West supposed to get out of it?

The treaty itself is either of purely symbolic meaning, or else it is an act of historical impudence without precedence in recorded diplomacy. If it is purely symbolic, it is because (a) France and China are not going to sign the treaty, so that what we have set up is a tennis game of doubles, with one member of each side declining to abide by the rules; and (b) the scientific world knows that the means are now available by which a country can go ahead and produce an atom bomb without much fear of routine detection (and anyway, the treaty's provisions permit a nation's withdrawal upon service of ninety days' notice).

The traditional, indeed until lately the only, means of producing the enriched uranium needed to make atom bombs has been by the so-called gaseous diffusion method, which is both hideously expensive, thus deterring the less wealthy nations, and overbearingly conspicuous (thus making concealment of the facilities difficult). The so-called centrifuge method is something else again, relatively cheap, relatively portable. So that a signatory power capable of coping with its conscience could go ahead and produce the stuff without attracting the attention of the international inspectors, who in any case are armed with ambiguous powers of prying about in the territory of the signatory nations.

If, on the other hand, the treaty is to be taken seriously, and we permit the assumption to flow out of it that only those nations that now have the bomb will ever have it, then it is a most remarkable piece of effrontery under the circumstances. Paul-Henri Spaak of Belgium said to me on a recent occasion that he could not understand a small nation signing such a pact, or a large nation asking a small nation to sign such a pact, in the absence of automatic, as distinguished from political, guarantees that atomic weapons would come to the aid of a small nation threatened by another atomic power. But how is such a mechanical guarantee to be made? Are we to have orbiting atomic platforms with programmed instructions to dump the bomb on Russia if Russia invades Belgium? But how could such a platform receive its instructions "automatically"? How would it know that Russia was advancing on Belgium? Aren't all such devices, in the last analysis, subject to the domination of the human intelligence—indeed, isn't that as it should be?

It took me many years to grasp that the reason acute Europeans like De Gaulle distrust U.S. guarantees to defend Europe by use of the bomb if necessary is that said Europeans, in American shoes, would do no such thing. Can you imagine President De Gaulle of the United States triggering his Minutemen and Polaris missiles in defense of President Nixon's France, knowing what then would happen to *la vieille gloire,* America? That is the reasoning behind France's *force de frappe.* That is why statesmen like Spaak oppose the treaty. Those Europeans who approve the treaty do so less because they trust America than because they have long since adopted a fetishistic position toward the atom bomb: the more you anathematize it, in treaties, in editorials, in sermons, the more likely it is to go away.

What the Soviet Union wants, pure and simple, is to prevent West Germany from getting the bomb, because it is West Germany perhaps alone that has the stamina to use the damned thing if necessary to keep the Soviet armies at bay. The Soviet Union accordingly desires maximum U.S. cooperation in the matter of keeping Germany from getting said bomb, and since we are a conscientious power (look at our efforts in Vietnam), we are likely to keep our word, discourage Germany from getting the bomb, and in the event that Soviet intelligence were to find the Germans clandestinely at work producing such a bomb and were thereupon to pounce upon her preemptively, the United States would be left powerless, muttering juridical formulas about the Great Treaty of 1969, and that would be the ball

game. It is comforting to think that Mr. Nixon has Henry
Kissinger around. My guess is that "part of the general
political settlement" will wag the proliferation treaty in the
weeks ahead.

The Great Week—June, 1967

ISRAEL TO THE RESCUE OF
THE UNITED STATES

June 10, 1967

Perhaps we should sign that mutual defense pact with
Israel—if only for our own self-protection. Let's face it:
that was a blood-stirring show she put on against the
Egyptian swaggerer with all his Communist tanks and
airplanes and all his jingoistic rodomontade. One can
hardly imagine a better military machine to help us out of
a jam than Israel's. There is courage, tenacity, single-
mindedness, skill—all of them put to essentially
nonimperialist uses, if you grant the legitimacy of the
Balfour Declaration, which at this stage you might just as
well do.

Nasser declared that the Mideast was too small an area
for the Arabs and for the Israelis, to which the Israelis'
only response—always assuming they were not prepared
neatly to dismantle their nation and march into the
sea—was that, under the circumstances, the Arabs would
have to move over. After thirty-six hours of an Israeli
blitzkrieg, the Arab braves have stopped war dancing long
enough to discover that they are surrounded by Israelis,

and that their great brothers in the Soviet Union were off at the United Nations jawing about cease-fires, and never mind the old borders, the new ones would be perfectly satisfactory.

Not only might Israel be of great military help to the United States in any future emergency; there is absolutely no limit to the psychological help she can be. Who else but Israel could have turned our doviest doves into tiger sharks? Who but Israel could, for instance, have persuaded Dwight Macdonald, that eminent tranquilizer, who walks out of the room rather than listen to Hubert Humphrey because Hubert Humphrey is committed to the proposition that the United States has to help small nations around the world when threatened by aggression; who else but Israel could have transformed Macdonald into Long John Silver, patch over his eye, dagger between his teeth, boarding the enemy's ship shouting, "Murder! Loot! Rapine!"

Difficult to believe? My friends, Gamal Abdel Nasser accomplished the impossible. We are being told to go out and defend the security and the survival of Israel and its people (which we should certainly do under the existing circumstances) in order to "uphold our own honor." That is the statement actually signed by Dwight Macdonald, who dismisses anyone as mad who brings up the same reasoning applied to South Vietnam. And it isn't only Macdonald. It is the whole clutch of them, who could not care less if it had been the South Vietnamese whose territory was threatened or whose ports were closed.

A single advertisement sponsored by the "Americans for Democracy in the Middle East," whose text I myself heartily endorse, is signed by Theodore Draper, critic of LBJ; Michael Harrington, a pacifist of sorts; Robert Heilbroner, the economist and critic of LBJ; Irving Howe, the critic and editor of *Dissent,* which is to the American left what the John Birch Society's *American Opinion* is to the American right; H. Stuart Hughes, who loveth man so, that he would have had the U.S. disarm unilaterally years

ago—leaving us, Sir Stuart, with what means of
implementing the action you call for now in Israel?;
Norman Podhoretz of *Commentary*, Joe Rauh of the
ADA, and so forth and so on.

Any nation with the strength to compel such men as
these to start talking in terms of international obligations,
the demands of honor, the necessity for the use of force
thousands of miles from home is a priceless national asset,
quite apart from the sentimental value of the country.
Indeed, one should consider giving to Israel a few square
miles of territory in South Vietnam, in West Berlin, in the
Straits of Formosa, and at other pressure points where
East and West are likely to meet on unfriendly terms.

The big question, of course, is what will have happened
to the bridge-building program with the Soviet Union. The
balance of power in the Mideast has been shattered. It is
unfortunately true that the stunning victories of the
Israelis are not likely to lead to any strategic tranquillity.
Israel will not settle for the old frontiers, and why indeed
should she so long as the Arab determination persists to
wipe out the Israeli state? Why not frontiers more easily
defended in tomorrow's war? The Arabs will be only
temporarily chastened. The battle cry against Israel—that
"foreign body" in the Arabic system—will be as
galvanizing as ever, probably the single reliable means of
effecting unity among a people atomized by myriad
differences.

New frontiers take years and years to consolidate, and
during those years the Soviet Union will see itself as *de
facto* defender of the Arab position, the United States as
de facto defender of the Israeli position, though both sides
will feign a certain neutrality and, even, urge restraint
upon their protégés. But the fact that the area is in flux
will greatly interfere with that tricontinental serenity which
has been advertised as the *mise en scène* for a true detente
between East and West, the great stage for what has been
described as the big kissing conference LBJ wanted to put
on with the Soviet Union via trade, treaties, disarmament,

and the like. Johnson's difficulties with Russia will now increase. But for a while, anyhow, he has most of the critics of our policy in Vietnam on the run.

THE SOVIET CONSTANT

June 13, 1967

I foresee (who doesn't) that one of the consequences of the recent events in the Middle East will be a consolidated enthusiasm for the proposition that we and the Soviet Union are now truly wedded and will march arm-in-arm together happily into history. The documentation will be simply that here was a world crisis, and yet apocalypse was averted by concerted action between the Soviet Union and the United States. QED.

It is true that we used the hot line, apparently for the first time, and used it effectively. So far as I am aware, there was never a good argument against the hot line, any more than there was ever a good argument against collaborating with the Soviet Union to devise means of preventing accidental wars. It is as much to the advantage of the United States as to the Soviet Union to avoid thermonuclearizing each other because a star-struck goose strays off the beaten path. And it is obviously to the advantage of both nations to have available mechanical means by which to exchange, without delay, the thoughts of their leaders. Western Union, which anyway would be busy if one rang it seeking to send through a communication to the Kremlin, is not enough. The hot line is a good idea, was always a good idea, and its successful use in the present crisis therefore proves nothing that was not already known.

But what about the collaboration between the United

States and the Soviet Union in the United Nations? One needs to ask: What was the purpose of that collaboration? A disinterested concern with peace in the world? If so, why can't the Soviet Union and the United States come together on resolutions concerning the aggression in Vietnam or the exportation of revolutionaries from Cuba, or the training of saboteurs in Zanzibar? The Soviet Union acted in the UN strictly with reference to her own best interests. It is naïve to suppose that there are no circumstances at all in which her best interests and our own coincide. That is on the order of opposing cooperation with the Soviet Union to prevent accidental wars. It was obviously in the interest of the Soviet Union to stop, on almost any terms, Israel's successful blitzkrieg.

At the rate at which Israel was moving, one or two more days of the same could have meant the total, as opposed to near-total, destruction of the Russians' Mideastern military exhibits. It was as if someone at Expo '67 had traveled through the Russian pavilion plugging in every one of the cocky exhibits of Communist industrial prowess, only to find that in each case they blew up in your face. Granted the Russian tanks and airplanes and cannon and rockets are not all like Mr. Tucker's car. It required Nasser's technicians to incapacitate them completely. But the effect was formidably embarrassing, and the Soviet Union wanted a quick end to it. Not only, of course, because of the apparent insufficiency of Russian hardware. But because the very existence of Russian hardware in the area in such great abundance presupposed political calculations.

And those calculations, it became obvious, were disastrously awry. It wasn't only that the tanks and airplanes were apparently no good. It was—much more serious—that they shouldn't have been deposited in the first place in such incompetent hands. The prestige of the Soviet Union was sinking rapidly, and her decision to join with the United States in calling for a cease-fire was analogous to what the stockbrokers call a stop-loss order.

If Mideast Revolution, Inc. goes below 70 on the open market, sell.

We should remember that at first the Soviet Union refused to join in our call for a cease-fire except on terms obviously unacceptable, namely, that the Israelis return to the prewar boundaries. It was only on the second day that the Soviet Union recognized that to retrieve that much was clearly hopeless and reconciled herself to what happened: a Soviet-backed Nasser thoroughly beaten, the blockade of the Gulf of Aqaba dissolved, the military situation pretty much at Israel's command.

It is symbolic of Russia's petulance that having, in her own interests, given way on the main thing, she nevertheless took a childish opportunity to taunt an American warship in the Mediterranean. Like the boy, abandoned by Jane in preference for someone else, subsequently refusing to give up his seat to her in the crowded bus.

There is a lot of flux in the Mideast at this point, and we shall have to try to mold it all (a) so as to advance peace; (b) so as to effect what justice can be got out of the irreconcilables in the situation; and (c) so as to introduce charity into the whole of the thing. But there are the coordinates of the situation that shouldn't be lost sight of. One is a continuing, even embittered hostility against the Israelis by the Arabs. The second is the continuing determination of the Soviet Union to press for any measures that will hurt the West.

AND WHAT OF THE UN?

June 15, 1967

"The war that has just exploded in the Mideast," writes *El Mercurio* of Santiago, "has seen the dissipation of the final remains of prestige that the United Nations had been left with and, as a lamentable paradox, it was precisely the Secretary General, the maximum executive functionary of the organization, who was responsible for its having happened in that way. If one had to give a name to this conflict, it could be said that this was the War of U Thant."

These words were written before the Israeli Army conveniently put an end to the War of U Thant. But if the indictment of Mr. Thant was correct to begin with, it is correct now, since it can hardly be contended that Mr. Thant exculpated himself by his skillful deployment of the Israeli Army. In other words, we need to go back and look at Thant's record; and to survey the role and current standing of the United Nations.

Millions of observers had the opportunity last week to familiarize themselves with the dramatis personae at the UN, and the impression was certainly confirmed that this is a surrealistic organization whose entire role is Aesopian. What mattered, clearly, was that the United States and the Soviet Union had agreed on a course of action. The rest was punctilio. And through it all U Thant, uniformly addressed with extreme unction by the diplomats even as, one can be sure, a spectacularly unsuccessful general is treated with extraordinary courtesy before being canned, sat with Oriental detachment. Indeed there was a lot for him to be detached about, since he had very well established at least his impotence, at most his utter incompetence, during the preceding period.

But even then, the UN showed itself to be not altogether useless. One has to keep reminding oneself that diplomats are to a very considerable extent just like little boys. And the UN is perfectly suited for childishness. For instance, there was the evolution in the Soviet Union's position—first the Russians said they would go along with a cease-fire only if Israel retreated to the prewar boundaries; then finally the Russians agreed to the *de facto* boundaries.

Now for a proud nation to go from Position A to contradictory Position B absolutely requires massive displays of petulance and bad sportsmanship, and sure enough it was at the UN that Russia had the opportunity. Time and time again Ambassador Fedorenko would weigh in with heavy Slavic sarcasm sometimes at the expense of Israel, mostly at the expense of the United States. Our Mr. Goldberg let him go on and on and on, catechizing us over our patronage of reactionary and aggressive and colonialist movements.

Somehow Mr. Goldberg resisted every temptation to tell the ambassador of the Soviet Union to go home and try a free election. Only once did Mr. Goldberg wax wrothful, and that was when Fedorenko publicly wondered whether Mr. Goldberg was there as ambassador from the United States or as ambassador from Israel. Failure to respond with proper indignation might have got Mr. Goldberg into trouble with the Anti-Defamation League.

The conquered nations also got visible relief from the opportunity to hurl abuse at Israel, and at the United States. Egypt and Jordan flatly refused to withdraw the manifest lies alleging U.S. naval complicity in the defeat of the Arabs. (The only relation between the U.S. Navy and Israel during the week in question was that the latter torpedoed one of the former's boats.)

Surely that opportunity for the losers to indulge themselves in a little spite is itself a justification for the United Nations. This is said with utter seriousness, by someone who believes that pride plays a great role in great affairs. The editors of *El Mercurio* are correct that the UN demonstrated its incompetence, but such a demonstration was redundant. Everyone knew all about its incompetence. What is important isn't what was demonstrated that was redundant, but what was demonstrated that is not generally recognized, namely that the UN is, as someone put it years ago, a "useful forum in which nations can meet together economically to exchange bribes, threats, insults, and conciliations."

TWO AFTERTHOUGHTS

June 17, 1967

1. Mr. Arthur Schlesinger, Jr., God bless him—if there is a God; if not, never mind—is still capable of a surprise or two. His native cunning prevented him, last week, from signing one of the hawkier statements calling for instant military intervention in the Mideast. The statement in question was distributed in behalf of Americans for Democracy in the Middle East by Mr. Charles Silberman, an editor of *Fortune* magazine. It is recorded that the sharp-tongued Mr. John Roche, who has no patience for humbug, called Mr. Silberman from the White House, where he sits at Arthur Schlesinger's old desk, and suggested that the committee's advertisement be signed "Doves For War." It is not known whether Mr. Silberman, who along with most of the other signers has been yelling his head off at Lyndon Johnson for using military force in Southeast Asia, was amused. If we had to guess, it would be that he was not.

And as for Mr. Schlesinger, whose sense of humor is not absolutely secure, he was, to begin with, annoyed at being asked to sign the declaration, admitting that signers of it were caught in an inconsistency. But when asked later to clarify his position, he gave other reasons for not signing, both of them extraordinary. The first is that he never signs any statement that he has not written himself. Suppose everyone adopted that position? It could only mean the end of the Joint Statement, something Mr. Schlesinger surely does not want to encourage. Who would then be left to sign Mr. Schlesinger's future statements? Nobody? Well, there's a point to be made in favor of that.

But it is indicative of how balled up Mr. Schlesinger became, that he should have invited speculation of that kind.

And then he gave as his second reason for not signing the statement that his views on the Middle East are nobody's business. Now that, surely, is the strangest position of all for Mr. Schlesinger to take, and one even wonders if he is quite well. Since when is it no one's business to consult the views of Mr. Schlesinger? Presidents and princes have been beheaded for failing to consult Mr. Schlesinger's views on public matters.

It boggles the imagination to suppose that the events of last week proceeded without a least one telephone call from General Dayan to Mr. Schlesinger. Let's just leave it that Mr. Schlesinger is overworked and pledge together to restrain the impulse to ask him his views on public affairs until he is quite well again. Even if it takes years and years.

2. The Anti-Defamation League has a genius for vulgarizing any subject it touches. The organization was originally founded to guard against anti-Semitism. In recent years it has gone in for the bigthink, taking firm positions on any number of social issues that have nothing whatever to do with anti-Semitism. But it regularly defames, as for instance in the series of books by Mr. Arnold Forster and Mr. Epstein, those whose views it disagrees with.

Most recently, the league announced that it would launch a national drive to uproot such anti-Semitism as it discovered during the Mideast crisis. Most virulent were the Americans who telephoned in to radio talk shows to give their views.

One such instance, cited by the league, was the man who called in to say, "Why should we send American boys to fight Israel's war?" The league's director wonders why the radio stations didn't interdict such sentiments, via the "holding devices" available to all radio stations.

Why is it anti-Semitic to say: "We have no business

fighting the Israelis' war?" Is it anti-Oriental to say: "We have no business fighting the Vietnamese war?" My own position is that the United States has essential interests in the Mideast even as we do in Asia, but people ought to be free to disagree with that position without being called racists. The Anti-Defamation League's arrogance, and its undisguised disposition to suppress the views of the opposition, had a chilling effect in a week in which Israel won the spontaneous admiration of the entire country.

Our Allies

DE GAULLE ON AMERICA

September 23, 1967

I have it from a friend who has it from a friend of Charles de Gaulle—what is bugging the general. De Gaulle has for several years now greatly vexed us. He has destroyed alliances, upset balances of power, spoken about us contemptuously as "the other hegemony," as if there were left no grounds for distinguishing between our own historical mission (which is to resist) and Russia's (which is to conquer). And his attitude has been all the more puzzling because De Gaulle would appear to be the quintessential conservative, loving God, country, and family. How could he, then, fail to love the United States?

Here is the answer. De Gaulle's misgivings about the United States had already begun, but when John F. Kennedy was shot down by Lee Harvey Oswald, De Gaulle began confiding to his friends that, in his estimate, the erosion of values in America had gone to landslide levels; that the rifle shot fired in Dallas was heard in the heavenly spheres and was just the beginning, the beginning of an age which would see the destruction of the United States by violence.

It is needless to note that the anarchy of the past few months tends to confirm the general's thesis. And it is no good asking De Gaulle why one demented assassin whose aim was true in Dallas means something about the United States at large, whereas the several not-so-demented assassins *manqués* who three times ambushed but failed to kill President de Gaulle a few years ago say nothing at all about France, not to mention the plastiqueurs. One does not debate with Charles de Gaulle, and in any case what concerns us here is not whether De Gaulle's estimate of America is correct, but what is De Gaulle's estimate of America.

The way it is in America, De Gaulle tells his intimates, is that we are through. Our society has broken down. It has broken down because of a confluential collapse of family (see the divorce rate, see the rate of illegitimacy, see the broken homes); of church (see the new skepticism, the playboyism of American theologians); of patriotism (see the growing popular resistance to the war in Vietnam, resistance which is traceable less to a specific opposition to the war in Vietnam, than to a general unwillingness to exert oneself greatly for a country one doesn't particularly love).

For Lyndon Johnson, De Gaulle has little respect, believing that Mr. Johnson has got his country hopelessly involved in an area in which we cannot impose our will, in part because of the practical problem of subduing a tenacious bunch of Orientals, in part because our own will is lacking in credibility, hence in force.

And he believes—most painful blow of all—that the probabilities are against our finding a solution to our racial problem, or even a *modus vivendi*. Once again he cites the collapse of the family. A recent dispatch in *Le*

Monde, believed to have fortified De Gaulle's convictions, cites American ideologues' refusal to listen to the arguments raised by the Moynihan Report pointing to the dissolution of the Negro family as being the center of the problem. *Le Monde*'s correspondent observes that even Patrick Moynihan was dismissed as a racist in influential quarters, suggesting the continuing preeminence of abstraction over reality—which is the crux of the American difficulty.

De Gaulle believes that our obsessive concern with ideal democracy will prove the likeliest cause of our demise as a great nation; certainly it will prevent us from making advances on the racial problem.

Our prodigious gross national product, De Gaulle reasons, our fancy technology, cannot overcome the disease America suffers from. Thus viewing us, De Gaulle's foreign policy is appropriate. If that's the way we are, then indeed France should not bank on us.

Of course, it isn't the way we are. And one would think that André Malraux, his closest consultant, would look around and report back to De Gaulle. If he looked, he would detect as much heroism among Negro and white Americans in Vietnam, and in the ghetto areas, and even in the academies, as he celebrated in a novel—*Man's Fate*—which, for all the penumbral gloom of it, stirred the optimism of a generation of intellectuals, causing Albert Camus to write about the revolutionary who is tossed half alive into the boiler of the locomotive, "*Il faut supposer Katow heureux*"—one must suppose that, in dying even thus, Katow was happy. So also, in that sense, America remains a nation of high morale, a nation that will bury De Gaulle.

LONDON: A MANAGEABLE BEDLAM

London, October 12, 1967

Although Mr. Harold Wilson got his votes at Scarborough and so avoided the formal tension that arises when the Labour movement finds itself in opposition to the Labour Party, the tensions are there and they rage away. Everything begins as mystique, is the aphorism, and ends as politics.

The theorists of Socialism in England are furious with Harold Wilson because he has conformed to the directives of monetary disciplinarians—to the strictures of the gnomes in Zurich, who should be borrowed from but not heard.

What Wilson ought to do, says Michael Foot, who is the heart throb of the British left wing and recently challenged Mr. Wilson's economics minister quite openly, quite futilely, but not altogether pointlessly, is (1) liquidate her overseas military responsibilities; (2) disarm; (3) impose tight restrictions on the export of capital and the import of goods; (4) devalue the pound; (5) mount a crash program of government investment at home sufficient to solve the problem of unemployment; (6) terminate the existing freeze on wages; and (7) withdraw the application to join the Common Market.

Wilson survives such assaults by the shrewd rhetorical maneuver of refusing to defend his measures in a context that begins before midnight last night or stretches beyond noon tomorrow. He has no more idea where he will bounce after he collides with the next reality than a billiard ball, and this of course not only keeps him tactically flexible, but keeps him strategically orthodox.

He would never say, to Mr. Michael Foot, for instance,

that Socialist theory has been proved wanting in this or the other particular. He will say only that the particular circumstances of the day required the particular course of action. He is, of course, impelled by a leftward bias so that when he is caught up adopting conservative solutions (*e.g.*, economic austerity), he refuses to accept the complementary conservative discipline (*e.g.*, a reduction in state spending), and everyone is left sullen but not mutinous, a condition which leaves Harold Wilson as First Minister to the Queen, which, one suspects, is Mr. Wilson's true idea of the *sine qua non* of the Commonwealth.

One suspects further that, as so often is the case, the left intuits its impotence and, for that reason, tends to get its kicks from rhetoric and from proposals whose effect on world events is about the equal of King Canute's on the rising tide. Thus, for instance, the clamor to dissociate from the policy of the United States in Vietnam.

Poor Mr. George Brown, the foreign minister, begged the conference not to vote down Mr. Wilson's policies, on the grounds that to do so would deprive Mr. Brown of such leverage as he is now able to exercise on our State Department. The conference nevertheless voted for withdrawal from Vietnam, which vote is not likely to have any serious effect on Mr. Wilson, whose withdrawal, should he ever decide upon such a policy, would not have a serious effect on events in Vietnam.

But for those on the left who cannot get their kicks from actively helping the Vietcong, they can get them from actively criticizing the United States. The Bishop of Woolwich, who is England's Bishop Pike only more so, announced recently from the pulpit of Canterbury Cathedral that he could not understand the morally outrageous position of the government in endorsing the Vietnam War, inasmuch as he had recently traveled to America and there found that "every Christian I met" was also opposed to the war—a statement which, if it is true, suggests that the bishop was given a Potemkin tour of the

United States, visiting only the fever swamps of the Christian left; or, and this is both more likely and more charitable, that the bishop does not know a Christian when he sees one, even as, one must conclude on reading his books, he does not recognize Christianity when he sees it.

But England struggles along. There is spirit there, and deep reserves of talent and good nature. The sun will never set on the British Isles.

APPALLED AT CHARLES DE GAULLE?

May 23, 1968

If it weren't so serious—as the saying goes—one would be tempted into just a little fugitive satisfaction at the detumescence of his imperial authority. Let's face it, human beings being, unfortunately, human, it is satisfying to a part of one's nature to see General de Gaulle's enormous nose being rubbed into his apparent inability to govern his own country.

We have been on the receiving end of many, many strictures about our own shortcomings. We are constantly being told that we cannot bring peace and good government to Vietnam—by a French president who cannot apparently bring peace and satisfactory government to his own country. Granted, the French people are very nearly an ungovernable race, as any student of modern European history will recognize. It is a part of their vaunted *gloire* that President de Gaulle has made so much of.

It may be that France works only as a stumblebum democracy, the kind of thing that went on during the thirties and fifties (during the forties, there was a period of repose under Pétain), or under Napoleonic rule, and nothing in between. But unless we are prepared to give way to such hopelessness, we have got to get together and pitch for Charles de Gaulle.

What happened? Surely, the salient question is, What didn't happen? Vietnam.

In this country, parts of which have certainly given way to unreason, explosions tend to be campus-size or even city-size. It has become the fashion to blame them on the Vietnam War. The litany has it that the war produced a great division among the people, which produced that general anomie which produced the alienated class, which joins with the dispossessed whose problems—education, housing, health—we are incapable of solving because of our financial and moral preoccupation with Vietnam. All our distresses are laid to war in Vietnam.

And, of course, in France, Charles de Gaulle took the position concerning the war which is popular with the left. He denounced the war and America's participation in it. He went further and appeased the French left and his own vanity by kicking the Atlantic Pact nations out of France. He denied England access to the Common Market on the explicit grounds that England is too closely related to the United States. He received Communist dignitaries from foreign lands and toasted their health and their governments.

And the left has now paralyzed France.

It is tempting to say that the left is only a factor in the paralysis, that deep discontents which are not under the control of the left have suddenly been unleashed. It is true that there are such discontents, but it is true also that there always have been, and very likely that there always will be, it being part human, and especially French, to be hypercritical of whatever is going on, with the exception of public love affairs.

The fact of the matter is that the crisis is national only because the hard, disciplined left is behind it. The overpoweringly large General Confederation of Labor is

Communist-dominated, and it has voted for a general strike. The left students are probably no more representative of the majority than the students who closed down Columbia University. The left parties in the Assembly have moved for censure of the government. De Gaulle is a constant stimulant to one's iconoclastic hormones, but, really, he is, from the theoretical point of view of the left, very nearly exemplary. In foreign policy, splendid. In domestic policy, he can be mildly faulted for continuing to believe in a free market place, for enduring progressive capitalism, and for tolerating his economics adviser M. Rueff. But there is a certain amount of capitalism going on in Russia herself, and the Kremlin tolerates its Liebermans. There is no doubting his personal capacity to govern; he is admirably trained and speaks a most elegant French. What else? Even so, the left demands revaluation.

I write these words before the great appearance he is due to make on Friday. I predict that he will overcome.

And recall William von Dreele's doggerel:

> *Je suis appalled at Charles de Gaulle*
> *I do not dig his gloire at all.*
> *I think the force de frappe a fraud*
> *La Rusie's hardly overawed.*
> *I worry when he mentions "moi."*
> *The overtones suggest le Roi.*
> *However, though de Gaulle's de trop*
> *They say he'll move to Fontainebleau.*
> *I'd like to borrow his esprit*
> *To stiffen les Etats-Unis.*

RHODESIAN FIASCO

March 14, 1968

You would think the Rhodesians had just finished executing Florence Nightingale, her mother, and her father. The reaction to the execution of the convicted murderers is one of the strangest phenomena of our inscrutable age. Consider.

1. India is furious. India is taking the position that the queen's word must be final in these matters. Herewith a show of homeguardism quite extraordinary under the circumstances, the circumstances being that India was the first and major defector from the empire, that India would be the first to howl out its resentment if the Crown were to intercede in a criminal case in India to dispense a royal pardon. The further circumstance being that the Government of England, which India is at the moment so avidly championing, has just finished writing into the statute books a law which officially declares that Africans of Indian descent may not come into England. An act of racism, one would think, which hardly argues the appropriateness of the moment to pursue the vendetta with Ian Smith.

2. Kenya is furious. Kenya has just finished making its Indian-descended citizens officially second-class, which of course makes it imperative to side noisily with anyone who criticizes a government which has done the same thing, only to black Africans.

3. U Thant is furious. Why? Isn't U Thant committed, above all other things, to anticolonialism? Why should U Thant yap about the authority of the Crown in remote territories, it being his explicit concern to undermine that authority wherever it emerges? When last

heard from, the United Nations was brooding over such colonialism as is exercised by the United States over Puerto Rico. Surely U Thant would be more consistent to have objected to England's officious intervention in the purely internal affairs of a country which was self-governing twenty years before the United Nations was a gleam in the busybodies' eyes?

4. The United States is furious. The State Department has announced that the execution, "we fear, drastically reduces the possibility of a negotiated settlement of the Rhodesian situation in accordance with the six principles put forward by the British government." Quite right. But then why isn't the United States sore at England, rather than at Rhodesia? It is England, not Rhodesia, that promulgated this crisis. As a matter of psychological fact, nothing could more surely have guaranteed that the execution would take place than the granting of a reprieve by the queen, the sole purpose of which was manifestly political, and everywhere obvious; namely, to challenge once again the legitimacy of Rhodesia's separation in 1965 from the Commonwealth. And then again, why is it the business of the United States to comment on such internal squabbles as Rhodesia's with England? Would we welcome pronouncements by Harold Wilson on our arrangements with the Virgin Islands?

5. And then England is furious. That one is my absolute favorite. "There were demands in the House today," reads the dispatch in the New York *Times*, "for prosecution of the Rhodesians if they can ever be brought before a British court. One Labour member, Andrew Faulds, even said 'the death penalty should not be excluded.' " The sun has surely set on British reason. Concerning the humane argument, it should be noted that England was hanging its criminals as a matter of course until quite recently and has no right to expect that other countries should necessarily follow England's lead in the matter of abolition. This is an important point to bear in mind; namely, that the queen's reprieve is justified purely on the grounds of the

categorical commitment that England now has against the institution of capital punishment. Concerning the guilt of the three men, no one raised a question, not even Mark Lane. Canada retains capital punishment. Would an English government dare to prop up the queen into calling off an execution in, say, Montreal?

No, what has happened is a pure venture in cynicism, the bloodier for having used three wretched murderers as the pawns. What emerges from it all is the infantile barbarism of the oldest Parliamentary government in the world: England's. The leverage England might have had on Rhodesia by which to leaven Rhodesia's policies is now lost, and the three men have been hanged; a typical accomplishment of the Wilson administration. God save the queen, she greatly needs His help so long as she is burdened by her present ministers.

WHERE'S BIAFRA?

August 1, 1968

I wonder how many readers will complete the reading of this column? Because it is about . . . Biafra. John Gunther once said that Americans will do absolutely anything for Latin America—except read about it. So it is with many other places, except in moments of flash-flood interest. Along comes Biafra, and the general reaction is, Oh, no, not another one of those African things!

Those African things having come frequently into the news over the ten-year period of decolonization. It began with the declaration of Ghana's independence, toward which our diplomats devoted much unctuous optimism. When the gentleman who was designated to lead Ghana to a New Dawn free of imperialism took to beating and imprisoning just any old somebody, and his cabinet ministers' wives began ordering solid gold bathtubs, we sort of lost interest in Ghana.

For a while the Mau Mau got our attention, and certainly they earned it. But Robert Ruark drew the full benefit of that uprising, and perhaps a little besides; and then old "Burning Spear" took over, and once again we were back to simply hating South Africa, and standing by to hate Rhodesia. Fortunately, there was that lodestar of stability on which all of us could count: the great Nigerian Federation, presided over by Sir Abubakar Tafawa Balewa.

Not, you understand, that Nigeria was a sleepy-time republic of altogether acquiescent plainsmen freed from the shackles of colonialism. It was a good robust democracy. *Time* magazine's cover story on the prime minister back in the halcyon days recorded the reception given in Parliament to the speakers on a typical day. "Each . . . was greeted with cries of 'Heah, heah' from his friends, and derisory shouts of 'Sit down, you wretched fool!' from his foes; from the rostrum came the perennial plea for 'Odah! odah.' "

And, of course, a very few years later Sir Abubakar Balewa was found dead, his face mutilated, and the reign of terror began; but by this time we had shut out our minds on African problems so long as they did not, as in Rhodesia and South Africa, involve white folks. And that is why so little attention has been given to the horrors of the Biafran secessionist war.

We are right to stay out of that political controversy. Few Americans have any idea of which is the right side and which the wrong side, and those who do make arbitrary commitments. But the point is that the suffering of the Ibo people is on a scale unparalleled since the Communist starvations of the kulaks in the mid-thirties, and somehow nothing is being done about it. The grisly estimate is that unless we act immediately—within a week or two—1,000,000 Biafrans, mostly children, will die.

And the rate will continue, at 1,000,000 per month, for six months.

The American Committee to Keep Biafra Alive has taken full-page ads, asking individual American citizens to write to Dean Rusk requesting that the U.S. government take steps to bring food to Biafra, and to persuade the Nigerian authorities to permit the passage of food through the blockade it is currently maintaining. Mr. Rusk should grant no greater priority to any other problem than this one.

But where, pray, is the United Nations? When last heard from, they were in uproar over the execution in Rhodesia by the white government of a couple of depraved murderers duly convicted by an integrated jury; how we did wail and gnash our teeth over that one. Since then, Colonel Benjamin Adekunle, commander of Nigeria's Army of Invasion, has described relief efforts to Biafra as "misguided humanitarian rubbish." Such food, the colonel argues, will go to soldiers who will prolong the war. "If children must die first, then it is too bad. Just too bad."

Where is the Herbert Hoover of the present situation? One wishes that some of those dogged signature collectors who want to reduce the suffering in Vietnam, or impose suffering in California on Ronald Reagan, or effect the impeachment of Earl Warren, would use their precious time to organize relief missions for Biafra. "How can I get people interested in my country," a Nigerian attending a Midwestern university once told me, "when they don't even know where it is?" It's hard. But the American people are a very generous people. The problem is to awaken them. Herewith my meager contribution.

BIAFRAN AFTERTHOUGHTS

January 17, 1970

Concerning the end of Biafra, a few reflections:

1. The United States' performance during the thirty months of war was—proper. In several respects. We recognized that the civil war was an internal matter, and that it posed, moreover, no threat to international peace. Still more, we acknowledged that England, which founded the modern state of Nigeria and gave it its freedom in 1960, was the relevant uncle in the Old World, and so we deferred to her, even as we would expect England to defer to us, let us say, in any future difficulty involving the Philippines.

So that we did nothing, except offer our good services, now and again, in the rather uncoordinated enterprise of bringing food to people who were starving. We were instrumental in delivering a lot of food to Biafra, but apparently not enough to keep an estimated 2,000,000 people from starving to death.

2. Two million people. The mind reels under the weight of the time we have spent during the past thirty months cursing the heavens and the bureaucrats over the war in Vietnam, which during the equivalent period cost the world fewer dead than 10 percent of those who died in Biafra. In the light of this spectral thought, was it enough that the United States should have acted—properly?

I do not mean to put the question rhetorically, but to confess a quite genuine moral confusion. In the postwar years the entire world was traumatized by the haunting knowledge that it did not do enough to prevent the slaughter of the Jews in Germany. A few seasons ago Mr. Rolf Hochhuth made a great hit in New York and in other cosmopolitan capitals by presenting a play the villain of which was Pope Pius XII who, according to the playwright, had done less than his utmost to rally world opinion to the necessity of an expeditionary force to save the Jews. The argument that such a thing is simply impossible in this day and age, when the enemy disposes of hydrogen bombs, is an argument that is serviceable to argue inaction when, say, word comes in that the Chinese Communists are practicing genocide on Chinese Christians.

But how is it to be used to argue relative inaction to save the 2,000,000 Biafrans? The Soviet Union, like England, sent arms to Nigeria. But one doubts that even the Committee for a Sane Nuclear Policy would have rallied to oppose an expeditionary force whose sole purpose was to enter Biafra in order to feed Biafrans on the ground that we were engaged in activity that might provoke a nuclear war.

No, our reaction was comparatively acquiescent, based on the inertia of the old argument that one should not interfere in the internal arrangements of other countries. A perfectly sound doctrine, as a general rule, but leaving unanswered the question: What are we supposed to have learned from the Jewish precedent? We continue to mourn. There is no way to bring the slaughtered Jews back to life, so that the purpose of the mourning is presumably to pledge corporately that such a thing will not happen again. Are we now to assume that ten years from now Mr. Rolf Hochhuth will write a play arguing that Pope Paul VI, and Lyndon Johnson, did less than they should have done to prevent the slaughter of Ibo Africans and that we will all applaud that play?

3. We are reminded, by the grisly events, of the inappropriateness of the fashionable argument about the cost of killing in the modern world. It is popular to remark that the cost of killing someone in Vietnam approaches, now, $500,000 a head, suggesting the indefensibility of it all by the fundamentals of moral arithmetic. Well, the cost

of killing Biafrans probably wasn't very much more than $40, $50, or $60 a head; suggesting that for all the moral bombast concerning Vietnam, the creepy insight begins to take form, that perhaps the more money spent on killing, in the acid terms of the actuaries, the greater the presumption of the value the killer attaches to human life.

LONDON LETTER

London, March 5, 1968

The talk everywhere is of the plight of the Kenya Indians who had been promised (everybody says) permanent rights to immigrate to England back when Kenya was turned over to old "Burning Spear" Kenyatta, who now officially discloses his intention to make the Indians second-class citizens. Mr. Duncan Sandys, who was at that time Minister in Charge of the Liquidation of the British Empire, insists that he gave no such promise but appears to rest his case on the formalistic argument that after all, he had no power to "tie the hands of Parliament." Already the government's measure to restrict the flow of immigration has passed the Parliament by a vote of about 80 percent, strongly backed by the public which fears an increase in racial antagonisms and unemployment.

Opponents of the Socialists' bill, who include Labour backbenchers and a few Conservatives, are stressing the obnoxiousness of a bill which could be compared to our old Oriental Exclusion Acts and, for the first time in English history, describes the color of a man's skin as relevant to his admissibility. They stress, also, that the Indians in question are for the most part highly skilled in various crafts and would be just the kind of people

England would be encouraging to immigrate if their skins were white. The most interesting argument being adduced is simply to the effect that whether England likes it or not, what Sandys now says or doesn't say, in fact the pledge was given, and the Indians' possession of British passports is evidence enough in the matter. Indeed the *Daily Telegraph*, which usually weighs in on the pragmatic side of such questions as these, published the facsimile of such a passport with the modified wording, *"Dieu et mon droit et votre* slightly attenuated *droit aussi."*

The Archbishop of Canterbury came in with the propaedeutic ethical consideration, namely, that "it involves the country in breaking its word, and that is very wrong indeed." (Unless, of course, the country is the United States, and the word is given to South Vietnamese.) His Grace is, of course, a member of the House of Lords, a chamber of aristocrats so genteel that they have never passed what the English refer to as a "guillotine" provision, the equivalent of our cloture clause, which enables the majority to close down debate. So that the good archbishop could, by rising on the floor of the House of Lords and ruminating for a few days on the angels and the saints, delay the passage of the bill by the fortnight that would be necessary for all of the aggrieved Indians to arrive safely at London Airport. Just a suggestion.

On other fronts in London, there is Mrs. Kenneth Tynan, the incumbent Mrs. Tynan, who was a guest of the gentle Mr. David Bruce, the American ambassador to the Court of St. James. Mrs. Tynan, who apparently learned her social manners from our own Dwight Macdonald, is, to the vast relief of most Englishmen, an American. In any case, she accepted the ambassador's invitation, and she buzzed about the residence sticking anti-Vietnam signs on the furniture, calling on us to bug-out. Only a few years ago, her husband was calling on the West to give over Berlin to the Communists, declaring manfully that he would sooner live on his knees than die on his knees. Mr.

Bruce, asked by the press for comment, replied: "Stickers? What stickers? It wasn't drawn to our attention." It is no wonder he is a successful diplomat.

On the book scene, the volumes on the British spy, Harold Philby, have received much attention, and at the hands of the Earl of Birkenhead, one sees a revival of that high pitch of British indignation which once awed the world. Philby was protected by co-spies Burgess and Maclean, and the earl reads with such stupefaction as Senator McCarthy—the bad Senator McCarthy—used to read, the record of the patronage by high officials of subordinate security risks.

"Each of these men"—Philby, Maclean, Burgess— writes the earl, "was cossetted by ministering, if moronic, angels; in the case of Burgess, who was another fanatical hater of America, by Hector McNeil, Minister of State in the Foreign Office. 'We must do something for dear old Guy' seems to have been McNeil's theme song, and so, stupefied by whiskey and richocheting from catamite to catamite, this splendid specimen of British manhood was gently detached from his frolics and sent—guess where—to Washington, with the rank of First Secretary, where he moved into Philby's house."

And Birkenhead concludes: "We shall never know how many agents were killed or tortured as a result of Philby's work as a double agent, and how many operations failed. He is now safe in Russia, and we must, alas, abandon any wistful dreams of seeing this little carrion gibbeted." One has, also alas, the feeling that if Mr. Philby were to reappear in England, he would go over to Oxford or somewhere to lecture on the transcendental cause he served and be instantly acclaimed as a prophet of the new and the sublime.

MR. GALBRAITH IN INDIA*

October 17, 1967

AMBASSADOR'S JOURNAL: *A Personal Account of the Kennedy Years*. By John Kenneth Galbraith. Houghton Mifflin. Illustrated, $10.

When President-elect John F. Kennedy asked Professor John Kenneth Galbraith to go to India as ambassador, he readily agreed and resolved to write a diary of his experiences during those years. This romp is the edifying and hilarious result.

When Galbraith goes fundamentalist, he is as easy to trip up as William Jennings Bryan. His disparagement of Portugal's ties to Goa and Goa's to Portugal even fluster him into the "bad English" which he begins his book by telling us that "no historical merit attaches to." Since he puts so great a stress on English, and since his own is the exemplar of correct and spirited usage, I pause to twit him over the Portuguese being "exempt, hopefully, from anti-colonialism." I wonder at so rigorous a critic of State Department prose recording that a massive move against Red China is "the kind of decision that is only taken if the Chinese push transpires," and note gravely that "Arthur [Schlesinger] has long been famous for his lofty disinterest in underdeveloped countries." I wonder whether Arthur seeks to emulate Galbraith's rhetoric?

Galbraith very much wanted this job, and he truly enjoyed it, notwithstanding the social and bureaucratic rigors. For a while he fretted that the Senate would deny him confirmation. "I always find the fiction that I am

* Reprinted by permission of *Life* magazine.

being done in by malign influences strangely agreeable." In the interim he solidly identified himself with the Kennedy administration, detailing his achievements: "I added [to the Inaugural Address] the sentence, 'Let us begin' at one point to give proper cadence, and a day or two later it was mildly historic." And finally, late one day in March, "word came in over the ticker that I had been confirmed. The Committee was unanimous, with Lausche abstaining." And then a characteristic footnote, of the kind that makes Galbraith-hating an impossible activity: "In 1968, Lausche was defeated for renomination. Asked to comment, I hazarded the guess that it was the result of the lingering resentment of the people of Ohio over this action. The explanation was not widely accepted."

Galbraith went to India with that unique confidence that is felt by the truly omniscient of this earth. "Once," he mused, on sitting down to draft Kennedy's first messages to Congress, "such responsibility would have worried me. Now I realize that I can do it better than anyone else who is available. Modesty is a vastly overrated virtue." Only twice does he confess ignorance of a current problem. Concerning the Congo: "I was handicapped by my uncertainty as to whether Katanga was the province and Mobutu the man, or vice versa." That ignorance he quickly overcame; not so an ignorance of the sources of Arab animosities, which, however, he comforted himself by recalling that not even scholars of the area are able to plumb.

Galbraith was determined to run a tight ship at New Delhi, to which end he used quite openly the prestige of his friendship with John Kennedy—by the way, a superb relation. Galbraith's letters to Kennedy (never mind the "ideology") are models of what a President might hope to get from his ambassadors, both as to style and substance. "One should scrupulously avoid using influence," Galbraith notes, "except when it is needed."

He had, moreover, every reason to expect totally harmonious relations with Washington. In February, dining at the White House mess, he had observed that "conversation is much like that at the Harvard Faculty Club, perhaps because it involves the same people." (Later in his diaries, on returning home for a fortnight and heading to the White House for dinner, he was to tell his diary that that would be his "*third* meal there of the week." And of the party, that "Everyone had also that fine glow that comes from being 'in.'")

He accepted gladly every usufruct of power and office and got himself a Convair even before arriving: "A good plane is obviously essential for a decent standard of living." "David Bell came in at midnight. . . . He was traveling tourist class as befits a former budget director. Happily, I have no compulsion to save money in this way, which is a great comfort." He threw his weight about with some relish. About his superior in the State Department he writes, "He is a liberal jellyfish. He told me that he tried to give equal attention to the pleas of all chiefs of mission. I told him brutally that I was to be considered a member of the administration, one of the policymakers of the Democratic Party, and that a special accommodation to my requirements was in order." Though he made many gestures to propriety, he treated himself to exemptions. "I have cut protocol activities to the bone," he writes toward the end. "Accordingly, this afternoon I substituted a note of apology for a pilgrimage to the airport to meet the Prime Minister of Malaya." When Governor Nelson Rockefeller, presumably for analogous reasons, thought to spare himself coming to New York City to greet Galbraith's Prime Minister and excused himself over the telephone by remarking that nobody would notice his absence, Galbraith became Mr. Protocol. "I said I was sure [the public] would, that in fact I was having a press conference that afternoon and would mention the Governor's absence. In the evening, Rockefeller was waiting at the Carlyle for Nehru."

His relations with Nehru were good, and he apparently visited with him incessantly. It is a weakness of the diaries that one gets no idea what Nehru was like and leaves the volume no better informed than before wherein lay the strengths of this singular man (perhaps they are as inscrutable as Arab animosities). Galbraith permitted himself, quite justifiably, to delete animadversions upon foreign and particularly Indian officials—a part of the continuing responsibility, he reasons, of any ex-ambassador. Even so, his irreverence occasionally shines through. "Municipal employees gathered by the hundreds to see me come and go. The damage to the public business may not have been irreparable. In India, the difference between working and not working is not always decisive." and he permits Indians to criticize other Indians. Shortly after the Chinese tore through the Indian lines in the war of the fall of 1962, Galbraith reports that on one day "several told me . . . That General Kaul had been taken prisoner. This was denied rather succinctly in the evening by President Radhakrishnan, who said, 'It is, unfortunately, untrue.' "

And so the economist-turned-diplomat presided over the U.S. embassy through crisis after crisis: Goa, the visit of Jackie, the China War, the eternal quarreling over Kashmir. Occasionally he was interrupted by the President for advice on other matters: "Monday [the stock market] took a terrible plunge, and as the Thucydides of the 1929 crash, I was immediately called by the President." Indeed, so frequent were his visits to America that he came in for criticism: "Some, it was said, felt not that I was neglecting India, but that I was insufficiently neglecting the United States." His schedule was always hectic: "All of this caused me to miss most of a luncheon for a visitng admiral, but I got in on the end of it and made a touching speech on sea power." The trials of office at one point almost caused him to depart from dogma toward spirited anti-Communism: "It is remarkable . . . how hard-nosed one becomes on China. I used always to take a relatively tolerant view. A few more months and I will be as warlike as anyone." (Alas, he was not vouchsafed a few more months, and never will be.) Although he had been lecturing Kennedy for two years on the advisability of retrenching from our military alliances, he ended by "wonder[ing] if we shouldn't take some dramatic action to ensure the peace such as guaranteeing the Indo-Pakistan border." He came with great glee to master the mechanics of public opinion: "I gave [at today's press conference] our reasons for seeking a Pakistan settlement. We seek to narrow differences as the Chinese seek to widen them. By mild implication, I suppose, anyone who fosters dislike for Pakistan is mildly pro-Chinese," which type of reasoning was not tolerated by Mr. Galbraith when used by Senator Joseph McCarthy.

It ended for Galbraith—he returned to Harvard, having run out of his leave of absence—only two months before it ended for them all, at Dallas. Galbraith resumed his diary to record the three days of grief; and then, like Sisyphus, we leave him composing the State of the Union address for President Lyndon Johnson.

Galbraith has given us memoirs which, like Sir Harold Nicolson's, are important for the events they record and engrossing in their telling. But Galbraith, though lacking Nicolson's sense of history, is ten times more entertaining, and therefore twice as endearing. "Confessions were being heard in a dozen stalls," he noticed on a visit to St. Peter's in Rome, en route back to the United States. "I was depressed by the thought of so much sin and refreshed by the thought, that, were I a Catholic, I would have so little to confess." It has been my conviction for years that history may not forgive Galbraith the evangelist, but that literature will add him to the roster of the saints.

The Bear

THE SPIRIT OF GLASSBORO

June 29, 1967

On returning from Glassboro after the second and final visit with LBJ, Alexei N. Kosygin held a press conference that lasted more than an hour, in the course of which he managed at least ten times to state that he could not smile upon the American people or their government until after we have shown that we will desist from further aggressions. For instance? Our aggression in the Mideast. No one doubts, said Mr. Kosygin, that we were behind Israel and made her aggression possible; and that, therefore, we were ourselves guilty in effect.

And, of course, there is our continuing aggression in Asia. Would he be satisfied if we stopped the bombing of North Vietnam? No; he will be satisfied only after we have pulled out of South Vietnam. Only then, said Mr. Kosygin, whose observations on political morality are more newsworthy these days than the Pope's—only then would the Russian government and the Russian people welcome a visit to the Soviet Union by LBJ.

In the same twenty-four hours that the President of the United States sat at Glassboro and took it, even as the press did subsequently in New York, there were other news items:

1. A reproduction of the front page of *Pravda* of the day before, which recorded that the coverage given to the first Glassboro conference between Kosygin and LBJ was

confined to thirty-seven (37) words, about as much space
as a major metropolitan newspaper devotes to the day's
weather. The same front page of *Pravda* announced
proudly in an editorial that the millionth Volga car had
come off the assembly line at the Gorky auto plant, a
news item comparable to something the Ford Motor
Company put out along about, say, 1911. The front page
also announced "nationwide support" (there is never any
other kind of support in the Soviet Union—nonnationwide
support, *e.g.*, in favor of free speech, expresses itself in
Siberia) for the Soviet Central Committee's denunciation
of Israeli "aggression."

2. A dispatch from Beirut, quoting observers who
have been witnessing the outpouring of Soviet military
equipment into Egypt. Fifty MIG fighters have already
arrived there, according to one estimate, in the past couple
of weeks, and one American counted ten Soviet vessels
unloading simultaneously.

3. The report of a refugee arrived in Miami, describing
his recent past under Communism in Cuba. He estimates
that 35,000 (a comparable figure using U.S. population
figures would be about 1,000,000) Cubans are in labor
camps for the politically unreliable, a typical sin of an
inmate being to have signed up to emigrate to the United
States.

"We had to work in the fields about twelve hours a day,
six and a half days a week," he said, "and every night
after work we were given classes in Marxism. I don't
really know what they tried to teach us, because we were
too tired to listen. Most of us were unaccustomed to hard
work in agriculture, and the food was scarce and often
uneatable. I lost over fifty pounds in the camp."

4. Not suffering from malnutrition are Soviet Communists in New York, who eat very well in order to
prepare themselves for the rigors of UN life at which they
berate with such stamina the aggressions of the United
States and Israel. "They're just like the rest of us—except
that they spend a lot more," said supermarket operator

Gil Shapiro who runs the neighborhood grocery nearest to the Soviet mission in Manhattan. The Soviet families, he figures, spend about $100 a day for their private food supplies, $700 a day during the current period, such are the demands of feeding Kosygin and the entire crew. "You ask what they buy? Practically everything. They're heavy on cornflakes. [You have to understand about the Russians, Whittaker Chambers once told a visitor. They can make bombs and intercontinental missiles, but they can't make shredded wheat.] You remember when Nikita Khrushchev was here a few years ago? He liked cornflakes so much he took back four cases of it. When they leave for Moscow or wherever they live in Russia, they come in and say good-bye like old friends. Usually, we know when they are going to say good-bye because of what they buy. They get lots and lots of bubble gum and chocolate bars."

5. "There is not, and there cannot be any neutralism in the struggle against bourgeois ideology," said the Communist Party of the Soviet Union in a manifesto on the fifty years of Soviet power, calling for a renewal of the struggle against the "imperialist world."

Couldn't LBJ, at Glassboro, at least have threatened the Russians, if they refuse to cooperate in the Mideast, with cutting off their New York supply of cornflakes?

THE FIFTIETH ANNIVERSARY

November 2, 1967

We are called upon today to celebrate the fiftieth anniversary of the Soviet Revolution, which I proceed to do by pledging Not to Forget, even as the Jewish community is pledged never to forget the tribulations it

suffered under Adolf Hitler—and never to countenance
the rise of power of any government so motivated, and so
powerful. One wonders, if Hitler had died in office, and
the Nazis had continued in power under, let us say,
Hermann Goering, whether the American kidney would
have assimilated, in 1938, an official celebration of the
coming to power of Adolf Hitler.

Forgive, yes; forget, never. It may be that Hitlerism
would in due course have been excreted by the National
Socialist Party. The assumption today, of course, is that
Stalinism has been excreted from the Soviet Union, a
contention which is made even athwart the face of
Soviet Russia's official vaporizing of Stalin's only
daughter—because she intuited the relationship between
Stalinism and Communism.

On the fiftieth anniversary one recalls a few lines from
Milovan Djilas' *Conversation with Stalin:*

> I am interested in how such a dark, cunning, and
> cruel individual [as Stalin] could ever have led one of
> the greatest and most powerful states, not just for a day
> or a year, but for thirty years! Stalin's present critics—I
> mean his successors—will only confirm that in good
> part they are only continuing his work and that they
> contain in their own make-up those same elements—the
> same ideas, patterns, and methods that propelled him.
> . . . [In fact] the ruling political bureaucracy of the Par-
> ty found use for just such a man. . . . The ruling Par-
> ty followed him doggedly and obediently—and he truly
> led it from victory to victory, until, carried away by
> power, he began to sin against it as well. Today this is
> all it reproaches him for, passing in silence over his
> many greater and certainly no less brutal crimes against
> the "class enemy. . . ." Despite the curses against his
> name, Stalin still lives in the social and spiritual
> foundations of the Soviet society.

Last week scientists revealed what had theretofore been

only an intuition; namely, that the human mind works in such a way as to forget the painful, even the unpleasant. Recently at the University of Moscow an American, seizing a moment of camaraderie with a high Soviet official, asked whether the moment would ever come when the Soviet Union would officially apologize for its purge trials of the thirties. The Soviet official froze, even as Khrushchev froze before the National Press Club on the eve of the Spirit of Camp David when asked about the tanks he had sent into Budapest. "Provocateur!" the Communist hissed, the old rhetorical evasion, by which over the generations Communists have hissed down criticisms of the policies of the Soviet Union. Their techniques tend to work: How many young Americans feel any communion with the millions who died, so that that government might survive, which today our ambassadors, glasses raised so high, are solemnly toasting?

All the statistics in the archives of the Kremlin cannot communicate the feel of the last fifty years as vividly as a few words from the artists, from those who feel most keenly. Whittaker Chambers wrote a few years ago to a friend, after reading Arthur Koestler: "If you re-read *Darkness at Noon* at this late hour you will see how truly it is a book of poetry. I re-read it recently. I came to the part where, after his breakdown, Rubashov is permitted a few minutes of air in the prison yard. Beside him trots the Central Asian peasant who has been jailed because, 'at the pricking of the children,' the peasant and his wife had barricaded themselves in their house and 'unmasked themselves as reactionaries.' Looking sideways at Rubashov in his sly peasant way, he says: 'I do not think they have left much of Your Honor and me.' Then, in the snows of the prison yard and under the machine-gun towers, he remembers how it was when the snow melted in the mountains of Asia, and flowed in torrents. Then they drove the sheep into the hills, rivers of them, 'so many that Your Honor could not count them all.' I cannot go on reading because I can no longer see the words. . . ."

Such words, imperishable, unforgettable, have been written by the master witnesses of the past fifty years. The honor roll will not be called at the celebrations. Their names should be in our hearts, and their words engraved forever in our memories. The honor roll includes:

The Case of Comrade Tulayev by Victor Serge, Doubleday & Company, 1950; *I Speak for the Silent* by Vladimir V. Tchernavin, Hale, Cushman and Fling, 1935; *Speak Memory: An Autobiography Revisited* by Vladimir Nabokov, G. P. Putnam's Sons, 1966; *The Captive Mind* by Czeslaw Milosz, Alfred A. Knopf, 1953; *Doctor Zhivago* by Boris Pasternak, Pantheon Books, 1958; *Assignment in Utopia* by Eugene Lyons, Twin Circle Publishing Company, 1967; *One Day in the Life of Ivan Denisovich* by Alexander Solzhenitsyn, Frederick A. Praeger, 1963; *The Burned Bramble* by Manes Sperber, Doubleday & Company, 1951; *Homage to Catalonia* by George Orwell, Beacon Press, 1952; *The Cypresses Believe in God* by José Maria Gironella, Alfred A. Knopf, 1955; *Bread and Wine* by Ignazio Silone, Atheneum Publishers, 1962; *Witness* by Whittaker Chambers, Random House, 1952; *I Chose Freedom* by Victor Kravchenko, Charles Scribner's Sons, 1946; *Darkness at Noon* by Arthur Koestler, The Macmillan Company, 1941; *The Journals of André Gide,* Alfred A. Knopf, 1956; *Ward 7* by Valeriy Tarsis, E. P. Dutton & Co., Inc., 1965; *On Socialist Realism* by Abram Tertz (Andrei Sinyavsky), Pantheon Books, 1960; *The Penkovskiy Papers* by Oleg Penkovskiy, Doubleday & Company, 1965; *Moscow Summer* by Mihajlo Mihajlov, Farrar, Straus & Giroux, 1965; *Conversations with Stalin* by Milovan Djilas, Harcourt, Brace & World, 1962.

To them on this occasion our tribute and gratitude.

MR. HUMPHREY'S DILEMMA

Chicago, August 29, 1968

The mood here is that if something doesn't happen, something bloody well should, to justify all the commotion involved in bringing the Democratic Convention into being. The odds, before the convention began, were heavily for Humphrey. But troubles arose, in connection with unit voting and Southern representation, the result of which was to somehow unsettle the hold Humphrey has been exercising on events. Funny, how a single banana peel can throw a giant off balance.

And then, late, late Saturday night, Mr. Humphrey appeared on a taped interview with Chicago's renowned Mr. Irving Kupcinet. Mr. Kupcinet, who is a very nice man, took pains to remind the listening audience that the interview had been taped a week before, back before the Red Army took over Czechoslovakia. I say Mr. Kupcinet is a very nice man. If he had been even nicer (but nobody in teevee could be expected to be that nice), he'd have sent the tape back to Mr. Humphrey unplayed, along with a little note suggesting that it might be appropriate, in 1969, to name Mr. Kupcinet as Ambassador to the Court of St. James. Certainly he'd have shown himself well qualified to serve as a diplomat.

Because there was old Humph, chatting along a mile a minute about his outstanding qualifications to serve as President of the United States. Why? Because he is so well equipped to accept change, to see things new and fresh, to discard the old, jaded, sclerotic ideas of the past. For instance—the TV audience heard poor Mr. Humphrey saying three days after Czechoslovakia was shattered—for instance, said Mr. Humphrey, the East European nations are by now "relatively autonomous."

I cannot think of an analogous blooper; oh, yes, I can. As a boy I sat listening to a Congressman delivering a speech on a Sunday afternoon against involvement in the Second World War. His speech, he said, would be composed of two parts. The first part was devoted to demonstrating that under no circumstances would Japan attack the United States. Having completed the first part, a messenger walked onstage to announce over the loudspeaker that Pearl Harbor has been attacked. "I shall now make my second point," the Congressman said genially. Oh, but they are a breed, are our politicians. If only they wouldn't also run for President.

Then Mr. Humphrey went right on. He was qualified, in a sense that Richard Nixon was not qualified, to preside over the glorious deliquescence of conflict between the United States and the Soviet Union. You see, Humphrey found himself saying in Chicago—thirty-six hours after United States Ambassador Ball in the United Nations accused the Soviet Union of not having changed, of being capable of the same monstrousness that made Stalin famous, of blithely clamping down on the minor efforts of a poor small country to be free—you see, explained Mr. Humphrey, unlike Nixon, I am not one of those "old cold warriors." The old cold warriors, Democrats like Truman, Republicans like Dulles, maintained such freedom as exists here and there to defy the Soviet Union. Now that the Soviet Union has once again demonstrated that either you make cold war against her or she is free to grind down any hope of Europeans to be free, Americans are, of course, entitled to conclude that if Humphrey is not a cold warrior, will a cold warrior please stand up?

It is considered dirty pool to consult yesterday's campaign platforms. But it is nevertheless instructive to do so. In 1964 the Democratic Party platform, uproariously approved by all the Democrats at Atlantic City, a platform on which the greatest electoral victory in history was won, contained among others, the following sentences:

"We pledge unflagging devotion to our commitments to freedom from Berlin to South Vietnam." Shall we at least acknowledge that the devotion is at least flagging? And,

"[We pledge] to speed the restoration of freedom and responsibility in Cuba." That has been the most unnoticeable speeding within memory. And,

"[We pledge to] encourage by all peaceful means the growing independence of the captive peoples living under Communism and hasten the day that [insert ten countries] will achieve full freedom and self-determination." What have we done?

Mr. Humphrey is a good man and a bright man. There isn't anybody in the world better than he at dissolving the edges of any question so completely as to reconstitute the question into a supporting case for Mr. Humphrey's current position. But his dilemma, though dramatized in the personal dimension by a mere week's passage of time between the taping of a show and the playing of it, is also the Democratic Party's.

ON MAKING FRIENDS WITH
THE SOVIET UNION

July 18, 1968

Mr. Hubert Humphrey announces that we should make love, not anti-Communism, and calls for a new era of international relations, which presumably would reach a climax of joy under a Humphrey administration. The New York *Times,* meditating on Mr. Humphrey's credentials to inaugurate such an era, points out that in the past, Mr. Humphrey has been guilty of anti-Communism. The point is that we should be charitable about people's pasts and prepared to believe that Mr. Humphrey can outgrow his.

Indeed it was Mr. Humphrey who in 1954 sponsored a bill which became the law of the land. It called for outlawing the Communist Party. Said act never amounted to very much for a number of reasons, one of them unenforceability, another the party's decade-long disappearance from formal politicalizing on election days. Still, it was a symbol, and there are those who have never forgiven Mr. Humphrey for it. But he is not going to be caught guilty of the sin of postmature anti-Communism.

We have now a fresh symbol for Soviet-American relations: a nonstop flight, inaugurated Tuesday, New York to Moscow, aboard Aeroflot Soviet Airlines. The institution of the service is announced in full-page ads around the country. I called the lady at the number listed, for fun, to inquire whether the Union of Soviet Socialist Republics' airline had a first-class section. She did not get the joke but answered matter-of-factly in a thick accent that yes, of course, first-class seats are available. But, then, in a Greta Garbo no-nonsense Ninotchka voice, she announced that any reservations would have to be confirmed so many (*sic*) howers ahett uff time. Presumably, there is no problem about confirmations from Moscow to New York, where the people's state is in charge of discipline. No-Shows Will Be Executed—see Ma? No hands.

The Soviet Union is, of course, different from the way it used to be under Stalin, and even under Khrushchev, back when Senator Humphrey called for illegalizing the Communist Party's American branch. Unfortunately, in many respects it isn't different. For instance, they are still the most unmitigated liars in the history of the world and care nothing at all about it; on the contrary it is a way of life. On the advertisement, for instance, it says, under "Aeroflot Soviet Airlines": "World's Biggest and Busiest Airline. 55 Million Passengers in 1967." I thought maybe I had missed a major development and maybe they have taken to flying all their political prisoners to and from Siberia.

I called a friend who keeps statistics. He cackled with mirth. "They might as well have said fifty-five billion passengers, while they're at it; and I'm surprised they didn't." In America we make a big point of commercial hyperbole. But we make distinctions. The Royal Typewriter Company, for instance, while perfectly capable of saying, "The world's finest typewriter," would not say, "In 1967 we sold 146 million typewriters."

Mr. Hubert Humphrey, who is in favor of continued sanctions against Rhodesia, is against any sanctions at all against a country which tolerates no labor unions, no political liberty, no freedom of speech, no freedom of assembly, no freedom of religion, no freedom of emigration, no freedom of economic movement; and besides that, makes hydrogen bombs and intercontinental missiles the purpose of which is to intimidate people and, if absolutely necessary, to liquidate people on a scale even more efficient than that developed by the old master, Joseph Stalin, whose memory is widely revered.

On the other hand, it isn't the same country. One reads in the morning papers that the Che Guevara guerrilla operation in Bolivia was messed up by the ineptitude of a Russian girl spy. It appears that the lady broke fundamental rules of espionage behavior and left clues strewn about like ladies' hosiery for the bourgeois-imperialist police to pick up, leading to the capture of Guevara. Alger Hiss would never have done that.

Well, Mr. Humphrey has proved that he can change with the times. If only we could contrive to elect him President of the Soviet Union, he might be in a position to prove that the times will change to harmonize with the requirements of the politics of joy.

TEDDY'S REALPOLITIK

March 29, 1969

The ironies are almost unbearable. Consider:

Time magazine: "It was an extraordinary scene. There, in Chancellor Kurt Kiesinger's antique-filled office in Bonn, sat Soviet Ambassador Semyon (Scratchy) ["Scratlhy" to whom? U Thant? Leonard Lyons?] Tsarapkin. Painstakingly, the Russian explained Moscow's grave concern over the first China border clash early this month to the head of a government long reviled by the Soviets as the chief villain and menace in Europe. Patiently, the German listened as Tsarapkin charged that the 'chauvinist foreign policy of Peking' threatened the cause of peace and stability in the world."

Had enough? No. The effrontery is incomplete. . . .

"It was probably [*Time* continued] the first time that any Soviet envoy had so formally attacked the policies of the other Communist giant. Behind Tsarapkin's words was a warning. . . . In Paris, Rome, and Tokyo, Tsarapkin's colleagues were giving the French, Italian, and Japanese foreign ministers roughly the same message. . . . The intent was clear: China, no longer a brotherly Socialist nation but instead a dangerous foe, should be expelled from the ranks of civilized nations."

This account of the Soviet Union's diplomatic offensive against Red China would alone animate an entire book by George Orwell. The notion of the Soviet Union ostracizing a nation from the "ranks of civilized nations" would provide the story line. It is all so ludicrous that one wonders how Prime Minister Kiesinger restrained himself from planting a few thumbtacks on Scratchy's chair. I cannot think of any other means by which the realities might have been reintroduced. The notion of an ambassador of the Soviet Union lecturing the head of the West German state on the nature of international proprieties. . . . *O Geordie, jingling Geordie, it was grand to hear the Baby Charles laying down the guilt of dissimulation, and Steenie lecturing on the turpitude of incontinence!*

The difficulty is that for every Communist incredibility there is in the West—a Kennedy.

Herewith, in the very shadow of Scratchy's impertinence, a statement by Senator Edward Kennedy. He wants the United Nations to recognize Red China. Now, if one thought that the Senator's maneuver was motivated by a desire to exasperate the Soviet Union, one would reason one's way happily through the anfractuous implications of his audacious suggestion.

But alas, a suggestion by Senator Kennedy is not to be confused with a suggestion by Senator Machiavelli. It isn't as if we were listening to someone who proceeded on the assumption that the enemy of our enemy is our friend. No, the analysis of Senator Kennedy turns out to be pure Eleanor Roosevelt. The recognition of Red China by the UN, he explains, should be done "without waiting for resolution of the complex question of Taiwan." That means, very simply, that the question of Taiwan—which is that Red China is governed without the consent of the governed—is to be ignored. But the best is yet to come. In UPI's paraphrase:

"Once the old policies were dropped, Senator Kennedy added, it might be possible for a political accommodation to be reached between the Communist regime on the mainland and the government on Taiwan, in which case Taiwan might be represented in the United Nations as an autonomous unit of China, similiar to the status of Byelorussia and the Ukraine in the United Nations as autonomous provinces of the Soviet Union."

To speak of the "autonomy" of Byelorussia in the constellation of the Soviet Union is something like

asserting the autonomy of Charley McCarthy. The sheer
idiocy of it all has the strange impact of reminding us that
Senator Kennedy is not an idiot. Which requires that we
consider the chilling datum that even as the Soviet Union
attempts to consolidate world opinion against Red China,
the leader of the American opposition is graduating Red
China from the Coventry to which it was relegated by four
American Presidents, including his own brother.

Senator Kennedy's rationale is the sentimentalist
rationale that Red China will dissolve into peacefulness
immediately upon imbibing one chocolate milk shake at
the UN. Mr. Nixon, as also the scores upon scores of
Democratic legislators who have stood up against the
recognition of Red China, has an opportunity to fondle
Senator Kennedy's suggestion back into the ideologists'
crib in which it lies. And, meanwhile, to take a lesson
from Soviet diplomacy. When the Soviets want something,
they do not hesitate to plant their demands right up on the
altar of the opposition. When will we do likewise? What if
Prime Minister Kiesinger had been in a position to say
that he would listen to Scratchy only after learning that
the Soviet Union had ceased shipping arms into North
Vietnam?

THE GREAT FREEZE

August 28, 1969

A researcher who works in the White House notes the
appearance here and there, including in unexpected
places, of sharply anti-Soviet commentary, such as has not
been in fashion for many years. Mr. Anatole Shub wrote
for the Washington *Post* last spring a brilliant series of
articles describing the hell of Soviet life, which got him

kicked out of the Soviet Union. Last week the New York *Times'* correspondent in Prague was kicked out for the sin of reporting what happened; namely, yet another jackbooted suppression of the impulse to freedom—on the anniversary of last year's repression.

It goes on and on. A few weeks ago it transpired that six Soviet author-prisoners, among them Ginzburg and Daniel, petitioned the Presidium of the Supreme Soviet to look into the condition of the political penitentiaries. The writers were most concrete. "For example," their petition said, "Major Annenkov, Chief of the Camp Section 172, has ordered that paper be confiscated from the political prisoners in punishment cells and recommends that they use their fingers in place of toilet paper.

"Another administrator, Duty Officer Lieutenant Taktashev, orders a political prisoner handcuffed and the guards, 'in performance of their duty,' beat the prisoner to boot." The Presidium of the Supreme Soviet of the USSR has not acknowledged the pathetic petition, and if you bring the matter up while in the Soviet Union, you are likely to be dealt with as the reporters of the Washington *Post* and the New York *Times* were dealt with.

In France, a Czechoslovakian Communist has published the record of his ordeal under Stalin in the early fifties, when he was falsely accused along with others and then set up, after months of torture, for a spectacular show trial. Miss Alice-Leone Moats, the talented journalist, describes one episode which will cling to the memory: "Rudolph Slansky, who had been secretary general of the Czechoslovakian Party, and ten others were hanged. Their ashes, in a potato sack, were carried in the same car that bore the three surviving prisoners to another jail outside of Prague. On the way, the car skidded and, to get traction for the wheels, a guard scattered the contents of the potato sack over the icy road."

Every now and then the Innocents travel to Moscow and, because they are otherwise intelligent, come back and write their stupefactions at what they witnessed. I think, for instance, of Arthur Schlesinger, Jr., and James Reston, who for at least forty-eight hours after each visit to Russia, achieve such a pitch of anti-Communist indignation as years ago Mr. Walter Lippmann condemned as vulgar. Unfortunately, we have not contrived a means of persuading Messrs. Schlesinger and Reston to stay in Russia.

A week ago the Miami *Herald* published an editorial under the heading "Rosy Hue Fades Away: Real Russia Is Rigid." The editorial quotes the views of Dr. Mose Harvey, "distinguished Soviet expert at the University of Miami's Center for International Studies." "Soviet liberalization," he says, "was a myth. The present leadership is based on a number of vested interests, a pool of conflicting interests. It is inflexible, and this will be very limiting in the matter of new departures."

"One basis of the despair," the paper observes, "about the possibility of liberalization was offered in the example that Russians speak of Stalin with respect and of Khrushchev with disdain. All this means that United States citizens must take off their rosy glasses and see the Soviet Union as it is: a giant deeply committed to a rigid system. The President properly seeks ways to tear down the fences and warm the relations, but as a practical matter it does not appear that the nation can expect any magical solutions."

The implications of the end of the dream of Soviet liberalization are infinite. But let us begin, to quote a famous phrase, and to begin is to wrench our way free of illusion. Mr. James Burnham, the political philosopher who was never confused on the matter, sums it up: "Those who put faith in Soviet 'thaws' are ignorant of self-deceiving. Though bureaucratic crystallization has permitted a decrease in the number of deaths, the Soviet Union continues to be what it has always been—the quintessential model of a terror-police state. But there is a profound change from Stalin's day. Many victims no longer participate—as nearly all in the purge trials of the thirties did—in their own degradation. Far from confessing as good and repentant Communists for the sake of the cause, they now reaffirm their words and acts, defy the police terror, and sometimes find ways to tell the world what is happening."

AND ON TO VIETNAM

December 2, 1969

The slaughter at Songmy (Mylai 4) raises those mind-
numbing moral questions which strike one with special
force on the eve of a visit to Saigon. I go there, by the
way, on official business for the United States Information
Agency, but—I take the time to put it into the
record—the statute is plain on the matter: The Advisory
Commission of the USIA on which I serve was intended to
work in behalf of United States information policy, as
distinguished from working for the United States
Information Agency, a distinction which even those
Senators who accept contributions from labor unions and
then find Judge Haynsworth unfit to sit on the Supreme
Court will perhaps recognize.

What should one especially look for in Vietnam? The
question plagues the individual who has no pretensions to
sophistication in military matters, and who resents efforts
by others to reveal what are the roots of public sentiment
in a complicated situation, after a short, or even a

protracted, visit to a foreign country. What, for instance, can be said at this point concerning the appalling situation at Songmy? What are the principal questions that ought to be asked? Mr. James Reston suggests the difficulty of the problem by asking what is the moral logic of a situation that calls for giving medals to pilots who bomb civilians, and court-martialing infantrymen who kill the same civilians with rifles?

A few preliminary observations:

1. What makes a killing especially abominable is the question of the necessity for it. A pilot 30,000 feet high, who is ordered to lambaste a city, village, or hamlet because it is a center of enemy activity and not otherwise neutralizable, proceeds with few moral scruples. In any event, those who ponder the deed worry not about the soul of the pilot who drops the bombs, but about the soul of the general who told him to do so.

In Songmy, it was different. There, or so the story goes, individual American soldiers squeezed triggers of rifles aimed at individual civilians who could not realistically be held to be a part of the enemy's war machine. For instance, children. Under the circumstances, if we are still inclined to the presumption of innocence, we examine other possibilities.

2. Could it have been panic? What is it that causes panic? It is a commonplace that soldiers who are being shot at, who do not know whether they will live to see another day, who are tired and calloused and excitable, do things that their consciences would not justify when in cool working order. Is there palpable, in the anxiety to denounce the soldiers who took part in the massacre at Songmy, that old anxiety to discredit the Vietnam War by any means? The facts may, and yet may not, answer convincingly that question. Thus far it looks like simple barbarism, like bloodlust sadism. The trouble with that explanation is that it does not easily reconcile with what we know about typical Americans. Were these atypical Americans? Were they the kind of Americans who, if they

had not found themselves in Vietnam with Vietnamese to
fire at, might have found themselves in Chicago or New
York or Los Angeles aiming their guns at bank tellers or
enemies of the local syndicate? And

3, and most important. Are we perhaps, in our common
rage against these soldiers, engaged, however subtly, in a
circle-squaring expedition? The same week that Mr.
Nixon expressed himself as quite properly horrified at
what happened at Songmy, he officially proscribed the use
of chemical and biological weapons by the United States
even in retaliation against their use by an enemy. It
seemed so simple, so wise, so humane, that few observers
paused to wonder why, if it was so simple, so wise, so
humane, it hadn't been done before. By, say, President
Johnson. Well, not Johnson, because we all were taught
that Johnson wanted to napalm little children. Well, John
Kennedy? Why didn't he come to the same conclusion?
Or, before that, Eisenhower the Good?

We are, it seems to one observer, engaged somehow in
trying to make war tolerable—which it isn't, for reasons
ontological. It does not follow that war equals the
massacre of civilians. But it may follow that war makes
inevitable the incidence of Songmy—and Hiroshima, and
Dresden. The prosecution of the guilty will, then, tell us a
lot about them, and not a little about us; and about those
who dream of wars fought from the turret of the good ship
lollipop.

TALK WITH AN ADMIRAL

Honolulu, December 8, 1969

Admiral John McCain is busy in the same ex-
cruciatingly geometric way that the powerful get busier

as their responsibilities increase. He is technically in charge of the Pacific area; indeed even General Abrams who is directly in charge of the Vietnamese operation reports directly to CINCPAC Hawaii (Commander in Chief Pacific) according to the chart, which is to say to Admiral McCain. But there are all those other duties. On November 29 he hurtled out of his residence in order to greet the astronauts from Apollo 12 who were freshly arrived on the *Hornet*, en route to Houston. They engaged together, through the microphone, in heroic pleasantries and congratulations. (President Nixon had just spoken with the astronauts over television, delivering a little graduation address jocularly promoting them to the rank of captain.) The astronauts, all three of whom are in the Navy, just to show that they were once again truly earthbound, produced a streamer visible through the porthole of their quarantined quarters: Beat Army. Admiral McCain was pleased. Although he suppressed any untoward expression of factionalist enthusiasm. After all, he is in charge not only of the U.S. Navy, but of the U.S. Army, and also the Air Force.

The admiral is a man of formidable character and charm. He might have served as the character around whom the entire concept of the tight ship was crystallized. He is of the school that understands the nature of duty and is quite prepared to face the consequence, as a realistic matter, that duty can be unpleasant, which isn't exactly how he would put it, given as he is to saltier description. He does not wear publicly his private badge of sorrow, which the visitor is discretely informed about, namely that he has a son, a prisoner of the North Vietnamese, shot down in action, in uncertain health, held virtually incommunicado.

He is asked at one point during a briefing session, what might have been the response to the seizure of the *Pueblo*. He responds, as in so many other situations, with instant reaction. He answers—mind that you understand this well—purely in terms of American military capacity, and he declines to weigh the political question which he tells you is outside his competence. And he therefore lists what might have been done when the *Pueblo* was seized. A visitor objects that it is inconceivable that the President would take action which might have resulted in the death of a hundred crewmen of the *Pueblo*. Hell, the admiral says, there are several hundred American military who risk their lives every day flying through enemy flak. The admiral is not among those who would enthusiastically have heralded the courage of Commander Bucher. It is left to the visitor to meditate how he would have reacted, by parallel reasoning, to the courage of Lyndon Johnson: This is most firmly forbidden territory. The admiral is as firm in his conviction that the civilian arm should give orders to the military as he is that the *Pueblo* should have taken its instructions not from North Korean gunboats, but from naval code books.

He stands there by his charts, assisted by staff officers of medium and very high rank, including a vice admiral who turns over the leaves of the briefing pad, which informs the visitor how we are doing in almost every aspect of the Vietnam operation, and by a lieutenant general, expert in many matters that come up under discussion.

When a question is put to the admiral to which he does not have the answer, his mode is to tilt his head skyward, at about ten o'clock. "I don't have the specific answer to that question. . . ." He pauses then, pregnantly, for maybe up to ten seconds. He is confident that before the ten seconds elapse, a member of his staff will come forward with the answer, the specific answer. One has the feeling that if the ten seconds go by, and the admiral is left to resume the briefing without the answers to the question, a private execution will take place at dawn the next day.

Oh, says the admiral, relaxed at his home, but never losing something of the coiled-wire tension appropriate to the CINCPAC, America has made a lot of mistakes, no doubt about it. But I do not understand (a theme which would become recurrent) why America doesn't take heart over the achievements which we are now able to record. For instance? Well, for instance, the replacement rate of the enemy troops. The rate is down, way down over what it was a year, let alone two years ago. For instance? The number of Vietnamese who are under the direct control of the enemy. The figure rose, during the height of the Tet offensive in 1968, to 33 percent. The figure is down now to an incredible 8 percent.

But the admiral, speaking in a Southern accent yet exercising Yankee skepticism, cautions the visitor to take carefully such statistics as these. It is impossible to vouch for them with any sense of statistical certitude. What he does vouch for is the graph. The relative figures. There is no doubting that, ever since the great offensive which was to have heralded the end of resistance to the Communists, the enemy has gone down and down and down.

Why is it, the admiral wonders, that more Americans do not take pride in these achievements, which although they may not be conclusive, surely seem to indicate how considerable, and how measurable, is our progress? If you discover the reasons—the admiral waved his hand as the visitor headed for the midnight shuttle to Saigon—let me know. The visitor thought this the least he could do, under the circumstances, for the CINCPAC.

MYLAI—WHOSE FAULT?

Saigon, December 12, 1969

General Creighton Abrams, who has a major war to think about, talks only reluctantly about the massacre of

Mylai. Those who suppose that this is because General Abrams is anxious to disengage from a subject which is acutely embarrassing to him (a) forget that General Abrams was not in charge of the Vietnam theater at the time that headquarters, after a perfunctory investigation, denied the rumor of a massacre at Mylai; (b) forget that even now the general is incompletely informed on the subject since the entire dossier was lifted from Saigon and flown to Washington, and (c) do not know General Abrams, who retreats from difficulty about as much as a moth retreats from the flame.

There is the further difficulty of the military-legal situation. So strict have the rules become, if we are to believe General Abrams, and why not, that any interference by a commanding officer, whether explicit or implicit, in a matter pending before a military court can have the effect of invalidating the proceeding.

Even so, he agreed to listen, on an *arguendo* basis, to what might result from the investigation of the Mylai massacre, the rules being that, for the sake of the discussion, we would accept the version of what happened which is generally current. What follows is a composite of opinions which are not necessarily his, but which were expressed in his presence without arousing his vehement dissent.

1. How many people were actually guilty? A very important question, because one struggles to define the limits of aberrancy. Jack the Ripper was not a corporation, so that we can think of him as aberrant. We cannot do that about, say, the Nazis under Hitler, or the Communists under Stalin. If it had been one company commander and one platoon leader, and maybe even one or at the most two or three sergeants, we may conclude that the behavior was utterly eccentric, *i.e.*, that no conclusions regarding the genus are to be inferred from the behavior of the particulars.

2. If, on the other hand, it transpires that ten, twenty, thirty, even fifty men concerted in the act of genocide,

then we must seek an explanation for why a cross section
of young America found itself capable of utterly barbaric
behavior. We have available to us two explanations. The
first, which is infinitely preferable, is that the guilty
company relapsed, as the result of a confluence of
extraordinary pressures, into a kind of catatonic frenzy, a
sort of collective fury, as unreasonable as a rogue sea. The
second alternative—the horrifying alternative—is that
America, in A.D. 1969, has bred young Americans who
can insouciantly murder grandmothers and little children.
Raising the question 3.—to dispose first of a mechanical
matter—how shall we, if all fifty of those soldiers are
found guilty and sentenced, define the immediate
responsibilities of infantrymen in forthcoming engagements? An example might be a lieutenant's ordering a soldier to fire at anyone leaving a particular
building which, in the lieutenant's opinion, is occupied by
a sniper. The lieutenant goes off to instruct another
member of his command, and at that point the infantryman sees the door opening slowly and out comes
—grandmother. Ambiguities to tax—to paralyze?—
the infantryman of the future, when he is faced with such a
situation as we describe?

4. But then back to the most absorbing question, which
is this. If it is agreed that it was a cross section of
American youth, out there at Mylai, and that there are not
available to them extenuating circumstances such as would
relieve them of true moral responsibility for their acts, then
who, and what, do we blame? Many American moralizers
came out with the answer instantly on the revelation of the
massacre. Why, what we blame is the Vietnam War. That
has brutalized clean and wholesome American youth, has
turned them into sadistic killers who think nothing of
gunning down children. That is one explanation.

It is insufficient. What is it about the Vietnam
experience that can transform a twenty-year-old into a
monster? The adage is that a woman bent upon virtue
cannot be seduced by her hypnotist. By the same token, it

is simply unbelievable that two or three months of combat can corrupt otherwise ethically stable young men. It must be—it must be what came before.

The twenty-year-old who, under the press of circumstances, can easily murder, after only a few months in uniform, is most likely a twenty-year-old whose ethical equilibrium was unbalanced well before he came to Vietnam. Unbalanced by a society which in quite other contexts we all have been criticizing over the years. A society deprived of the strength of religious sanctions, a society hugely devoted to hedonism, to permissive egalitarianism, to irresponsibility, to an indifference to authority and the law. Such a society as—dare we say it?—produced the kids who are attracted to the iconoclast of the day. I would contend that a better explanation for what happened, according to this analysis, is—not Vietnam but, to reach for a symbol—Berkeley.

Breaking out now from the shackles of our assumptions, I would expect (and here I speak only for myself) that the court will discover either that it was the aberration of the few, or that it was temporary mania of the many—rather than that it was the considered act of the many. But if it should prove to be the latter, beware of blaming Vietnam for it. The danger is closer to home.

HUE—A FULL DAY

Danang, December 10, 1969

In the morning, Ellsworth Bunker, chatting with the visitor, reminisces that on a very recent trip to the United States he came across Averell Harriman. "I've known Ave Harriman" (Yale, 1913), said seventy-five-year-old Mr.

Bunker (Yale, 1916), "for sixty years," which struck the visitor as a long time to have known Mr. Harriman, "and I reminded him that the tacit understanding back when they were telling us to stop the bombing was that if we did so the North Vietnamese had agreed to do three things: (1) stop infiltrating across the demilitarized zone; (2) desist from shelling the population centers in the cities; (3) agree to talk directly with the South Vietnamese government at the negotiating table. And," said the tall, angular, poised, incisive ambassador to South Vietnam, "of course, the enemy has observed not a single one of the three provisions."

What did Mr. Harriman say? the visitor wondered. "Oh, well, he said that conditions had changed."

Mr. Bunker bears no grudges, let alone against friends he made sixty years ago. But he sees straight, out of his straight and lean body, and although he guards strenuously against synthetic optimism, so much does he fear that the credibility gap of yesteryear will affect his own usefulness that sometimes it seems as though he husbands the good news as though it were a government secret. Even so, the good news is there, notwithstanding the routine duplicities of the North Vietnamese, who persuaded the United States to stop the bombing in return for—a heightened contempt of the United States by the North Vietnamese.

You fly to Danang, the great sea and military base up on the coastline a hundred miles from North Vietnam. Then a helicopter to Hué. Hué. The very sound of it. That was where, during the Tet offensive in 1968, the enemy moved in most tenaciously, holding the old capital city, the quiet aristocratic religious center of 150,000 people, for a couple of weeks, before he was finally dislodged.

What happened was this. The Vietcong and the North Vietnamese, exuberant at the apparent success of the winter offensive, gave back the news to Hanoi of their victory. Hanoi, reasoning that a little general optimism was in order—150-odd assaults on South Vietnam cities had been programmed for what Hanoi thought would be a general takeover—decided to proclaim victory. Whereupon the underground at Hué surfaced. And several thousand people suddenly saw that Mrs. Jones' chauffeur was a Vietcong, now giving orders, and also Mr. Smith's greengrocer, who was all over the place telling people what to do; and on down the line. The consequences were unthinkable: blowing the entire hidden VC population. So the leadership decided on an easy solution. They would round up all the residents of Hué who had come to know who they were. And . . . eliminate them.

They have not finished finding the bodies. But because the Vietnamese and the Americans are nowadays anxious to avoid any danger of exaggeration, the official count is only of those bodies actually discovered, *i.e.*, 2,750. They were killed here and there. At one spot, southeast of the city, you look down on the calcified area of that part of the earth's surface, and you see long, low general cavities. That is where they were buried. They have been retrieved by their families, who did not trouble to recover the paraphernalia of execution or the sediments of death. Some of these human caches were discovered only a few weeks ago, so that the bones of the decomposed corpses here and there are visible; and, every few yards, the remnants of the Wirz grass that served to tie behind their backs the wrists of those who were to be killed. A line was then run through the makeshift handcuffs, and the VC began shooting. At the lucky ones. Others, whether to save ammunition or to silence the noise of gunshot, were clubbed, and then dumped down into the open communal graves. It made no difference that many of them were not killed by the blow of the club, so that they died slowly, of asphyxiation. They were, as the saying goes, buried alive.

You go forward, to within the shadow of the DMZ; and are briefed by a proud colonel from ARVN; *i.e.*, the Army of Vietnam. There are no American troops left in this critical area. They were withdrawn by the President, so that now the natives feel, and exercise, the responsibility.

The area is, to be sure, largely pacified. You return to Danang, to bed down there that night, and the helicopter pilot asks for clearance, which means, now at sundown, that he does not desire to fly through a practice artillery range. He is given a course, which takes him, unexpectedly, just past a point where suddenly mean-looking radiant rockers are zapping up toward the top of the mountain. The pilot guns his chopper heavenward and comments, laconically, that such weapons as we see going off "seldom go above 2,500 feet," which was reason enough for the pilot to take our plane up from 2,300 to 4,000 feet.

BLOODY, BLOODIER

Saigon, December 18, 1969

I have read about in fiction, but never supposed, that such a document ever existed—the blank execution warrant; that is to say, a form ordering the execution of whatever individual is so hapless as to get his name written in where now a blank space exists. The form I have in front of me bears the official seal of the "People's Revolutionary Committee of Saigon-Gia Dinh, Fourth Precinct" and requires nothing more to set it into motion than, as I say, giving the name and one or two particulars about the man you are condemning. Not even a human signature is required—not a bad idea, that: Perhaps the North Vietnamese have learned from the Nazis' meticulous attention to detail how dangerous—and how unnecessary—it is to affix upon a piece of paper the name of the responsible executioner.

The form is of macabre interest. It is headed: "Death

Sentence." The text, only slightly abbreviated, says:

"In accordance with the judgment and resolution of the Fourth Precinct People's Revolutionary Council dated — [filled in].

"A sentence of death has been pronounced on —— [name] —— [address] . . . the culprit [having] been found to be a cruel tyrant who has committed the following crime: . . .

"A collaborator of the country-grabbing pirates and U.S.-Thieu-Ky-Huong counterselling lackeys who has [sic] . . . opposed the revolutionary undertaking of our entire people.

"All military, civilian, administrative authorities are required to carry out this sentence."

I also have here translations of a few enemy documents which exist in profusion and are workaday accounts both of the achievements of the Communists and of the character of the instructions that flow down from the Revolutionary Committees.

One of them, for instance, reports a rather anemic day's work: "Agents of the District Armed Reconnaissance Unit gave a pack of poisoned Cotab cigarettes to some field policemen. After smoking these cigarettes, eleven field policemen were poisoned; one died and ten others were cured after being evacuated to the hospital."

Another reports on a more fruitful day. "Killed twenty-four men, including hamlet and village administrative personnel and informants who owed the people a blood death. Wounded four men and warned thirty others before a crowd of eighty people. Four of them confessed to their crimes, and their families agreed to be responsible for their conduct. In addition, we sent letters of warning to thirty-eight hamlet and village administrative personnel and interfamily chiefs."

Here is an order issued last June and addressed to a "Village Party Committee": "A complete roster of local administrative personnel must be swiftly established, with full names, activities, and private residences. The roster should include the wicked village delegates, policemen, hamlet chiefs and assistant hamlet chiefs, intelligence agents, spies, and betrayers who have committed blood debt [*sic*] against our people. We must arrest or kill the above tyrants on the night of June 5 and 6. . . ."

And again, addressed to "various agencies": "Every armed reconnaissance cell must kill at least one chief or assistant chief in each of the following: Public Security Service, District National Police Service, Open Arms Service, Information Service, Pacification Teams, and a district chief or an assistant district chief. In addition, every cell must exterminate three wicked tyrants living in a district seat or ward, and warn thirty other enemy personnel that they will be punished if they do not conform by rallying to our cause."

I note, too, the decentralization of the authority to execute: "To cope with the present situation and to properly prepare to fight the enemy in the days ahead, the high echelon has decided that from now on the District Current Affairs Committees have the right to examine the death sentences passed by village security sections and party chapters. These sentences will also be executed at the request of the District Security Sections."

And on and on. But here, finally, is one whose awful resonance should freeze the banter of those who prattle about the likelihood of amnesty in the event of a Communist victory: "We must counter the aggressive war not only in the present but also in the future even when our Fatherland is completely liberated. The people's struggle will continue to take place, fierce and complicated, especially the struggle against spies, reactionaries, henchmen of the U.S. imperialists, reactionary elements in the religious community, and ethnic minority groups [report to the security agency of VOSVN on September 30, 1968]."

The day I left Vietnam, *Stars and Stripes* carried a short item, the news of a housewife who had been kidnapped from a hamlet on the outskirts of Hué. A notice was in due course sent to the village announcing that she would be executed, a retaliation for her husband's collaboration with the antipeople's movement. That poor woman is no more guilty than, say, 12,000,000 South Vietnamese who are equally eligible to find their names on one of those execution forms.

Discussing, a week ago, the massacre at Songmy (Mylai), the *Economist* of London wrote:

> It would be a harder sum to work out if last year's massacre at Hué [the full measure of which has only just been revealed] was being anxiously discussed this week in *Nhan Dan* or *Pravda*; if Hanoi radio was interviewing the men who did it; if Mr. Truong Chinh had said it was abhorrent to the conscience of North Vietnam. What happened at Songmy is a terrible commentary on the cruel, or weak, men who committed the act. The fact that it was belatedly but inevitably discovered, and the reactions now that it has been discovered, are a better commentary on what the war is being fought for.

A DAY IN LAOS, AND AN EVENING

Vientiane, December 15, 1969

Pity the poor Laotians, however depleted your reserves of pity. There aren't very many of them, just over 2,500,000; they are very, very poor; earning per capita fifty dollars per year, which the United States practically doubles with its various projects—military, economic and social—in Laos. The country is split right down the middle, the eastern half dominated by North Vietnamese soldiers who use it as a conveyor belt to feed the war against South Vietnam. That line oscillates wildly, depending on who is in control of a central plain to the north, which the government now controls, but which the Communists are always threatening to overrun. The war costs the Laotians, on a typical day, 13 soldiers dead. Multiply that by 100, and you have an idea what would be a comparable loss to the United States—1,300 dead per day, or just under 500,000 men per year, far, far worse than our burden during the worst days of the Second World War.

Probably Laos will survive or not depending on whether South Vietnam survives. It is so in all of Southeast Asia, which is like a mobile, which rises, or lowers, its component pieces, maintaining their relative position to one another, as one lifts or lowers the halyard. Souvanna Phouma, the Prime Minister, told the visitor sadly, philosophically, that for so long as that war continues, Laos is definitely in danger, because the enemy needs the Ho Chi Minh Trail, which is on Laotian territory. But if South Vietnam survives, even then it will be a struggle, because the North Vietnam Communists are greedy, and they will continue to prey on Laos.

Yet the country breeds a rugged kind of optimism, or so it seems. The American ambassador, Mac Godley, is energetic, exuberant, determined. So also are the Americans who help in every conceivable way, with education, agriculture, public health, military security. It isn't an easy job. For one thing there is the language problem—more generally, the problem of communication. There are a total of 7,500 copies sold per day throughout Laos of all the daily newspapers combined. Very few Laotians speak English, indeed very few Laotians read Lao (75 percent are illiterate). So that one needs to start from the very bottom, which Americans have undertaken to do, helping, for instance, to train Laotians to fly airplanes, an indispensable accomplishment for any nation that decides to protect itself. As one Lao put it to one

American official, complaining of the insecurity of travel,
"The activities carry out quite well, but feel worry one
thing, that is no any boss go along the trips. I have
complained this question several times but boss is afraid
to die." Not all bosses are afraid to die.

Incredibly, there are now more than fifty Laotian pilots,
some of them taken right off their water buffalo, who are
now flying four and five sorties per day against the enemy.
It requires eighteen months to train such a pilot, who first
must be taught the rudiments of English so as to be able
to perform simple acts of maintenance. It was after dinner,
away down in Savannakatt, across the river from
Thailand, when it occurred suddenly to a young
intelligence officer that we could see for ourselves. There
was a brand-new gun, or rather guns, which are bolted
down on the floor of an old DC-3, the three muzzles
protruding out the windows, and they shoot off an
incredible 6,000 rounds per minute, in short bursts, after
the flares are tossed out illuminating the area of
infiltration, as word of it comes to a central intelligence
post; they call the airplane Puff the Magic Dragon, and its
pilot, Spooky. Would we care to see the operation?

He telephoned; yes, a Laotian crew will be going out
momentarily. We climb aboard in the bitter cold, and the
plane roars up into the night shatteringly loud, the cold air
roaring in through what once was a door, now is an
aperture through which the crew will toss the brilliant
white flares. All very informal, not to say anarchical, and
we don parachutes not because we are instructed to do
so—the pilot and crew are most permissive—but because
they keep us a little warmer. But since we do have them
on, the pilot leans over and shouts through the noise, "If I
make long bell we crash," so that we know that if we hear
long bell, to jump out the door, count slowly to two, and
pull the handle appropriately perched over the heart.

But the pilot made only short bells, after each one of
which a big flare was jettisoned, itself to parachute down
toward the enemy. An hour or so of this, but no firing,

then suddenly off to the southeast, more flares and suddenly the whole side of the plane becomes a machine gun, the three parallel beams describing, at 100 rounds per second, a golden tracery to the ground. The noise is as if you found yourself inside the walls of an engine. Four, five bursts, and the 9,000 bullets have been fired, and it is time to reload and return to the ground, which we greet with great reverence. The Laotian pilots are matter-of-fact about it, strolling into the little room with the radio. They expect to go out again that night, maybe even twice more. The passengers would sooner retire to where the water buffalo roam.

I do not know why heroism and stamina and simple determination in a just cause are so unexciting nowadays to so many who have never had to fight for the freedoms they so often abuse, certainly who have never had to fight against such awful odds as the Laotians, whose introduction to the wonders of the modern world finds them, late at night out in the cold, foraging through the blackness for those who are bent on taking from them the very little that they have. But the memory is indelible, and the sadness overpowering, because the laws of nature will not be suspended, and they speak as certainly as they spoke for the pilots who volunteered to save Britain against the falling of the night, saying, surely, that one day, maybe not tomorrow, the men we flew with will have to make a long, and endless, bell.

THE WORLD'S ANGRIEST MAN

Bangkok, December 23, 1969

If one of our Telstars were given the assignment of singling out the world's angriest man, it would freeze over

Bangkok, Thailand, more specifically over the rooftop of
Dr. Thanat Kohman, the Foreign Minister of Thailand for
the past eleven years. He is angry with us because he
believes that the United States is nowadays represented by
such as Senators Fulbright and Symington, which
gentlemen the foreign minister believes to be engaged in
policies which, in moments of conversational relaxation, he
denounces as "sterile."

The meeting took place a day after the newspapers
reported that the United States had in effect paid to
Thailand $1 billion in order to bribe the Thais into
sending a single division of men into South Vietnam. Dr.
Thanat Kohman's howls have no doubt been heard in
Washington. To begin with, it isn't true. In the second
place, says Dr. Thanat Kohman, Thailand is unusual in
this world in that it has not presented the United States
with a great bill in return for receiving the United States'
favors. Perhaps, he says bitterly, that was a mistake.
Perhaps Senators Fulbright and Symington would think
better of Thailand if she had followed an ambiguous
foreign policy over the years, alternating her favors
between the Soviet Union and the United States. Instead,
for the eleven years that Dr. Thanat Kohman has
administered the foreign policy of Thailand, his country
has firmly and unequivocally joined with the United States
in regional defense pacts and obliged the United States by
giving us such facilities as we have needed in order to
discharge our obligations. Why can't the United States
realize this?

At this point the visitor began to fidget and reminded
His Excellency that Senator Fulbright is not the United
States. Well, why don't Americans reject Senator
Fulbright? he asked directly. Americans, said the visitor,
have never been given the opportunity to reject Senator
Fulbright, but if ever they were, the visitor had no doubts
that they would do so enthusiastically. Well, said the
foreign minister, if Senator Fulbright's views are rejected
by the people, how come he is still in the Senate? The

visitor despaired of explaining Arkansas politics even to so learned and cosmopolitan a citizen of Thailand, and thought it best to take the offensive. Look, Mr. Minister, how do you think American feels about the criticisms of us? You're getting criticized by individual members of the United States Senate. We get criticized by whole governments for doing things we are not getting anything out of concretely. For instance? Dr. Thanat Kohman asked, visibly concerned that he was called upon to share his sense of outrage with anyone else. Well, for instance, said the visitor, the government of Sweden, which just voted to extend $45,000,000 credit to North Vietnam. So, said the foreign minister, what do you want? Do you want us to declare war against Sweden? All right, we'll declare war against Sweden, if that's really what you want. But meanwhile, what about Fulbright?

The visitor thanked the minister most cordially and said that perhaps the declaration of war against Sweden should await a more propitious season; and anyway, however sympathetic the visitor was to those who deplored the ingratitude of American Fulbrights, still, he stressed, they are in a minority, and meanwhile, what was Thailand doing about the nonparticipation in Asian burdens of such countries as Japan?

Japan, said the minister, is the principal profiteer of the Vietnam War. She has taken every commercial advantage from it and is clearly prepared to sail into history devoting only 1 percent of her gross national product to defense, for so long as she can depend on others to do her work.

And talking about burdens, the minister perked up at the memory of another grievance. Not only is the United States reducing its foreign aid to Thailand to the merest trickle, under our Public Law 480, which permits the sale at exaggeratedly low prices of agricultural surpluses under special circumstances, we have directly cut into Thailand's exports, aggravating her already grievously distorted imbalance of payments. What did the visitor have to say about that?

Well, he would certainly take up the matter with Senator Fulbright when he got home—which, at that point, couldn't be soon enough. But he left deeply concerned that the friends of the United States should feel so keenly the apparent indifference of the United States toward those few countries in the world which have stood by us—uncomplainingly, I almost said.

SUMMING UP—I

Hong Kong, December 20, 1969

The temptation is to sum up a short visit to Vietnam by giving figures which suggest how the situation there is tilted at this moment. To that temptation I partly succumb.

Here, first, is some bad news. We have not succeeded in devising the means of persuading North Vietnamese soldiers to defect. This is not a tribute to their ideological constancy, so much as testimony to their home-mindedness. Defection means for them a permanent separation from their families and, not inconceivably, retaliation against their families. There is abundant evidence that the North Vietnamese tire not only of the rigors of the war but of the manifest futility of it. Still, the tendency is to do what one is told, and to dream of repatriation. Defection is for the few, the very few who will live apart from their families. Fewer than 1,000 North Vietnamese have defected. By contrast, 120,000 Vietcong have defected.

An enormously important, and ominous, datum —inasmuch as the conduct of the war has passed dramatically in the past year or so from the hands of the Vietcong on over to the North Vietnamese, who although they were always responsible for the direction and provisioning of the war, did depend heavily up until recently on indigenous units. In the space of a little more than a year, the ratio almost exactly reversed, from 70 percent SVN and 39 NVN, to the exact opposite. One might call it the North Vietnamization of the war. All the more discouraging that the defection rate is so low among the most crucial element in the current struggle.

More bad news. Although the enemy, as we shall see, is reeling from successive disasters, he retains the technical capacity to regenerate himself at about the rate at which we have been killing him. An estimated 100,000 healthy males not designated for specialized training turn eighteen every year. That is about how many soldiers, on an average, have been killed per year over the course of the war. The bright side of it, in the macabre figuring of the military statisticians, is that something like an entire generation of North Vietnamese males has been killed during the past seven or eight years. The sobering side is that they grow 'em as fast as we kill 'em. One recalls the blood-chilling comment of Wellington surveying the carnage after a great battle against Napoleon in Spain, and sniffing that the English dead were no greater than the number of men who would be conceived the next Saturday night in London.

The enemy, the North Vietnamese, have enough men left over to keep 50,000 of them engaged in Laos, where, as in South Vietnam, they shoulder the overwhelming burden of pressing their imperialism. Did I forget to mention that there are only 75,000 Vietcong? More-over—another grim statistic—the matériel that crosses the borders of North Vietnam en route to the slaughter of Americans and South Vietnamese does so with less than the difficulty—thanks to Lyndon Johnson's suspension of the bombing—that an American tourist experiences in crossing over, say, to Canada.

We are talking, for the most part, about Soviet goods;

Soviet weapons, Soviet trucks, Soviet oil. Two figures, purely suggestive. There are more North Vietnamese infiltrating into South Vietnam right now, than in 1966 or 1967. As of December 1, 4,500 vehicles were landed in support of the Communists, which is 800 more than the figure for a year ago. During October alone, 52,000 tons of fuel went into North Vietnam, a figure which I reduce, straining the limits of my mathematical prowess, to approximately 15,000,000 gallons. It is generally supposed that all of the infiltration of the goods of war comes down through Laos and the Ho Chi Minh Trail and then insinuates east across the long South Vietnamese frontier. In fact a great deal of matériel laps into the port of Sihanoukville in Cambodia and treks its way leisurely east into the southernmost area of Vietnam, the Delta region, which is what the war is all about, that being where the rice is. Why, why we do not ourselves close off that port, or, with a salute to Vietnamization, why we do not give the South Vietnamese the means to do so remains a mystery, too subtle for me or Spiro Agnew to understand.

But the point is made. The enemy neither has to give up, nor is, apparently, disposed to give up. Which does not mean that we are not winning the war, achieving our objectives, and facing, in a controlled situation, far brighter prospects. We are, in fact; so stay tuned.

SUMMING UP—II

Honolulu, December 21, 1969

I have struggled for a formulation, and it is this. There is insufficient evidence that Washington has thought through the meaning of Vietnamization. It is perhaps unfair to put it in quite that way, so let us settle for saying that there is abundant evidence that Washington has not communicated to the American public the true meaning of Vietnamization.

You need to keep reminding yourself, when you think of Vietnam, that there was never a war like it fought in history. You see whole legions of pilots and bombs and machine guns and helicopters and godknowswhat which are entirely but entirely unnecessary, because their sole function is to track down and eliminate supplies which entered into the country in the first place via a couple of bottlenecks visible to every seagull on the coastline of North Vietnam and Cambodia, let alone our super-bombsights. Why do we not block these accesses? There is no questioning that that would be the humane thing to do. Blocking those accesses would save not only American lives, not only South Vietnamese lives, but also North Vietnamese lives.

Well, we have become accustomed to the argument that we do not block those great ports because to do so would be to provoke directly the Soviet Union in particular, whose merchant fleet is busy supplying those ports with the materials of war. Provoke her and possibly also provoke China, which though to a lesser extent also uses the harbor at Haiphong, although most of her help flows down a railroad line which also could be easily interdicted.

Now it is a question for diplomatic strategists to dispute whether the reasoning that stayed the hand of Lyndon Johnson, and now Nixon, is ultimately sound. But there is no argument at all about the military inanity. The military feels that its job is to erect the Empire State Building, but to skip the first floor.

Now, any military authority capable of neutralizing a peashooter would proceed at once to do at least some, and probably all, of the following: (1) block the harbor at Haiphong; (2) block the harbor at Sihanoukville; (3) effect an amphibious landing north of Haiphong cutting a swathe across central North Vietnam and dividing the country; (4) march a column of troops west extending (roughly) the Demilitarized Zone, thus cutting off the Ho Chi Minh Trail.

Now the question before the house is: With the assumption by the South Vietnamese of military authority and, progressively, the human brunt of the war (during the week I was there, 80 percent of the battle casualties were South Vietnamese, 20 percent United States), are we also prepared to rescind the political considerations which have hampered our own movements? It is one thing to say that blocking Haiphong or invading North Vietnam would be interpreted as a threat by the United States to Red China. It is altogether something else to suppose that South Vietnamese action of the identical kind would represent a threat to Red China. China is as much threatened by South Vietnam as we are threatened by Costa Rica. South Vietnam's enemy, North Vietnam, cares nothing at all about violating the territory of Laos, or of Cambodia, for the purpose of introducing aggression into South Vietnam. So under what reasoning should South Vietnam care about moving into Cambodia and Laos in order to repress that aggression?

How would it look for the Soviet navy—for all that it is given nowadays to swaggering about in the Indian Ocean—to command its dreadnoughts to shoot down South Vietnamese gunboats engaged in closing down a harbor which it is entitled to do under international convention when the harbor is being used to supply aggressors against it? Now there would be true escalation, calling for reprisals by the United States, symmetrical or asymmetrical. But that is our problem. It ought not to be the problem of South Vietnam.

True, the South Vietnamese would be using our matériel; so what? The enemy continues to use matériel made in the Soviet Union and in Red China. True Vietnamization would set up true equilibrium, but the question now is whether we are so stuck in our fear of escalation that we will seek by reflex action to impose on Vietnam inhibitions which are only questionably defensible as they weigh down the United States but would be unquestionably indefensible as they weigh down South Vietnam. If we pass along our political repressions to South Vietnam, the strategic outcome is clear: Victory for the enemy.

OUTSTANDING

San Antonio, October 9, 1969

"It helps, ma'am," he said spiritedly, "if you tell me who you are." The nurse identified herself so that he was then able to refer to her by name. Would he care to join us for some coffee? "I never turned down free coffee in my life," and he climbed down off his bed and struggled with his bathrobe. Unsuccessfully.

The visitor sorted it out and helped him on with it. He chattered on, wanting to know the latest word on New York City politics. He extended his left hand, fastening it on the visitor's right arm, and told him to go ahead. "If we pass any pretty girls, tell me and I'll whistle. I don't know whether there are any around here, but I wouldn't be surprised." (But there were only doctors and nurses as they strolled down the corridor, and the maimed bodies of servicemen.)

He talked on in high spirits, touching on Louisiana politics, concerning which he was expert. He majored in history at LSU and knew and obviously cherished the brawling politics of his home state. "Real upheaval now. The old Huey Long base—the white redneck and the Negroes—is breaking up, since the integration business. The governor is in deep trouble. And you know that

Louisiana never votes for the winning President. Not since 1956. Earl Long was my man. I worked for his election when I was nine years old. Outstanding. He knew politics. The trick is to play politics and not to get enmeshed in them. He had a way with the voters. 'The South may not always be right,' he said, 'but it's *never* wrong.' One governor said he hadn't run for public office in order to take a vow of poverty. Next I saw of him was a picture, alongside the president of LSU, cutting sugarcane in a chain gang."

Getting into the car confused him, because it was one of those new models, the rear doors opening up to leeward, so that he began to step in facing the rear. At that, you would not know that his experience with blindness is so short. It happened on June 9. William Fullerton was squad leader, instructed to reconnoiter on a hilltop south of Danang.

"We got up there all right, but the area was booby-trapped. Half the platoon was hit. My squad—twenty men—had twenty-five casualties during the preceding period, so we were under-strength. I thought, God we're going to be ambushed, and I worried because I couldn't see my gun. But the choppers were there in no time. What a sound when you hear those blades. Outstanding. Thirty minutes later I was in a hospital. Three days later in Japan. I got here the fifth of July, how's that?"

American logistics, the visitor admitted, are better than American foreign policy. "They ought to fight that war to win, or pull every man out of there tomorrow. If I could see, I'd go back tomorrow, if we'd agree to fight to win. I didn't have to go last time. I was 1-Y. I just figured I'd go and do my Hemingway thing."

What now? "My own doctor says an operation could bring sight back to my right eye. But the people here disagree; they say the eye is too far gone. So I'm headed for Chicago. They'll discharge me there, and I'll go to the Veterans' Hospital where they specialize in blind people. If they agree to operate there, fine. If not, I'd have to go and get it done privately, and that costs two thousand dollars. But I suppose it's worth it. I'd like to go back to LSU and take law. But I'll have to wait. They'll teach me Braille at Chicago. Maybe that way you can get to understand Louisiana law. The constitution is the longest in the world. I started to read it once. Didn't get past the preamble."

It was time to go back. A corporal greeted him in the street outside the hospital door. "Hey, George," he returned the greeting, "what about the kidneys?" George said the doctors hadn't succeeded. "Oh, well, George, just think, you could be ugly, too." George walked off, and Fullerton leaned over, his face deeply grieved. "Awful. He has three children. But with his kidney condition, he can't live more than fifteen or twenty years."

Back at the ward, he stood erect by his bed, smiling, and on finding the visitor's hand, shook it. "Outstanding," he said, "I've had an outstanding time."*

---

* William Fullerton, Jr., was operated on by the famous New York surgeon Ramon Castroviejo in February, 1970. Seven weeks after the operation he was able to distinguish colors, and there is daily improvement.

VI. APOLLO

CAN MEN MAKE MIRACLES?

Cape Kennedy, December 28, 1968

I write on the assumption that Apollo 8 will complete its mission, though my spirit is dogged by the direful premonition of a poet who, moments before the lift-off, confessed to me that something would go wrong. Intuitions being for poets to have, I found my thought turning gloomy. But science has done so much, surely it will not fail. Remember what Mr. Kearns told us yesterday as he took us around and showed us what went into that launching. . . .

He said that the scientists put it this way: There are 5,600,000 parts to Apollo 8. Obviously that means to count every screw as one part. Still the figure is very nearly unfathomable, like the venture those parts combine to attempt. Anyway, the scientists tell you that they look for a performance of 99.6 percent. That is to say, four-tenths of 1 percent of the parts of Apollo 8 can fail and still the project can be made to come off. That means that 56,000 parts can fail.

Now obviously among those 56,000 parts you cannot indulge the failure of specified parts, say the steering wheel, or whatever is its counterpart. When Apollo 7 went up and came down, the scientists computed its success at 99.99, or as nearly perfect as our asymptotic universe permits. So then permit us, O Lord, our optimism, even if it means to gainsay our poets.

Our poets. I found myself wondering about them there at the press pad with several hundred journalists scampering about, some of them talking into microphones strung out to their constituencies thousands of miles away, some focusing cameras (one gentleman from Zurich had a telephoto lens about as long as a short Cadillac), some of them scribbling a little self-consciously on their stenographic pads, others filing through the little cafeteria trailer ($.15 for coffee—the $361,000,000 Apollo cost did not include free coffee for the press); all of us dizzy with excitement as we saw first in the blackness the penetrating beams that illuminated the enormous rocket 3.4 miles away, which is the nearest they allow you to be.

Then the dawn, and the rocket is seen in relief against a Homeric sky. And finally the sun is up, and the countdown meters show that there are only twenty-eight minutes and thirty seconds to go. The science reporter of *Time* magazine breezes by, and you ask him whether he is the gentleman to whom technical questions should be addressed, and he answers, Do you happen to have seen the moon? Surely a lunatic inquiry you think, as you look up to point to it, but it isn't there, and suddenly you recognize the mad piquancy of it all: Is it conceivable that the scientist forgot that there is no moon visible for the astronauts to aim at? You shake yourself loose and think again about the poets. . . .

What would Robert Lowell be thinking if he were here? What a terrible tug. On the one hand the poet in him would, must, celebrate the nearest thing to total beauty that science ever created (after all, penicillin isn't beautiful to look at). On the other hand there is the ideological part

of Robert Lowell which might just constrain him to say:
Do you realize that instead of this we might have had
64,000 new housing units in Bedford-Stuyvesant? No, no,
you say, not even Robert Lowell. You feel that surge of
magnanimity, so intoxicating that you find yourself
saying not even William Sloane Coffin. But your thoughts
are obviously getting out of hand. Enough of that.

Two minutes. You are told by a veteran observer to get
out forward of the stand. That way you can crane your
neck back and follow the flight without suddenly running
into the roof of the reviewers' stand. And then you see the
flames, pouring out of the base of the rocket, in total
silence. There is the paralyzing suspense. You are trained
to know that it is sheer physical agony to lift this weight,
and that in order to do it we are consuming fuel at the rate
of 5,000 tons per second. Still, it merely arches up, and
you feel certain that it will get up only just so far, and then
plop over on account of the failure of the fifty-seventh-
thousandth part. But when the roar reaches you, and it
begins slowly to go up, then faster and faster, and you
know it is up and going, and the imperturbable Frank
Borman is heard to have communicated that everything is
just fine, thank you.

All of this is science? Don't believe it. We have reached
into God's territory, and if it were written that there would
be no trespassing, then the poet's premonition would have
been correct.

MOONSTRUCK

London, July 24, 1969

As a freshman at college seeking grist for the
undergraduate newspaper, I approached a famous
astrophysicist, Lyman Spitzer, and asked if it was true that

he intended to fly to the moon. He replied frostily, "I shouldn't know what to do if I got there."

And indeed the scientific community went back to somnambulism, leaving the moon to science fiction, until the great Soviet Union worked their way through to the White House and John F. Kennedy wrote a memorandum to Lyndon Baines Johnson: "Do we have a chance of beating the Soviets by putting a laboratory into space, or by a trip around the moon, or by a rocket to land on the moon, or by a rocket to go to the moon and back with a man? Is there any other space program which promises dramatic results in which we could win?"

Here in London the Sunday *Times* is quite explicit about it all. The editors regret the choice of the American flag over against the choice of, say, the flag of the United Nations to plant down on the moon but concede that "without Old Glory standing there alone the objective set by President Kennedy when he sent America to the moon in 1961 would have been betrayed in the last stride." The gentleman is saying that America suffers from *amour propre,* which is true; which should be true. Lord Ritchie-Calder is a professor of international relations at the University of Edinburgh and a past chairman of the Association of British Science Writers. He is quite forlorn about Apollo 11. "Dare one utter the heresy 'fugitives into space' and confess that it is an evasion and an exasperation of the problems of our planet?" His lordship observes that "If Sputnik had not got into orbit first, if American prestige had not been affronted, if it had not been made the excuse for the 'missile gap' furor, we would not have had the technologically bombastic competition between the superpowers and the yip-hurroo of 'man on the moon by 1970. . . .'" And, he concludes, ". . . the world is crying out for bread and is being offered moondust."

The American press has diligently plied the line that the discovery of a means of reaching the moon is going to have great material benefactions for the earth. My absolute favorite, I mean my all-time favorite, was *Time* magazine's exclaiming that in the years to come it might prove economical to manufacture certain kinds of vacuum tubes on the moon, since there are vacuum-type conditions already there, suggesting that we have all these years overlooked the possibility of manufacturing ice on the North Pole, since it is already cold up there.

We cannot doubt that much will be accomplished of a material meaning by the space program—indeed much already has been, and the great achievement will be the mastery of weather, which will give Lord Ritchie-Calder the bread he wants so badly. But that isn't, let's face it, what the moonshot was all about. It was also an Englishman—Mr. Peregrine Worsthorne of the *Telegraph*—who said it best about the whole lunatic venture: "Western man is desperate for a new horizon. Let there be no hypocrisy here. Space is not a philanthropic exercise. It will not help to feed the hungry or clothe the naked. It is, in a sense, highly irresponsible and selfish, almost an aristocratic gesture of contempt by the privileged nations for the bread-and-butter concerns of the less fortunate people and classes. But it is difficult to believe that this is wrong. The advanced nations and classes cannot limit their aspirations to the goal of material philanthropy for the backward. To be policemen or guardians to the world—perhaps. But the role of nanny is not inspiring, at least as a full-time job. Unless Western man was to atrophy in boredom, he needed some more forceful dynamic than guilt and some inspiration more magnetic than charity."

It was indeed that—an aristocratic venture. All the more so as one emphasizes, rather than deemphasizes, the commercial inutility of it all, so perfectly expressed years ago by a professor who had no idea what he would do on the moon if suddenly he were plopped there. But how unmitigatedly glorious it was, and how universal the elation! At Canaveral, surrounded by the mighty and the calloused, the blast-off swept us all off our feet, and at

London for the touchdown, the crowds at Trafalgar Square were no more excited, I would wager, than the royal family huddled about their telly in Buckingham Palace.

As so often is the case, the world was given a complementary symbol, as when briefly Robert Manry, arriving alone on his 13-foot *Tinkerbelle,* competed with Apollo 3's eight swings around the earth in 1965. Now the Englishman John Fairfax comes into Fort Lauderdale after rowing *Britannia* 180 days across the Atlantic. As the lady said years ago, bringing a quick end to a donnish conversation exploring the motives of space travel, "Don't you see, boys will be boys?" To which one adds, once again, "Yes, and men will be heroes."

IN THE SPIRIT OF APOLLO

August 7, 1969

The President was visibly pleased, on stepping off the airplane, by his trip around the world, most noticeably pleased by his reception in Bucharest, which he identified as the warmest received in any of the sixty countries visited in his career. He quickly modified that statement, like diplomats should, by explaining that he by no means intended to depreciate any of the other countries that had welcomed him, etc.

And then he said that he thought that no doubt the enthusiasm expressed for him was in fact an enthusiasm expressed for America; and that the enthusiasm for America had greatly increased on account of the achievements of the astronauts. It is the spirit of Apollo, he said, which we must call our own. That spirit, he said, shows us the world is one, and shrinking every day. "The spirit of Apollo," he extemporized, "transcends political differences."

Poor Mr. Nixon, poor world; how we grasp at straws. It was said at the funeral of Edward VII that the sorrow on the passing of a monarch, which brought together the crowned heads of state of all of Europe, showed the essential unity of Europe. Ten years later the principal monarchs were deposed, a dozen million people had been slaughtered, and absolutely no point of any historical longevity had been established, save possibly that Communism was loosed upon the world, and where it will end, we do not know, neither knoweth Mr. Nixon, nor even Neil Armstrong.

Alas, human perversity transcends the spirit of Apollo. The aching of Rumanian hearts for the exhilaration of human freedom will not be satisfied by the achievement of Apollo. Mr. Nixon's other tumultuous reception was in Warsaw. Back when he was Vice President. How do the Poles fare, ten years later? How will the Rumanians fare in 1979? What can we do for the Rumanians who cheered Mr. Nixon in 1969? As much as we have done for the Poles who cheered him in 1959?

The spirit of Apollo. What was that spirit? If it was anything at all, beyond merely a mechanical projection, it was two things: (1) the acceptance of an overwhelming challenge; and (2) a venture in great audacity. But the spirit of Apollo, which lifted us onto the moon itself, was a spirit we could indulge in relative safety. At most, we stood to lose a score billion dollars (5 percent of our GNP) and the lives of a half-dozen brave men.

What would we stand to lose if we stood behind the Rumanians who wanted their liberty? What might we have lost (I use the conventional reckonings) if we had come to the aid of the Poles in 1956 or the Hungarians that same year or, twelve years later, the Czechs? Perhaps the whole world, it is whispered hauntingly. Look what we have lost in defending Vietnam, and look how the American appetite falters even there!

If we had given up as easily on space as so many Americans have done on Vietnam, we would not have got our heads out of the sands of Canaveral, where our earliest rockets landed so ignominiously. Certainly we would not have survived the fire that ravaged three astronauts two years ago.

There is a great pathos in the applause that is given by the legions of slaves to the leader of a free nation. How hard it must be to accept their tribute while knowing that you must conspire with their leaders and their leaders' leaders, to keep them enslaved, beyond even the moment when Americans succeed, in the spirit of Apollo, in landing a man on—Mars.

The day before Mr. Nixon was greeted in Rumania, the Russian Kuznetsov defected to Great Britain, leaving his wife and children and disavowing his poetry and his prose, composed under the stress of tyranny. If he hadn't got his passport, he said, he'd have swum out—anything, anything to achieve his destination. *That* was in the spirit of Apollo; that is what we must hope for, and pray for, for all the Rumanians who have expressed (forlornly?) their enthusiasm for Mr. Nixon, and for us.

VII. RELIGION, ESPECIALLY CATHOLICISM

JFK AND CATHOLICISM*

May 14, 1967

JOHN F. KENNEDY AND AMERICAN CATHOLI-
CISM. By Lawrence H. Fuchs. Meredith Press. $6.95.

Professor Fuchs of Brandeis University devotes the first
half of his latest volume (he is the author of *Political
Behavior of American Jews*) to an historical account of
Catholicism in America. It is a fine piece of work,
informed, informative, and readable, notwithstanding the
author's mildly irritating insistence on transfusing
something to do with John F. Kennedy ("We talked
animatedly for more than a half hour in the Senator's
bedroom" is the beginning of a chapter on Colonial and
Early Republic history) into the introductory paragraphs
of every single chapter, even as the novelist nowadays feel
the necessity to program an aphrodisiac at regular intervals

---

* Reprinted by permission of The New York Times Company.

just in case the attention should stray. Although the treatment is mostly sober and detached, there are here and there echoes of the cheerleader egging American Catholicism on toward its glorious destiny as a truly Americanized "religion culture" (Mr. Fuchs' most frequently used term), a religion primarily concerned with "encounter" (Mr. Fuchs' next most frequently used term). In a few dramatic chapters he reminds us how it used to be in the bad old days—when anti-Catholics were bent on persecution (Harvard's Paul Dudley established a lecture series devoted to exposing Romanism's "damnable heresies, fatal errors, abominable superstitions"); and disruptive Catholic leaders were explicitly bent on the antipluralistic goal of converting their fellowmen to the True Faith ("Everybody should know," said the incredible Archbishop Hughes in the 1850's, "that we have for our mission to convert the world—including the inhabitants of the United States—the people of the cities and the people of the country, and officers of the navy, and the marines, commanders of the army, legislatures, the Senate, the Cabinet, the President, and all!").

Matters progressed, Mr. Fuchs records. So much so that by the time Mr. Kennedy began to seek the Presidency, hostilities were pretty well reduced to two fronts, lackadaisically manned at that. Lines were more or less drawn on (a) the use of public money for church schools; and (b) a Catholic's qualifications to serve as President of the United States. The balance of Mr. Fuchs' book is an account of how Mr. Kennedy overcame the obstacle to the final, symbolic integration of Catholicism into the American political system, a victory accomplished, the historian concedes, by capitulating on front (a). Mr. Kennedy, the most prominent Catholic in the land, forswore any rights of students attending religious schools to the use of public funds.

Mr. Fuchs reminds us, in his autopsy of the election, that Mr. Kennedy took only 3-6 percent more Catholic votes than Mr. Truman took in 1948, a negligible increase considering the religiocentric pressures of the Kennedy campaign; indeed Mr. Fuchs discovers that a far higher percentage of Negroes and Jews voted for Mr. Kennedy than of Catholics. That datum suggests that many Catholics were reluctant to exchange their political predispositions to Republicanism and/or their claims to participation in public money for private schools in return for the honorific of a Catholic President. Recent events in Wisconsin, where an overwhelming majority of a secular-minded citizenry voted in early April to reverse themselves and permit public transportation for students of church schools, suggest that Wisconsin Protestants are more open-minded on the subject than Kennedy Catholics. At any rate, the figures seem to show that in 1960 Mr. Kennedy was not able to offset the presumptively anti-Catholic vote by coming in with the presumptively pro-Catholic vote.

Mr. Fuchs reveals, moreover, that by September of 1960, Mr. Kennedy's computers tumbled to the conclusion that he had lost as many votes as he ever stood to lose on account of that much of his Catholicism that was ineffaceable—but also that the same computers serendipitously discovered that there were votes to be had from publicly stressing and restressing his independence of the Catholic Church so as to appeal to the fair-minded who desired to vote against prejudice. Thus it was that Mr. Kennedy decided to go to Houston, Texas, there to drive the point home that as far as the American people should be concerned, he was a Catholic only by accident of birth; there to make it finally plain that, as Mr. Fuchs who knew and loved the late President puts it, "religion was something one accepted as decided by birth, like blue eyes or the fact that one's right leg was shorter than one's left. It should not be necessary to defend one's blue eyes. . . ." At Houston Mr. Kennedy faced a Protestant ministry, mostly Baptist, which he hugely impressed by the dissociative whacks with which he severed himself from Rome. It was not widely noticed, though it is a charming confirmation of John Kennedy's genuine innocence of the

Roman coils, that in answer to one minister who asked him how he could reconcile his protestations of liberalism with the drastically antiliberal encyclical *Syllabus of Errors,* Mr. Kennedy (who was to earn a record as the best-briefed candidate in the history of Presidential contention) gave an answer that would have amused novitiate Catholics and anti-Catholics alike. The *Syllabus,* Mr. Kennedy replied according to Professor Fuchs' paraphrase, was concededly still "a part of church doctrine" (it isn't), but on the other hand, the encyclical was from "several centuries in the past" (it was promulgated in 1864). Mr. Kennedy went on to restress on Constitutional grounds his "absolute" opposition to any form of public aid to church schools. He had checked out his speech, Mr. Fuchs informs us, with the fabled Jesuit scholar (of theology and of the American political system) Father John Courtney Murray. The reader's inference is that Fr. Murray had wholly approved the speech, which is altogether mystifying considering that Fr. Murray's book *We Hold These Truths* was at that very moment on its way to the best-seller lists. In that book the pluralistic-minded Fr. Murray reached the conclusion that the "moral canon of distributive justice . . . would require that a proportionately just measure of public support should be available to such schools as serve the public cause of popular education, whether these schools be specifically religious in their affiliation and orientation, or not."

Indeed Mr. Fuchs acknowledges, not out of any discernible sympathy for their position but because of his own high scruples as a historian, that in the opinion of some highly responsible non-Catholics and non-anti-Catholics, Mr. Kennedy's declarations of independence from his own religion were perhaps . . . fulsome. (Prominent Catholics were, mostly, silent as a tomb during that period, and mostly remain so even now—as some might put it who reason that Mr. Kennedy's acts of ingratiation were at the expense of principle—well after the cock has crowed.) Dr. Robert McAfee Brown, the liberal Protestant theologian, remarked in *Christianity in Crisis* during the campaign that Mr. Kennedy had demonstrated not merely that he was a rather irregular Catholic, but that "he is a rather irregular Christian." And the editor of the *Christian Century,* the liberal and adamantly Protestant Mr. Martin Marty, observed that Mr. Kennedy had revealed himself as "spiritually rootless and politically almost disturbingly secular."

After the election was all over, Mr. Murray Kempton, who is *not* quoted by Professor Fuchs, posed the big question, which Mr. Fuchs' book does not illuminate: "We have again been cheated of the prospect of a Catholic President in a nation where religion is so sacred a subject as to be outside the realm of engaged discussion." If Catholicism (or Unitarianism or Judaism) is nothing more than the color of one's eyes or the irregular length of one's right leg, then what was it that was proved by the election of Mr. Kennedy other than that most ethnic and religious groups, particularly Negroes and Jews, became convinced that blue-eyed and stump-legged men may go on to the Presidency? What would have happened—the question continues to haunt us—if Mr. Kennedy had said at Houston that although he would not permit his Catholicism to stand in the way of his constitutional duties, neither would he for a moment suggest that his own conscience and attitudes were uninfluenced by Catholicism? Or that his position on public aid to parochial school children would not be influenced by any desire to appease voters if he became convinced that their position was constitutionally irrational.

Mr. Kennedy was never a lot of things, and especially never a venturesome campaigner. No doubt he could have devised ways more discreet of handling provocative questions than, for instance, Hilaire Belloc did when he was asked jeeringly, while running for a seat in the House of Parliament, whether it was true that he was "a Papist." "Madam," *all of Belloc* replied, reaching into his pocket and taking out a rosary, "Do you see these beads? I say them every morning when I rise, and every evening when I go to bed; and if *you* object to that, madam, I pray to *God* that he will spare me the *ignominy* of representing *you* in Parliament." That kind of thing would not have gone over very well in Houston, and Mr. Fuchs would probably not have had a book to write if Mr. Kennedy had been that kind of candidate. Indeed the book would yet be unwritten chronicling the ascendancy of a Catholic—that kind of Catholic—to the White House. As it stands, Mr. Fuchs has written an absorbing book celebrating, however, what the history of religion and politics in America may, upon meditation, write off as a pseudoevent.

THE MARCH OF AMERICAN CATHOLICISM

July 13, 1968

The Archbishop of Canterbury, to judge from the recent record, is more worried by orthodoxy abroad than heresy at home. He has just criticized Pope Paul for reasserting the essential dogmas of Roman Catholicism, one of them being that the Roman Catholic Church is the designated vehicle of the word of Christ. It is difficult to see why the reassertion of that claim should bother the archbishop. It is one thing to dispute the claim; it is another to fret about its being made. Rather as though an American in London were to pop up from his seat at Albert Hall and say, "But wait a minute, Britannia does *not* rule the waves!"

I don't mean to imply that the assertion of the Catholic Church is merely a matter of tradition, but that it is at least a matter of tradition, and that therefore it is sort of, er, dumb for His Excellency the Archbishop to get lathered up over its restatement. And it wasn't only

Anglican dignitaries who were disappointed by the Pope's dogmatical assertiveness, but also a lot of Catholics, for instance the so-called progressives in Holland, one of whose spokesmen pronounced that the Pope's words were like stones in his stomach which, come to think of it, may be what Purgatory feels like.

The strategy of the Pope, meanwhile, is presumably to try to do something about the dissolution, yes, dissolution, of the Catholic Church—to prevent happening to it what happened to the Archbishop of Canterbury's church in England like maybe a hundred years ago. Auberon Waugh perhaps oversays it: ". . . in England we have a curious institution called the Church of England. . . . Its strength has always lain in the fact that on any moral or political issue it can produce such a wide divergence of opinion that nobody—from the Pope to Mao Tse-tung—can say with any confidence that he is not an Anglican. Its weaknesses are that nobody pays much attention to it, and very few people attend its functions." Perhaps he oversays it; but not by much.

Presumably the Pope is alarmed at some of the results of modernization. There are many examples, some of them reaching right into the tabernacle of Catholic Christianity to mess around with what they used to call the *depositum fidei* before Latin was abolished as antisocial, or whatever. There are data less astounding, but hardly insignificant. I sat next to a most beautiful and lively young Catholic girl the other day at a public function who spoke to me of Catholicism at Vassar, which she attends. The Catholic chaplain there is modern-minded and in a brief space of time has so succeeded in his evangelization that nowadays only about 13 percent of the Catholic girls in Vassar bother to attend Sunday mass, the failure to do which, in the Catholic Church, is analogous to defying the Constitution in the civil world, with, one assumes, even graver consequences.

A non-Catholic lady in California writes me that she recently attended a mass at a Catholic high school. "It was held in the auditorium. A poster directly behind the altar was of an enormous catsup bottle and the message, 'If you're a plump tomato, Hunts has an opening for you.' On either side of the altar were 'box-art' figures, about five feet high, of Martin Luther King, Bob Dylan, John Lennon, the Maharishi what's his name, Gandhi, Thurgood Marshall. Above the altar was suspended a large mobile made of pieces of broken glass and tin cans and a sign asking, 'What's your story, people?'"

Recently I was visited by a faculty member and a dozen seniors from another Catholic high school, St. Mary's in Mount Clemens, Michigan. I found them all charming, poised, and intelligent, but a little bit out of breath, as though they had just finished scaling a very high mountain; and indeed I learned that the reverend sister, the superintendent of their school, had decreed that if they consummated their plan to visit with me, they would be deprived of their right to participate in their forthcoming commencement exercises and stripped of their academic honors. Now the Church quite rightly cautions its sheep to avoid occasions of sin, but it is going to take me a while to get used to the notion, post-Vatican II, that I am, by the modernists, to be treated like a brothel.

There are, of course, Catholics who are on the side of the Pope. But they speak in whispers and walk about furtively, lest the new religion of love and understanding espy them and eat them up.

PAPAL GAUCHERIE

April 8, 1967

Pope Paul VI has released an unfortunate encyclical (*Populorum Progressio*), particularly unfortunate because its naïveté in economic and other secular matters drowns out passages of eloquence which, had they gone unencumbered by confused and confusing ideological detritus, might have served to remind the responsible community of the inspiring ardor of the Pope's passion for human reconciliation and the exercise of charity on a universal scale.

One wishes one might dwell on these passages. But it is not they, unfortunately, which are newsworthy. Around the world the press has elected to feature passages in which the Pope seems to be calling attention to the limitations of capitalism and the need for the further redistribution of wealth between the "rich nations and the poor nations," and another acknowledging that the control of the birth rate (by "moral means") is desirable.

The most specific of the encyclical's passages seem to be directed at the Latin American latifundia, the landed estates sometimes owned by an absentee millionaire and operated primarily by peasant sharecroppers. ". . . it is unacceptable," he writes, "that citizens with abundant incomes from the resources and activity of their country should transfer a considerable part of this income abroad purely for their own advantage, without care for the manifest wrong they inflict on their country by doing this."

The difficulty with this generality is that if it is kneaded for meaning, it can be made to say a good many things that obviously were not intended, such as that the pharaoh was quite right in resenting the exodus of Moses and all the Jews from Egypt. There are a lot of selfish Latin American millionaires with bank accounts in Switzerland. On the other hand, there are a lot of Latin American ex-millionaires who stuck around and were impoverished—and maybe shot—by demagogues who justified themselves by using the kind of language the Pope uses.

Any Brazilian or Argentinian—or Indonesian—who took his money to Switzerland before Goulart or Perón or Sukarno took over the management of those countries contributed more to social well-being by investing his capital via Switzerland in productive enterprises than by leaving it around to be squandered by the three left wingers who in the name of human progress reduced the economic structure of their nations to ashes and set back by a generation any hope for improvement in the material condition of the people.

It is nothing more than a repetition of elementary Biblical injunctions to urge the rich to share what they have with the poor. It is another thing to urge that this process be executed primarily through the taxing or expropriating power of the state. In fact, the richest nation in the world, the United States, though giving in direct foreign aid only one-half of 1 percent of her gross national product, is even now having serious difficulty in balancing her gold accounts, a final failure to do which would result in the devaluation of the dollar and the impoverishment of a score of poor and semipoor nations which hold billions of dollars as their principal reserves.

History has repeatedly shown that the most durable benefactions are not those that are mulcted from the people by a government to be sent disorientedly abroad, but those that flow abroad in enlightened search of opportunities, providing capital, jobs, and productive activity. There have been two forms of aid to Latin America by the United States during the past thirty years, direct financial grants of the kind the Pope presumably favors, and investment by Americans and American companies in Latin America. The results of the former are, to say the least, exiguous. The results of the latter have been to furnish jobs for 20 percent of the Latin American labor force.

And so it goes. He enjoins upon "government officials"—"above all"—"to make [your peoples] accept the necessary taxes on their luxuries and their wasteful expenditure in order to bring about development and to save the peace." The terrible congestion of misinformation in that sentence! Tax *all* the luxuries of the rich and you don't have enough money to buy all the Vatican treasures—it is the middle classes and the lower middle classes who are shouldering the great economic load today, for the simple reason that the rich, if you took away everything they had, could not relieve the world's poor for a single week. The peace is not most usually disturbed by the poor, but by the power-hungry, rich or poor: the great peace breakers of this century—Russia, Japan, and Germany—were not poor nations by common standards. It all reminds one of St. Thomas Aquinas' warning that, outside the field of morals and doctrine, the Church is quite capable of erring, *"propter falsos testes"*—on account of bad information.

Those who have worked hardest and most productively for the diminution of human misery and know that the preconditions are (1) political stability, and (2) economic freedom will be disappointed not at the goals, exquisitely described by the Pope, but by the suggested means, illusory and self-defeating, which, if followed, would have the contrary effect to that desired by this intense and holy man.

ANOTHER LOOK AT THE POPE

January 4, 1968

Pope Paul VI continues to disappoint a number of people, most recently some Protestant churchmen who showed great chill when asked to react to President Johnson's visit to Rome en route back from Australia. There is no doubting that there was a bit of the old denominationalist jealousy here. The President vaulted from Vietnam to Rome, granting a few minutes to the President of Pakistan only—one got the impression—because he couldn't bear to sit around doing nothing while his jet was being refueled. And then on to Rome, to spend an hour with the Pope, whose usefulness as a mediator in the Vietnam controversy the two gentlemen are said to have discussed.

It was then, for some people, bad enough that Paul should have been unofficially recognized as the leading religious spokesman for the West. Resentment also came on account of the nature of the Pope's recent Christmas message, wherein he took the ground from under the same theologians and church activists who have come very close, in recent years and months, to unlicensing war under any circumstances. The Pope bore down very hard on pacifism and, in the course of doing so, acknowledged what many people know, but dare not say; namely, that the motives of some, repeat some, of the young opponents of the Vietnam War are, to say the least, ignoble. What is more, in the very same passage, the Pope reintroduced into the analysis of specific wars certain conventional terms which the relativists have been getting away from. The Pope spoke about good and evil, justice and injustice, freedom and the lack of it; and did so in such a way as to endorse the official view of what we are doing in Vietnam. This was a considerable moral setback for those who refuse to make distinctions. His words exactly:

"Accordingly, in conclusion, it is to be hoped that the escalation of the ideal of peace may not favor the cowardice of those who fear it may be their duty to give their life for the service of their own country and of their own brothers, when these are engaged in the defense of justice and liberty, and who seek only a flight from their responsibility, from the risks that are necessarily involved in the accomplishment of great duties and generous exploits.

"Peace is not pacifism; it does not mask a base and slothful concept of life, but it proclaims the highest and most universal values of life: truth, justice, freedom, love."

Now if those words had been uttered by a fire-eating Pope who obviously lusted for world conflict in pursuit of religious colonization, the words would have meant less than they do from a Pope who is the most ardent peace seeker in recent papal history; who, indeed, came to the United Nations and demanded: No More War.

The rumors now are that the Pope is an ambiguist, that he says one thing one day, another another; and that he is just perhaps a little bit naïve about world affairs. Concretely, some of his critics mention his disqualifications to serve as a negotiator in Vietnam in the light of the fact that the Catholic population of South Vietnam is a strong, vested cultural-political interest. Others have mentioned the curious point, namely, that in his encyclical last spring, the Pope referred to modern capitalism in terms appropriate only to nineteenth-century capitalism and so showed himself out of touch. A curious point not because it isn't so (it is), but because it has come from people who do not customarily take offense at any misrepresentation of capitalism. In this case, their irritation at the Pope appears to have transcended their hostility to capitalism.

Notwithstanding the points the Pope will have lost in some quarters, he has encouraged others, others who have wondered in the past whether the Pope was beginning to lose sight of the essential political drama of the day. It would appear that he has not. And it would appear that, in his continuing commitment to the cause of justice over the cause of pacifism, he is showing the tenacious concern for the end of genocidal activity in the Far East which Pope Pius XII was accused of not having shown when it was the Jews who were being victimized by Nazi Germany.

THE AGONY OF PAUL VI

New York, April 10, 1969

Pope Paul has released now two *cris de coeur*, most appropriately during Holy Week, lamenting the disintegration of Catholic unity. He warned most specifically of schism in the Church, and besought the faithful to unite behind the doctrines of the Church and the authority of the Church's hierarchy. He spoke of "a practically schismatic ferment [which] divides [the Catholic community], breaking it into groups . . ." "Above all" he laments those who are "jealous of arbitrary and basically egotistical autonomy, masquerading as Christian pluralism or liberty of conscience." And he asked whether the Church is still "truly animated by that sincere spirit of union and charity" such as to permit its flock to observe without hypocrisy "our most holy daily mass."

The crisis of the Catholic Church is much written about. *Look* magazine celebrates it every couple of issues, and its editors have even volunteered to rewrite the Apostles' Creed, reaching a new high in reader service. There is a strange sense of almost universal concern. Back in the old monolithic days of Pius XII, the Church was regularly assaulted for its autocratic ways, and the most popular notion in the Bible Belt was that Catholics weren't really Americans. Not only the Bible Belt. Peter Viereck observed twenty years ago that anti-Catholicism was the anti-Semitism of the intellectuals.

But now that the Church has gone modern, not only have dissatisfactions within the Church magnified. Somehow even much of the non-Catholic world seems somehow disturbed. Perhaps because Rome has always been something of a shelter for dogmatic Christianity. To observe Rome, year after year, century after century, defending the essential tenets of Christianity somehow made it easier for schismatics to improvise their own doctrines and beliefs. In such a way is the Constitution useful even to the most experimental Supreme Courts.

The Pope calls for charity, but of course charity and discipline are under certain circumstances incompatible. The exercise of charity by the Pope is presumably what caused him to refer to "a practically schismatic ferment." It is "practically schismatic" in the same sense that Richard Nixon is practically President. A recent publication called *Spectrum of Catholic Attitudes* lists views on Church issues by a half-dozen Catholics, one or two of whom take positons which would make Unitarians uneasy.

Where does charity lie? In permitting such "Catholics" to continue so to label themselves; or in excommunicating them? The Pope is unquestionably reluctant to excommunicate. That is the ultimate sanction of the Church, not to be used loosely. On the other hand, the sanction itself dissipates if the Church deteriorates into amorphous impotence.

Professor Jeffrey Hart of Dartmouth, a recent convert to Catholicism, wrote recently that he wondered why the left wing (so-called) of the American Catholic Church does not do the obvious thing: namely, embrace some form of Protestantism. Because the objections of the left wing relate in almost every case to distinctively Catholic features of Christianity: the authority of the Pope, indeed his infallibility when speaking on faith or morals; the singular position of Mary within the Church; priestly celibacy; the position on birth control and abortion; and so on. How easy to dispose of these difficulties by the simple expedient of turning to any number of Protestant sects.

It may be thought to be a minor matter alongside questions so grave, but the Pope's reference to "our most holy daily mass" and attendance thereat takes no recognition at all of the great scandal of Catholicism at least in the United States: which is that going to mass has become an aesthetic ordeal.

On Palm Sunday, reciting the translation of St. Matthew approved by the Catholic Bishops, the priests read out from the pulpit: "Now Peter was sitting in the courtyard when one of the servant girls came over to him and said, 'You too were with Jesus the Galilean,' but he denied it in front of everybody. 'I don't know what you are talking about. . . .' Again he denied it with an oath: 'I don't know the fellow.' A little later the bystanders came over to Peter and said, 'Obviously you are also one of them, why, even your accent gives you away. . . .' 'I don't even know the fellow.' Just then the cock crowed . . ."

(*"Now Peter sat without in the palace; and a damsel came unto him, saying: Thou also wast with Jesus of Galilee. But he denied them all saying: I know not what thou sayest . . . Surely thou art also one of them; for thy speech betrayeth thee. Then he began to curse and to swear saying: I know not the man. And immediately the cock crew."*)

There may be a case for turning over the Bible to Bob Dylan for translation. But there is none at all for turning it over to the translating machine exhibited at the World's Fair, which alone could come up with the "modern" version. The common denominator between the two problems is loss of standards: doctrinal, aesthetic. The Catholic Church has been historically the tablet keeper. The surrendering of its convictions at so many levels is a cause of the sorrow of Paul VI and of so many of his flock.

WORLD COUNCIL SNAFU

July 20, 1968

The World Council of Churches has made the headlines by endorsing the principle of selective objection to "particular" wars. The effect of that resolution is to put the sanction of organized Protestant Christianity behind the movement to permit individuals to select the wars they desire to participate in. The practical effect, for instance in this country, is to assist the campaign of which the Reverend William Sloane Coffin is the most conspicuous spokesman: to encourage the defiance of the laws of the United States which at this moment permit the government to conscript an army in order to implement its foreign policy.

The argument for civil disobedience is, in other words, greatly assisted. The dissenter will now take comfort in being able to say that, to be sure, he is breaking the law as narrowly understood, but the law is an unjust law, *vide* the World Council of Churches. Theoretically it is of no matter that there should be differences between positive and religious law. In fact, laws that defy strongly asserted religious positions are greatly weakened, particularly in an age of moral opportunism.

The moral problem posed by the World Council is, in the long run, even more disturbing than the political problem. The council's declaration has the effect of saying that wars are justified if they are wars of personal passion. That statement is profoundly anti-Christian and indeed recidivist, suggesting the spirit of the more fanatical Crusaders. The Christian doctrine as understood during the Enlightenment is that all wars should be painful and, in human terms, objectionable (love thine enemy).

Wars are justified only under clinical circumstances, *e.g.* and primarily, in order to defend sacred things of great value, to use the phrase of Pius XII; to defend the homeland.

But who is to decide when those things of great value are threatened? The Western practice is that such decisions are made by elected governments. Under the reasoning of the council, what matters is the individual attitude toward a particular war. The individual becomes not merely the absolute moral arbiter on whether he is (as a pacifist) prepared to commit violence under any circumstance; but whether he is prepared to commit violence under this particular circumstance. In other words, if he disagrees with the political reasoning of the duly constituted authorities, he is, by the council's reasoning, free to cut himself out.

An extension of this view of the individual's sovereignty is pretty frightening. The state is, in the general moral understanding, permitted under given circumstances (*e.g.*, Eichmann) to take a man's life, say for the crime of genocide. But the individual is never permitted to do so. Why not?—if the individual is supreme? If a Christian is going to deny the role of the impartial mechanism of the state in making binding decisions involving the use of violence—whether war, or electrocution, or the use of tear gas—then what is to prevent the individual from asserting his own conscience at such moments when that conscience declares that he believes violence to be necessary?

Are we not being driven, by the well-meaning lords spiritual of the World Council, back whence we came so painfully: back to the age when wars were holy wars (burn the heretics!) and individual acts of violence were the accepted protocols of ultimate moral self-assertion?

The World Council is continuing in the general march of organized Christianity toward a confused sort of secular idealism. The other two recommendations call for admitting Red China to the United Nations, concerning which problem the council is as equipped to speak as

Groucho Marx is to remove an infected appendix; and a call for the economic boycotting of racist nations, which is a splendid way to increase world misery and, considering that the majority of the nations of the world are racist in one sense or another, to drive the nations of the world toward the autarky which the world-minded council theoretically opposes.

It is a pity, the mess the gentlemen are promoting.

GURU-BOUND

London, February 29, 1968

The doings of the Beatles are minutely recorded here in England and, as a matter of fact, elsewhere, inasmuch as it is true what one of the Beatle gentlemen said a year or so ago, that they are more popular than Jesus Christ. It is a matter of considerable public interest that all four of the Beatles have gone off to a place called Rishikesh, in India, to commune with one Maharishi Mahesh Yogi.

The gentleman comes from India, and the reigning chic stipulates that Mysterious India is where one goes to Have a Spiritual Experience. Accordingly, the Beatles are there, as also Mia Farrow, who, having left Frank Sinatra, is understandably in need of spiritual therapy; and assorted other types including, the press reports, a space physicist who works for General Motors. It isn't altogether clear what is the drill at Rishikesh, except that—and this visibly disturbed a couple of business managers of the Beatles—a postulant at the shrine of Mr. Yogi is expected to contribute a week's salary as an initiation fee. A week's salary may not be very much for thee and me, but it is a whole lot of sterling for a Beatle, and one gathers from the press that the business managers thought this a bit much and rather wish that the Beatles could find their spiritual experience a little less dearly.

The wisdom of Maharishi Mahesh Yogi is not rendered in easily communicable tender. It is recorded by one disciple that he aroused himself from a trance sufficiently to divulge the sunburst, "Ours is an age of science, not faith," a seizure of spiritual exertion which apparently left him speechless with exhaustion; I mean, wouldn't you be exhausted if you came up with that? It is reported that the Beatles were especially transfigured when the Maharishi divulged, solemnly, that "speech is just the progression of thought." One can assume that the apogee of their experience was reached upon learning, from the guru's own mouth, that "anything that comes from direct experience can be called science." It is a wonder that the entire population of the world has not gravitated toward the cynosure capable of such incandescent insights.

I am not broke, but I think that if I were, I would repair to India, haul up a guru's flag, and—I guarantee it—I would be the most successful guru of modern times. I would take the Beatles' weekly salary, and Mia Farrow's, and the lot of them, and I would come up with things like: "Put on, therefore, as the elect of God, holy and beloved, bowels of mercies, kindness, humbleness of mind, meekness, long-suffering; forbearing one another, and forgiving one another, if any man have a quarrel against any; even as — forgave you, so also do ye. And above all these things put on charity, which is the bond of perfectness. And let the peace of God rule in your hearts, to the which also ye are called in one body; and be thankful."

To the especially worldly, I would say: "Walk in wisdom toward them that are without, redeeming the time. Let your speech be always with grace, seasoned with salt, that ye may know how ye ought to answer every man." Can it be imagined that I would be less successful, quoting these lines, from a single letter of St. Paul, than Maharishi Mahesh Fakir has been? The truly extraordinary feature of our time isn't the faithlessness of the Western people; it is their utter, total ignorance of the Christian religion. They travel to Rishikesh to listen to pallid seventh-hand imitations of thoughts and words they never knew existed. They will go anywhere to experience spirituality—except next door. An Englishman need go no farther than to hear Evensong at King's College at Cambridge, or to hear high mass at Chartres Cathedral; or to read St. Paul, or John, or the psalmists. Read a volume by Chesterton—*The Everlasting Man, Orthodoxy, The Dumb Ox*—and the spiritual juices begin to run, but no, Christianity, is, well, well, what? Well, unknown.

The Beatles know more about carburetors than they know about Christianity, which is why they, like so many others, make such asses of themselves in pursuit of Mr. Gaga Yogi. Their impulse is correct, and they reaffirm, as man always has and always will, the truism that man is a religious animal. If only they knew what is waiting there, available to them, right there in Jollie Olde Englande, no costlier than 2/6d at the local bookstore. It is too easy nowadays to found new religions, though the vogue is constant. Voltaire was once abashed at the inordinate iconoclasm of one of his young disciples who asked the master how might he go about founding a new religion. "Well," Voltaire said, "begin by getting yourself killed. Then rise again on the third day."

VIII. CIVIL DISORDER

HAVE WE BECOME UNGOVERNABLE?

July 27, 1968

The (London) Sunday *Times* features an extensive article entitled, "How the Democrats Are Tearing Themselves Apart," which leads off with a startling quotation, or rather misquotation, from Mr. Gerry Bush of the staff of Mr. Hubert Humphrey. "We can win the nomination in Chicago okay," Bush is quoted as saying in behalf of Humphrey. "We can win the election in November. But then—can we govern the country?"

Mr. Bush is identified in the article as "an able young Democrat who has emerged as one of the most effective members of Presidential candidate Hubert Humphrey's campaign team. His concern was serious, and he is not alone."

Actually, says Mr. Bush, his stated worries were by no means confined to the difficulties that a Humphrey administration would have in governing the country. He meant that the serious question has arisen: Can *anyone* govern the country? I asked him whether he agreed with

303

the thesis that what one might call the McCarthy wing of American politics has acquired a singular leverage, inasmuch as they are the people who threaten ungovernability, not the others. If Hubert Humphrey is elected President, the followers of Richard Nixon and Ronald Reagan are not going to start burning down their Union League clubs or their Masonic lodges. But some of the followers of Eugene McCarthy are, as some of them have put it, disposed to burn, baby, burn. Does this mean that the unruly left has maneuvered into a position whence blackmail is effectively exerted? Vote our man in—or else we shall disrupt the republic?

Mr. Bush shrinks from what he calls a partisan rendering of his misgivings, and indeed he remarked dutifully that the threat of disruption from the right is potentially just as great as from the left. We couldn't, in the few minutes' conversation over the telephone, come up with any right-wing analogue of the doctors and preachers who are calling for civil disobedience, or of the students who prevent other students from exercising their civil rights and who occupy whole campuses (Mr. Bush came into government via UCal in Berkeley), or of the left winger who every now and then shoots a President or a Presidential aspirant.

One has to go back to the Ku Klux Klan to come up with Violence on the Right; but the Klan and its following is, blessedly, diminishing, and even George Wallace disdains any association with it. An extreme right wing which was unsuccessful in getting a single Congressman to call for the impeachment of Earl Warren is not likely to make America ungovernable.

No, Mr. Bush—and Mr. Humphrey presumably—are on to something very, very important and very alarming and are understandably reluctant to acknowledge that the trouble tends to come from people whose votes they will shortly be soliciting: the American left. It is true that the American right is a possible source of disorder only in the sense that the American right, at the margin, would no doubt resort to force in order to reestablish order. In that sense, it can be said that the American right is as much of a threat to America as the generals were to Argentina and Brazil who finally got around to kicking out Perón and Goulart.

Would Senator McCarthy himself contribute to the dissolution of government? Would he run on a separate ticket? "At the moment," says the *Times*, "he says no—and must, of course, till convention time. But he says he might support it. If the year has established anything about that complex personality, it is that McCarthy is most dangerous when he thinks he has been double-crossed, as when Robert Kennedy moved in after New Hampshire, or his New York supporters were railroaded a few days ago. Each time, his staff detected a renewed appetite for battle; and a raw deal in Chicago or on the way to Chicago might well shatter his loyalty to the Democratic Party." Leaving only his loyalty to the republic.

DO THEY REALLY BREAK THE LAW?

December 5, 1967

The morning's news brings yet another defi from the lawbreakers, couched this time in language most provocative. The idea is to "close down" an induction center in Manhattan by physically interfering with anyone who seeks to enter the building. It all began, as ever, with a press conference, Dr. Benjamin Spock, the baby doctor, and Mr. Dwight Macdonald, the critic, presiding.

These gentlemen, who even now will swoon with dismay at the mere recollection of Senator McCarthy's "methods," are in fact not particularly interested in testing the validity of certain Congressional statutes authorizing the draft and prohibiting seditious resistance to the draft. They are interested in any method of interfering with the prosecution of a particular war, the war in Vietnam. Nevertheless, they find it rhetorically convenient to frame their case against these laws in generic language. It makes you sound more philosophical if you say, "I am against the killing of women and children," than if you say, "I am against the killing of those women and children who are accidentally killed as the result of our defense effort in Southeast Asia."

Accordingly, Dr. Spock talks as though the law against counseling young men to refuse to register were unconstitutional (that law was upheld unanimously in 1917 by the Supreme Court and, indirectly, in 1956). "The government," said Dr. Spock, "is not likely to prosecute us. Its bankruptcy in the moral sense is proved by its refusal to move against those of us who have placed ourselves between the young people and the draft."

A reporter fished around for the meaning of that statement and then asked the gentlemen whether they didn't in fact suspect that the Justice Department was avoiding prosecution because it feared to take steps that might be interpreted as suppressing dissent? "No," Mr. Macdonald answered unequivocally. "What we're doing is not just dissent; it's a deliberate violation of the law."

That would appear to remove such doubts as might have existed concerning defendants' knowledge as a mitigating factor. Mr. Macdonald is being as plain as any man can be. He appears to desire to break the law. And Dr. Spock, egging on the Justice Department, dares it to defend such laws as, in their sovereign wisdom, he and Dwight Macdonald choose to break.

So I called the U.S. Attorney Mr. Robert Morgenthau and asked him, Has Washington instructed him not to prosecute?

No, he replied.

Well, then, would you feel free to prosecute on your

own initiative, or would you refer such a matter as this to Washington?

In such a case as this, with national implications, he would probably consult Washington.

Well, do you intend to prosecute, or to ask Washington whether to prosecute?

The U.S. Attorney's Office does not, as a matter of policy, hand out advisory judgments.

I reached a gentleman with a full working knowledge of how these things go, and he advises me that the heroic lawbreakers are for the most part a foxy lot, who are engaged in psychological rather than legal gambits. They call their press conferences and make their speeches. But they keep a subtle ace up their sleeve. The draft card turns out not really to be a draft card, but a facsimile. Take them to the grand jury and all of a sudden, in the privacy of the chamber, they will plead the Fifth Amendment, and the government will not have a prosecutor's case. Most of the lawbreaking you read about in this field, my informant advised me, is mock lawbreaking.

One wonders whether Dr. Spock and Mr. Macdonald are, on top of everything else, breaking the rules of lawbreaking. Surely it would be worthwhile finding out just who is funking what, under laboratory conditions. I therefore cordially invite Mr. Dwight Macdonald to violate the law, at 3 P.M. on Thursday, the fourth of January, at my offices at 150 East Thirty-Fifth St., New York 10016. He is invited there and then, in the presence of witnesses and a television camera, to counsel young men to refuse to register and serve in the armed forces. Young men will be provided. A representative of the Justice Department will be invited upon receipt of a written acceptance to this invitation. We shall see who is lacking the moral courage Dr. Spock refers to.

A REPLY FROM THE LAWBREAKER *MANQUE*

December 16, 1967

I have a reply from the aspirant lawbreaker, Mr. Dwight Macdonald, the literary critic.

"Mr. Buckley challenges me to put up or shut up about civil disobedience and lawbreaking. He proposes a High Noon shootout in the offices of his magazine on January 4 at exactly 3 P.M. (tick, tock, tick, tock), and he offers to provide young men for me to attempt to subvert into refusing conscription for the Vietnam War, in the presence of TV cameras, a representative of the Department of Justice, and of course, himself. I must regretfully decline the gambit, for several reasons. How does he get into the act, in the first place? Who appointed *him* sheriff? Assuming the government needs more evidence of my lawbreaking than I've given in writing and verbally (twice with TV cameras in action), why should I provide it in the offices of the *National Review?* . . . Martyrdom, if it comes to that, can be staged under more dignified conditions than a publicity stunt. . . .

"But I deny his assumption that the Department of Justice needs any more evidence than Dr. Spock and myself have copiously, tediously provided, including what Mr. Buckley quotes from our remarks at the press conference that set him off. . . .

"As for 'taking the Fifth Amendment' (which Mr. Buckley implies I might do on being confronted by a grand jury), we would be as illogical as Mr. Buckley if we did so since it would negate the two purposes we have in mind by taking a stand of civil disobedience: to make it awkward for the authorities to continue to prosecute young draft refusers without also prosecuting their elders who are breaking the same law, and to bring about a trial, which the press would not ignore, in which the immorality, and the illegality, of the Vietnam War could be thoroughly explored by the defense. I agree with Dr. Spock that the authorities have no ardent wish for such a trial. . . . If they decide to risk it, there will be no need of High Noon melodramatics presided over by Sheriff Bill."

If you detwaddle that statement, what Mr. Macdonald is saying is: I continue to hope that there is just enough of a blur in my lawbreaking to keep the authorities at bay, and I hope to be able to distract the attention of the public by wheezing along about publicity stunts.

My return observations: (1) Mr. Macdonald is in constant search of publicity for his "lawbreaking." It was he, not I, who called a press conference announcing, with his customary bravura, how his conscience has Transcended the Law. (2) The reason I suggested the offices of *National Review* is that those are the only offices of which I dispose. I should be glad to arrange for Mr. Macdonald's breaking of the law under laboratory conditions at the grand ballroom of the Waldorf-Astoria, which would be neutral territory, or even at the offices of *Mad* magazine, in Macdonald territory. (3) It is one thing (the Justice Department contends) to blurt out one's intention to defy the law ("I shall counsel students to evade the draft"), another actually to defy the law ("You, Jones, tear up your draft card, evade the draft").

I leave it, then, (4) that Mr. Macdonald is not willing, under intense public scrutiny, to break the law particularly, preferring to tweak the law by rodomontade; but also (5) that the Justice Department—not, presumably, because it is afraid of testing a law the constitutionality of which has been twice affirmed by the Supreme Court, but because it believes it has more to worry about than tracking Dwight Macdonald around with a photographer in case he should ever actually engage in the act—chooses to ignore Dwight Macdonald. Which is universally tempting.

THE BRUMMAGEM HEROISM OF
DRS. COFFIN AND SPOCK

January 11, 1968

At last, the Justice Department has moved. There were plenty of targets, but you can't hit them all at one time, any more than you can stop everybody who is speeding. In his wisdom, the Attorney General selected two especially provocative targets and three lesser types. The two heavies were Benjamin Spock, the baby doctor, and our old friend William Sloane Coffin, the Yale chaplain. Dr. Spock immediately called a press conference at which he was from all accounts, elatedly impenitent, obviously looking forward to the auto-da-fé, which is scheduled to take place in Boston, probably in the next two or three months.

Now please note something that is already beginning to happen in connection with United States *v.* Spock and Coffin, namely, an effort to elide their deeds from moral on over to legal grounds. Neither Dr. Coffin nor Dr. Spock is a lawyer; indeed it is unlikely that either of them would recognize the Constitution of the United States if it crept into bed with them. Neither of them was ever heard to question the constitutionality of the Selective Service Act before the act was invoked to conscript soldiers to fight in this particular war. No, the gentlemen have most clearly been emphasizing not that the Selective Service Act is unconstitutional, but that the war in Vietnam is immoral, and that the higher demands of conscience enjoin them to do what they can to prevent the war's prosecution; specifically, to advise young men to evade the draft, that is to say, to break the law.

But lo, the American Civil Liberties Union has offered to represent the defendants, and Mr. Melvin Wulf, who is the chief lawyer for the union, has declared that the indictments are unconstitutional. His reasoning will be that you cannot punish an American for anything he says, it being unconstitutional to constrict anyone's freedom of speech. That argument, though eccentric, is not entirely forlorn. It is the argument not only of fanatic lawyers in the American Civil Liberties Union, but also the argument of Justice Hugo Black. Some years ago, accosting that argument, Justice Black's colleague Mr. Harlan went to painstaking lengths to show Mr. Black that it is highly traditional even in the most permissive societies to proscribe some forms of speech; for instance, slander, fraud, blackmail—and sedition. The United States has always had sedition laws, and indeed if Messrs. Spock and Coffin were now to win a legal victory in the Supreme Court on the grounds of the unconstitutionality of some of the provisions of the Selective Service Act, not only would sedition vanish as a legal offense, so also would the concept of conspiracy to violate a law.

But here we are, analyzing the legal merits of the Coffin-Spock position, which is what the defense is most likely to do unless Messrs. Coffin and Spock forbid them to do so. What they want is a showcase trial aimed not at clarifying the relationship between the First Amendment and the Selective Service Act, but a trial at which they will have gaudy opportunities to denounce the Vietnam War, invoking God, baby health, Nuremberg, Thoreau, and U Thant. What would be absolutely ideal, as far as they are concerned, is if they could have that opportunity—and then go back home, saved by a deft introduction of the First Amendment argument. If, in other words, they could both have their cake and eat it. And that is the point that needs especially to be watched, so as to guard against the crystallization of such sympathy as would naturally go to a lawbreaker whose motives were merely to test a particular law—a Henry Mencken going out on the Boston Common to read a book, in order to test the local obscenity law.

What Dr. Spock and Dr. Coffin have been saying and have been doing adds up to the assertion of the right of every individual to pass a personal veto on the making of American foreign policy. Theirs has been a call to anarchy, and they have shown that they are prepared, in behalf of their obsession concerning Vietnam, to undermine the structure of civil order, the law.

It would do them both more honor to go before the judge and plead guilty. Theirs then would be an uncomplicatedly moral position. Their apparent appetite for a trial on the legal question reduces the integrity of the drama, as if Socrates, upon being handed the hemlock, suddenly announced that his advocates had discovered reversible error in the Athenian trial. It would be a pity if, having already done their best to undermine the ideals Americans are dying for in Vietnam, they should go on to undermine the ideals of civil disobedience they themselves have been publicly honoring.

ON RIOTING

September 5, 1968

I dare say that the resentment and bitterness at Chicago last week had something to do with the public's philosophical unwillingness to decide, really, how to deal with rioters.

The outrage, so lavishly displayed on television, was only one part ideological. There are those who are always against the cops, on the traditionalist grounds that associate policemen with the repressive establishments of history. But even those who have worked their way out of that emotional snare *were* horrified at what they saw, because what they saw included the redundant blow of the nightstick, at the head or shoulder or rump of a victim already incapacitated; included, on one notorious occasion, policemen calling for the vacating of a street at a speed with which, literally, unpracticed sprinters could not comply.

But then the police and their supporters counterattacked, and their general case was compelling. They began by boldly challenging the terminological myths—on the one hand the big sadist Gestapo-minded policemen; on the other hand the sun-spreckled, gentle-minded young idealists; Otto Preminger versus Harvey. That didn't take too long, what with the (belated) revelation that the gentle folk had taken intensive training in the arts of public disturbance, featuring, among other select disciplines, how to capture public sympathy by provoking police into the use of unnecessary force.

The avowed intention of the high command of the rioters was to paralyze the convention. Most of those who expressed themselves on the question dismissed the strategic objective as palpably idealistic and, therefore, unrelated to any justification for what the police did. Still, the confidence of the anti's was shattered. At this point the convention was adjourned, leaving questions unanswered.

1. Do we really desire to enforce police regulations adamantly, or do too many people suspect that such regulations, promulgated under pressure, are arbitrary and constricting, and therefore lacking in sufficient moral authority to justify automatic acceptance? There were those in Chicago who were saying, in effect: Was it worth the bloodshed to hold the line at Avenue A when, after all, there were all those avenues in between it and Avenue X?

Question: Can the public be persuaded to grant the police the right to designate, from their command posts, their own Verduns, beyond which rioters will not pass? Or must the police announce these boundaries well in advance, in order to attempt to persuade the doubters of their plausibility?

2. Do the excesses of policemen reflect the tendencies of their superiors? We were hotly urged on to this conclusion at Chicago, and it required an ice-cold shower in the realities to bring us out of it. On Sunday night, Daley having declined to endorse Humphrey, he was on his way to becoming a hero. If on Wednesday he had announced his support for Gene McCarthy, the flower children, so help me, would have been accepted, and graven into history, as the modern counterparts of the Hitler youth movement by 6 P.M., CBS news time, Thursday. I kept wondering why no one meditated on the event of last spring, when Superimpeccable Mayor Lindsay gave orders to Superimpeccable Commissioner Leary to superimpeccably bust Columbia, nevertheless resulting in howls and screams about police brutality which are even now the roar at Columbia. Suggesting,

3. That Americans really haven't made up their minds concerning aspects of the problem which absolutely require attention before we can handle such phenomena as the Chicago riots with any sense of self-assurance. But our minds are not disposed to seek resolution. What it comes down to, I think, is that the opinion makers prefer a highly plastic line between the law and the defiers of the law, believing as they do that salients struck across the line by the defiers of it are matters that require urgent democratic attention; that if young rioters in Chicago throw themselves into police lines, they are saying to us things which we ought to hear. I suspect that that is why if Thomas A. Edison were to appear on the scene tomorrow with an antiriot weapon which would totally immobilize rioters without causing them as much pain, physical or intellectual, as a minor sunburn or an editorial in the New

York *Times,* Mr. Edison and his machine would be quickly proscribed by law, in the company of that long list of unpopular riot-controlling weapons, which have been serially pounced upon, from fire hoses, to cattle prods, to tear gas, to Mace.

The initiative, at this point, is with the intellectuals who should tell us-folk how to square off to these problems.

THE KERNER REPORT

March 16, 1968

The Kerner Report on the riots last summer is likely to engage the attention of a generation of politicians and moralists as the central document of the period, accounting for our revolutionary summers and laying the blame for them squarely on the culprit—our old friend, honky. Floyd McKissick, the director of CORE, was made a happy man, perhaps for the first time in his tortured life. "We're on our way to reaching the moment of truth," he said exultantly. "It's the first time whites have said, 'We're racists.' " And then, the typical American response: Buy your way out. Two million jobs, 6,000,000 new housing units, vast educational programs, welfare, anti-poverty, you name it.

Now there is a very good case for trying very hard to improve the lot of the Negro in America. But it has nothing to do with summer rioting. A few years ago, our moralists used to tell us that the way to curb Communism abroad was to increase welfare at home, a most tortuous non sequitur, it being supremely immaterial to the Communists how much welfare we enjoy in America.

Rioting in the ghetto is merely the slum variant of what Drs. Martin Luther King, Benjamin Spock, and William

Sloane Coffin are busily engaged in doing, to the applause
of a significant sector of the intellectual community. The
riot in Detroit was merely a proletarian version of well-fed,
well-housed white students preventing McNamara from
speaking at Harvard, or a police car from leaving the
premises of the University of California. One would have
thought that the old stomach argument about how to
prevent riots would have died for intellectual under-
nourishment after the riots in New Haven and
Detroit, model cities from the positivist point of view
which guided the thinking of the Kerner Commission.
What caused the riots isn't segregation or poverty or
frustration. What caused the riots is a psychological
discord, which is tearing at the ethos of our society as a
result of boredom, self-hatred, and the arrogant contention
that all our shortcomings are the result of other people's
aggressions upon us.

The Kerner Commission is committing the same
mistake that the Freedom Nowers committed beginning a
decade or so ago. All those civil rights bills, all those
Supreme Court rulings, all the heaving about for forced
integration; very good arguments can be made to defend
that activity. But once again, they are not justified as
bringing Freedom Now, and the high expectations
cultivated by the dreamy rhetoric of Martin Luther King
standing at the Lincoln Memorial in 1963 bred
only frustration and resentment, not composure and faith.
We need St. Paul, counseling patience and forbearance,
and reminding us that true justice is reserved for another
world; not the gnostic utopianism of those who tell us how
Congress can vote in paradise.

The commission, so far as one is able to judge, has
added nothing at all to one's knowledge of the
imperfections of our society that is unavailable to, say, the
reader of Claude Brown's *Manchild in the Promised
Land*. But by its emphasis on the material elements of the
problem, it fails totally to account for a malaise which is
mistakenly thought of as a Negro problem. Last week

Negro sociologist Harry Edwards said, "I'm for splitting up in twos and threes, killing the mayor, getting the utilities, and poisoning the goddamned water." And last week Robert Bly, the poet, on receiving the National Book Award, said, ". . . It turns out, [America] can put down a revolution as well as the Russians in Budapest, we can destroy a town as well as the Germans at Lidice, all with our famous unconcern. . . . In an age of gross and savage crimes by legal governments, the institutions will have to learn responsibility, learn to take their part in preserving the nation, and take their risk by committing acts of disobedience."

The problem is biracial, and nothing said by the Kerner Commission is relevant to its solution.

IX. CONTROVERSY

ON EXPERIENCING GORE VIDAL*

August, 1969

I have here a recent issue of *The East Village Other* featuring a piece entitled "Faggot Logic" which is about me, or more precisely about a column I wrote on Senator McGovern which highly displeased this demimondaine journal. "Following faggot logic," my critic writes, "is disturbing at any time of year, and Buckley's spiteful spewlings today have just pissed me off, even more than usual." That is certainly an icebreaker, even in *The East Village Other*, and I read on, my interest aroused to learn something about the nature of faggot logic. "On the Right," the author went on, referring to the logo of my thrice-weekly column, "is nearly invariably an exercise in faggot dialectic. And since I think this peculiar mode of intellect is worthless at best and generally inimical to the

* First published in *Esquire* magazine.

318

public weal, then I'd like, just once—Christmas season notwithstanding—to engage in a point-by-point vivisection of one of his scabrous evacuations."

Alas, many, many words later, the reader is left knowing nothing he didn't know before about the nature of faggot logic, which in my case was nothing at all, and moreover glumly aware that he would not likely come to apprehend the meaning of anything in any· way elusive under the guidance of the writer in question, whose thought proved to be as barren as his wit: so that after jogging alongside him over an endless stretch of indignation, one arrives at the cheerless conclusion (hardly reassuring to poor Senator McGovern), that the author likes the Senator, dislikes me, and thinks we should get out of Vietnam instantly.

Even so the piece sticks in the mind because here is a licentious rhetorical effort at homicide—in which the author arms himself with all the bad words; and yet he selects as the killer word: "faggot." That was the warhead. Very interesting. And particularly revealing in the context of the general attitude of that journal toward faggotry, the unmetaphorical practice of which it explicitly panders to, or so it would seem. On page 17 of the same issue there are advertisements as plainspoken as Macy's for garden furniture. "NUDE MALE FILM CLUB. . . . There will be continuous screenings nightly . . ."—is just one display ad. Another, discreetly sequestered in the classified section, positions wanted, "WHEEL AND DEAL": "Bi-Sexual, nude model, handsome, tall, trim, blond, hung, well-built, 30, will pose for sketches or you name it. $20 per session. . . ." And for those choosy readers who desire a synoptic view of the area and its possibilities there is the "1969 Gay Guide for gay guys, 'N.Y., N.J. baths, bars, glory holes, restaurants, movies, etc.' "

Why is faggotry okay, but the imputation of it discreditable? Is there a platonic coinage which is bad —even as the real thing becomes okay? Is that a culture lag, of sorts? Rather like saying about somebody that he is impious (which is unfriendly) even though, as everybody knows, explicit impiety is perfectly okay.

At this point my mind moved to Gore Vidal, and the dismal events of the summer of 1968, when he and I confronted each other a dozen times on network television, leading to an emotional explosion which, it is said, rocked television. Certainly it rocked me, and I am impelled to write about it; to discover its general implications, if any; to meditate on some of its personal implications, which are undeniable and profound; to probe the question whether what was said—under the circumstances in which it was said—has any meaning at all beyond that which is most generally ascribed to it, namely, excessive bitchery can get out of hand. But first the narrative.

In the late fall of 1967 I had a telephone call from Mr. James Haggerty, vice-president of the American Broadcasting Company and former White House press chief for President Eisenhower. Would I, he asked, consent to confer with Mr. Elmer Lower and Mr. William Sheehan concerning ABC's coverage of the 1968 political conventions? Yes, I said—obviously. We met then, the heads of ABC News and Special Events and of ABC Television News, and they disclosed their plans for 1968. Instead of covering the political conventions "gavel to gavel," ABC would condense the day's events into ninety minutes of nightly television, divided into five segments. The fourth segment was conceived as broad-ranging commentary on the convention, and the forthcoming election, and on politics in general.

They had in mind that two people would share that time, one of them a conservative, the other a liberal. Would I?

I asked a few mechanical questions and indicated it would probably work out, and then asked them who would be my adversary. They replied that he had not been selected. Did I have any suggestions? I thought awhile and gave them eight or ten names, among whom were some of the obvious people (Schlesinger, Galbraith, Mailer), and some a little less obvious (for instance, Al Lowenstein, Carey McWilliams, Jr.). Was there anyone at all I would refuse to appear alongside? I wouldn't refuse to appear alongside any non-Communist, I said—as a matter of principle; but I didn't want to appear opposite Gore Vidal (I said), because I had had unpleasant experiences with him in the past and did not trust him. A few months later the announcement was made that Gore Vidal had been selected as my opposite number. "We knew we wanted Buckley," Elmer Lower told a reporter in Miami at the outset of the Republican Convention, "because we were well familiar with him. . . . It was a question of who would best play off against him. We considered a number of people and did some 'auditions,' sort of surreptitiously, that is, watching people on the air without them knowing we were watching them. It looked as though Buckley would play better with Vidal than any of four or five other people." In one sense he was right. Even before Chicago—a good week or ten days after Miami—there were those who took pains to record their misgivings. For instance—not exactly typical, but singularly interesting—Stephanie Harrington, who wrote in the *Village Voice,* looking back on our first series of encounters at Miami:

What political analysis ABC did try for turned out to be the most embarrassing ingredient in its grand innovation. This was its attempt to elevate the affair to the level of intelligent discussion by bringing together nightly Gore Vidal and William Buckley for their comments—which [discussions] had far more to do with their contempt for each other than [with] their impressions of the convention. It was clearly a sequel to that painful moment some years back when Buckley, during a televised debate with Vidal, descended to his unique level of argument and in a typically Buckleyesque display of dirty debater's tricks, destroyed his opponent not by logic but by using his personal life against him. [I interrupt Miss Harrington to bring you a special announcement: remember that phrase, "personal life."] Indeed, he tried again this time, dismissing Vidal's political opinions on the grounds that he is the kind of man who would write a book like *Myra Breckinridge*. It was obvious that Buckley's heroics about the show going on despite the broken collarbone he suffered in a fall on his boat [—heroics? I simply went. Heroism, maybe; heroics, no—] had less to do with interest in the convention than with eagerness to get his claws into Vidal again.

Now under the stress of my conversations with ABC, we see that the anchor of Miss Harrington's argument is uprooted, and her analysis drifts away into fantasy. *Still,* she did say a few things concerning which there has been considerable speculation which *is* relevant: so that (fulldisclosurewise) I now divulge the history, abbreviated but not censored, of my dealings with Mr. Vidal, acknowledging Miss Harrington's and others' suspicions that those dealings figured, yes, indeed, in the meetings at Miami and Chicago.

1.

In January of 1962, appearing on the Jack Paar program to promote his play *Romulus,* Vidal went out of his way to observe that I had "attacked" Pope John XXIII for being "too left wing"; which sorrowful recording of my impiety drew from the audience horrified tremors.

Paar was evidently pressured to invite me to reply, which he did and I did, on an evening Paar once reminisced about as having been among the most memorable of his career, such was the ensuing uproar. Said uproar, for once, directed not against me, but against Paar's assault on me after I had left the studio, which assault stimulated, by the count of one NBC spokesman, 7,000 (anti-Paar) telegrams of protest and one (pro-Paar) phone call from the White House. That is by the way—what I liked most in terms of the theater of the episode was that instants after I left the studio, Paar ingenuously announced to the studio audience, *"I just got a call here. Gore Vidal's coming back tomorrow night!"* Now Paar's shows were taped three hours before they were telecast. So that he couldn't have received a telephone call from Gore Vidal reacting to my appearance—because the show would not go out over the air waves for another three hours. (And they talk about Tricky Dick.)

Anyway , Vidal showed up, and after cooing about him ("Notice the difference in manner and approach and reasoning") for a few minutes, Paar asked, what *had* I actually said about the Pope and the encyclical.

Vidal: *Yes, well what he actually said—and I went back and looked it up . . . in the month of August, Buckley attacked the Pope in a piece in his magazine, and the piece was called "A Venture in Triviality."*

a. I did not "attack the Pope." b. There was no "piece," merely a one-paragraph, unsigned editorial. c. The paragraph was not called "A Venture in Triviality"; it bore no title; one phrase in it said, "[The encyclical] must strike many as a venture in triviality coming at this particular time in history.")

V.: *It was a vicious piece and* America, *which is the Jesuit weekly in the United States, attacked Buckley in an editorial declaring that he owes his readers an apology, unquote.*

(The demand by *America* for an apology was unrelated
to the editorial in question.)

V.: *And Buckley's answer to the Jesuits was: "You
are impudent."*

(My answer to the Jesuits was in 2,500 words, one
sentence of which stated that it was impudent for *America*
to ask a non-Catholic journal of opinion to apologize for
a transgression—even assuming that that is what it
was—against exclusively Catholic protocol; and of course,
I was right.)

V.: *I mean, who is he? Here's a guy who has never
worked for a living . . . has never had a job.*

(I had held down one part-time job, as a member of the
faculty of Yale, 1947-1951; and three full-time jobs
before going to work for *National Review,* in 1955, which
is at least a full-time job.)

V.: *He's got two sisters.*

(Six.)

V.: *One said while she was at Smith . . .*

(It was ten years after she graduated.)

V.: *. . . that the faculty was filled with Communists.*

(She said four faculty members had Communist-front
connections, which was true.)

V.: *The other was at Vassar and started the same thing
at Vassar.*

(She said that at Vassar the bias in the social science
departments was predominantly liberal, and of course she
was right; ask Mary McCarthy.)

V.: *Meanwhile their brother was at Yale and wrote*
God and Man at Yale *and said that was full of
Communists.*

(My book did not charge or intimate that there was a
single Communist at Yale.)

V.: *He feels free to correct, through this little magazine
of his, the actions of all our Presidents and the Pope, and
philosophers . . . on the subject of philosophy—I thought
this might interest you, Jack—of Albert Schweitzer—who
is one of the great men of our time, and whose philosophy*

is reverence for life—he wrote of *Albert Schweitzer,
quote: He is more destructive than the H Bomb, unquote.*

(The quotation is not from me, but from a book review
in *National Review*—by a PhD in the classics. I do not
censor the book reviewers.)

V.: *On the subject of integration, Mr. Buckley wrote,
quote (Segregation is not intrinsically immoral, unquote.
Well, that's a double negative which means I don't quite
dare to come out and say I'm in favor of segregation, so
I'll put it in a double negative.*

(a. It isn't a double negative. b. It is a litotes and
should be recognized as such by a professional writer. The
litotes has been around as a necessary rhetorical
refinement for years; was used, for instance, by that old
evader, Homer. c. I didn't in fact write that phrase, I
spoke it in the presence of a Catholic liberal, John Cogley,
who d. agreed with me.)

V.: *. . . but that's exactly what it means, which goes
against not only Catholic doctrine but I would think any
humane*—*you put your finger on it, you know, when you
said there's no humanity there.*

But Mr. Vidal was not through.

V.: *I was just going to say one more thing struck me,
listening to Mr. Buckley. He said (and I was quite
fascinated because it's amazing the things perhaps you can
just get away with, this side of libel) . . . he said that
Harry Truman had called Eisenhower an anti-Semite and
anti-Catholic.*

Paar: *Yes, he did say that. But what*—

V.: *There's no evidence that Harry Truman ever said
this. Now I would like to say right now, on the air, that I
will give one hundred dollars to the* National Review,
*which is Buckley's magazine, if he can prove that Harry
Truman ever said any such thing; and if he cannot prove
it, why, I think he should then be regarded as what he is,
which is an irresponsible liar. . . As someone once said
. . . [the Buckleys] are sort of the sick Kennedys.*

I flew early the following morning to Switzerland, leaving a telegram to be dispatched to my office to Jack Paar. It read: "PLEASE INFORM GORE VIDAL THAT NEITHER I NOR MY FAMILY IS DISPOSED TO RECEIVE LESSONS IN MORALITY FROM A PINK QUEER. IF HE WISHES TO CHALLENGE THAT DESIGNATION, INFORM HIM THAT I SHALL FIGHT BY THE LAWS OF THE MARQUIS OF QUEENSBERRY. HE WILL KNOW WHAT I MEAN. WILLIAM F. BUCKLEY, JR." The telephone was ringing when I reached my destination in Switzerland, as I half expected it would be. Come on now, calm down, whaddaya say, forget it, write a piece about the whole thing instead. So I finally withdrew the telegram and contented myself instead to send a letter to Jack Paar:

"Dear Mr. Paar:

[I have been informed of what Mr. Gore Vidal said on your show on February 1.]

"1. The documentation, taken in each case from the New York *Times,* is as follows: On October 9, 1952, President Harry Truman accused the Republicans generally of supporting 'the discredited and un-American theory of racial superiority.' On October 17, Assistant Secretary of State Howland Sargeant read a message from Mr. Truman to the Jewish Welfare Board in Washington. Eisenhower, Truman said, 'cannot escape responsibility' for his endorsement of Senator Revercomb, 'the champion of the anti-Catholic, anti-Jewish provisions of the original D.P. bill.' Truman charged that Eisenhower 'has had an attack of moral blindness, for today he is willing to accept the very practices that identify the so-called master race although he took a leading part in liberating Europe from their domination.'

"2. The following day, Rabbi Abba Hillel Silver, ex-President of the Zionist Organization of America, expressed 'shock that an irresponsible statement of that character could be made. The attempt by implication to identify a man like General Eisenhower with anti-Semitism and anti-Catholicism is just not permissible even in the heat of a campaign.'

"3. Please instruct Mr. Vidal to make out a check for $100 to the National Conference of Christians and Jews."

Paar, directed to do so by NBC's lawyers, read, or rather caused to be read, the letter aloud over his program, during a station break, following which he made no reference to it whatever. Vidal made no acknowledgment, tendered no apology, did not reply in any way to a couple of letters asking him to make out the check.

2.

It is not my habit to review the material that appears in the back of the book section of *National Review*, so that I saw for the first time in the published magazine, weeks later in Switzerland, a review by Noel E. Parmentel, Jr., of Vidal's play, *Romulus*. The review was unfavorable to the play, but generous—one should say accurate—in its appreciation of Vidal's talents as a playwright. One aspect of *Romulus* the reviewer found offensive and was not alone in the critical community in doing so. "All in all," he wrote, "*Romulus* adds up to (with the possible exception of *Sail Away*) the most offensive instance of 'inside' theatre, which such diverse types as the late Ernie Kovacs and New York *Times* drama critic Howard Taubman have chosen to call 'effeminate' and which the boys in Lindy's are calling '*la nouvelle fague.*' "

Parmentel went on. "Although the critics have generally ridiculed the Vidal literary product, he is far from being a jejune hack. He has certainly traveled an odd road. During his early career as a 'serious' novelist, he evinced an interest in homosexuality equalled only by that of the editors of *One*. Many of his novels and stories are clinical, apparently informed commentaries on the problem. [Notice what Vidal would consider the planted axiom— the *problem*.] In spite of all this high purpose, critic William Peden was once moved to note that the Vidal output constituted 'a rather dreary landmark in the literature of homosexuality.' "

And there followed a crack I confess I have repeated here and there mostly because I thought it funny, still do. "Always the seeker after truth, Vidal lived for a time in the ruins of a sixteenth-century monastery in Guatemala, where he gathered material for an anti-United Fruit Company novel—positively, as a local wag observed, the *only* anti-fruit novel Vidal ever wrote."

And then, more seriously, "At another point he made a pilgrimage to the bedside of André Gide. It is reported that the great French writer liked Vidal and gave him an inscribed first edition of his controversial *Corydon*. Vidal carried his almost obsession with homosexuality into the movies. Although he is quite a proficient scriptwriter, he once wrote a scenario about Billy the Kid, acted by a bewildered Paul Newman, in which the legendary outlaw appeared as a misunderstood homosexual. It was only natural that Sam Spiegel should call on Vidal's specialist skills for Tennessee Williams' *Suddenly Last Summer*."

The operative word is "obsession." And it wasn't only *National Review,* as Parmentel made clear, that thought it a—problem. Our sister publication on the left, *The New Republic,* carried a review of *Romulus* by Robert Brustein who is now the dean of the Yale Drama School. He wrote that Vidal had "transform[ed] Dürrenmatt's tough parable into an effeminate charade. . . . To make the Romans into homosexuals," he concluded, "is simply in bad taste." *Why* bad taste?

The months passed, and David Susskind asked me if I would appear *mano a mano* with Vidal on his "Open End"—just the two of us. And discuss what? I asked.

Everything, said Susskind. All right, I said.

Now no discussion of "everything" nowadays can be counted upon not to touch on sex. Accordingly I was prepared, should the subject arise, to attempt to state the case, biological, cultural, and religious, for heterosexuality (that sounds funny, doesn't it?)—prepared to go as far as to defend its "normalcy"; to defend, even, the idea that normalcy in this instance at least is related to what is normative: to defend, one might say, the conservative position.

It seemed to me utterly natural—one is tempted to say utterly normal—that in defending heterosexuality I should furtively consult my own preferences in that direction, and accordingly that in defending bisexuality, the question of Vidal's preferences would reasonably arise. I had read, in preparation for our meeting, his book of essays, *Rocking the Boat*, in which his own intellectual sympathies, at least, were quite candidly stated. "Now it is an underlying assumption of twentieth-century America," he wrote —and the student of rhetoric knows already, the "now" being a dead giveaway, that the writer is about to introduce an assumption with which he disagrees—"that human beings are either heterosexual, or through some arresting of normal psychic growth, homosexual, with very little traffic back and forth. To us, the norm is heterosexual; the family is central; all else is deviation, pleasing or not depending on one's own tastes and moral preoccupations. Suetonius"—Vidal was reviewing a translation of *The Twelve Caesars* by Robert Graves —"reveals a very different world. His underlying assumption is that man is bisexual and that given complete freedom to love—or, perhaps more to the point in the case of the Caesars, to violate—others, he will do so, going blithely from male to female as fancy dictates. Nor is Suetonius alone in this assumption of man's variousness. From Plato to the rise of Pauline Christianity, which tried to put the lid on sex, it is explicit in classical writing. [Nonsense, as it happens. *E.g.,* Aristophanes, who mocked Plato's homosexuality; Juvenal, who stigmatized the Greek-aristocratic homosexuality; Catullus, who found Caesar's bisexuality, in the words of Gilbert Highet, 'ridiculous and disgusting.'] Yet to this day Christian, Freudian and Marxian commentators have all decreed or ignored this fact of nature in the interest each of a patented approach to the Kingdom of Heaven. . . ."

Now in fact the subject did not come up, though the question was raised, I think (I do not exactly remember, and I do not have the transcript), as to whether practicing homosexuals working in sensitive government agencies were security risks, like, say, drunkards. I have never been convinced, by the way, that they are, but I did recite the reasons given by security officials (susceptibility to blackmail, primarily), and I do not know whether I loosed an inflection that burrowed into the memory of Miss Harrington. I cannot conceive that if I had made a major, or even a minor statement, about Gore Vidal's "personal life," that it would have escaped the attention of every single one of the television critics who watched and reported on the program, and there were apparently many of them, none of whom made the slightest reference to the cause of Miss Harrington's trauma. Could she have had in mind a personal reference to Vidal's relations to the Kennedys? But the only thing I knew about his private life in that connection (Vidal had not yet fallen out with the Kennedys) was that his sometime stepfather is Jacqueline Kennedy's incumbent, a nexus that connects an awful lot of people with an awful lot of people and is neither newsworthy nor scandalous.

On the other hand, I gather that I spoke sharply to Vidal (I should hope so!). One reviewer, who was also covering the opening of Lincoln Center that night, wrote that every so often he "would switch over to an independent channel where a fair-haired barracuda named

William Buckley, Jr., was nibbling at the flesh of a young sea robin named Gore Vidal. . . . In the only complete sentences spoken on this piscatorial orgy, we heard Mr. Vidal saying he couldn't imagine Mr. Buckley in the role of an abolitionist and Mr. Buckley saying that he was an abolitionist for the slaves of Eastern Europe, which Mr. Vidal wasn't." There was no masking, I gather, the mutual dislike, which in Mr. Vidal's case was spontaneously generated, in mine evolved as a reaction to his hit-and-run network disparagement of my family and myself earlier in the year. "The debate," another reviewer wrote, "got entrenched in so much personal opprobrium nothing really was decided other than Buckley's clear debating superiority. . . . When it came to historical and political facts and interpretation, Vidal, frustrated in realistic fencing, resorted to personal disdain, never an attractive effect. . . . Both indulged the sort of *ad hominem* needling that dazzles and spins off sparks and delights viewers who adore such exercise of forensic fisticuffs, but it does keep issues muddled while delighting the more sadistic semantic fight fans." Vidal said a while later on the Les Crane program that I had beaten him badly and gave as the reason that he, Vidal, had permitted himself to become "emotionally involved," whatever that means.

3.

It was during the Republican Convention at San Francisco in 1964 that I resolved I would not again debate with Gore Vidal. It was the memory of that encounter, added to everything else, that made me suggest to ABC that I'd prefer not to debate with him, and now I gather that his exclusion graveled him. Indeed over the intervening years I had never asked him to appear on "Firing Line," which was launched early in 1966. "The one forum on which they have not met is Buckley's

syndicated series, 'Firing Line,' " a reporter wrote, after
interviewing Vidal. "Buckley invited the novelist to the
program, but 'I refused to give him that much help' Vidal
smiled thinly." (I'd have smiled thinly, too, if I told a
reporter I refused Ed Sullivan's invitation to tap dance on
his show because I didn't want to give Sullivan that much
help.) At San Francisco it wasn't just the usual things that
aroused me, but an insight I got into what I now concluded
was more than a merely episodic insensibility to the truth.
Specifically, Vidal announced on a television program,
once again "moderated" by Susskind (Susskind's
advocacy of Vidal's positions competed with the positions
themselves in burdening Vidal), that I had that very
afternoon importuned Barry Goldwater to accept a draft
of an acceptance speech I had written for him, and that
Goldwater had brusquely turned me down, all of this in
the presence of Ed Knellor, a Goldwater aide. I told him
(a) that I had not laid eyes on Goldwater that afternoon;
(b) that I had not written or suggested to anyone that I
write a draft of Goldwater's acceptance speech; and (c)
that although I knew very well who Ed Knellor was, in
fact I had never laid eyes on him in my entire life. Vidal
not only refused to modify let alone to withdraw his
allegation; he reasserted it several times. The next day,
Susskind (over Vidal's protests, Susskind subsequently
told me) read over the air a letter from Knellor confirming
my denials. (Goldwater, it happened, had tuned in on the
program and was as nonplussed as Knellor.)

There were one or two other instances of the same kind
of thing, and I remember that it occurred to me then, as it
did a couple of times in Miami and Chicago, that perhaps
Vidal makes his own reality, which is, all things
considered, sufficient reason to understand his philosophical melancholy, even as the order of reality
would be melancholy if it had conceived Vidal. At any
rate, one wants to stay away from such people, at least
publicly. Yet once again the debate had been lively. One

reviewer, who took pains to disavow any sympathy with my politics, said that, in the service of "the radical right, [Buckley] was far more successful than Susskind and Vidal on the medium left . . . Susskind and Vidal rocked back and forth like two old harpies and spat at him with no visible effect on their target nor, I suspect, on viewers." The other reviewer "got the impression . . . that Susskind was a zookeeper trying to prevent two hissing adders from killing each other. But the hissing was always wreathed in benign smiles." August 7, 1968, the Rockford *Star*: " 'I haven't seen Buckley since 1964 at the Cow Palace,' Vidal recalled. 'His last words to me were that he never wanted to see me again.' " Needless to say, I did not say those words. But they represented, accurately, my thoughts.

I find only two unpleasant references to Vidal written by me between 1964 and 1968. Commenting on an article by Vidal in *Esquire* on the Kennedy family, I wrote, "It is of course ironic that Mr. Vidal, the super-liberal super-thinker who in pursuit of the good life has tried everything, but everything in the world, including icon-smashing with a vengeance, now engages an icon he had a hand in molding." The other reference was exhumed by the drama editor of the Miami *Herald* who wrote at the beginning of the Republican Convention that "Vidal is worried the broadcasts may be a bit dull, feeling the allotted twenty minutes or so won't really give them time to get into things. That seems like an obscure worry as only a couple of years ago, in his newspaper column, Buckley referred to Vidal as 'the playwright and quipster who lost a Congressional race a few years ago but continues to seek out opportunities to advertise his ignorance of contemporary affairs.' "

4.

Bent on promoting their forthcoming programs, the
people at ABC set up a lunch for me to meet the area's
television critics, and subsequently did as much, I assume,
for Vidal. Such meetings, as every writer knows, are
something of a strain: because you are generally made to
feel that you can only please by being viperish. What will I
want to say about the conventions when face to face with
Vidal? I didn't know. My line on Vidal was that I thought
his dissatisfaction with America and with American
politics was such as to make him almost necessarily sour
on anything that was likely to happen at either convention.

Vidal was evidently much more detailed. One critic
wrote that according to Vidal he had "accepted ABC's
offer, even though he was to be teamed with Buckley, a
man with whom he has had video encounters before and
for whom he has utter contempt." Another quoted Vidal
as saying, "Bill, of course, will try to personalize our
shows. He thrives on insults. But I'll try to stick to
politics. He never sticks to a subject because he's on such
weak ground." Another wrote that Vidal "was not the
least bit reluctant to discuss his adversary. Vidal
welcomed the chance to be quoted. Apparently he relishes
the vaudeville team approach to interpretative journalism
employed by ABC television for the national conventions
and is anxious to allow the churlish nature of their onscreen rapport to carry over into off-screen conversation.
. . . 'Though I don't like being brought down to his level.
That's the reason I've refused to appear with him over the
last four—or is it six?—years. . . . Buckley is frivolous,
superficial, and often very entertaining.' "

And he told Mr. Hal Humphrey, whose column is
widely syndicated, that he would "stipulate at least one
ground rule. . . . 'When I'm talking I want the camera on

me and not on Bill's face doing all those wild expressions of his while I'm just a voice offstage.' " Later he told a correspondent that he had complained to the director of getting insufficient camera time, and the director had promptly complied with his requests. On these and related matters he proved most fastidious. "Buckley," a Miami reporter wrote, ". . . is as conservative about being pictured in the makeup chair as he is in his political philosophy. He submitted to a brief [makeup], a quick swish of a comb by his wife, Patricia, who had accompanied him. On the other hand, his fellow program jouster Gore Vidal was thoroughly liberal about being touched up. No hurry-up job this. Miss May leisurely cleansed the skin with antiseptic lotion, added a cream-type foundation and powder, and commented on his hair-line: 'He has a good hairline.' 'I don't have a wig,' he quipped. 'Tell your photographer not to make me look as though I have. Past pictures have. See how vain I am. I'm letting you take my bad side,' gesturing to his right."

In general, the press anticipated the forthcoming debates with unmitigated glee. In Toledo the headline was "POLITICIANS ARE FOREWARNED/BILL, GORE MAY STEAL SHOW." The Washington *Post* announced that "The best show during the Republican and Democratic conventions next month will not be on the convention floors or in hotel corridors but in an ABC studio. . . . In Buckley and Vidal, ABC has a dream television match. They are graceful, shrewd, cool antagonists: paragons of caustic wit and established observers of the American political scene." "It's anybody's ball game," wrote the New York *Daily News* about the GOP Convention, "as they've been telling us the past couple of days, but right now the inside dope at the convention is that Bill Buckley and Gore Vidal have it practically sewed up. As a team, Buckley is in the No. 1 slot, naturally, since he's thoroughly committed, with Vidal, an expert sniper, as his running mate. And the beauty part of it is that, disliking one another intensely and both gifted in invective (they are far and away the best infighters in Miami Beach), they're a cinch to provide challenging leadership." "A rare stroke of good television programming . . ." said the Philadelphia *Daily News*. "As an ABC spokesman puts it, 'We fully expect the fur to fly when those two come together,' and there wasn't a dissenting comment from his listeners."

So there we were, Saturday, August 3, on duty for our first broadcast, suddenly rescheduled in a makeshift studio at the Fontainebleau Hotel because the ceiling had caved in two days before over the studio at the convention site. We were instructed that we must prerecord an initial statement of a sentence or two, and I knew, when I heard Vidal's, that the session was going to be grim.

"To me," he said, *"the principal question is, can a political party based almost entirely upon human greed nominate anyone for President for whom the majority of the American people would vote?"* Now there was an interval of eight or ten minutes before we swung into the live portion of the program. Diagonally across from us, William Lawrence was well into his political forecast, which had followed a pastiche of the day's events screened by ABC producers. Across from us was Howard K. Smith, suave, intelligent, mildly apprehensive, rehearsing with his lips the lines he would presently deliver, directly in touch with the controls, where twenty officials and technicians called the signals, to Smith, to Lawrence, to the thirty-forty-fifty technicians, reporters, directors, who filled the enormous room, at one corner of which, earphones attached, Vidal and I awaited the sound of the bell. We had exchanged minimal amenities, and I scribbled on my clipboard to avoid having to banter with him, and he did the same, and I felt my blood rising in temperature as I reflected on the malevolent inanity of his introductory observation, and then the resolution evolved that I would

hit him back hard with a *tu quoque* involving *Myra Breckinridge*—which I had not then read. . . . But Howard K. Smith derailed me by asking me not, as I had expected, to initiate the exchange by commenting on Vidal's description of the Republican Party, but rather to answer a specific question—who, in my judgment, was the Best Man at Miami? We were off.

I answered: Reagan and Nixon, and said why, more or less. Vidal came back with Rockefeller—*"I cannot possibly imagine Richard Nixon President of the U.S."* He backed this failure of his imagination by reciting an arresting catalog of Nixon's sins, so livid up against the exigencies of the day:

"And here you have a man who when he was in Congress voted against public housing, against slum clearance, against rent control, against farm housing, against extending the minimum wage . . . He said, 'I am opposed to pensions in any form as it makes loafing more attractive then working.' And now today he offers us a program for the ghettos which he's made much of, and what is it? Well, he is going to give tax cuts to private businesses that go into the ghetto and help the Negroes. Now in actual fact private business is set up to make private profits . . . So I would say that so far as Mr. Nixon goes he is an impossible choice domestically."

Now up against an extended barrage like that, a debater·has problems. Point-by-point refutation is clearly impossible. As a rule one doesn't have handy the relevant material for coping with such arcana. And anyway, in network situations, an elementary sense of theater (which if you don't have it, you won't ever face the problem of what to do in network situations) disciplines you in the knowledge that you simply don't have the time it takes for detailed confutation. Nixon hadn't been in Congress for *sixteen* years. Just to begin with, whatever Nixon did in Congress between 1947 and 1952 was largely irrelevant. Apart from that, what on earth does it mean, Nixon "voted against," say, "rent control"? Rent control survived in only a few places, primarily New York City. How can *any* attitude he took toward "farm housing" eighteen years ago bear on his present qualifications for the Presidency? And what sort of a "farm housing" bill did he vote against? How can we know?—maybe it was the same farm housing bill that the Americans for Democratic Action also opposed. And anyway, wasn't Nixon selected in 1952 by Eisenhower because he had a reputation as a domestic liberal (one of Christian Herter's boys) and as a tough anti-Communist—a good combination in 1952? Hadn't Nixon's preference for Eisenhower over Taft situated him in the liberal wing of the GOP?

And then there was the problem of the directly quoted sentence. Vidal quoted Nixon as saying, *"I am opposed to pensions in any form as if makes loafing more attractive than working."* The debater knows by the application of rudimentary discriminatory intelligence that no politician in the history of the world ever said that, and most probably no nonpolitician; and certainly not anyone who ever contemplated running for the Presidency. The mind needs to work quickly in such situations, canvassing rapidly the possibilities that a direct challenge might lead him into a carefully planned ambush. . . . So one comes in on the subject from the other direction: If Nixon had ever uttered a sentence so preposterous—condemning pensions paid even to ninety-year-old widows, on the grounds that they are conducive to sloth—wouldn't a fatuity so lapidary have instantly become a part of the political folklore, like, for instance, Mr. Agnew's "If you've seen one slum you've seen them all"? The answer is, of course, yes; so that in debate, under these circumstances, you can feel safe in saying, *"Nixon never said that"*—even though such a denial is itself (a) unprovable, and (b) silly; since no one on earth is familiar with every statement Nixon ever made; and no one therefore can know as a certitude that he never made *any* particular statement. What to do?

I decided to do nothing. To go back and challenge the over-arching axiom planted by Vidal at the outset—more damaging, more readily exposable, than what he said about Nixon. . . .

B.: *It seems to me that the earlier focus of Mr. Vidal here on human greed—you remember that he said he found himself wondering whether the party that was devoted to the concept of human greed could ever hope to get a majority of the American people to vote for it. Now the author of* Myra Breckinridge *is well acquainted with the imperatives of human greed—*

Vidal broke up—reacted quite extraordinarily. . . .

V.: *Ha, ha, ha. If I may say so, Bill, before you go any further, that if there were a contest for Mr. Myra Breckinridge, you would unquestionably win it. I based the entire style polemically upon you—passionate and irrelevant.*

B.: *That's too involuted to follow. Perhaps one of these days you can explain it—*

V.: *You follow it.*

I didn't and don't. In any case, we were off.

B.: *For Mr. Vidal to give us the pleasure of his infrequent company by coming back from Europe, where he lives in order to disdain the American democratic process, and to condemn a particular party as one that has engaged in the pursuit of human greed requires us to understand his rather eccentric definitions. . . .*

I went on to point out that Senator Robert Kennedy, not Nixon, had first suggested the tax rebates, and that the Republican Party's support of the costly Vietnam War was hardly an exercise in greed. Vidal answered that the Republicans were big businessmen who made profits from the war, I pitched for the free enterprise system, he said the Republicans denigrate the poor and the minority groups, and that if by some terrible accident Nixon became President, "I shall make my occasional trips to Europe longer."

B.: *Yes, I think a lot of people hope you will. As a matter of fact, Mr. Arthur Schlesinger, Jr., who is a member of your party, not mine, [has] remind[ed] you of your promise to renounce your American citizenship unless you get a satisfactory party in November.*

V.: *Now, now, Bill, that isn't quite what I said. I said it would be* morally *the correct thing to do, but I can behave as immorally as the Republicans.*

B.: *I can believe that, too.*

What Vidal had written, in the book *Authors Take Sides on Vietnam*, published only a few months before Miami, was "*For myself, should the war in Vietnam continue after the 1968 election, a change in nationality will be the only moral response.*" So already, *pre-Gethsemane*, the statement turned out to be nothing more than moral bravura.

Vidal returned to the theme of Republicans-as-believers-that-welfare-is-immoral. He managed to intrude a feline reference to Ronald Reagan, which, so help me God, if I had said such a thing about Adlai Stevenson, I hope I'd have gone off and joined the Trappists. He warmed up by attributing to Reagan, as he had done to Nixon, a statement Reagan never made—

V.: *Meanwhile, with several denunciations [by Reagan] like I quoted to you, on free-loaders on welfare and how it encourages immorality and divorce—I assume he was on unemployment insurance when he divorced Jane Wyman—*

And on he went. Another evening (August 6) he would motivate Reagan's liberal-to-conservative switch in the early fifties on Reagan's falling in love with the daughter of "a very prominent brain surgeon." I asked how come, under the circumstances, Reagan had achieved the extraordinary plurality of 1966. Well, the people make mistakes.

Vidal suddenly switched the topic, electing to allude to my "intimacy" with Reagan and Nixon. In order to do so, he assigned to the word "neurosis" a meaning I have never heard it given, not even by conventional neurotics.

V.: *. . . Since you're in favor of the invasion of Cuba, in favor of bombing the nuclear potentiality of China, since you're in favor of nuclear bombing of North Vietnam, I'd be very worried about your kind of odd neurosis: neurosis being a friend of anybody who might be a President. If I were one of the candidates I'd say, Bill Buckley, don't stay home. I know, I know, I don't get it either.*

B.: *I'd be very worried, too, if you had such a hob-goblinized view—but I've never advocated the nuclear bombing of North Vietnam.*

V.: *I'll give you the time and place if it amuses you.*

B.: *Well, you won't.*

V.: *I will.*

B.: *I advocated the liberation of Cuba at the same time that Mr. Kennedy ordered the liberation of Cuba.*

V.: *No, no, Bill, keep to the record. You said we should enforce the Monroe Doctrine and invade Cuba the sooner the better in your little magazine whose name will not pass my lips in April 1965. You favored bombing Red China's nuclear production facilities the seventeenth of September, 1965, in* Life *magazine . . .*

I had said to *Life*: "I have advocated bombing Red China's nuclear production facilities. But it becomes more and more difficult to do . . . as Red China takes pains to diffuse and protect its facilities. But technically, it is still possible. How do we justify the bombing in terms of world opinion? On the grounds the good guys of this earth have got to keep the bad guys from getting nuclear bombs."

V.: *. . . and you suggested the atom bombing of North Vietnam in your little magazine which I do not read but I'm told about, the twenty-third of February, 1968. So you're very hawkish, and if both Nixon and Reagan are listening to you, I'm very worried for the country.*

I told him he was misquoting me.

V.: *No, Bill Buckley, let me make it clear to you that the quotation is exact . . . Are you saying that you didn't say that?*

B.: *I'm saying that I didn't say it, that your mis-quotations—*

V.: *Tune in this time tomorrow night and we will have further evidence of Bill Buckley's cold war turned hot. . . .*

I responded limply, and Howard Smith relieved us, and I would suppose the national audience, from the misery, by telling us how "enjoyable" it had been to hear us "articulate" our "points of view."

That was August 3. Today (as I write) is February 19, 1969, and I have just now reached for the bound volume of *National Review* 1968, and leaf through to find the issue of February 23, 1968. It does not exist. I look back, to the issue of February 13—surely that was what he meant? Nothing there about nuking North Vietnam. Perhaps the following issue—February 27? Ha! P. 206: "Vietnam and Partisan Politics" by W.F.B., second column, third paragraph. "If Lyndon Johnson's reasoning is correct that bombing the North is justified, then it is also correct to bomb the harbor of Haiphong and prevent the delivery there of the hundreds of thousands of tons of matériel being used against us so effectively." That is the most bellicose paragraph is the issue. Could Vidal have had in mind a column, written about that time, though never published in *National Review*, advocating the use of tactical nuclear weapons in Vietnam? Who knows? Yes, I have advocated (and most ardently continue to do so) their use, only after pointing out that they are conceived as more efficient than conventional artillery, under certain circumstances, and that their firepower is more discriminatory, and therefore less damaging to extramilitary targets than, for instance, the mass bombings by the B-52's used in the defense of Khesanh.

I wondered what, say, a court would have done under parallel circumstances. "You know," the prosecution declaims, "on February 23, 1968, the Supreme Court, in Minelli *v.* Illinois, declared that anyone who. . . ." And, later, an inquisitive legal researcher discovers that the Supreme Court didn't declare *anything* on February 23, 1968, and that Minelli and the State of Illinois, far from fighting with each other, were always on the best of terms. What happens? Contempt of court? Reversal? Disbarment? I'll tell you what happens when the audience is not the judge, the jury, and Minelli's kinfolk, but 10,000,000 people. What happens is nothing.

5.

Reflections on the first meeting?

From Vidal: *"I don't mind his condemning my books,"* he told one reporter. *"The president of Bantam Books, which is bringing out the paperback edition in September, phoned me last night and asked me to encourage the attacks on* Myra *because the book wholesalers have been calling all day with orders. . . . Bill refuses to deal with the issues because he doesn't know what they are, so he uses the personal attack. I spend my time reading statements of Nixon, Reagan, and Rockefeller, and I'm able to deal with their positions. Buckley doesn't do much reading. He just arranges his prejudices."* Vidal was very pleased by his performance. The television people, he explained, learned greatly from it. "Did you notice," he asked another critic, "that after our first meeting the other commentators began to change their style—to try for wit and candor? Even Cronkite tried to be funny. It's possible that ABC is exploiting our names and reputations. But I couldn't turn down the audience. Just think of how many millions of people who never heard of us now know who we are," he crowed. "He went over each encounter," the critic reported, "claiming that he 'absolutely destroyed' Buckley in their first preview meeting. . . . 'The camera did focus on Buckley too much during Tuesday's session, but I put a stop to that,' Vidal said. 'The next night there were not so many full-face reaction shots of him.' "

The press wasn't, or at least not all of it, quite so appreciative. Dean Gysel, who had talked about the dream team, referred to the shows' "waspish bitchery." "Vidal was expecially guilty of making personal attacks," said another reviewer. "There was something positively obscene"—wrote Terrence O'Flaherty, who had written four years earlier about the San Francisco encounter, sounding a note of warning—"about . . . [the] face-splitting exchange [which] was irresistible as well as embarrassing. . . . It was not the dialogue itself that made the conversation obscene; it was the expression of almost sensual relish which flashed across their faces as they thrust and stabbed—for obviously they enjoyed these duels as much as the audience. [Point: What is obvious may not be true, and in this case, speaking authoritatively about my own state of mind, I not only didn't enjoy the evening, I detested it.] [But] suddenly the conversation gets the teeth on edge." And Jack Gould, of the New York *Times*: "[Their] petty confrontations should qualify them as the week's major bores in Miami Beach. . . ." Sure, there was also the world of the satisfied. "Both stress style over content," one critic wrote, "but it is high style. Both may be irrelevant, but they are passionately irrelevant. The polemics are such that the rubber band often breaks, but then they define their positions." And the ratings were very high.

My own feeling was that the encounter had confirmed my misgivings. On Sunday morning I telephoned to Wally Pfister, the producer, and suggested the possibility of alternative formats: perhaps two or three minutes of Vidal, followed by two or three minutes of Buckley, but no cross-talk. He reported back the conclusion of the brass that that would make for uninteresting fare. To a television critic he spoke without making reference to my expressed dissatisfactions: "Pfister revealed that the day after the first debate, Vidal called him and said, 'I sure took care of him [Buckley] last night, didn't I?' Later Buckley called him and said, 'I certainly made him [Vidal] look silly, didn't I?' The mighty are human, too," the critic concluded. The mighty are unmighty, too, he'd have better concluded.

Vidal's political philosophy is, I discovered fairly early in our association, elusive. His attitudes, if you look them up in the yellow pages, are neatly left-liberal in purely conventional terms. However there are anomalies. There is a strain of populism. But populism, after all, should be popular. I have heard John Kenneth Galbraith call himself a populist, always on the understanding that he does not thereby deprive himself of his right to intellectually aristocratic habits, *e.g.*, in the case of Galbraith, cultural elitism, and in the case of Vidal, that much at least; and, touching on the point already raised, sexual singularity as well. But on the whole, populists should be not only expert but enthusiastic at reasoning through to the justification of the people's demands. Vidal isn't good at this at all: or rather, one comes across an impenetrable barrier to the understanding. Toward "the people," he has ambiguous relations, though he appears not to be able to do without them, at least not for as long as twenty network minutes. Even though "they" are, strangely, always out to get him. "Vidal expresses the hope," wrote Hal Humphrey in a syndicated story, "that security provisions at the conventions are especially good because, he says, for the first time in his life (he's forty-two) he has a fear of physical danger to himself. 'I get more threatening mail each day, and from reading it I wonder that there isn't more violence in our country than there is. You know, of course, that one of every five people in the U.S. is mentally disturbed?' " (The influence is that he gets threatening mail from those who are disturbed, rather than from those who are undisturbed.)

Now anyone plugged in to reality will recognize this as sheer fantasy. If Vidal got five threatening letters in 1967, I'll deliver him J. Edgar Hoover as a bodyguard. But it was a cherished theme: "While in Miami Beach," reported Tom Mackin, "he was the subject of considerable hostility. 'I hear hissing in the lobby of the Fontainebleau and people shrink from me,' he said."

Possibly his difficulty in understanding "the people" accounts for his rather extraordinary record as political forecaster. In 1963 he wrote that Goldwater could not be nominated in 1964, in 1968 he predicted that Reagan would be nominated, at Miami he said that Nixon could not be elected, a few days later he predicted that he would be elected—but having predicted something which actually came to be, he left the impression that he made this prediction not so much because his observation of political events led him to the conclusion, as because he needed to massage his *Weltschmerz* which he proceeded to do in *The New York Review of Books*, after the nomination of Nixon, with masturbatory diligence. Gloom is his chic, and when he remembers to blame "them," it is "the people" who are responsible for the melancholy state of public affairs. On the occasions when he forgets to blame the human condition on "the people," it is the people's leaders who are responsible, the people's leaders being the Vested Interests. "*I think*," Vidal told a writer for the *Saturday Review*, who asked him what his thoughts turned to on contemplating the city of Rome, "*I think*," said Vidal, "*not only of Marc Antony, Caesar and Cicero, but of our own representatives who take their name from this*"—he pointed to history—"*the Roman senate. I contemplate their follies and mistakes. I see Washington in ruins as something perfectly portended. . . . Americans have no sense of the past, and indeed hate it.*" (Even though they are reactionaries.) "*. . . We're in the third world war* *already,"* he sighed to an interviewer in the Washington *Post* last winter, *"and it is going straight to the terminus."* It isn't exactly clear why we have not yet reached the terminus. Away back in 1961 Vidal was writing that *"we have become a passive, ill-informed, fearful society,"* whose right wing *"has not yet had the courage to propose that some people be allowed to vote and some not to vote according, say, to the size of their income, but that is what they* [who?] *are after. For they mistrust and dislike the majority."*

Now wait a minute. The right wing mistrusts and dislikes the majority. As much as Vidal mistrusts and dislikes the majority? Indeed, shouldn't we *all* distrust and dislike the majority—if, among other things, the majority's memory "is about four weeks at best," as Vidal announced it to be in Miami? *"One must never underestimate the collective ignorance of that informed electorate for whom Thomas Jefferson had such high hopes,"* he told us in the spring of 1963. And now, a few years later, the majority was in even worse odor. Because *"it could be said that with almost the best will in the world, we have created a hell and called it The American Way of Life."* On the other hand, in other moods, and to suit other purposes, it is "the people" who are the foilees, rather than the foilers. At Miami, Vidal wrote, *"The public liked Lindsay but the delegates did not. They regarded him with the same distaste that they regard the city of which he is mayor, that hellhole of niggers and kikes and commies, of dope, and vice and smut. . . .* [One is left to infer, by Vidalian logic, that "the people" should—and one supposes, really *do*—approve of dope and vice and smut.] *So they talk among themselves until an outsider approaches; then they shift gears swiftly and speak gravely of law and order and how this is a republic, not a democracy."* "The people" were pronounced good by Vidal in an opening statement at Chicago. *"At Miami Beach,"* he reminisced about the people, *"the people*

*wanted Rockefeller but the politicians wanted Nixon.
Here, in Chicago, the people want McCarthy but the
politicians seem to want Humphrey. On Wednesday night,
we shall discover just how democratic the two political
parties are.*" Two days later he was saying in despair that
the Presidents we tend to get saddled with, in the instant
case Lyndon B. Johnson, "*reflect the mood of the
country.*" Which would certainly appear to be "the
people's" fault, it being "the people" who make up the
mood of the country, right? At a moment when the
Gallup poll was showing that Nixon was decisively and
exactly equally ahead of both Humphrey and McCarthy,
Vidal simply ignored the McCarthy showing, his endeavor
being, at that moment, to prove that the people were
against Humphrey. "*. . . there is a poll about to be
released,*" he said, "*. . . which is going to show that
Humphrey has got something like twenty-seven percent of
the vote against Richard Nixon who's got something like
sixty in that trial heat. . . .*" But of course the trouble with
putting Humphrey down, vis-à-vis Nixon, was that to do
so required that Nixon be put up; and, of course, this
interfered hugely with the antidemocratic melodrama of
Miami Beach, where Vidal had announced that if Nixon
were nominated, in the teeth of the demands of the people
who wanted Rockefeller, the people would not forgive the
Republican Party. . . .

By election night, of course, Vidal was utterly confounded, because "the people," in going toward Nixon,
obviously weren't behaving themselves. "*I have always
felt,*" he explained, "*that we must never underestimate the
essential bigotry of the white majority in the United
States.*" If the white majority is bigoted, why did it want
McCarthy at Chicago and Rockefeller at Miami? Or, all
along, did he really mean the *minority*? Let's see—the
minority who wanted Rockefeller—McCarthy; or the
minority who is bigoted? And then at Chicago (August
25) Vidal had said, "*Well, it is the greater wisdom, finally*

*to trust the people. In any case, we are trusting the people,
since the major politicians are entirely dominated by what
the polls say, as we witnessed at Miami Beach. . . ."* So:
the people—who are good—even though their memory is
only four weeks old—but they are wise—and wanted
Rockefeller and McCarthy—in spite of their essential
bigotry—but the politicians paid no attention to the
people—even though the politicians are entirely dominated
by the people:—and so on, into the mists of
unintelligibility.

Whatever difficulty Mr. Vidal had with "the people,"
he had none at all with the poor people, with whom he
identifies altogether. He does have difficulty in deciding
how many poor people there are all told, though he is
quite certain on the point that they will not be cared for by
a Republican administration.

"The United States," he announced on August 5, *"has
thirty million poor people in the ghettos, people that I am
afraid voted against you so heavily when you ran for
Mayor, Bill, when you kept reminding the Negroes in
Harlem, in one of your first efforts, to throw the garbage
out the window for that."* [I don't know, you figure it
out.]

I challenged the figure but was sharply rebuked.

*"I would say that Mr. Buckley as always has misstated
the case on poverty as he has on so much else. There are
over thirty million people living at the poverty line and the
Republican Party, according to the platform, which I read
very carefully, is going to benefit the insurance
agencies, the private interests, in great detail and nothing
at all for the people."*

Vidal's little-Marxist assumption that material interests
always govern occasionally got him into trouble. When he
was challenged to recite the practical evidence that
McCarthy knew the mind of the public, and was therefore
qualified to serve as President, Vidal first cited McCarthy's

support of Humphrey's anti-Communist bill of 1954, and then

V.: . . . *also, on two occasions,* [McCarthy] *supported the . . . oil lobby on the depletion of oil resources allowance of which I must say liberals take a very dim view, but I suspect you, with your oil interests and liking for that sort of lobby, would find quite commendable. So he can indeed make these "practical elisions" that you so much admire. I think he is a practical man.*

B.: *Do you think that Minnesota is such a heavy oil state?*

V.: *If Minnesota—what has that got to do with anything?*

B.: *What was the advantage in* [McCarthy's] *yielding to the oil interests?*

V.: *I dread to think but I—*

B.: *I know you dread to think. That's obvious. . . .*

Two days after giving the figure of thirty million, Vidal suddenly rescued millions of Americans from poverty.

"*As far as the mutiny in the land which Mr. Buckley refers to, of course, there is mutiny in the land. When you have sixteen million people in poverty and six million in abject poverty—these are actual statistics—and when something like ten to eleven billion dollars is needed to end it all according to Health, Education, and Welfare, I suspect that you are going to need some sort of a program.*"

So now there are not "over thirty million" but twenty-two million poor (whose poverty will end, we note in passing, with a one-time subsidy of $500 each). That was Wednesday. That weekend, Vidal wrote an article for *The New York Review of Books,* bewailing the events of Miami Beach, and speaking gloomily about the prospects, under a Republican Administration—"*for the forty million poor.*"

6.

In the interval between Miami and Chicago, I read *Myra Breckinridge*. I have thought and thought about it and resolved finally to describe and evaluate it and its purposes mostly by quoting from reviewers of the novel who cannot be suspected of sexual or cultural homeguardism.

"*Really*," said Gore Vidal during the spring after his novel's appearance, to an interviewer from *The National Observer*, "*the state of reviewing in this country is so low. There is so much dealing in personalities, even in respectable publications. You know, I had originally intended to let* Myra *go under a pen name—not because I was ashamed of her, but because I wanted her to stand on her own. I wish now I'd done that. . . . [But] I wanted to make* Myra *the kind* [of book] *I'd read myself. I did. I'm delighted.*"

From *Myra*, a sample—a bowdlerized sample:

I touched the end of [his] spine, a rather protuberant bony tip set between the high curve of buttocks now revealed to me in all their splendor . . . and splendor is the only word to describe them! Smooth, white, hairless except just beneath the spinal tip where a number of dark coppery hairs began, only to disappear from view. Casually I ran my hand over the smooth slightly damp cheeks. To the touch they were like highly polished marble warmed by the sun of some perfect Mediterranean day. I even allowed my forefinger the indiscretion of fingering the coppery wires not only at the tip of the spine but also the thicker growth at the back of his thighs. Like so many young males, he has a relatively hairless torso with heavily furred legs. . . .

In England, the authorities did not permit the distribution of the American original. However, the *New Statesman* observed:

> Despite the famed mutilations, the British *Myra* hasn't been severely ravaged: the operation leaves no fiery scars. The cuts are mainly in the rape scene: pink sphincters, rosy scrotum, 'the penis . . . was not a success.' The cruelty of this particular charade is so triumphant that it survives censorship. Also, it's far more gruesome than erotic—for those who don't love pain. In fact, *Myra* is more cerebral than bawdy.

Indeed.

"*Oh,*" said Vidal on the Merv Griffin show (November 18, 1968, "*Myra's not pornographic. It's extremely graphic, I suppose. It's a—describe certain sexual activities in great detail but I don't think—pornography is written to stimulate people, in order to make money for the writer. And I was not—I didn't—I don't write books to make money.*"

Griffin: "*You don't?*"

Vidal: "*People, though I'm not—I think now, I must say, in a way I would be more interested in exciting people perhaps than in writing for money.*"

Indeed. Vidal, the reviewers seem to agree, was engaged in other pursuits than moneymaking, even if he did not resent the pennies from heaven; it is gratifying, in fact, to make money from intellectual pursuits. "In an 'Afterword' to his revised early novel, *The City and the Pillar,*" the *New Statesman* observes, "Mr. Vidal announced that everyone is bisexual, while 'the idea that there is no such thing as "normality" is at last penetrating the tribal consciousness. . . .' "

In order to establish the abnormality of normality, the vehicle is homosexuality. "Not only are these nasty consequences in Vidal's little morality tale," wrote Marvin

Barrett in *The Reporter,* "he takes his lofty homosexual theme of twenty years back (then all high-toned sentiment), grinds it to sludge, and flushes it away with a lewd satiric chuckle.

"Only half kidding," Barrett continues—and there is the operative phrase—"he has Myra/Myron say: 'In the Forties, American boys created a world empire because they chose to be James Stewart, Clark Gable and William Eythe. By imitating godlike autonomous men, our boys were able to defeat Hitler, Mussolini and Tojo. Could we do it again? Are the private eyes and denatured cowboys potent enough to serve as imperial exemplars? No. At best, there is James Bond . . . and he invariably ends up tied to a slab of marble with a blow torch aimed at his crotch. Glory has fled and only the television commercials exist to remind us of the republic's early greatness and virile youth.' "

"Glory" has fled, along with—necessarily with?—the convention in favor of heterosexuality as the "normal" sexual relationship. We move in a different direction, as we are emancipated from surely the only prejudice commonly shared by St. Paul, Marx, and Freud. . . . "Some novels," writes Michael O'Malley in *The Critic,* "smell of beer, others of marijuana or perfume. . . . This one is soaked in estrogen. A tone entirely estrous: everyone in continual heat, an itchy, yowling, manic, pussycat heat that is right out of *The Pearl* and as ludicrous, as depressing. . . . The whole thing seems to have been written from a point of observation to the rear of the characters and about eighteen inches off the pavement. This may be a privileged angle to some but for me it produces almost at once a severe pain in the neck. The story itself is Odds and Ends. Rear ends. There are more bottoms here than in *Twenty Thousand Leagues Under the Sea.* The heart of the book—and the part where you throw up your hands *and* your lunch and realize that you're dealing with yet another pale echo of Genet's

masturbatory daydreams—is this rape. It just goes on and
on with an interminable homosexual nittyness. . . . Other
Odds against you include a masochist with a touch of
nymphomania, the rapee who turns sadist homosexual, a
Negro queen called Irving Amadeus, the profoundly
lesbian Miss Cluff, a rock group that practices bestiality,
the bisexual Gloria Gordon, a bit of a satyr, the obligatory
Hollywood orgy scene, and some business lifted from
Catullus to add tone. Catullus did it better."

But then Catullus had other things on his mind,
whereas *Myra* is plainly intended as allegory, in the
continuing crusade of Gore Vidal not only to license
homosexuality but to desacralize heterosexuality: in the
interest of a *true* understanding of human nature, such as
has not been nobly or ignobly understood by any
dominant philosophical or imperial figure since Plato and
the Twelve Caesars; and (bonus!) is in any case desirable
if only as the humane solution to pressing social problems.
"In other words," *Time* magazine commented, "the
remedy for overpopulation might be homosexuality."

But the allegory fails, straining vainly against
paradigms artistic as well as moral. "Is this *Paradise
Lost*"—asks *The Times Literary Supplement,* in a review
entitled, "Pathetic Phallusy"—"or merely a *Golden Ass*
penetrated? Milton, Blake said, was 'of the Devil's
party without knowing it'; Vidal, it seems, is of the Devil's
party—and knows it. For he connives with his temptress,
his tutelary female, the eternal aggressive whore, or *porné*
incarnate, deflating, deflowering the tumescent males.
Myra Breckinridge herself sees all life as a naming of
parts, an equating of groins, a pleasing and/or painful
forcing of orifices. Which is the essence, after all, of
pornography. All is referred to the phallic point, the
reductio ad absurdum of the genitalia. Nor is the response
spiked, but silkily sensuous to male buttocks, nipples,
pubic hair, and the whole repertory of male adornment
from jockey briefs to T-shirt and jeans. . . . Pornography,

then, is exhibited as the final metamorphosis of Existentialism: 'The only thing we can ever know for certain is skin.'

"Today," the *T.L.S.* concludes—even as the *New Statesman* sighed that "the sexual cook-outs will disturb many, as they are meant to; but the trans-sexuality can't be rejected as fantasy; since a fantasy that's so popular has surely acquired universal flesh"—"Today," *T.L.S.* succumbs, Kinseylike, "sex is metamorphosed as freely as fancy dress. And in his role of *arbiter elegantia,* Gore Vidal can write, without recourse to preposterous tableaux:

> It is the wisdom of the male swinger to know what he is, a man who is socially and economically weak, as much put upon by women as by society. Accepting his situation, he is able to assert himself through a polymorphic sexual abandon in which the lines between the sexes dissolve, to the delight of all. I suspect that this may be the only workable pattern for the future, and it is a most healthy one.

Vidal has thought seriously about the future. One year after writing *Myra* he proposed (*Esquire*, October, 1968) the dissolution of the family. Breeding complications? None he cannot handle: "The endlessly delicate problem of who should be allowed to have children might be entirely eliminated by the anonymous matching in laboratories of sperm and ova."

There is nothing left to be said about *Myra*. It attempts heuristic allegory but fails, giving gratification only to sadist-homosexuals, and challenge only to taxonomists of perversion: for the rest, for the millions, only the same excitement that depravity gives, that De Sade has given to six generations of people altogether healthy. But the homiletic failure of the allegory does not rob it of the seriousness of the effort. *Myra* is indeed more intellectual

than bawdy, even as De Sade was. Vidal is fond of
recalling that Alfred Whitehead once said that one gets at
the essence of a culture not by studying those things which
were said at the time, but by studying those things which
were not said. It will surely be said about *Myra
Breckinridge*, not that the shrewdest readers of it failed to
get the message, but that the responsible community
betrayed itself, finally, as indifferent: to so acute, so
crazed an assault on—traditional, humane sexual
morality; on the family as the matrix of society; on the
survival of heroism, on the very idea of heroism. It may be
that the cognoscenti consider that Vidal is a trivial literary
figure, and hardly a philosophical menace; that their
toleration of his effronteries, indeed their ignoring of
them, is merely an application of the Jeffersonian
principle that one's tolerance of those who would tear
down the republic is a monument to our democratic self-
assurance. But Jefferson said that such toleration was
appropriate on the assumption that "reason is left free to
combat" the nihilists. Reason is free all right. But who is
using it? ABC-TV? The half-dozen young black racist
anti-Semites in the New York public school system are not
about to usher in Buchenwald. Even so, reason and
passion were quickly and decisively mobilized against
them. The editor of a prominent news weekly, renowned
for its liberal opinions, told me that *Myra* was the only
book he had taken pains to hide from his adolescent
daughter—who probably read it before her father did,
assuming she can get the $1.25 to buy the paperback
edition and has a normal curiosity. Censorship is probably
not the answer. But with the repudiation of censorship,
something very strange happened. The corollary was
unthinkingly accepted that no one is censurable. "And on
my left, Mr. Gore Vidal, the liberal author, and
playwright, and novelist, whose most recent book is *Myra
Breckinridge*. Mr. Vidal, could we have your views on the
moral qualifications of the Republican nominee, Mr.
Richard Nixon, to serve as President?"

7.

And so we met again, at Chicago. No need to describe the surrounding tumult. The unhappy delegates could not give satisfaction. Lyndon Johnson was still powerful, but not so much so as to risk a personal appearance, not even to celebrate his birthday. Eugene McCarthy—it was somehow intuited—simply wouldn't do; indeed the Kennedy forces had, in inexplicit recognition of McCarthy's Presidential shortcomings, extruded Senator George McGovern, who, in his few personal appearances, had captivated the beholders; but he was a staying operation, clearly so—his practical role being secondarily the tacit repudiation of McCarthy and primarily a foot in the door for a blitzkrieg by Senator Kennedy.

For a while the official attitude toward Mayor Daley was tolerant—his was an adamantine history of pro-Kennedyism, and he forswore on Sunday the expected endorsement of Hubert Humphrey. So that the pressure on Daley mounted, and his ensuing ineptitudes might have been stagemanaged by Lowenstein and Unruh. In the turmoil, the delegates—and the public—reached hagiologically for the single nominee they knew they could not conscript, because Bobby Kennedy was dead. But his name, especially now that he was dead, was holy; even as Goldwater's would have been, if he had been assassinated minutes after triumphing over Rockefeller in the California primary (I can see John Lindsay at the Communion rail).

I trafficked on Robert Kennedy's prestige, though not, I like to think, in a way he'd have disapproved of. . . . It was on Tuesday, and the Vietnam plank was on the agenda. After a while Vidal made a pass at realpolitik. He yearned for the diplomacy of the nineteenth century, shorn of morality and pietism, and wondered whether, in fact, it wouldn't be clever of the United States to back Ho

Chi Minh, on the grounds that he and Mao Tse-tung were
natural enemies. (Virginia Kirkus was to comment on
Vidal's *Reflections upon a Sinking Ship*: "Vidal seems
fatally addicted to the worldly skeptical tone with a Boy
Scout aria tagged on at the end, rather like Vidal imitating
Talleyrand imitating Walter Lippmann.")

At the mention of Ho Chi Minh and the Vietcong, I
saw an opening I had been waiting for. . . .

B.: *Mr. Vidal's suggestion that perhaps it would be in
our interest to support Ho Chi Minh suggests* [to me] *that
as a matter of testamentary integrity, I should reveal a
concrete proposal contained in a letter sent to me by
Senator* [Robert] *Kennedy about six months ago,* the
P.S. of which was:*

"*I have changed my platform for 1968 from 'Let's give
blood to the Vietcong' to 'Let's give Gore Vidal to the
Vietcong.'* "

V.: *May I see that?*

B.: *I think, however, that* [giving Vidal to the Viet-
cong] *would be immoderate.*

Vidal was reeling.

V.: *I must say. . . . I must say, I am looking at this.
What a very curious handwriting. It also slants up, sign of
a manic depressive. I did see that. Whether you forged it
or not, I don't know. I would have to have my
handwriting experts, the graphologists would have to look
at it. I put nothing beyond you, not even in the Dreyfus
case when we had such evidence brought into court.* [Poor
Vidal had been reduced to blithering unintelligibility] *. . .
But it is very, very amusing and has nothing to do with the
case. In fact, his writing you letters makes me terribly
suspicious of him as a Presidential candidate. I will say
that. . . . Yes, I realize that, I recognize the handwriting.*

* I should have said "about a year ago." The letter was sent in
early April, 1967.

*Makes me very suspicious of what he might have been like
as President.*

Vidal had been oh-so-careful to stay clear of the history
of his feelings toward the Kennedys, for reasons both self-
serving and charitable. He had begun as an ardent admirer
of JFK. Then there was the affair at the White House,
after which he turned anti-Kennedy. It was rather hard for
him to become convincingly anti-JFK, in the teeth of his
own fulsome praise of him; but he took it out against the
Kennedy family and Bobby in particular (Vidal worked
conspicuously for Senator Keating against Bobby in
1964) in two interesting and discerning articles published
in *Esquire*. But now Robert Kennedy, freshly assassinated, had emerged as the stricken savior of young
idealism, so that not once had Vidal, in all the previous
sessions, spoken about Kennedy. Indeed shortly after the
assassination, Vidal had treated it as a personal affront,
final proof of everything he had been saying for years and
years and years about America. Interviewed by *Stern*,
he gave a most remarkable explanation for the murder of
Robert Kennedy, namely, the intensity of the hatred of
Kennedy in the town of Pasadena which, he explained to
his German readers, had housed and reared the killer.

*"Sirhan grew up in Pasadena, a center of the John Birch
Society, a center of radical right reactionaries, a despicable
blot on this earth. The people of Pasadena are well off.
They hate the Jews, they hate the Negroes, the poor, the
foreign. I find these to be really terrible people. Sirhan
grew up in this atmosphere and I do not doubt that he
heard many anti-Kennedy speeches. He simply accepted
the way people in Pasadena think. He decided that Bobby
Kennedy was evil and he killed him. . . ."*

One wonders what exactly the people of Pasadena read,
that so inflamed the assassin's heart.

*"There is no doubt that when Bobby goes before the
convention in '68 he will seem beautifully qualified. . . .*

but there are flaws in his persona hard to disguise. For one thing, it will take a public-relations genius to make him appear lovable. He is not. His obvious characteristics are energy, vindictiveness, and a simple-mindedness about human motives which may yet bring him down.

Was *that* the passage that caught the eye of Sirhan?

"To Bobby the world is black or white. Them and Us. He has none of his brother's human ease; or charity. . . . He would be a dangerously authoritarian-minded President."

Can't permit such a man as that to become President, can we, sons of Pasadena?

"In their unimaginative fierce way, the Kennedys continue to play successfully the game as they found it. They create illusions and call them facts, and between what they are said to be and what they are falls the shadow of all the useful words not spoken. The cold-blooded jauntiness of the Kennedys in politics has a remarkable appeal for those who also want to rise and find annoying—to the extent they are aware of it at all—the moral sense . . . to entrust him [Bobby] with the first magistracy of what may be the last empire on earth is to endanger us all."

The words, of course, are all Vidal's—did Sirhan read them? Vidal did not speculate on the question. The reporter from *Stern* did not question him on the subject. Vidal had little to fear from a reporter who accepted unquestioningly Vidal's learned intelligence that Sirhan Sirhan came by his anti-Semitism from the public school children of Pasadena, California.

8.

By nomination Time, Vidal had catalogued a considerable indictment of the opposition, and of me. The Republican platform was "war-minded"; Ronald Reagan was merely an "aging Hollywood juvenile actor"; I was what he had in mind in writing *Myra Breckinridge*; Nixon had "no discernible interest except his own" for running. He had denounced Nixon as a hypocrite who accepted racist support. He had deplored my "almost Stalinist desire to revise history," and pronounced me "the leading warmonger in the United States."

Chicago was seething with tension, objectified in the demonstrators' encounters with the Chicago police. ABC devoted itself, in the filmed segment preceding our own commentary, to an impassioned excoriation of the Chicago police superintended by ABC commentator John Burns. Vidal was thereupon asked by Howard Smith for the usual preliminary statement.

V.: *One of the more vivid pleasures* [what a strange word to use] *of Chicago has been the spectacle of a Soviet-style police state in action. The police here are brutal. The citizens are paralyzed, and the right of peaceful assembly has been denied by Mayor Daley, who believes in order without law.*

B.: [Trying to focus on the political vectors—after all, Humphrey had just been nominated.] *The selection of Mr. Humphrey is what in a Republican context would be hilariously applauded as the choice of a moderate over against an extremist. But the American left are very poor losers and therefore it means trouble for the Democratic Party.*

The attempt to bring the discussion around to the nomination of Humphrey as Presidential candidate was ignored.

V.: *I think there's very little that we can say after those pictures that would be in any way adequate. It's like living under a Soviet regime. . . .* [He proceeded heatedly along the same lines until finally,]

Howard Smith: *I wonder if we can let Mr. Buckley comment now for a short while?*

B.: *The distinctions to be made, Mr. Smith* [I had

found that, under stress, I was better off addressing the moderator than Vidal], *are these: Number one, Do we have enough evidence to indict a large number of individual Chicago policemen? It would seem, from what Mr. Burns showed us, that we do. However, the effort here—not only on your program tonight, but during the past two or three days in Chicago—has been to institutionalize this complaint so as to march forward and say that, in effect, we have got a police state going here, we have got a sort of fascist situation.*

One young man approached me last night and said, "Are you aware that Mayor Daley is a Fascist?"—to which my reply was, "No. And if that is the case, why didn't John Kennedy and Bobby Kennedy, whose favorite mayor he [Daley] was, indict him as such, and teach us that we should all despise him as a Fascist?"

The point is that [some] policemen violate their obligations just the way [some] politicians do. If we could all work up an equal sweat and if you all would be obliging enough to have your cameras handy every time a politician commits demagogy or a businessman passes along graft or bribes, or every time a businessman cheats on his taxes, or every time a labor union [man] beats up people who refuse to join his union—then maybe we could work up some kind of impartiality in resentment. As of this moment, I say: go after those cops who were guilty of unnecessary brutality, [and] develop your doctrine of security sufficiently so that [you can know] when you don't have as many cops as you should have had—for instance, in Dallas, in November of 1963. You don't [then] go and criticize the FBI for not having been there, for not having taken sufficient security measures. But don't do what's happening in Chicago tonight, which is to infer from individual and despicable acts of violence, a case for implicit totalitarianism in the American system.

Vidal responded emphatically that nothing less than a

constitutional issue was at stake, that the demonstrators had sought nothing more than constitutionally guaranteed opportunities to voice their dissent.

V.: *These people came here with no desire other than anybody's ever been able to prove, than to hold peaceful demonstrations.*

B.: *I can prove it.*

V.: *How can you prove it?*

B.: *Very easily. By reciting the recorded words of Mr. Hayden of the SDS, of Mr. Rennie Davis of the Coordinating Committee—whose object has been to "break down the false and deceptive institutions of bourgeois democracy sufficient to usher in a revolutionary order." Anybody who believes that these characters are interested in the democratic process is deluding himself. I was fourteen windows above that gang last night, [above] these sweet little girls with their sun-baked dresses that we heard described a moment ago, and the chant between eleven o'clock and five o'clock this morning, some four or five thousand voices was sheer, utter obscenities directed at the President of the United States, at the mayor of this city, plus also the intermittent refrain, "Ho Ho Ho/Ho Chi Minh/The NLF/Is sure to win!"*

This is the way [they have chosen] of accosting American society concerning their brothers, their uncles, their fathers, who are being shot at by an enemy which wrongly or rightly nevertheless we are fighting. I say it is remarkable that there was as much restraint shown as was shown for instance last night by cops who were out there for seventeen hours without inflicting a single wound on a single person even though that kind of disgusting stuff was being thrown at them and at all American society.

Smith: *Our reporter, Jim Burns, said there ought to be a different way to handle situations like that.*

B.: *I wish he would invent it. Why don't you ask him*

*next time—maybe tomorrow?—to tell us how to handle
it. Because I'm sure the Republican Party and the
Democratic Party would* [gladly] *form a joint platform
which would suggest how to do it. . . .*

V.: *The right of assembly is in the Constitution, in the
Bill of Rights.*

B.: *Nothing on earth is absolute.*

V.: *That's right. We live in a relativist world. However, it is the law, it is the Constitution and . . .* [Vidal,
agitated—as I was—groped frantically for his ideological
querencia] *and let us have no more sly comments in your
capacity as the enemy of the people.*

The discussion turned blisteringly to the question of
what does the Constitution guarantee, what doesn't it,
with Vidal insisting on the blamelessness of the
demonstrators. . . .

V.: *When they were in the parks on Monday night,
when I observed them, watched the police come in like
this from all directions, standing. They were sitting there,
singing folk songs. There were none of the obscenities
which your ear alone seems to have picked up.* [What I
and my wife had heard, fourteen stories high was:
F — LBJ! . . . F — Mayor Daley! . . . —How do you
begin producing witnesses when there are, say, 50,000 of
them available?] *They were absolutely well behaved.
Then, suddenly, the police began. You'd see one little
stirring up in one corner. Then, you'd suddenly see a bunch
of them come in with their night clubs and I might say,
without their badges, which is illegal—*

Smith: *Mr. Vidal, wasn't it a provocative act to try to
raise the Vietcong flag in the park, in the film we just saw?
Wouldn't that invite—raising a Nazi flag in World War II,
would have had similar consequences?*

Vidal explained that there are different points of view

about the Vietnam War, and that *"I assume that the point of American democracy is you can express any point of view you want—"*

B.: (garbled).

V.: *Shut up a minute.*

B.: *No, I won't. The answer is: They were well treated by people who ostracized them and I am for ostracizing people who egg on other people to shoot American marines and American soldiers.*

And then it came—

V.: *As far as I am concerned, the only crypto Nazi I can think of is yourself, failing that, I would only say that we can't have. . . .*

Smith: *Now let's not call names.*

B.: *Now listen, you queer. Stop calling me a crypto Nazi or I'll sock you in your goddamn face and you'll stay plastered—*

Smith: *Gentlemen! Gentlemen! Let's not call names.* . . .

B.: *Let Myra Breckinridge go back to his pornography and stop making allusions of Nazism . . . I was in the infantry in the last war.*

V.: *You were not in the infantry; as a matter of fact you didn't fight in the war.*

B.: *I was in the infantry.*

V.: *You were not. You're distorting your own military record.*

Through it all one hears the pleading voice of Howard Smith: *Gentlemen, please, gentlemen, I beg of you;* and then, taking the conversation by the horns:

Smith: *Wasn't it a provocative act to pull down an American flag even if you didn't agree with what the United States is doing?*

V.: *It is not a provocative act. You have every right, in*

*this country, to take any position you want to take
because we are guaranteed freedom of speech. We've just
listened to a certainly grotesque example of it.*

I muttered something about lawful acts which are
nevertheless provocative, citing the projected hate-Jew
rally that George Lincoln Rockwell had planned to stage
in New York City a few years before, which Mayor
Wagner aborted by denying him a license. Vidal
maintained that such freedoms are absolute, and Smith,
reacting to instructions from the control board at which
the mesmerized executives finally rallied, no doubt to tell
him to get the two madmen off the air, interrupted:

Smith: *I think we have run out of time, and I thank you
very much for the discussion. There was a little more heat
and a little less light than usual, but it was still very worth
hearing.*

But it wasn't over. Situated as we were, in one corner
of the immense studio, at other parts of which ABC
continued ineluctably with its live broadcast for another
twenty minutes, we had, as was customary, very quietly to
unharness ourselves from our ear sets and then tread
noiselessly out of the room. My pulse was racing, and my
fingers trembled as wave after wave of indignation swept
over me—and then suddenly, about to deposit the
earphones on the table stand, I stopped, frozen. Vidal,
arranging his own set, was whispering to me. *"Well!"* he
said, smiling. *"I guess we gave them their money's worth
tonight!"*

I reached my trailer after taking great strides through
the maze of technicians, operators, executives, reporters,
guests—all of whom looked at me as I stomped by and
then, quickly, looked away; afraid, perhaps, that I would
greet anyone guilty of a lingering glance with a sock on his
goddamn face. I reached my trailer, and there was chaos
there among my half-dozen friends, and my wife, who had

watched on the closed-circuit television. Everyone spoke at once, and then the door swung open—it was Paul Newman, longtime friend of Vidal. I want you to know, he said, working his jaw like Hud, I think that was the foulest blow I ever saw. I approached him feverishly: "Have you ever been called a Nazi?" I spat the words out at him. His voice mellowed. "That," he explained, opening his hands wide as one does in expressing the obvious, "was purely *political*. What *you* called *him* was personal!" I despaired; and motioned to the door, a gesture which the clamorous company, silent since Newman's arrival, by the strain of their necks and the inflection of their eyes, seconded by acclamation. And he left, slamming the door behind him.

The reaction was voluble. There were those who did not conceal a sense of bawdy-house excitement. *Time* magazine wrote that "Commentators William F. Buckley, Jr., and Gore Vidal made Mayor Daley and his cohorts look like amateurs in invective." ABC, which was in uproar, withheld the entire exchange from the western United States, where it would normally have run two hours after being seen live in the rest of the country. That would account for some papers' (*e.g.*, the Oakland *Tribune*) otherwise unaccountable failure to remark the provocation—"The boys were discussing the police violence, Vidal attacking the police and Buckley defending them," wrote Bob MacKenzie. "The insults became more and more heated. Finally Buckley blew his famous cool entirely. . . ." The New York *Daily News'* Kay Gardella delivered a prim rebuke for our "disgraceful" language and reported that a spokesman of ABC-TV had said that after the telecast Vidal "apologized to Buckley in his trailer office at the convention site. . . . [However] an apology was adamantly denied by Vidal when reached in his Ambassador Hotel

suite in Chicago. 'What would I have apologized for?' he
asked. 'It's Mr. Buckley who begins the personal attack.
I simply respond in kind.' " "ABC official Elmer Lower,"
the same story reported, "referred to the verbal volley
yesterday as 'intemperate language.' He said that 'ABC
was upset about what happened, but what can you do
except talk to the individuals and ask that it not happen
again?' " Well, you can of course do that much, which in
fact ABC did not do.

I wondered as the clippings came pouring in at the all
but universal conclusion that my outburst had identified
me as the equal of Vidal in intemperance. And worse.
Commentary magazine, shrewd and deliberate, wrote that
"it was really rather irresponsible to choose this pair as
the chief editorialists on the ABC team. Though their
political opinions certainly added up to a rather perilous
balance, the shameful pleasure of watching them match
wits had less to do with a search for political
enlightenment than with such archaic or illegal enter-
tainments as cockfighting, duels to the death, and
fliting. The effect was the opposite of edifying. Certainly,
Dr. Frederick Wertham must have been worried by
Buckley's scarcely controlled ferocity as he shook his fist
and drawled. . . . After drama like that, who could be
content to turn back to the maunderings of Carl Albert?" I
wondered that the editors of *Commentary*, of all people,
should apparently think it irrelevant to specify what it was
that catalyzed the scarcely controlled ferocity. One
wonders how the editor of *Commentary* would have
reacted if he had been called a crypto Nazi in the presence
of a dozen million people. Would he take the position that
that was merely a *political* charge, in a response to which
one has no reason to lose one's cool? If, in nonacademic
circumstances, you call a man a Nazi, are you evoking
ethnocentric nationalism—or Buchenwald? A single
editorialist—in the Arizona *Republic*—caught the point:

This was a smear of the worst kind. The New York *Times*, which was so mad it couldn't see straight when Spiro Agnew said Hubert Humphrey was soft on communism, ignored it completely. . . . In order to put the incident in better perspective, just suppose that Buckley had called Vidal a pro or crypto Communist. . . .

For days and weeks, indeed for months, I tormented myself with the question, What should I have said? Obviously my response was the wrong one if it is always wrong to lose one's temper, as I was disposed ("the wrath of man worketh not the righteousness of God") to believe that it is. Was my mistake that of going on TV at all, in the light of the abundant warnings, with Vidal (who says A, must say B)? Assume that. But even so, the question is not then answered: What *might* have been done within the narrow context? Could it be that my emotional reaction was defensible and even healthy, but that my words were ill-chosen? "The higher the stakes," C. S. Lewis wrote, "the greater the temptation to lose your temper. . . . We must not overvalue the relative harmlessness of the little, sensual, frivolous people. They are not above, but below, some temptations. . . . if they had perceived, and felt as a man should feel, the diabolical wickedness which they"—let us say the Nazis—"[were] committing and then forgiven them, they would have been saints. But not to perceive it at all—not even to be tempted to resentment—to accept it as the most ordinary thing in the world—argues a terrifying insensibility. . . . Thus the absence of anger, especially that sort of anger which we call *indignation*, can, in my opinion, be a most alarming symptom. And the presence of indignation may be a good one. Even when that indignation passes into bitter personal vindictiveness, it may still be a good symptom, though bad in itself. It is a sin; but it at least shows that those who commit it have not sunk below the level at which the temptation to that sin exists—just as the sins (often quite appalling) of the great patriot or great reformer point to something in him above mere self. If the Jews cursed more bitterly than the Pagans, this was, I think, at least in part because they took right and wrong more seriously."

Can it be that the rhetorical totalism of the present day has etiolated *every* epithet? It was a commonplace at Chicago to call the police and the mayor Fascists and Nazis, and the country yawned, indeed much of it expected that so should the police and mayor have yawned. Everybody gets away with everything. Paul Krassner of *The Realist,* addressing the kids at the Coliseum at LBJ's "unbirthday party," attaches the highest importance to impunity. "I have it on good authority," he yelled into the loudspeaker, "that when someone privately asked LBJ why he kept up the war, he answered, 'The Commies are saying F — you LBJ; and nobody gets away with that.' Well, tonight, as a birthday present, we are all going to say 'F — you LBJ—*and get away with it.*'" To that Coliseum William Burroughs dispatched a congratulatory message calling the cops dogs, and Jean Genet topped him and called them mad dogs, and Terry Southern said they weren't dogs but swine. Can such men understand the causes of anger in others? Understand the special reverence we need to feel for that which is hateful? I do not believe that anyone thought me a Nazi because Vidal called me one,* but I do believe that everyone who heard him call me one without a sense of shock, without experiencing anger, thinks more tolerantly about Nazism than once he did, than even now he should.

And then finally, the word I did use, which was "personal" in the understanding of Paul Newman—and a few others. Perhaps if I had merely threatened to hit him, that would have been all right. But to call him a queer—"I've been aware of you," one man wrote to me,

---

* This proved to be dead wrong.

months after the affair, and apropos of nothing, "since the old days when you were on the debating team at Yale and I sat and watched and listened. I admired you then, and since—until you called Vidal a 'homosexual' on TV. This reminded me—somehow and so much—of *Of Human Bondage* when Mildred called the doctor a 'cripple'. I mean, he *did* have a clubfoot, a limp, true, but it was wildly cruel of her to mention it. Dramatic, yes, but really hitting below the belt. I can't recall your doing this sort of thing in New Haven. Have you changed that much—and if so, why?" I don't know. I hope not (though unquestionably Yale hopes so). But don't you see, Vidal does not consider that he is clubfooted, rather that the conventional morality is. He is no more reluctant to suggest his tastes than Swinburne was—and everyone from Carlyle to Edmund Wilson has spoken and written about them—intending to be wildly cruel. *"In some ways,"* Vidal has written, *"I was lucky to be brought up with no sense of sexual guilt. I was never told that . . . it was particularly wicked to go to bed with boys and girls. I also went into the army a month after my seventeenth birthday, and there was very little [there] one didn't do. That established a promiscuous pattern which I'm sure has had its limiting side. But there have been compensations."* Vidal as usual writes loosely. One must suppose that very little of what we know is "wicked" we know because somebody took us aside and told us so. I don't remember, *e.g.*, being "told" that it was particularly wicked to kill someone, but I have nevertheless always supposed it to be so. And anyway, what does Vidal mean by the "limiting side"? And has that limiting side any obligation to try to survive? Evangelists for bisexuality must endure evangelists for heterosexuality. And the man who in his essays proclaims the normalcy of his affliction, and in his art the desirability of it, is not to be confused with the man who bears his sorrow quietly. The addict is to be pitied and even respected, not the pusher.

Such then have been my thoughts, acknowledgedly self-serving, but not empty, I think, of objective interest. It remains a fact that, as I began by acknowledging, faggotry is countenanced, but the imputation of it—even to faggots—is not. There may be occasions when the clinical imputation is justified, such occasions as were mentioned earlier—Robert Brustein's reviewing a play. But the imputation of it in anger is not justified, which is why I herewith apologize to Gore Vidal.

DON'T EAT GRAPES ALONG WITH ME

June 28, 1969

We have a softness for Ethel Kennedy, and therefore we weep. Imagine coming out of political retirement (incidentally, how fine it would be if she remained in political retirement and continued to inspire us all as a mother and a woman) in order to not eat grapes at a big social party in Southampton hosted by Ann Ford Uzielli, Charlotte Ford Niarchos, the Carter Burdens, the George Plimptons, the James Nivenses, and, as the press puts it, "maybe Anthony Quinn." That is what she is up to. Herewith, respectfully submitted, a few observations for Mrs. Kennedy, general and particular:

1. The ban-the-grapes movement centering upon the efforts of Cesar Chavez to unionize the grape hands in Southern California is, to say the least of it, incompletely informed. The grape boycotters are contending that the grape hands live in inhuman conditions and that all of this is the result of a few grape-growing monopolists who take ruthless advantage of the misery of immigrant Mexican farmhands, whose liberation is the cause of Cesar Chavez.

In fact, the situation is not as depicted. Two prominent Canadians who figured in the Toronto grape boycott a while ago have just came back from a tour of Delano—the center of the struggle—to report that the squalid living conditions Chavez speaks about are largely fictitious, that the workers oppose a union because they fear that it would limit their working hours and therefore their earning power: and that there are reasons to suspect that the high pressure being put on the area is rather imperialistic than compassionate: that what the AFL-CIO desire is a foot in the door to ease their way into the national scene as bargaining agents for all farm workers, which position would put their hands on $84,000,000 per month.

2. Ninety percent of the pickers are not migrants but permanent residents. Wages? The average farm worker wage in California is, according to the Department of Agriculture, the highest in the nation at $1.69. The average wage of the grape pickers is more than $2 per hour. Far from being owned by large corporations, all but two of Delano's seventy ranches are family-owned and operated.

3. If the grape boycott is finally successful, what will happen is very simply this: The grape growers will convert their vineyards into wine grapes, which do not need the human care that the other grapes need. That will result in the loss of thousands of jobs.

4. And now at a more general level, if we are in the mood to boycott people who displease us, it would appear that one ought to shop around a little more discriminately.

Does Mrs. Kennedy know that the beautiful people regularly eat Polish hams? These are produced by a state in which living conditions are materially poor, and in which there is a total lack of political freedom.

Isn't it possible that the clan will gather at Southampton in automobiles that use Liberian rubber? *Liberian* rubber. Have you ever been to Liberia and seen the working conditions there? Might they, at the party in

Southampton, offer tea? Tea from Ceylon? Nepal? Where the tea growers earn maybe $.10, $.15 an hour? Those who feel they'll need to flex their courage a little to prepare to boycott grapes might order vodka from the bar. Vodka made in Russia, for all we know, in concentration camps. With vodka, of course, one eats caviar, preferably Russian. It gets chilly in Southampton at night, so the girls may wear their sables, also tracked down by slave labor from the frozen wastes of Russia. If the customs authorities want to bust the party, I flatly guarantee them they will find some Cuban cigars, grown by—would you believe it?—un-unionized labor.

It will, in any case, be a dressy affair, so the ladies will wear their diamonds. Mined in South and Southwest Africa, by black men earning a pittance, working under inhuman conditions. Then, after the speeches, they will toast Cesar Chavez—with champagne, distilled from grapes picked in the champagne country in France by grape pickers who earn less than one half what they earn around Delano.

5. On the other hand, if we are to boycott coffee, sables, diamonds, cigars, caviar, and vodka and champagne, how will the beautiful people survive? They can't *eat* Ethel Kennedy. I mean, politics isn't *everything*.

6. So that the moral, dear Ethel, is never, ever, ever, ever join any committee, not even a committee to clean the streets, if its members are the Ford girls, George Plimpton, Carter Burden, and James Nivens. They are my brothers and sisters and I love them, but politically, well, you may as well ask Zsa-Zsa Gabor to rewrite the Constitution.

ON GAINING SOCIAL RESPONSIBILITY WITH
JACK NEWFIELD AND "JIMMY" BRESLIN

February 1, 1969

It has been remarked about Richard Nixon that he has made the effort, having been elected President, to embrace dissident political factions by honeyed ecumenicisms. He has earned a short season's tranquillity —Mr. Tom Wicker, for instance, couldn't find the grounds to criticize Mr. Nixon's first press conference; but he will, he will; never underestimate the willpower of ideology. I am myself experienced in the difficulties faced by Mr. Nixon's *mutatis mutandis*. I am not aware that I have made such overtures as the President has made to gentlemen of the left to come-on-over to my tent, folks. But the disconcerting thing about many of the lefties is that they consider themselves to have been courted even by gentlemen who are barely aware of their existence—a form of narcissism, no doubt, which is a very useful affliction in some people, particularly in those who, if they did not love themselves, would eliminate the entire potential field.

For instance? Well, for instance, Mr. Jack Newfield. STOP. Have you ever heard of him? I mean—other than you curators of the ideological zoos? Well, Mr. Newfield thinks you have; thus he writes matter-of-factly in a recent book review, "Everyone knew I was a personal friend of Robert Kennedy's." "Everyone" being, so far as I can figure it, everyone except everyone who didn't know that Jack Newfield was a friend of Robert Kennedy, indeed, who didn't know who Jack Newfield *was* a friend of; indeed, who didn't know who Jack Newfield was or, for that matter, is. Well, *I* know who Jack Newfield is, and indeed, I even recognize him on sight, because he approached me on an airplane one time last spring and chitchatted with me for quite a couple of minutes, about this and that. And that very evening, at Nashville, Tennessee, espying me in the lobby of the hotel, he introduced me to Mr. Tom Hayden, who is the founder, sort of, of the Students for a Democratic Society. Mr. Hayden greeted me about as Commander Bucher would greet the prime minister of North Korea if he happened on him at a motel in Nashville, Tennessee; leaving Mr. Newfield, who is advancing upon middle age, transparently terrified at having emulated such decadent middle-class values as civility; leaving him, in a word, positively uptight.

So Mr. Newfield looked for an opportunity to affirm the fidelity of his vows to incivility; and has now done so by proclaiming his personal immunity from my blandishments—which, if he proved it, would gain him that immortality he is otherwise unlikely to earn. "Wm. F. Buckley," he announces in print, drawling obviously over the sainted syllables, taking the same pleasure experienced by the Jacobinical court that sent the king to the guillotine, "has always been the favorite right-winger among literary radicals. His social friendships with Murray Kempton, Dwight Macdonald, and Norman Mailer have been well publicized. Buckley, in fact, has seemed to covet and thrive on these relationships: They give him . . . social respectability."

Now, I have enormous admiration for the gentlemen in question, and it is true that I have from time to time met socially with them, at which meetings we have discussed everything on earth save possibly Mr. Jack Newfield. But concerning social respectability, I am certain that no three people on earth would more quickly agree with me than the gentlemen in question on the proposition that did I covet it, I would perhaps begin by avoiding, rather than soliciting, their company. I last broke bread with Mr.

Mailer in 1964, with Mr. Macdonald in 1960, and with Mr. Kempton in 1967. I should be happy to share breakfast with them tomorrow morning. But it can hardly be suggested that anything I covet that ardently, I should pursue that indolently. Except by Mr. Newfield, who, everybody knows, was a friend of Bobby Kennedy.

Then there is Mr. "Jimmy" Breslin, who has announced in his syndicated column that I "head" his "list" of people he will not "nod to" during 1969. It is good that he published this declaration, else his proscription might have gone unnoticed, inasmuch as any actuary will give you a thousand to one that I would not in the course of a typical year find myself so situated as to give Mr. Breslin the opportunity to deny me his regal nod. "He thinks he's such a big shot," writes Mr. B. "In August in Miami Beach he went into a meeting—and at the end he said that anybody who had Jimmy Breslin hanging around him deserved a drink." Ah, so. What I said, commenting on that morning's column by Mr. Breslin reporting that John Wayne had traveled directly from the podium of the Republican Convention to the bar at the nearest hotel, was that so would I have done if I had had Mr. Breslin following me. I thought this, at the time, to be an exercise in rhetorical moderation, inasmuch as, when looking for a bar and in the company of Mr. Breslin, one hardly needs to search out an adjacent hotel.

Well, well. Mr. Nixon will not find it adequate, coveting social respectability, to seek out Mr. Newfield; and he must not, after a bout with Mr. Breslin, seek out the narcotic relief of the White House bar. But these are among the many trials of Mr. Nixon, as everyone knows: everyone, at least, who knows who Mr. Newfield is; and then some.

CRAWFIE STRIKES AGAIN

July 8, 1969

I do not intend to read the account by Mrs. Gallagher of the years when she served as secretary to Mrs. John F. Kennedy, but one must assume that the reports of that book which have been published in the newspapers diligently collect the most sensational revelations about Mrs. Kennedy—and they are utterly unsensational.

What is one to do, for instance, with the item that Mrs. Kennedy, even while living in splendor, instructed her staff to make the household purchases at stores which issued green stamps? I cannot see any meaning on the shady side of quaint that we can attach to that wholesome determination to take advantage of the little economies life makes available even to First Ladies.

It is not known whether Queen Elizabeth has given complementary instructions to her equerries, but it would not be antitraditional. During the war, King George would not permit his royal bath-pourer to put more than three inches of hot water in the tub, thereby joining in the common sacrifice to save fuel. (Most of England has had generations of experience in saving bath water, so that the ordeal was bearable.) Harry Truman was visited on the day that he left the White House by John Mason Brown, who thought to write about what a President does during the two-three hours before driving off with his successor to the inauguaration. What Harry Truman did was float about the offices opening drawers, and taking paper clips and 3 x 5 cards and pencils and putting them in his pockets, which he would periodically empty into a large vat destined for Independence, Missouri. Who thinks less of Mr. Truman for his husbandry?

Mrs. Gallagher attempts to make a contrast. After all, she rebukes her, wasn't Mrs. Kennedy spending $50,000 or more a year on clothes? So what? Lyndon Johnson was spending $150 billion a year on odds and ends, and ordering the lights turned off in the White House, in order to effect a few savings. Who thought less of him for that? Add up the cost of those little economies, and you have a major economy, as any householder knows. What point could Mrs. Gallagher be striving for?

That Mrs. Kennedy was stingy because she declined, at first, to raise Mrs. Gallagher's salary? But salaries are, in a free society, a matter for negotiation. Wages and prices are set, according to the wisdom of the ages, *secundum aestimationem fori*—according to the estimate of the marketplace. It may be that Mrs. Kennedy figured, quite shrewdly, that Mrs. Gallagher was being amply repaid in the light of the absolutely predictable commercial uses to which she would one day be putting her intimacy with her employer. If Mrs. Gallagher thought her salary too low, she had the option of quitting, an option which Mrs. Kennedy, looking back, must certainly wish she had exercised.

Mrs. Gallagher is obsessed with money. She writes that she was always convinced that there were two things John F. Kennedy wanted in his home, and that one of them was "no money worries." Alas, she sighs, Jackie was not able thus to satisfy her husband, if, in fact, he felt the press of money worries. The founding father was an unstinting provider, and it is estimated that John Kennedy had income from about $10,000,000, which at 5 percent means $500,000, plus $100,000 salary as President, makes $600,000, less taxes, makes $200,000, plus loopholes makes, say, $300,000. One's reserves of compassion somehow do not extend to worrying about John F. Kennedy's money problems.

And then Mrs. Gallagher says, "I sometimes thought it would be nice if Jackie would eat breakfast with the Senator." I think she meant to say, "I thought it would be nice if sometimes Jackie would eat breakfast with the Senator." On the other hand, one is about ready to settle for her saying simply, "I sometimes thought." Not often enough.

I cannot imagine anything in the world more exemplary than breakfast quite, quite alone, wherein to suffer, in solitude, the ordeal of reading the New York *Times*. I think it most understanding of Mrs. Kennedy to permit Mr. Kennedy the solitude of his breakfast hour, and I think more of her now than ever. Indeed if ever I accumulate a surplus, I shall send her some of *my* green stamps.

X. THE KIDS

THE TROUBLED CONSCIENCE OF ADAM PARRY

November 16, 1967

Sir Arnold Lunn once described a liberal as a man who defends the rights of conservatives, which definition would exclude a whole lot of ladies and gentlemen who think of themselves as liberals but would sooner die (though not in Vietnam) than extend to conservatives such rights as conventional courtesy.

Anyone who chooses to collect specimens has only to pick up the nearest net and go gamboling to the nearest college campus and catch the limit—I promise—before the sun has shaken the sleep from its eyes. My favorite recent example involves the impending invasion of Yale University by Governor Ronald Reagan, which some members of the university are wondering whether Yale can possibly survive *virgo intacta*.

The background is an extraordinarily modest bequest made to Yale, in years gone by, by an insurance gentleman called Chubb, proceeds from which are to be used to lure to Yale men engaged in public affairs, so that they might meet informally with students of Yale who desire to know something about life on the shady side of the ivory tower. The executor of this fund has been, in recent years, a scholar-aesthete of obstinate liberalism, Professor Thomas Bergin, who dreams at night of the beauties profound of Dante Alighieri, and of the urgent necessity to get out of Vietnam, more or less 50-50.

Professor Bergin has in the past ten years invited a great many Chubb Fellows to Yale, and by no means has it ever been suggested that he has slighted the liberal men of affairs, ridiculous and sublime, among whom have been Soapy Williams, Clement Attlee, Adlai Stevenson, Jesse Unruh, and Stephen Young. Occasionally Mr. Bergin has invited a conservative, *e.g.,* Barry Goldwater in 1963. And, on the fifth anniversary of Senator Goldwater's visit, he invited to Yale another conservative: Ronald Reagan of California.

Pregnant silence from the university. Until, a few days ago, a young professor of classics, Mr. Adam Parry, broke the silence and demanded that the invitation to Mr. Reagan be withdrawn. His reasons are that Mr. Reagan's politics are, of course, "odious," and that the invitation to him to be Chubb Fellow in fact confers upon the governor "money [$500 for three days] and honor."—and this implicates Yale in third world wars, atomic holocausts, and anti-intellectualism.

Professor Bergin replied calmly, as is the gentleman's wont, suggesting that Mr. Parry has altogether missed the point: that Chubb Fellows are not invited to Yale because their views are endorsed by Yale, but because they are men of affairs whose views and attitudes of mind Yale students might profit from having a look at.

Professor Parry replied indignantly that Professor Bergin clearly didn't understand that Yale was acting as a leg up for Mr. Reagan's alleged Presidential campaign. "To say that the Chubb Fellowship is not an honorary degree is a sophistic [the professor of classics meant 'sophistical'] evasion. It is an honor here being paid by a great university to a political aspirant, and will certainly be taken by the world as such." (The world will be amused at Yale's self-consciousness. Rather like when the littel town of Rome, Texas, telegraphed to the League of Nations in 1935 that lest there should be any confusion on the subject, it should be made clear that it was Rome, Italy, not Rome, Texas, that had launched the invasion of Ethiopia.) And then Professor Parry clinched his point aesthetically.

How could a decent intellectual be persuaded to mingle with Ronald Reagan? Parry replied. "The other fellows of the College are expected to drink and dine and engage in friendly conversation with him. My conscience revolts at the possibility."

Professor Parry's conscience is certainly a matter of universal concern, and I would be the last to suggest that it is anything less than dangerous to fail to humor it. But for those who believe that Mr. Parry is safely tucked away in the ideologue's isolation ward, there is the upsetting view of the undergraduate newspaper, the *Yale Daily News*, whose Donald MacGillis, surveying the objections of Professor Parry, comes out against withdrawing the invitation to Governor Reagan—on the grounds that to do so would be to create a national scandal from which Governor Reagan might take political advantage. "Across the country, headlines would trumpet Yale University's slighting of Ronald Reagan, a little man out in California who never presumably asked to be invited to Yale University. . . . The best answer . . . is that a retraction would be a worse mistake than the invitation. . . ."

Poor Professor Bergin. "I cannot well report how I entered it, so full was I of slumber at that moment when I abandoned the true way." That is what his liberal friends desire to hear from him, words of Dante which he never thought to apply to his innocent invitation to the governor of the largest state of the Union to visit a university which speaks so often of the virtue of toleration. Just think. A decade hence, ex-President Reagan, retired, might be able to say that he owed his office to the marginal nudge of Adam Parry of Yale University, who might then be persuaded to leave off his studies of the Golden Age of Greece, in order to report, at first hand, on the Golden Age of America, and his own glorious role in it.

AN EVENING WITH THE KIDS

May 6, 1969

In front of you in the cool spring air are a few thousand college students spread about, Tanglewoodlike, in the grassy amphitheater.

The campus is in tension. A court has issued a ten-day standing injunction against any further attempt to occupy one of the buildings. Illegally. This is deemed, by the black militants and the SDS, as an affront on the dignity of revolution. The president of the student council, a young man of spectacular poise and ability, introduces you and is occasionally interrupted by hecklers who call out against the injunction. You rise and begin an address in which you attempt an analysis of the causes of the student disorders.

With great difficulty. Because on your left is a band of black militants. They will laugh uproariously without provocation, carefully beginning and ending at the signal of their concertmaster. Over on the right, the apparently segregated white SDS uses the tactic of applauding at incongruous points in the address, *e.g.*, at the mention, in a passage on crime, of the slaughter of a student by a gang of marauders. The technique is clap-clap-clap-clap-clap, which is taxonomically different from the traditional booing and hissing of the heckler, but whose effect is, of course, the same in that it prevents the audience from hearing the speaker, who is in turn distracted.

But along he plods, thinking that surely the thousands will in due course discipline the few, to permit themselves to hear a speech which, after all, they came to hear. But they are silent, so that after about fifteen minutes, the speaker gathers together his notes and announces that he is finished speaking under such circumstances and strides back to his chair.

There is tumult, and the chairman rises and pleads with the militants to be quiet. They roar their disapproval of life in general, of the pervasive injunction, of the irrelevance of it all. The aroused majority begins to shout back. One young man rises and accosts the leader of the black militants and shouts, "Black is beautiful, but black can be stupid, too!"

The speaker is meanwhile whispering with the studer seated next to him, "Why do you people put up with i' "Because," he said, "the last time we ejected one of t' people, the chancellor gave us hell. We just can' anything, period. Especially not if they're black."

The council president shouts down the demonstra. and asks the speaker please to try again, which he does. This time the two flanks keep not exactly quiet, but quiet enough so that the others can at least discern the speaker's words. At the end, there is much applause from the thousands, which is their way less of complimenting the speaker, than of rebuking the demonstrators.

The question period is cut down after the second question, which takes the form of a tirade from a young man against the speaker and his failure to remark the cruelty of Americans in Vietnam, concluding with the charge that the speaker had condescended to him. To which the speaker replies that if anything he said had suggested that he condescended to such as the questioner, that was precisely what he had intended to communicate. The crowd goes wild with voluptuous delight. The speaker then adds that the country is at war in Vietnam and spending $80 billion a year so as to furnish an opportunity for the questioner to cultivate his ignorance and grow his beard. Delirious pleasure for the students, heated animadversions from the demonstrators, of the racist-pig variety.

The chairman thinks it best to call the program to an end and escorts the speaker through a throng of excited enthusiasts, apologizing for the disruptions. The SDSer tags along explaining that his beard grows without any encouragement at all from the Pentagon. The speaker reaches the sanctuary of the automobile, and the evening ends, the speaker confirmed in his suspicion that there is nothing at all wrong with the overwhelming majority of the students, whose intimidation is less the result of the raucous minority, than the result of the intellectual and moral abdication of their faculty and deans, who are made, like their cousins in Ithaca, out of Cornell jelly.

HARVARD AND THE POLICE

April 17, 1969

The whole nation, one gathers from the attention of the press, hangs in suspense wondering what Harvard will do. Understandably so. Because Harvard is the oldest university around and because Harvard's continuing reputation as (in some respects) number one derives in part from its sense of self-assurance. Harvard, it is popularly supposed, is even capable of being reactionary and getting away with it.

Will it—the melodrama has us at the precipice—actually *punish* the malefactors? Or will it go the usual route and produce a professor of whatever who will patiently explain in behalf of the faculty why it was—perhaps deplorable—but in certain ways understandable—taking every factor into consideration—never losing sight of the psychological strains of the day—bearing in mind the necessary consequences of the Industrial Revolution—to say nothing of the French Revolution—why it is perhaps understandable that some students should feel it necessary to sling college deans over their shoulders, march them down the stairs of the Administration Building, and fling them to the ground. After all, they did not fling them into the Charles River, which suggests the triumph of moderation. Up Harvard.

It will be a while—an eternity maybe—before us plain folk will arrive at an understanding of the faculty of Harvard, who so narrowly declined to censure President Pusey for calling in the police.

But the time surely has come to examine the psychological aversion to the institution of the police, which, one gathers, figured so largely in the discussions of the faculty. The position at Harvard, like the position a year ago at Columbia, is that the police are an evil thing. And it follows that to summon an evil thing to the campus is an evil thing to do. One professor at Harvard put it explicitly when he said that it is next to impossible to excuse the introduction into a college campus of policemen.

It is time to reevaluate the policemen. It is popular among American liberals in particular, but also among many American conservatives, to conceive of the policeman as the agent of repression. It is certainly true that most "governments" have, in history, used cops to repress rather than to liberate. Hitler's cops and Stalin's, like Genghis Khan's and Caligula's, were not engaged in expanding human freedom. The attempt to project that Cop as the same Cop who was summoned by Mr. Pusey is at least a failure in imagination; certainly a failure of intellect, which is supposed to be the thing that Harvard professors are best at not doing.

When, a year ago, Columbia was beleaguered by the revolutionists, Professor George Stigler of the University of Chicago wrote to the New York *Times* to observe that precisely the index of the successful college was the absence of any necessity for a resident constabulary.

Ideally, a college should have in it not a single campus policeman—well, maybe one who shepherds home the occasional boy who has drunk too deeply of the draught of fraternity life. To suppose, by such reasoning, that Columbia, or Harvard, would have hanging around a body of men sufficient to cope with 100 or 200 students who decide to ignore all the rules, occupy buildings, paralyze the educational process, belabor university officials—such a force does not and should not exist within a campus. The question then is: Do you call in the cops, or do you yield to such pressures as the whole of education teaches you to guard against: the pressures of brawn and fanaticism?

The point of this lesson is that policemen are, in certain circumstances, precisely the agents of civilization and humanity. Their availability is something that the forces of reason and enlightenment should celebrate, rather than deplore. The dogmatic rejection of the police by so many members of the Harvard faculty is sad testimony to their ignorance of the necessity, under certain circumstances, for the use of force. One wishes, forlornly, that the Weimar Republic had had more policemen, and that they had succeeded, back when it might have worked, in rescuing those who were so permanently, so tragically, victimized by the uproarious students who fought and bled for Hitler.

THE ROTC GAME

May 10, 1969

The first thing the president of the typical university does, upon announcing that henceforward ROTC students will receive no academic credits, is to assure his audience that the decision of the faculty was reached without any thought to the political situation, absolutely none at all.

That is, of course, sucker bait, and the presidents know it, but they have become so much accustomed to dissimulation, which they practice upon the alumni as if they had PhD's in the subject, that they can manage to keep straight faces while saying such crooked things. Sure, anti-Vietnam sentiment had nothing to do with deciding to drop ROTC credits, and the New Hampshire primary had nothing to do with Lyndon Johnson's retirement. Sure, ROTC doesn't warrant academic respectability, but Eldridge Cleaver does. . . .

Here are a few points which the college presidents have not treated. One of them is: Why—if properly taught—*shouldn't* ROTC training earn credits? It is widely imagined that ROTC consists in marching up and down the quadrangle with rifles on one's shoulder. Sure, there is some of that. But much more is the classroom work. Now if the classroom work is unimaginative and consists only in the rote learning of drill manuals of one sort or another, then obviously academic credits are not in order.

But if that *is* the case, one wonders why the administration and faculty voted to give credits to ROTC in the first instance. It is not widely known that ROTC appears on campus not because the Pentagon, at some point in the past, dispatched a military expedition to the local college, posting nonnegotiable demands. A contract is negotiated and signed, and these contracts have called for the granting of academic credits. If university officials did not take the trouble to ascertain that the ROTC staff would devise a curriculum of academic consequence, then the dereliction is the university's.

Or are they saying that there is no body of knowledge presentable by an ROTC? That would be a strange position to take, particularly by those militants who hug to their bosom the collected works of Mao Tse-tung and Che Guevara and the gang, on the tactics and psychology of guerrilla warfare. If there is a body of knowledge to revolution, surely there is a body of knowledge to counterrevolution? Why, if the subject is academically jejune, do we acknowledge the "science" of warfare? What of the related paramilitary subjects, concerning which some of the most interesting theorists of human behavior have addressed themselves, stressing diplomacy, public psychology, propaganda, and the rest?

Is it idle to study military history? Or geopolitics? Or strategic geography? Or the relation between the psychology of a culture and the relevance of the weapon? Couldn't a highly instructive semester—at the very least—be devoted to an examination, for instance, of the intellectual relevance of the arguments and the tactics of the North Vietnamese during the currect war?

And then the other point. The movement now is not merely to deprive ROTC students of academic credit, but to ban ROTC from the campus. Why? I mean, why does the majority of the student body, or of the faculty, undertake to dictate to an individual student what he can do in *his* spare time? If he desires to drill with a master sergeant, or to otherwise satisfy Reserve Officers Training requirements, what business is it of the busybodies on campus, who prate about academic freedom—while designing a curriculum geared to their own neurotic lusts? The ROTC—here is an interesting and, so far as I know, heretofore unpublished datum—has, at this writing, received not one communication from one college in America announcing the abridgment, or rescission, of an outstanding contract. That means that students are entitled even to academic credits, until that contract expires. What then? Is ROTC to set up shop, like Berlitz Schools, unrelated to the college in any formal way?

What, then, will the student and faculty do, in pursuit of their goal of unconditional victory? Ask that any student who spends his afternoon at the local Berlitz-ROTC institution be punished? Expelled? Publicly flogged? One weeps for the end of reason.

COMMENCEMENT DILEMMA

June 19, 1969

It was a dramatic scene, helped out by wind squalls that rattled the canvas that stretched over the dignitaries who sat, the archbishop on his throne at the center, facing the bleachers at Roosevelt Stadium to witness the commencement ceremonies and to confer a half-thousand degrees on the graduating class. There had been preliminaries. During the "Star-Spangled Banner" a half-dozen students and spectators raised their clenched fists, a general symbol of undifferentiated defiance made popular by a black athlete at Mexico City during the Olympics last fall.

Then the valedictorian came to speak, a grim and intelligent young man, whose words were indistinctly heard because the wind and the canvas were now flogging and whipping like a badly trimmed sail. But the idea was plain, and about one-fifth of the students were rapturous: The college was no good, the system was no good, America is no good, and things had to change NOW! Boos from the majority, lusty applause from the minority. Then thirty or forty students walked ecstatically out of the stadium intending to register that for them, the commencement was over.

But the climax was to come. The class prizes were distributed. The president of the college called out the recipient who came, received the award, and accepted the congratulations of the archbishop, shaking his hand or kissing his ring. One girl, taking the prize, walked directly to the old archbishop, turned her back on him, and raised her hand in the salute of defiance. No umpire was ever booed more vociferously at Roosevelt Stadium, and the applause was a little tentative. Had she overdone it?

As we sat there, Nelson Rockefeller was speaking at Dartmouth College, explaining the plight of the cities, and receiving yet another honorary degree. Forty students stood throughout the duration of his speech, their backs turned on him. Why? Because he is a member of the Establishment.

At Harvard, moments before the commencement exercises, the SDS approached President Pusey and informed him that unless one of their number was permitted to speak, they would disrupt the entire proceedings. Capitulating, President Pusey granted the speaker ten minutes. He took eighteen.

At Brown University, three-quarters of the senior class stood and turned their backs on Professor Henry Kissinger. Why? Because he serves President Nixon as a principal adviser and has not, manifestly, prevailed upon the President to do in Vietnam what the majority of Brown seniors would do in Vietnam if only they were President.

Sir Harold Nicolson wrote in one of his books that he

suspected that the persecution of the early Christians came about less because the Romans found the Christians' dogmas offensive, than because they found their manners intolerable. It is the manners of the current dissenters, more even than their deeds, which arouse true, deep, even savage antagonisms. At Roosevelt Stadium, as a part of the ceremony, several dozen seniors received their commissions in the Army after four years in the ROTC. A perfectly normal ceremony, and the young men were entitled to the polite applause of the crowd. But what they got came closer to adulation. The near-hysterical applause was in direct reaction to the provocations of the dissenters.

The reason why is obvious. One protester, heckling the principal speaker, was seized by the cops and dragged out —so much for that. But what does one do about the man who burns the flag, the girl who violates sacerdotal proprieties, the band of students who turn their backs on someone who is called on the scene to be honored? Where reason does not obtain, power will, and this is the ugly truth the growing consciousness of which is haunting more and more people. You cannot have ceremony without a certain decorum, and you cannot have a workable society without ceremony. The choice society is being handed is to abandon ceremony, or to repress demonstrators.

MIDDLE-CLASS VALUES

March 27, 1969

I thought I had seen everything—I hoped I had—in the student world of unreason. But the all-time champion effrontery was as yet uncommitted. It was left to a

seventeen-year-old Negro boy called Rickey Ivie whose
Black Student Union has touched off disorders in a Los
Angeles high school in a demonstration against "racist
training." An example of that training is the inclusion in
the curriculum of the music of Johann Sebastian Bach. He
is described by Master Ivie as "that old, dead punk." "In
the world of music," he explains, "the schools keep
imposing middle-class values in teaching us about Bach."

I sat next to a middle-class French countess the other
day who announced to me that she did not like Bach. I felt
like asking her, did she like color, or fresh air, or
trees—when suddenly I realized that she figured that her
dislike of Bach was *Bach*'s fault—such is the egomania of
democratism. If one really doesn't like Bach, why I
suppose one shouldn't listen to him. But one should then
be disturbed about oneself, not about Bach.

The remarkable thing about young Ivie isn't, one
supposes, that he doesn't like Bach—probably he has
never let himself listen to Bach. It is that as author of such
a remark as he made about Bach, he hasn't become the
laughingstock of his fellow students. Eccentricity is one
thing (the late publisher of the New York *Times* specified
that no Mozart should be played at his funeral). To call
the greatest genius who ever lived an "old, dead punk,"
the least of whose cantatas will do more to elevate the
human spirit than all the black student unions born and
unborn, is not so much contemptible as pitiable:
conducive of that kind of separation one feels from
animals, rather than from other human beings.

George Tyrrell once observed that there is as much
difference between a Christian and a pagan as there is
between a pagan and a dog. The point survives the
exaggeration. Those who cannot love Bach are to be
pitied. Those who believe that Bach should not be
admired should be despised.

One sees, over and over again, the use of "middle-class
value" as a devil term. In playing Bach one is practicing a

middle-class value. Yes, says Rickey, "the only culture the schools deal with is WASP culture. That's why we are deprived." Take, for instance, Van Gogh. "They teach us about Van Gogh. What did he do? He cut off his ear and sent it to a prostitute. That art is no good."

More likely, that art teacher is no good. Though one supposes, sadly, that that art teacher, having spent years in cultivating his admiration for the masters, can only hold the attention of the children by telling about how Van Gogh cut off his ear and sent it to his prostitute. Like teaching *The Federalist* by recounting that Hamilton was killed in a duel.

The middle-class values we are supposed to contemn. One wonders what exactly they are. Bach and Van Gogh? If so, middle-class values are off to an unimpeachable start. Materialism? But Rickey's BSU never ceases demanding material benefits. Color teevee? But nothing is so popular in a good riot as color teevee, and whiskey. Whiskey? It is disdained by Elijah Muhammad, but it is not by any means universally abhorred by the new left. Thrift? Is that a middle-class value? Perhaps. And without it there would be no surplus. And if there were no surplus, Rickey would be having to pay for his own education, which, come to think of it, he would be manifestly better off without. "The history they teach is not factual," he complains. "George Washington was a slave owner. They don't include black people in history books." But if they don't, how does Rickey know that George Washington had slaves?

It is very depressing, because the rhetorical escalation is totally out of hand. If Bach is a punk, then the human dislocation is total, and nothing at all is worth striving after, not peace, or freedom, or good relations between the races.

ON LOWERING THE VOTING AGE

March 8, 1969

During the Presidential campaign, Mr. Nixon made an unfortunate commitment to lower the voting age to eighteen. Now he has asked the Attorney General to advise him whether this ought to be done by a constitutional amendment, so as to lower the age uniformly for all federal elections, or whether the President should simply encourage the individual states to reform their own laws, as Nelson Rockefeller has been urging the legislature in Albany to lower the voting age. At first glance one would hope that Mr. Mitchell will make the second recommendation or that if he makes the first, Congress will promptly disobey him.

Lowering the voting age has become something of a cause among very young people, who believe that as things now stand they are denied effective participation in democracy. That is, of course, true—although participation in a democracy is not necessarily the highest value, the higher value being freedom. At some colleges and universities which are governed by students, the student is less free than at some which are governed by faculty and administration. It is the kind of government one has, rather than who it is that midwifes it, that matters; and this surely has a bearing on the question of whether to lower the voting age.

To begin with the voting age is arbitrary. If it is contended that nowadays youth are mature at age twenty-one in the relevant sense in which they were not mature at twenty-one when the Constitution was written, then the struggle is over the question—is that true or is that not true? There are those who believe that the contrary is true. That 200 years ago young men and women had much earlier than today to take active responsibilities. They married, bore children, earned their living, protected their homes, participated in civic enterprises, and generally exposed themselves to the consequences of government the form of which they were accordingly better qualified to express opinions on.

Such in any case is the countercontention, and one wonders whether Mr. Mitchell will give a moment's thought to that particular question or whether, more likely, he will be asked to weigh the political consequences of any action publicly advocated by Mr. Nixon. In any case, the question of whether youth are more or less mature than they were in previous centuries is moot, and the only sensible way to retreat from the arbitrary age of twenty-one is to specify that anyone may vote at any age upon passing a rudimentary examination.

Ah, but that, of all measures the most suitable for measuring the claims of youth, is least likely to satisfy them. The trouble with examinations is that some people fail them. And in democracies, people must not fail examinations—that hurts people, who then proceed to hurt the politicians. And anyway, it is also common knowledge that some of the people who are first-rate at passing examinations shouldn't be allowed to vote for a kindergarten teacher. Imagine a society governed by people elected by Susan Sontag!

What other claims might be called reasonable? That if someone is old enough to die in Vietnam, he is old enough to vote? But, of course, it does not follow. He is, after all, old enough at age fifteen to breed children, which does not make him old enough to be a father. After all, would the reverse apply—that when a man becomes too old to fight for his country, he becomes too old to vote for it? Bad logic, all the way around. What, then, are we left with?

As usual, the political question. It is generally recorded by political scientists that newly enfranchised voters are, for a period of time, grateful to the party that enfranchised them. The Whigs made a big thing of it during the nineteenth century in England, as did the Republicans and then the Democrats here in vying for the Negro vote.

Nixon is on the spot because he made the commitment, specifically, while campaigning. Although it is perfectly honorable, upon the consideration of additional evidence, to change one's mind, it is unlikely that Nixon will change his on the general proposition. So that although Mitchell would be wiser to recommend that the matter be left to the states, he would probably be more prudent in recommending a Constitutional Convention. Because the former course of action might actually move some states, whereas the latter would almost certainly fail of passage.

MY PYGMALION

November 27, 1969

I have found myself—assuming he will agree—an ideological Pygmalion. He is nineteen years old, a second-year student at a big college in Pennsylvania, all beard and beads from the chest up, and below that, scruffy gabardine. I cannot describe his face, never having seen it, and he sat next to me one evening in the car that took me to the airport after my lecture, driven by another student, with yet others in the back seat, one of them with a tape-recording machine asking such questions as "What do you and your son talk about?"

My Pygmalion is interested in grander themes. To say that he comes to politics with *tabula rasa* would cause the founding of a Tabulae Anti-Defamation League. My Pygmalion says things like, "Like, I jus' don't figure how you come and give a speech and say you're for Vietnam and collect your fee and then jus' go away, like man, you don't know what it means, you make war sound cool. I'm not going to Vietnam and have my face blown off or my arms or something, why should I?" I looked at him and wondered, from the depths of my fatigue, where to start, where to start. I tried the usual analysis. Look, I said, wars are not beloved of the warmakers, at least not as a general rule. Look, I said, wars are because there is something worse than wars, like life in Russia or in China or in North Vietnam. Look, I said, if you don't want to live in America because you think America is diseased and makes decisions that involve other people's heads and limbs being blown off, you can do something about it, including leave America.

"If I'm going to split," my Pygmalion said, "I'm going to think about it first." I didn't say that that experience might prove more painful even than going to Vietnam. "I went to the Iron Curtain countries this summer," he said, "like even to Albania," he said, "and they weren't so bad. On th'other hand,"—he speaks gently, like St. Francis speaking to the birds—"I know they didn't show me what they didn't want to show me." He smiled. We reached the airport in time to have a drink or a coffee before the flight. The others ordered a daiquiri or a whiskey sour or a beer, but Pygmalion ordered a coke; he doesn't drink booze. At the gate he said he wanted to tell me something private. I leaned over, and what he said was, "Look, if you want, I'll go on the plane with you to New York and you can explain all those things. Don't worry about the money; I'll use my student pass." No, I told him—abruptly, I fear—it's too late at night. But I sensed that he felt the shock of rejection, so I said, Look, call me up, here's my private telephone number. "When?" "Between two thirty and three thirty tomorrow afternoon." I got to my office at

2:35. He had already called and was told I wasn't in. He did not leave his number, or call again, and I knew that he thought that I had put him on, like the military-industrial complex.

But then a week went by and his easy-soft voice came over, like he was coming to New York to work for Lindsay before the election, and did I want to visit with him. Of course, I said.

He got there a little early and slipped into the secretary's office wearing a weather-beaten coat, which he took off and plopped smack in the middle of the floor, and then he leaned on the filing cases and made some gentle talk. Miss Bronson gave him a book of mine and he slid it between his back and his belt, where it rested comfortably, and in due course he came in and we chatted.

Mostly about marijuana, which was on his mind, and in any case was less depressing a subject to discuss than John Lindsay. What the matter with grass? Well, I said, nobody knows exactly, but just to take one specific thing, you can't tell if someone's had grass, but people who have it lose control and, for instance, can run over kids. Grass doesn't affect a driver's control, said my Pygmalion. Yes, it does, I said, because I know a doctor who says so and who writes for the New York *Times*, and nobody who writes for the New York *Times* and is a doctor doesn't know what he's talking about, right? He smiled his shy smile, and I felt terribly inadequate. We drove off, I took him to the subway to catch his train to Brooklyn, where he was poll watching for John, and now I have a letter from him:

"Dear Mr. Buckley,

"During our discussion on pot you said something to the effect of one of the results of legalizing pot would be an increase of auto accidents due to stoned drivers. I must confess that during the time we visited I was completely stoned. The reasons that I smoked pot before I came to see you were several and one was not because I thought it would be cool to see 'Mr. Buckley' from a stoned vantage point. But rather (a) a complete stranger gave me a few joints (b) I was afraid to carry joints on my trip to see you (c) I met a groovy cop who wanted to turn on so naturally I turned on.

"I hope that during the time we met I conducted myself in a fitting manner (whatever that may have been) and if so I present proof that a person can control himself while being stoned. Therefore I hope I have dismissed your fears that legalizing pot will increase the rate of irresponsible acts committed by heads. Sincerely — I thank you most gratefully for meeting with me."

Well, as I was saying, the rines in Spine fall minely on the pline.

XI. MANNERS, MANNERISTS

HAIR

May 7, 1968

"This, folks of the Psychedelic Stone Age," says Claude, in the Broadway musical production *Hair*. Claude opens the show by declaring that ". . . I'm a genius genius/ I believe in Gawd/ And I believe that Gawd/ Believes in Claude/ That's me, that's me." Of course, Claude doesn't believe in Gawd—nobody does in the cast of *Hair*, because they are far too sophisticated, provided one understands that paganism is sophistication.

The stage notes are explicit. *"Hair,"* which is called an "American tribal love rock musical," is about "what's happening now. The tribes are forming, establishing their own way of life, their own morality, ideologies, their own mode of dress, behavior; and the use of drugs, by the way, has a distinct parallel in ancient cultures, in trival spiritual tradition, both east and west."

Indeed it does, and whoever said that the hippies are any different from the Adamites? "Note should be taken," the notes continue, "of the spiritual theme running through the play; outer space, astrology, the earth, the heavens, interplanetary travel, mysticism . . ."

And so a great deal of energy—and talent—go into the production of this psychedelic extravaganza. It serves up everything from the shock counter: Boys love boys, American flags are desecrated, all of those tired old four-letter words are used, there is male and female nudity, a leavening of sacrilege. The music and action are engagingly energetic, without having that frenetic feel which, like when Jimmy Durante starts breaking the piano, is a snake-bite substitute for entertainment. The obscenities fail somehow to shock. The nudity is less remarkable by far than the posturings at the stripper joint. There are a few very false notes, as though an IBM programmer calculating a continuous shock, had accidentally blipped into normalcy, disturbing the evenness of the iconoclasm. But in the end the experience is saddening. "Now that I've dropped out/ Why is life dreary dreary/ Answer my weary query/ Timothy Leary dearie," Claude comments. But Dr. Leary never answers the weary query; and never will.

How could he? Or anybody else? The hot blood of youth today *begins* tired. "Hey, lady, can you spare a handout, something for a poor young psychedelic teddy-bear like me? To keep my chromosomes dancing?" Quite impossible. The chromosomes react only to narcotic transfusions of drugs and iconoslasm, and even in *Hair,* the iconoclasm begins to cloy. And the uplift is, well, somehow just a little square. "I'm/ Uncle Tom and Aunt Jemima/ Voodoo zombie little black Sambo/ Resident of Harlem/ and President of/ the United States of Love."

The fun stuff here and there turns you on, with such oxymoronic posters as "Ronald Reagan Is a Lesbian." The ideological exhortations are pretty drear, out of the poetry section of the *Daily Worker:* "What do we think is really great?/ To bomb, lynch and segregate/ What do we

think is really great?/ To bomb, lynch and segregate."
There is an element of self-doubt, as though the young
authors knew intuitively that the hocus-pocus is, somehow,
done by rote. "Hair hair/Hair hair hair/Hair hair hair/
Flow it/ Show it/ Long as God can grow it/ My hair
Let it fly in the breeze/ And get caught in the trees/ Give
a home to the fleas/ In my hair."

The moralizing is, well, embarrassing. One is here and
there breath-catchingly suspicious that in spite of the
occasional spoofing, there is a hint of self-seriousness.
"Oooooo, these boys love to dress up like this. . . . I love
them. . . . I love all of you. . . . I wish every mother and
father would make a speech to their teen-agers: 'Be free
. . . no guilt. . . . Be whoever you are. . . . Do whatever you
want. . . . Just so you don't hurt anyone.' "

But the trouble, of course, is that you do hurt someone.
You hurt yourself, just to begin with. André Malraux
once put an end to a hectic discussion about the
shortcomings of modern art by saying simply, "But that's
the way our painters paint."

In a sense Malraux was quite right: If that is the way
the painters paint, and this is the way a creative section of
our youth writes musicals, then we must necessarily take
them seriously. What is interesting is less what comes out
of the misdirection of their talents, than that they should
choose so to utilize them. Youth is very mixed up—so
what else is new? Adults are very mixed up, too, which is
one of the reasons why the youth are as they are. Let them
be. But the responsibility of the adult world is to hang on
to one's sanity. Seeing *Hair* makes one just a little
prouder of middle-class establishmentarian standards.

HOW I CAME TO ROCK*

August 24, 1968

I speak for those who have had difficulty cultivating a convincing admiration for the popular culture of the rockers, foremost among them, of course, the Beatles.

Those who were not born into the movement can usually remember their first experience with it. Mine is vivid. I first remember engaging rock on learning years ago that a Mr. Alan Freed (1) was very famous; (2) was generally credited with launching the new musical form; and (3) had bought the house a couple of dwellings down from my own in the country; whence (4) he was broadcasting three hours daily as a network disc jockey.

He and his wife came calling one day. It was late on a summer afternoon, and I had been up the night before, and my mind wandered as he talked about this and whatever. My watchful wife managed, unnoticed, to nudge me. I jerked back into consciousness and, fumbling for something apposite to say, ventured with, "Tell me, Mr. Freed, do you know Elvis Presley?" This elicited for my wife a shaft of social despair such as to make me feel that I had just asked Mr. Gilbert whether he had ever heard of Mr. Sullivan. Alan Freed, upon recovering, explained to me that he had *discovered* Elvis. I couldn't think what was appropriate to say under the circumstances, but, having to say something, I asked, "Is he nice?" "Is he nice!" Freed responded, clearly indicating that I had moved from ignorance into idiocy. "Why, do you know, he makes *ten*

* Reprinted by permission of the *Saturday Evening Post*.

times as much as I make, and *he* calls *me sir!*"—he slapped me on the knee, so that I might share with him the full force of the paradoxes of life. I had, by that time, come to and was now a working member of the band. I knew—I have a sense, baby, for that kind of thing, only just warm me up—I knew where to go from there, and all those bits and pieces of information I had run across in years of traversing the newpapers and magazines since first the phenomenon had occurred focused into the question which was totally to redeem my previous ineptitudes: "But will the rock and roll movement last?" My guest was made a happy man. He answered that question as lustily as the evangelist being asked whether God exists. Will it last! Why, he said, I must have appeared on one million panel discussions where they asked me just that question, and I told them all, I told them, rock and roll is here not just for a month or two, not like Davy Crockett and hoola hoops, it's here *forever*. What was my opinion? he asked dutifully. I don't know, I said, I've never heard it. He told me numbly that the next day he was giving a party, down the road at his house, celebrating an anniversary, and Fats Domino and his orchestra were going to play, and would I like to hear some real rock. Indeed I would, I said; and we strolled over, my wife and I, not at the hour of seven, as suggested, but at ten, knowing the likely length of the preliminaries; but when we got there, we found Fats and his entire group, fully clothed, in the swimming pool, their instruments somehow unavailing. But Mr. Freed, still shaken by my question of the night before, was clearly concerned that I should not arrive at the impression that here was a sign of the deliquescence of the art: "Don't you forget it," he said—only a few months before being indicted for provoking to riot by musical orgy, and a very few years before his sad, unrhythmical death—"Rock is here to stay." He was, of course, right.

And he had persuaded me to make a serious effort. I

spent an evening—a very short evening—listening to one part of my son's collection. I found the noise quite scandalous. I remember a critic, writing for *National Review* after seeing Mr. Presley writhe his way through one of Ed Sullivan's shows, remarking that an extrapolation from the demure bumps and grinds of Frank Sinatra, on to the orgiastic b's and g's of Elvis Presley, suggested that future entertainers would have to wrestle with live octopuses in order to entertain a mass American audience. The Beatles don't in fact do this, I observed at the end of that brain-rattling evening, but how one wishes they did, and how this listener wishes the octopus would win. I proceeded to write a most unfortunate judgment. "Let me say as evidence of my final measure of devotion to the truth," said I in a newspaper column, "the Beatles are not merely awful, I would consider it sacrilegious to say anything less than that they are God-awful. They are so unbelievably horrible, so appallingly unmusical, so dogmatically insensitive to the magic of the art, that they qualify as the crowned heads of antimusic."

The response was, to say the least, emphatic. I received more than 500 letters denouncing—not my musical judgment, or my stodginess, or my Philistinism—but my infidelity. To manifest truth and beauty. I picked out one letter to reply to, because I found it so wonderfully direct, and eloquent. "Dear Mr. Buckley," the young lady wrote from San Francisco, "you are a ratty, lousy, stinky, crummy idiot. P.S. You are too crummy to be called a person." After an exchange of four or five progressively amiable letters, I came upon the final effusiveness of the human spirit. It was Christmastime, and my new girlfriend sent me, by registered mail, a square inch of white cloth. She explained that it was exactly 50 percent of her entire holdings in life, since she had sold or mortgaged everything in order to participate at a public auction the week before. She had been able to bid for only two square inches of the sheet on which Ringo Starr had slept while at the St. Francis Hotel. Thus did the Lord melt the heart of the pharaoh.

I mean, how can one prevail against them? The answer is: One cannot. And even if they are hard to listen to, there is an exuberance there that is quite unmatched anywhere else in the world. Imagine a group calling itself the Peanut Butter Conspiracy! You figure it can't ever be beaten, and the next day you run into the Strawberry Alarm Clock. And then you see the peace feelers. Truman Capote in *Playboy*, telling us that the young popular musicians are the most creative people around. Ditto, of course, such youth watchers as Jack Newfield. *Time* magazine, relenting, puts the Beatles on the cover. Suddenly one day, riding in the back of the car, you look up, startled. That was *music* you just heard, blaring out of the radio. It's gone now, but not long after, you hear it again. And soon, like the ordeal of Gilbert Pinfold, it is coming in regularly, from everywhere. And you realize, finally, that, indeed, rock is here to stay.

THE MESS ON BROADWAY

April 10, 1969

It wasn't hard to predict (I did so at the time in as many words), when the Supreme Court ruled that the states could not suppress reading matter or, by extension, movies, provided that they included something of social interest, that that was the end of antiobscenity legislation, notwithstanding the Supreme Court's reassurances to the contrary.

New York being a vigorous city, full of entrepreneurial verve, it is not surprising that it has emerged, in the few years since the Court's decision, as the metropolitan center of pornography. It had, to be sure, a long underground apprenticeship. A witticism of John Lindsay is recorded that when he was the Congressman for Manhattan and voted on a single day against a subversive control bill and against an obscenity control bill, he commented to an aide that Congress was trying to crack down on his constituency's two major products.

Now the social-interest bit is intellectually confusing. In the first place, anybody can insert social interest into a sex book or a sex film in about, oh, ten minutes. In the second place, the term "social interest" is itself meaningless. Why is it not of social interest to read about the sexual affairs of Mr. Satyriasis and Madame Nymphomania? Certainly Freud would have found it socially interesting, inasmuch as sexual relations lead to psychological insights which are of social interest. In other words, the Supreme Court acted either thoughtlessly or disingenuously; thoughtlessly if it really thought that fine lines would ensue from its decision; disingenuously if it pretended to salvage antiobscenity legislation but actually foresaw that within a few years people would be lining the streets outside theaters in New York to see copulating couples onscreen.

The interesting questions at this point are the responses of the community. It is probably fair to say that much of the community is outraged. But my notion is that the Supreme Court and the Congress have trained us well to accept rulings by the Supreme Court as irreversible. Four years ago the Supreme Court ruled that we could not recite a common prayer in the public schools, not even one which the community's priests, ministers, and rabbis approved of. On that occasion, forty-nine out of fifty governors of our states came out for a constitutional amendment, and see what happened. As much is likely to happen in the drive to control obscenity.

What is most discouraging is the level of analysis. The incomparable Mr. Art Buchwald was on television the other night and professed his utter unconcern with the subject. His point was that love is a perfectly wholesome thing, by contrast with, for instance, violence. Rather, he said, the sex act onscreen than somebody sticking a knife into somebody. Now the trouble with analysis carried on at that level is that it takes us away, not toward, an understanding of the issues.

To dispose of the analogy, it does not follow from the wholesomeness of anything that it is appropriate to conduct said anything on a public stage. The tradition of "clothing our nakedness," as the Bible puts it, is not to be confused with the Manichean tradition of loathing one's body or despising natural bodily acts. Such violence as we see onstage is feigned and reminds the viewer of an unenviable aspect of the human condition. If all the viewers were sadomasochists, the same objections that nowadays apply to promiscuous sexual encounters onstage might be plausibly raised. But the purpose of the kind of theater we are here referring to is not to edify, or to instruct, or to ennoble; but, at the expense of the players, to slake—or stimulate—the public lust. And it is as much a community decision whether this is desirable as it is a community decision whether there should be public brothels.

The reason why it is especially important to elevate the level of public discussion on the matter is precisely that the legislatures and courts are unlikely to overcome the institutional inertia. There is something to be said, as Professor Ernest van den Haag has written, for underground pornography. But the operative word is underground, and that is where, if the critics would concert to distinguish between art and obscenity, it could even now be relegated by public pressure.

THE MANNERS OF CONTROVERSY

June 12, 1969

The manners of those who engage in public controversy are always interesting. The rules in America are: (1) Thou shalt be robust in the expression of your views; and (2) Thou shalt, if at all possible, exaggerate. The tradition of the tall tale is firmly grounded in American habit, such that nobody ever noticed it when Mark Twain was comparing politicians unfavorably with the denizens of hell, or much later when Mencken observed that politicians tend to compare themselves at political conventions with the rising of the sun and the aurora borealis. Exaggeration continues, and that's okay, but it is laced nowadays more by rancor than by wit, and witless intemperance is a heavy burden. One wishes that the Port Huron Statement of the Students for Democratic Action had got around to denouncing it. It is about the only thing the kids forgot to denounce.

Consider, for instance, the behavior of SDS Guru Tom Hayden, who appeared a while ago before the House Committee on Un-American Activities, now the House Committee on Internal Security. The committee members were endeavoring to find out something about the background of the principals involved in the great Chicago rumble of last August. Quite naturally, they turned to the kids' kid, Tom Hayden, cofounder of the SDS. His manners were very bad, very bad.

Q. What jobs have you held in the political area?

A. I consider myself an organizer of a movement to put you and your committee out of power, because I think you represent a racist philosophy that has no meaning anymore in the twentieth century.

Now that is pretty heavy going, isn't it? "I think you represent a racist philosophy"—never mind the hyperbole. In the revolutionary cant, America is "racist" not because America declines to interfere with Nigerians who are killing Biafrans, or Moslems who are killing Hindus, or brown Egyptians who are killing browner Sudanese, or Chinese who are killing Chinese, or strong Latin Americans who are oppressing weak Latin Americans. We Americans have lived in relative internal harmony except for one major convulsion the principal purpose of which was to put an end to slavery. But we are wandering, having set out merely to observe that such racism as does survive in America is far from being philosophical, it is habitual, and that in any case Mr. Hayden is confusing when he says on the one hand that America depends on a political philosophy and on the other that that philosophy has no meaning. Obviously it has meaning if it prevails; even as voodoo has meaning in Haiti.

Poor Mr. Hayden. But the explosion of his wit was yet to come. After pages and pages of the same kind of thing, a Congressman finally asked him, "Mr. Hayden, I have one final question for you. Don't you think that the young people who follow you . . . should take a second look at you before they place their lives and their responsibilities in the hands of you?" To which the resourceful young leader replied with a single word, in four letters.

In refreshing contrast is the recent confrontation between Professor John Greenway and D. Chief Eagle. Professor Greenway of the University of Colorado published an article in *National Review* magazine challenging the fast-growing myth of the American Indian as the noble savage savaged by the white man. That isn't how it was at all, not at all, says anthropologist Greenway, drawing from a lifetime's study of the subject. Uproar. The student council of the university, exercising that conscience which we are called nowadays to yield to, voted to censure Professor Greenway without even reading the disputed article. At which point the beleaguered professor received a threatening letter from Chief Eagle, a survivor of the Sioux. The professor has replied to Chief Eagle in a letter which shows us that notwithstanding the kids, the spirit of the Celebrated Jumping Frog of Calaveras County survives:

"How!

"White brother readum chicken tracks of red brother, makeum paleface heart heavy; tears of sorrow flow all over floor of teepee like great river.

"Lo, many moons ago Injun smokeum peacepipe, promise Great White Father puttum down tommyhawk, no makeum war forever no more. Now me thinkum, *Injun speak with forked tongue.*

"D. Chief Eagle he says he invade white brother own hunting ground and castum lance at white brother. What kind talk this talk? Maybe D. Chief Eagle heap big silly humbug; maybe better watch out, you thinkum? White brother maybe lift up Injun hair pretty damn smart, hey? Maybe bury hatchet in D. Chief Eagle head, he come up here steal land, steal woman. Makeum damn good Injun right quick, by Chrise.

"Ugh!

> John Greenway
> Heap Big Chief Medicine Man
> Professor of Anthropology"

HAVE A PANTHER TO LUNCH

January 20, 1970

If it blurs in the mind just what and who are the Black Panthers, why, they are an organization founded a few years ago on the doctrine that the United States is a racist-oppressive country best dealt with by the elimination of its leaders and institutions. Suggestive of its rhetorical style is the front page of its house organ which featured on the day after his death a photograph of Robert Kennedy lying in a pool of his own blood, his face transformed to the likeness of a pig.

Do you think Robert Kennedy was a pig? I asked Eldridge Cleaver a while ago. Yes, he said. Did he believe in the elimination of pigs? Yes, he did. Well, why not begin with Nixon: surely he is the chief pig? I observed. Mr. Cleaver, who has had intimate experiences with the law, advised me that he knew enough not to counsel directly the assassination of the President, but that if in fact someone did kill him, that would be one less pig in the world. They don't think that white people are the only pigs. Julian Bond is also a pig. And in New Haven a year or so ago a young Negro who decided that he had had enough of the Black Panthers was tortured to death. Bobby Seale, the chairman of the organization, and a few others have been indicted for the murder. Perhaps the jury will find that they did not actually do it. If so, it would not be for reasons of scruple, to judge from the flavor of their communications, but from oversight.

So what do we do about the Black Panthers? Why, if we are Leonard Bernstein, the conductor, we have a big cocktail party to which we invite a local representative of the party, and at the cocktail party we are so ingratiating that the Ford Foundation should have brought back Alistair Cooke so that the hungry of this world, like you and me, might have been permitted via television to be present at the love-in.

Mr. Bernstein was modishly dressed, in turtleneck sweater and double-breasted jacket, and had obviously been studying up on the idiom of the times; indeed so thorough is Mr. Bernstein that it is altogether possible that he staged a rehearsal or two, because a dialogue with a Black Panther is every bit as difficult to perform as a symphony by Schoenberg. Anyway, the Black Panther, Mr. Cox, began by announcing that if business didn't provide full employment, then the Panthers would simply take over the means of production and put them in the hands of the people, to which prescription it is recorded that Mr. Bernstein's reply was, "I dig absolutely." Asked just exactly how the Panthers would proceed, Mr. Cox replied that that depended on the tactics of the opposition: "The resistance put up against us dictates strategy," he said. Mr. Bernstein didn't wholly understand, asking, "You mean you've got to wing it?"

Mr. Cox told the gathering how very pacific he and his confederates are, that ultimately of course they desire peace, but that they have been attacked in their homes and murdered in their beds and have the right to defend themselves. "I agree one hundred percent," Lenny said, neglecting to ask Mr. Cox to explain to what defensive uses his confederates intended to put the hand grenades and Molotov cocktails that were discovered in the raids.

One lady present, wife of a Black Panther who is in jail on the charge of planning to kill a few pigs and conspiring to dynamite midtown department stores, eliminating pig buyers who were patronizing them, expressed great indignation at the interruption of her husband's activities by the police, who recently arrested thirteen Panthers, holding ten of them on $100,000 bail. She brought along her lawyer, who asked the distinguished gathering of artists-capitalists for donations. Someone who desired to be anonymous promised $7,500. Sheldon Harnick, the lyricist, came in with $250. Burton Lane, the composer, gave $200, and Mrs. Harry Belafonte gave $300. Lenny said proudly that he would donate the proceeds from his very next concert. He is too shy a man to say how much he earns per concert, but he didn't want to appear a tease, so he said that the sum would be in four figures.

The Panther and the conductor ended the meeting by professing their mutual esteem, hugging each other, and going off to Mr. Bernstein's dining room to have dinner.

We should study the Bernstein Approach. It is a singluar contribution to conviviality. No doubt Mr. Bernstein curses himself for having only just now discovered it. Just two years ago he might have invited George Lincoln Rockwell and his Nazis into his apartment, to ask him to explain the causes of his grievances, and raised a little money for those frequent occasions when Rockwell found himself on the shady side of the law, though to be sure Rockwell would have not been so romantic a quest, as he never actually advocated killing anyone. On the other hand, there are surely still around enough members of the Ku Klux Klan to fill Mr. Bernstein's living room, or at least most of it.

I remember, in the hour I spent with Mr. Cleaver, the one thing I said to him that made him truly angry. It was that the Black Panther Party exists primarily for the satisfaction of white people, rather than black people. The white people like to strut their toleration, and strip themselves of their turtleneck sweaters to reveal their shame. The Panthers have only a few thousand black members, because the mass of the black people are too proud, too unaffected, to join the Panthers, to attend Leonard Bernstein's parties.

HOW TO SAY IT JUST RIGHT

January 14, 1969

Inasmuch as I am encouraged by my colleagues to fill this space as I please, I take liberties. Or do I? What follows is primarily of interest to syntacticians. How many of . them are there? Not many. But—ah!—how many voyeurs? What follows is interesting, also, to students of friendship, nothing less than an assiduous case of which could have prompted the redoubtable Professor Hugh Kenner to such heroic efforts to demonstrate the demerits of a single English sentence. . . .

HK to WFB Sept. 19, 1968:

. . . Garry [Wills] under pressure tends to deliquescent metaphor (*vide* his Miami piece, *NR*), as does WFB to filigree syntax (*vide* current *Esquire,* first sentence, which while it parses [to say which is to say that a chicken coop does not collapse] resembles less a tensioned intricacy in the mode of M. Eiffel than it does a toddler's first efforts with Tinkertoy).

WFB to HK Oct. 1

. . . You are surely wrong about that lead sentence? I reread it, found it springy and tight.

HK to WFB Oct. 15

. . . about that *Esquire* lead: it reads in my copy:

"Robert F. Kennedy had a way of saying things loosely, and it may be that that is among the reasons why so many people invested so much idealism in him, it being in the idealistic (as distinguished from the analytical) mode to make large and good-sounding generalities, like the generality he spoke on April 5 after the assassination of Martin Luther King, two months exactly before his own assassination."

"Springy and tight" my foot. Those aren't springs; they're bits of Scotch Tape. Have your syntactic DNA checked for mutations; it just isn't governing the wild forces of growth as of yore.

WFB to HK Oct. 17

Come on now, you are a goddam professor of English, so stop name-calling and get to work. . . .

HK to WFB Oct. 25

. . . Okay, that sentence:

One way of putting the problem is that it's not discernibly heading anywhere; it ambles along, stuffing more and more odds & ends into its elastic bag, until it simply decides to sit down. Mr. Niemeyer has ridiculed my interest in syntactic energy, countering my regret that Johann Sebastian Bach should be taking out the garbage with his pleasure that it's being taken out, whazzamatter, don't I want a tidy house? Yet I revert to the concept: something, something corresponding to tension and relaxation, to the turn of the key and the swing of the door, to departure from and return to the tonic, makes us willing to accept the necessity of a long sentence being one sentence and not three spliced by mispunctuation. Back to the exhibit: if there were a period after "loosely" no one would feel that a flight had been arrested in mid-course. Or after "him," or after "generalities." I think one test of the long sentence is that if it's stopped before it's over the reader should sense the incompleteness. This is sometimes a matter of formal grammar: if we start with "because" the reader won't accept a full stop until he's been accorded a principal clause. It's sometimes just a matter of promising in the opening words or by the opening cadence (a device of Gibbon's) some amplitude of concern the reader expects to see implemented. But here the offer to develop the proposition that RFK had a way of saying things loosely creates no syntactic expectation because it's capable of standing as a sentence by itself; nor does it restrospectively command the rest of the sentence, because the sentence has managed to end not with an amplification of RFK's looseness but with a triplicated irrelevancy about the date.

"Robert F. Kennedy had a way of saying things loosely: large and good-sounding generalities which being in the idealistic (as distinguished from the analytical) mode help explain why so many people invested so much idealism in him: generalities like the one Martin Luther King's assassination prompted him to utter on April 5, just two months, as it happened, before he was assassinated himself."

A possible improvement, if one *must* include all those components. The main difference is that by putting the colon after "loosely" one gives notice that the opening clause will preside over the remainder, not simply join to the next section of track. Then repeat of "generalities" to hitch the peroration to the second member. And rearrangement of terminal items keeps the mention of King and l'affaire Sirhan from sounding like doodles irrelevantly prompted by "April 5." I do not offer the improved version as anything but an exercise; I wasn't writing the article and haven't in my blood the points you anticipated making, so all I can manage is a piece of engineering.

I do not fuss about your occasional sentences to

preserve a professorial edge. I merely call attention to dangers when I chance to see them. You revise carefully, I know, and it never hurts to have a few explicit criteria of revision. One is the rationale of the long sentence, as above (and failing that rationale, or failing time to adequate one's drafts to the rationale, *vita* being *brevis* and deadlines being yesterday, one ought, I think, to cut spaghetti into shorter sentences where natural stopping places occur). Another is that grammatical lint is best picked: in my suggested version I've avoided "that that," "reasons why" (your ear had told you to eschew yet a third "that"), and "it being." These all have rhetorical uses, as colloquialisms bounced off girders, but strung along in a row like old peanut shells they suggest WFB just plain improvising while he awaits a glimpse of daylight, and suggest to les Dwight Macdonalds that the Scrambled Egghead Method is to talk till one figures out what one is saying. This method is of course frequently necessary, and offensive, *viva voce*, say on TV, but its appearance should be avoided in print.

WFB to HK Nov. 4

. . . I worry about that confounded sentence, as one worries upon failing to appreciate something which one is prepared to postulate as good, to wit your criticism of it. I shan't even apologize for belaboring the point, because I know that you will know that by talking back, I am proving that I have not put you to such inconvenience merely for my own amusement.

"*Robert Kennedy had a way of saying things loosely*" followed by the colon you suggest means to me that I am about to demonstrate my allegation, or give an example of it. Followed by a period, the lilt of the sentence is, it seems to me, self-consciously dramatic, as in "John F. Kennedy had a way of seducing women." Followed by a comma, I thought it to be leading rather gradually to a point I did not want for a while yet, until the mood set in, to crystallize: whence. *", and it may be that that is among the reasons why so many people invested so much idealism in him"*—again, if the period had come here, I'd have attempted, or so it strikes me, a stolen base, and the reader would have been annoyed by the intimation that I have proved my point; or that I infer that the reader will merely permit me to asseverate it. When, *i.e.*, by way of further explanation, begging the reader's indulgence so to speak, *", it being in the idealistic (as distinguished from the analytical) mode to make large and good-sounding generalities"*—department of amplification, not without—yet—the example I am about to furnish, and spend several hundred words confuting, *", like the generality he spoke on April 5, after the assassination of Martin Luther King"* surely writing about what Kennedy said about another man's assassination a few days after Kennedy's own assassination (which is when I wrote this article), gives a certain spooky suspense, which is ratified, Robert-Louis-Stevenson-wise, with the adverbial clause," *two months exactly before his own assassination.* That last I take to be a fair substitute for "two months exactly, as it happened, before his own assassination." Seems to me that, although the sentence is long it is not impossibly long, and that although the commas appear somehow to be loose and thoughtless linkages they are justified by their meiotic contribution to the plot I am contriving. Hell, it merely disturbs me that while I *understand* your generic points, my ear does not grant them a pre-emptive relevance in this instance; and I repeat, that I worry because undoubtedly you are right and I wrong. Anyway, I shall remember the generic advice. Believe. Me. Pal.

HK to WFB Nov 7

. . . Not to wrangle, I'd make a final suggestion: that your inability to relate my comments, which you follow, to the sentence, the intentions of which you expound convincingly, is perhaps based on this, that you're not reading the printed sentence but hearing yourself speak it. By pause, by suspension, by inflection, by variation of tone and pace, you could make the "little plot" you speak of sing. The written language provides no notation for such controls, and your intention as graphed by printed words leaves the reader too much to supply, and too many options for supplying the wrong tacit commentary, *e.g.*, that WFB is standing in an open space scattering peanut shells.

We have no such public style as Pope could posit, and vary from minutely, in an aesthetic of microsopic unappropriatenesses. We have instead the convention that the writer creates his operating conventions *de novo*. "Robert Kenndy had a way of saying things loosely." —followed by a hypothetical period, you say, its lilt is self-consciously dramatic. Yes, but those are the very first words of a long essay; we are just tuning in to station WFB; his eschewal of the self-consciously dramatic is not yet an operative principle; and one of the options open to us is to suppose that a dramatic opening was intended but muffed by a fault of punctuation. I think your rebuttal to my statement that the sentence could be terminated by a period at several points without creating a sense of incompleteness consists in an appeal to nuances of taste: it would make nuanced differences to cut it off here or here. So it would. But the reader hasn't yet a feel for the governing structure of taste in the piece before him. *Especially* in an opening, the reader would be well served by a syntactic tension, as inevitable as gravitation on an inclined plane, which makes it essential that the sentence incorporate, as it proceeds, the members it does, or else fall down. . . . *Mais passons.*

WFB *urbi et orbe*, Jan. 1, 1969: Who's right?

THE MANNERS OF A CANDIDATE

November 28, 1967

Soon after the mayoralty campaign in New York in 1965 a young gentleman who had been conscripted to write speeches for John Lindsay and has therefore grown old before his time told me about his first encounter. Mr. Lindsay had contracted to do a piece for a national magazine, something on the order of Whither the Republican Party? The beginning sentence of the Lindsay draft was: "Politics is the art of the possible." The new ghost-writer began his duties by crossing out those seven words. Why? Mr. Lindsay, patron of the arts, demanded to know. Because, said his ghost, delicately explaining the facts of literary life to a man old enough to be his father, "you just *can't* begin an article with a cliché like that." Mr. Lindsay was uncomprehending and ordered the cliché restored, with pomp and circumstance.

Things are different now. In one of the most remarkable pieces of journalism I have ever seen, Mr. Richard Reeves of the New York *Times* writes about the recent trip to Los Angeles by Mr. Lindsay. Not only is Mr. Lindsay accepting the services of a ghost-writer, the ghost-writer's identity is revealed, as also it is revealed that his duties include the formulation of all those spontaneous witticisms Mr. Lindsay is now strewing about the country. "Although he has the timing of a professional actor," writes Mr. Reeves, "Mr. Lindsay's spontaneous wit is often ineffective and can sometimes be embarrassingly crude. The man who writes the Mayor's public jokes and almost all of his speeches is James R.

Carberry, a thirty-six-year-old former newspaperman. Mr. Carberry, who left the Washington *Post* to publish an upstate weekly before joining Mr. Lindsay in 1965, has one of the toughest speechwriting jobs in the nation." You can say that again.

And then, too, Mr. Lindsay, according to this report, does not travel about without his own television man, responsible among other things for the mayor's cosmetics. "Mr. Garth, a television producer who works without salary"—why?—"was on hand to supervise makeup men and technicians before Mr. Lindsay appeared on local television" in Los Angeles. He "is usually huddled with Mr. Lindsay just before any on-camera appearance."

Well, as they say, politics is certainly the art of the possible. The possible being the emergence of Mr. John Lindsay, who is a good sort but hardly what the youth of the nation have in mind, which is a Carberry-Garth creation, as a man of eloquence and wit.

Recently, a worldly young editor of *Time* magazine was shocked to learn from a former fellow student at graduate school that he could not join him for a weekend, because he had to write a book review for John Lindsay. The young editor knew, as all of us know, that ghosts have been with us for many years. And indeed we should all be grateful to the profession, else we would be hearing speeches that begin with the statement that politics is the art of the possible. But to assign to a ghost a review of a book which one is not even going to read—well, that is a kind of job automation which shocks even worldly young editors of *Time* magazine.

Is there a line to be drawn, somewhere? As a general rule, good writers (*e.g.*, Adlai Stevenson) don't make good politicians, and good politicians (*e.g.*, John F. Kennedy) don't make good writers. And therefore good writers should help politicians from time to time, even as good politicians sometimes help good writers by, *e.g.*, pulling their books out of their pockets in front of TV.

But there is something spooky about so total an amalgamation as, for instance, Mr. Lindsay seems to be perfecting. They say that TV is a useful democratic instrument because it reveals the true character of a man to the voters. One wonders whether that in fact is true, under the developing circumstances. Perhaps the Federal Communications Commission should take a role here? After every appearance of Mr. Lindsay on TV, the credit lines: "Mr. Lindsay's Speech by David Carberry. Mr. Lindsay's Makeup by David Garth. Mr. Lindsay's Ad Libs by Harry O'Donnell." Now there is a proposal for lodging more power with the federal government which Mr. Lindsay could quite consistently support, if Mr. Carberry will permit him.

THE RIGHT PEOPLE*

June 9, 1968

THE RIGHT PEOPLE: *A Portrait of the American Social Establishment.* By Stephen Birmingham. Illustrated. Little, Brown. $10.

Mr. Birmingham would have written a more interesting book if he had written a book more objectionable, whether more snobbish or more loutish, more overawed or more underawed. He breezes in on society neither over there in the company of bracing iconoclasts like Tawney or Orwell; nor over here in the company of the wonderfully self-assured like Sir Harold Nicolson ("Only one out of a thousand people is boring," he recorded in his diary, "and

* Reprinted by permission of The New York Times Company.

he is interesting because he is one in a thousand") or Sir Winston Churchill ("We are all worms, but I do believe that I am a glowworm"). As it stands, Mr. Birmingham is both too unctuous and too impious; too admiring and too cynical. The book lacks an axis of true conviction. One thinks what Belloc could have done with the material. Or Chesterfield. Or, for that matter, Mencken. A book about Society which is written by a careless fellow traveler is like a book about the Catholic Church as told by Browning's bishop ordering his tomb at St. Praxed's Church. It is a pity, because Mr. Birmingham has amassed some interesting material, though, if one must be frank (which can be Bad Form), not *terribly* interesting.

Mr. Birmingham does have an eye for the nice society, or antisociety, story: the kind of thing that would have appeared in one of Oscar Wilde's lesser plays. He begins early in the volume (p. 6) with an autobiographical paradigm, involving his clumsiness as a fifteen-year-old at his first formal dance when, attempting to balance his and his lady's dinner plates and Sauterne glasses, he slipped and poured the food up his sleeve. Recounting his misfortune to a dowager the next day, he elicited the comment: "Do you mean they served Sauterne and not Dubonnet? How dreadful!"

Two pages later he is at it again, recounting a quite hilarious-tragic experience of honeymooning socialites in Philadelphia who spend such a wedding night at the Bellevue-Stratford Hotel as Walter Lord could write a minute-by-minute account of—which elicted from a local grande dame the comment: "*Nobody* would ever spend their wedding night at the Bellevue-Stratford." (Note, by the way, the exclamation point in the anecdote above, and the italics in this one, and meditate the probability that Mr. Birmingham is better as a raconteur than as a writer. His writing style, while we are at it, is better than merely serviceable. But it lacks finesse and force. It is bearable because he is witty and knows the journalistic imperative—the book is a collection of pieces from *Holiday* magazine—of briskness and anecdote.)

I do not intend to leave the impression that these two examples are high points in Birmingham's collection. The author is himself cleverer than his stereotype dowagers. I consider as a genuine improvement on the old line about how much it costs to maintain a yacht, Mr. Birmingham's disapproval (in the name of society, for which, by the way, he is, I think unconsciously, prone to speak, with such implied authority as, say, Madame Tussaud speaking from Madame Tussaud's Museum) of the question being asked of anybody, "Where did you go to school?" or "What do you do?" "If you have to ask such questions"—he intones as grandly as Groucho Marx talking about the disqualifications of country clubs that would consent to have him as a member—"you have no right to the answers." The snob-genre joke is perhaps a little easy, but Mr. Birmingham has out a net for the best of them, *e.g.*, again, "Of the same era was the Porcellian stroke of the Harvard crew of whom it was said, 'He's quite a democratic chap. He knows every man in the boat but the three up front.' "

This reviewer is not equipped to evaluate the accuracy of Mr. Birmingham's specific observations concerning social hierarchies in, for example, West Hartford, Palm Beach, St. Louis, and Westchester. One's confidence is unsettled by strangeish things he says about niches with which one happens to be familiar, *e.g.* (p. 100), "Yale men are supposed to go into banking," a remark obviously not intended to be taken literally, but a remark intended to be taken as meaning *something,* which is more than, in fact, the remark means. He is mixed up about Yale sociology, and in fact in the course of a single paragraph you can observe him conceiving, experimenting with, and then proclaiming a thesis, as when (p. 145) he begins a paragraph by saying that at Yale, Scroll and Key *"often* comes out a social notch or two ahead" of Skull and

Bones, which evolutionizes, a few sentences later, into
"Scroll and Key *inevitably* emerges occupying a place
considerably in front of first." In his best-selling *Our
Crowd,* Mr. Birmingham, in pursuit of a racy sociological
fix, cited Levi Jackson, the Negro football player, as a
member of Skull and Bones (he wasn't) and remarked
that if he had been named Jackson Levi, he would not
have been a member (two of Jackson's classmates were
both Jewish and members of Bones). While we are at it,
Mr. Birmingham is occasionally given to distracting usage
that derives no doubt from the occupational hazard of
prolonged association with *dah*ling people. *E.g.,* in the
same passage: "There are two ranking senior societies at
Yale, Skull and Bones, and Scroll and Key—known
affectionately as 'Bones' and 'Keys . . .' " They are indeed
known as such, but it is no more affection that induces the
economical contraction than it is affection that induces the
world at large to refer to International Business Machines
as IBM.

Enough. It is, mostly, badinage. Competent badinage.
Nothing there like the truly condescending sparkle of the
syndicated Suzy. And no truly serious theories to expound
about Real Society, as he calls it, or about the governing
class. Mr. Birmingham is aware of historical contexts, but
when he invokes history in order to adumbrate a thesis, he
is as ill at ease as when he poured all that food down his
sleeve while making the egregious mistake of sipping
Sauterne. He is much more comfortable back at the
listening post, focusing on the colorful wash of imperious
types who are always ready to talk about this and that.
Here is the illustrious Mrs. Marietta Tree talking about
her archetypal family as "The people who built and
administered the schools, universities, boys' clubs, and
hospitals. They were the sinews of society. They gave
generously of themselves for the public good and
prudently lived on the income of their incomes. They
valued educated women, as well as educated men; daily

exercise; big breakfasts; President Eliot; beautiful views; portraits by Sargent; waltzing; Harvard; travel; England; comradeship between the sexes; Patou dresses for 'swell' occasions; long correspondence with family and friends; J. P. Morgan; mahogany and red plush; and, most of all, they believed that if you tried hard enough, you could make the world a better place. And you *must* try." That very last bit sounds like Mrs. Tree's mentor, Adlai Stevenson, who was uneasy in the company of educated women, didn't exercise daily, ate light breakfasts, lived in a house with a routine view of the countryside, would not have looked twice at a portrait by Sargent, went to Princeton, and thought J. P. Morgan the type of person enlightened government mobilizes against. Yet Mr. Birmingham comments: "Few better, or more succinct, lists of upper-class values have been compiled," which is probably true, and certainly suggestive of the meagerness of the literature on American "society." Mr. Birmingham correctly points out that we are not given, in this country, to the ideal of class responsibility, which is why it is all so very ephemeral and, somehow, self-conscious. The dominant class in America is the people John O'Hara writes about, and he is a much better portraitist than the panting taxonomists who, like Mr. Birmingham, sweat up pseudotheses around which to drape loose talk about rich and squirish Americans, some of them interesting, some of them dull; like the pages of Mr. Birmingham's book.

ON UNDERSTANDING THE DIFFICULTIES
OF JOE NAMATH*

October, 1969

My attention hadn't coupled on Joe Namath when I was asked to ruminate on the ethical questions, a week or so after Mr. Namath's lachrymose but, it was generally assumed, irresolute resignation from professional football. Have you ever stood by the television set biting your nails while your team suffered prolonged humiliations from the enemy, only to see something suddenly coalesce—the gathering of a spirit? The final rewards of meticulous training? A rally to the charisma of a great leader?—which, in fits and starts, with lightning rallies of first downs and long forward passes, with field goals and end runs and down-the-center juggernauts, suddenly takes you from behind, to stunning victory? Have you ever experienced that elation? Well, I haven't. I have never seen Joe Namath on the football field or on television. I saw him in person once, at the opening of *Oh! Calcutta*. He sat, perched on the back of the seat ahead of him, facing listlessly not the stage but the audience for ten full minutes before the curtain went up; Paris-style. I do not know what he was looking for, or what he was looking at. People looked at him all right, but listlessly in turn: They had come greedier than to feast their eyes on the face of Broadway Joe. He'd have made quite a hit if he had turned his back on the stage after seeing what was being exhibited there, but although Joe Namath has been unconventional, he has not been that unconventional; and

* First published in *Esquire* magazine.

certainly he has not been unconventional in the direction of seeing evil in sexual unabashedness. Whether he has been hearing evil is a matter of quite relevant conjecture. He doesn't, so far as one can judge, speak much evil. He takes great pains, whenever the opportunity is given him, which is once or twice a week, to speak no evil about anybody. What he said about the quarterback of the Baltimore Colts—he said he was a not very good quarterback—shocked sports-world decorum but was finally judged to have been nothing more than an "unkind truth." For the rest, he has always taken great pains to profess his great respect for just about everybody in sight, his coach at high school, his coach at college, the coach of the professional team he joined on leaving college, his teammates, the fans, his family, the law, Vietnam; indeed, he combines his crabby individuality with a general institutional *Gemütlichkeit,* a nice balance. What he does not like is the press, which, he tells us, misrepresents him 90 percent of the time, by which we must understand, in a world of hyperbole which so naturally accentuates in the world of sport (how excruciating it must be for the sportswriter who cannot report that Joe Namath ran 200 yards for a touchdown!), that occasionally we have got him wrong. He does not like the press, and he does not like anything that stands in the way of his exercising his "principles," his principles being, as one probes the question, that he should be quite utterly free to do as he likes when—as he likes to put it—he is away from the football field, a defense of which principle led him to the historic secession of June 6, when he announced that he would quit professional football rather than accede to the demands of the commissioner plenipotentiary in charge of maintaining such discipline as, in the commissioner's opinion, is necessary in order to safeguard the integrity, which is to say the profitability, of professional football, whose name is (I sound like Jimmy Breslin, God save me) Pete Rozelle.

I dallied to acknowledge my own inexperience with Mr. Namath's magic (I quickly add that I am capable of being overwhelmed by far lesser beings exhibiting far less talent in far less dramatic pursuits), thinking that although manifestly unqualified to speak with authority on the intimate problems of football, perhaps my innocence qualifies me to speak with whatever authority attaches to the noncommunicant; a noncommunicant who is nevertheless impressed by what Mr. Namath has apparently succeeded in doing to other people. I take as the elegiac, which no doubt he will wish to put on his tombstone, Mr. Jimmy Breslin's, who, in recording the events of an evening spent in the company of Mr. Namath, remarked what it was that happened to New York City as a result of the victory by the New York Jets at the Super Bowl on January 12, 1969: "His name [alas, even Breslin writes like Breslin] is Joe Willie Namath and when he beat the Baltimore Colts he gave New York the kind of light, meaningless, dippy and lovely few days we had all but forgotten." That is a popular judgment, but it is not unique, let alone perverse. The editor of a most illustrious journal, whose reflexes one disregards only at the risk of imperiling one's own basic journalistic coordinates, says of Mr. Namath that he is the "center of the world." "These are extraordinary tributes, which require, even among confirmed democratists, special consideration. Is it the case that Joe Willie Namath is bigger than the Lilliputian rules which looked as though they would put a premature and tragic end to his career, even as they did to the career of Cassius Clay? What are the special responsibilities of the mighty when they see that they are up against individuals whose heroic proportions shatter the conventional mold? Shouldn't the rules yield? Was such a problem posed by Joe Namath?

First things first. Are there reasons for extraordinary

vigilance in the world of sport? Manifestly, there are. Sport places the ultimate reliance upon sincerity. Excepting those matches which are programmed in the full knowledge of the viewer as entertainment rather than competition (professional wrestling), the suspense— which is what brings the people—requires that one repose one's confidence in each party's earnestly struggling to do his best. Mr. Namath has regularly attempted to compare sports to other activity, in order to ask rhetorically just why the former should be persecuted by special, prurient scrutiny. But the analogies break down. It is the case, as Mr. Namath insists, that we are all of us gamblers. Mr. Namath would not be upbraided for entertaining Messrs. Merrill, Lynch, Pierce, Fenner, *or* Smith at Bachelors III, notwithstanding that these gentlemen are more surely gamblers than the senior partners of Cosa Nostra, who when they gamble have as a rule arranged the odds in concrete. The difference is that in the commercial world it is very seldom that there are levers about that put pressure upon the individual to do less than his best. In government service, sure: There is the venal government official whose services are bought by the enemy, but let us, at least this time around, detach government activity from commercial enterprise. The typical merchant, the typical entrepreneur, is unlikely to find himself so situated that it would be worth his while to do less than his best in order to serve his obvious interests. Who is lurking in the shadows to persuade the Ford salesman to do less than his best to convince a customer to buy a Ford? *Cui bono?* Not necessarily Chevrolet's, if only because disenchantment with Ford does not necessarily mean enchantment with Chevrolet; and anyway, the process becomes too mechanically complicated to repay the exercise of a grand suborning ingenuity. Now if Chevrolet could get to Henry Ford II, that is something else; but what on earth would General Motors need to pay Henry Ford to persuade him to, say, reintroduce the

Edsel? More money, one assumes, than even General
Motors would be willing to dispose of, yet less money, let
us also assume, than could possibly tempt Henry Ford to
damage his strategic interests in the Ford Motor
Company—all of these observations not taking into any
account at all such moral inhibitions as in another context
we would, of course, presumptively put forward as
conclusive deterrents. But now the point is raised
concerning Joe Namath, that after all he is worth a couple
of million dollars already and, as things were going on
June 5, would likely retire worth four, five, six times that
amount of money: How much would a gambler have
to pay him in order to seduce him into throwing a game?
Not to speak of the practical difficulties for the
quarterback who desires to throw a game? . . .

These points most obviously occurred to the
commissioner. Which raises the question, Was his
invocation of Rule 3—which specifies that professional
football players may not mingle with known gamblers and
underworlders—formalistically invoked? That is to say,
did Mr. Rozelle and his advisers say to themselves:
Although the chances are overwhelmingly against Joe
Namath's being bribed to throw a game, still we must
apply Rule 3 against him, because any failure to do so
would argue either (a) that Namath is too big for mere
rules to apply to, which would be demoralizing; or (b)
that the rules are somehow anachronized? The answer to
the latter question must have been easy. No, they are not
anachronized, inasmuch as dissimulation remains quite
possible in the world of sports. The argument that a
quarterback cannot fool his colleagues easily by calling
the wrong play or throwing an inept pass is not conclusive
for so long as there are value judgments as to which would
have been the best play under the circumstances, and for
so long as there is the accepted phenomenon of erratic
performance. Namath played very badly on a couple of
occasions during 1968, and if a prosecutor desired to

elbaorate the case that he had played badly for unnatural causes, he could have got himself an audience. Never mind that Namath would easily have won a jury vindication on the grounds that one is innocent until proved guilty. What matters to the professional football leagues is that *the public* consider you blameless. And the combination of erratic performance and close physical contact with gamblers sets up a circuit of suspicion which is the reason for all the commotion; and Namath of course knew it, and, who knows, his knowing of it, his sensing the commissioner's point, may have been the cause of those tears that inundated the sports world. Those tears of frustration.

What, then, about the first argument, that the rules should, in this particular instance, be waived? The argument is not *eo ipso* irresponsible. Remember that the discussion thus far is extramoral: We are talking not about the integrity of professional football but about its financial health—we force ourselves to wonder whether they are detachable. It could be cold-bloodedly contended that such is the popularity of Joe Namath that the fans would crowd to him even if they suspected that he were fickle to the integrity of the game, that they would transcend their own demands for sincerity—*quod licet Jovi non licet bovi*. It has happened before in analogous situations. Jimmy Walker was a popular mayor of New York, though, to be sure, it has never been expected of politicians that they be as honest as athletes, merely that they should express their indignation at dishonesty more volubly. It was widely suspected by bullfight audiences during the closing years of the great duels between Dominguin and Ordonez that their equerries were surreptitiously shaving the horns of the bulls, thereby greatly minimizing the hazard of pressing their heroic contests. The protests came primarily from the purists, the crowd being disposed to accept the minimization of the risk to these lives, these limbs. On the other hand, their reaction might have differed if it had transpired that the horns of the one matador's bulls, though not of the other's, had been manicured. Even so, the public might resent it less if, say, the rumor were passed around that the quarterback of the Jets and the quarterback of the Colts had arrived at a gentleman's agreement: each one of them to misdirect, say, five passes each in the course of an afternoon's contest. Not feasible, one concludes; wearily. If only because one team or the other has to win in a contest between the Colts and the Jets, whereas in a *mano a mano* between Dominguin and Ordonez a clear-cut victory isn't necessary and, in any case, a stylistic victory depends not at all on the sharpness of the bull's horns. So that the analogies are finally reduced to helplessness, and the commissioner is left grappling with the dumb facts, which are that though it is unlikely that any gambler would attempt to corrupt Joe Namath; and although it is unlikely that Joe Namath would succumb to corruption; and though the disciplinary exclusion of Joe Namath would greatly jeopardize the prospects of the fledgling American Football League, the financial complexion of NBC, the very psyche of America—still, Rozelle did the right thing.

But now that Mr. Namath's technical difficulties have taken up so much of our time with no benefit to him, let us, before dropping the matter, pay tribute to one of his inadequately elaborated insights. He said to the reporters that, what the hell, he keeps company with gamblers all of the time, indeed the owners of the New York Jets are gamblers, in the generic sense of the word: more precisely, if you insist, speculators. Why, as an ethical matter, should he be civil to one gambler, while being rude to another?

Now Namath is being hugely disingenuous. He has, in fact, been caught being civil to a whole lot of people whose professions are by any man's definition very, very ugly.

Almost everyone nowadays sulkily acknowledges this, and Namath didn't talk much about the inaccuracies of the press in the days after *Life* and *Newsweek* and *Sports Illustrated*—having presumably corrupted state or federal police in order to get their information—published descriptions of the kind of people Namath was consorting with at Bachelors III and elsewhere, and accounts of the uses to which these gentlemen were putting the pay telephones at Bachelors III, which had become a sort of subganglion of the underworld. Namath, it transpires, had been more or less officially informed that certain of his patrons were outcast members of society. But it was not until after Mr. Rozelle laid down his ultimatum that Namath most publicly hired himself an ex-FBI agent to screen out at least the most conspicuous undesirables. Namath, then, appears to have acted a little bit unconvincingly on the matter of how-could-he-know that Killer Joe was a killer.

But hark the big point, which he hit cleanly, using a trajectory as spare as if firing a ball to a receiver 20 yards downfield. Why, he wondered, should he be asked to distinguish between those whom the law does not distinguish between? One assumes that the president of the New York Jets would be welcome at Bachelors III, even though he is the president of the Monmouth Racetrack. It happens that the gambling done by the president of the Monmouth Racetrack is technically legal, and that which is done by the Cosa Nostra types is illegal. Interesting point Number One: Precisely the only thing the government is in a position to do which would for sure drive the gamblers out of business is to legitimize their profession; which would however gravely encumber the advantages of such gentlemen as the president of the New York Jets, who profit hugely from the oligopolistic privileges of their racetracks. Interesting point Number Two: If the people who frequent Bachelors III are engaged in illegal activities, why in hell aren't they in jail, instead of ordering drinks at Bachelors III? How is it that, on the one hand, one can be so certain that Joe is shaking hands with a king of the underworld, but not be certain enough of the point to put said king in jail? If the police are not certain enough of their man, why should Joe be certain of him? Has Namath penetrated to the subtle dilemma, which is that there are, and there should be, metaphysical difficulties in enforcing laws that—shouldn't be enforced? And isn't Namath to that extent innocently victimized by the law's hypocrisies, and the law enforcers' ineptitudes? Why—Namath's complaint rises up from the shambles of questionably legal tapped telephone contents illegally passed on to *Newsweek* magazine which questionably legally publishes them, whereupon identifying the nefarious activities of questionably illegal men who are, after all, out of jail—why, in that mess, do they want *Joe Namath's* scalp?

Ah, the virginal purity of his position. It has some force, and that is one reason why the fans are restive, notwithstanding the tightness of Rozelle's analysis which, in the context in which he draws it, is unassailable. Thus it was with Cassius Clay: Everybody was right, and everybody was wrong, and you sided with one person or the other according as you accepted this or the wider circumference of the argument.

And, inevitably, there are those—and Namath knows this surely—who take a certain pleasure out of his humiliation, because he has taken great pleasure—has our Broadway Joe—out of humiliating the mores and the folkways of the republic. Oh, he is *very* proper when he speaks his institutional reverences to the public press—yes, sir, says James Bond to M, I will apprehend Her Majesty's enemies and neutralize the threat to the empire at whatever risk to my gimpy knees, but, by God, sir, I'll screw all the beautiful women who will assuredly lie between me and the consummation of my appointed task. Just so he likes it to be known that he keeps a harem, and defies the coach's orders ad libitum, and spits Fu-Manchulike his tobacco juice into the poshest receptacles, and stays out drinking and wenching every night before a big game. That is his *machismo*. When after seven or eight martinis he took the hand of a young woman writer at a cocktail party and moved it to his fly and said, "That's all America wants from me," he was not entirely drunk-talking, even though he might not have said what he said in the way he said it to a relative stranger under steadier circumstances. In fact, the girl was quite taken with Namath's intuition and would have celebrated it in her article but for one mortal failure in the story: She could not overcome the conviction that he had heard the line before and was living up to a role of himself which he had not been able, in behalf of himself, so neatly to externalize. But he was, even so, on to something. I once saw a famous and temperamental bullfighter in Mexico who had been hooted and booed and laughed at by the crowd in response to his clumsy preliminary handling of the bull, so that when the moment came to dedicate the bull, he walked to the center of the arena, where the matadors go when succoring favor to hold aloft their *capa* and turn slowly a full circle of obeisance to the crowd. He took off his *capa*, dropped it on the ground, lifted his hand with only the middle finger thrust skyward, and slowly and reverentially turned the ceremonial circle. The crowd went wild with delighted indignation, the police rushed into the arena and dragged him off to jail; and, all night long, the fans serenaded him outside the jailhouse and passed him up myrrh and honey. Namath has been doing a little bit of that, and while he has delighted the majority, he has also caused the juices of propriety to run, all those little Mexican policemen spilling out from everywhere into the bullring. They got their man. And they should have got him. But he is still a hero. And must be a hero.

XII. RIP'S, TRIBUTES, DEMURRALS

FRANCIS CARDINAL SPELLMAN

December 7, 1967

In fact, Cardinal Spellman was not popular among all Catholics, though there were none who doubted his benevolence. I heard a Catholic intellectual remark contemptuously a while ago that Cardinal Spellman had only twice in ten years assumed the pulpit, and on both occasions to denounce dirty movies. Indeed, in the modernist intellectual-literary underworld Cardinal Spellman became an eponym, as in Spellmanize, v.t., to parochialize, vulgarize, as in to approach an issue in the manner of Francis Cardinal Spellman.

They very seldom attacked him publicly. That was difficult to do on account of the aforementioned benevolence: It is just plain difficult to go after a rubicund man of steadfastly genial disposition who whenever he said that he prayed for the well-being of his fellow Americans meant that he prayed for the well-being of his fellow

Americans. And then, too, he was a very powerful man. His power was greater over politicians than over literary critics, one of whom (the Cardinal chuckled when he recalled the occasion) remarked that the only good thing about the Cardinal's book *The Foundling* was that proceeds from the sale of it were going to charity.

In recent months the Cardinal's critics, detecting no doubt his physical deterioration, pounced on him, once actively when he came out for winning the war in Vietnam, once passively at the last Alfred E. Smith Dinner, which was the Cardinal's equivalent of the command performance.

The Cardinal pledged, at the battlefront last spring, to pray for a victory in Vietnam, and opponents of the war, most of whom as a matter of fact do not take theology very seriously, found the Cardinal's statement theologically shocking and threatened the Cardinal with the displeasure of the Pope himself who, said they, has called for reconciliation and for negotiation, rather than for victory. The Cardinal, as was his wont, declined to answer his critics, though he generously acknowledged the support he received from his friends. He was not a garrulous man, and he figured that if this was not a war concerning which we felt free to pray that we win it, then it was not a war we should be fighting, and if that reasoning was too simple for his sophisticated critics, why, then, let them proceed on their complicated paths in search of nihilism.

At the Alfred E. Smith Dinner, there was muted scandal. Neither the President nor the Vice President nor a titular head of the Republican Party was present. That never happened before. And then—incredibly—two gentlemen who were listed on the printed programs as speakers did not appear. Governor Rockefeller had the excellent excuse that he was cruising with the governors at the annual conference, though, in fact, if it had been an election year, it was the general surmise, and if Cardinal Spellman had been a few years younger, the governor would have hired himself a Lear or something and come home for the evening.

And then Mayor Lindsay—the Mayor of New York must be hospitalized to permit him to be absent from that dinner—was off in the Virgin Islands, sunning himself, and sent instead to speak for him a deputy only dimly recognizable.

But Cardinal Spellman was determined, during this last season, to defeat the Blaine Amendment in New York, which he viewed, correctly in my judgment, as a lingering codified—prejudice against Catholic education. But in order to defeat the Blaine Amendment, it was necessary to endorse the entire, and entirely unsatisfactory, new state constitution; and this even some of the Cardinal's most faithful friends declined to do. He was disappointed, but his spirit was not broken. Shortly before he died, I sent him, jocularly, a button bearing the legend "National Committee to Horsewhip Drew Pearson," and heard back from an aide, "The Cardinal says he hoped it wasn't vanity, but he did think he deserved the largest one in town."

Indeed he did. Only once did the Cardinal speak out directly against those whose activities he thought were motivated by anti-Christianity. That was the famous episode involving Eleanor Roosevelt. An episode that ended with the Cardinal's calling on her, exhibiting that charity which he not only preached, but practiced. He knew intuitively that the differences between our own world and the one he hoped to enter are greater even than the imagination can conceive. And that there will always be doubt, and doubt is best answered by even greater efforts to maintain one's faith, and to live as best one can with reference to it. The Cardinal's faith was as specified in the Nicene Creed, and probably the only charge that truly astounded him was the one so often made explicitly, and even more often whispered, namely, that allegiances to the Catholic Church and to the United States are

mutually incompatible. That was not the impression of
anyone who saw him, winter after winter, giving comfort
to American soldiers in battlefronts all over the world,
and praying for their well-being and for the American
cause, which even now, those who know him can be sure,
he is pleading, benignly, patiently, adamantly.

MR. EISENHOWER'S MEMOIRS

December 3, 1963

MANDATE FOR CHANGE. By Dwight D. Eisenhower.
Doubleday. $6.95.

Why this book? Mr. Eisenhower is a public-spirited
man and feels the average man's desire for self-
justification. Put the average man in the White House, as
we recently did, and the desire for self-justification will
spill over into a very long book, even as happened with
the quintessentially reserved Mr. Coolidge. Yet while it
may have satisfied Mr. Eisenhower to write this volume, it
will not greatly satisfy the people who read it, except
perhaps those who are truly reassured to know that
anyone can be President.

But he must have his due. Dwight Eisenhower is not a
man of average skills. He is, on his feet, far more
eloquent than most; his personality is infinitely more
magnetic than yours or mine; he is a supercompetent
administrator and, incomparably, the master of his own
career. He has—and the contrary opinion notwithstanding, I believe this is as surely his gift as
Marian Anderson's voice is hers—an absolutely perfected
political sense. There never was, in all American history, a

more successfully self-serving politician. Eisenhower did
nothing whatever for the Republican Party; nothing to
develop a Republican philosophy of government; nothing
to catalyze a meaty American conservatism. But he was
unswervingly successful himself. He never went after
anything involving himself that he did not get; and I have
no doubt that if—as recently he confessed to reporters he
sometimes dreams it did—it had happened that the
Twenty-second Amendment to the Constitution were
repealed, he would even now be President of the United
States.

Mr. Eisenhower tells in this book the thoughts he took,
and the acts he engineered, while President of the United
States during the first four years. A sequel is to come.*
What does he add to our understanding of him? In respect
of the thinking that underlay his decisions, nothing at
all—we knew it all before, had plumbed its awesome
philosophical emptiness, had taken comfort or despaired,
according as we were of the political right or left, over the
torque of his superficial opinions. There is nothing here to
give substance to Progressive Moderation as political
philosophy, if that sacred word can be used to describe the
aglutination of ideas, hunches, prejudices, reflexes, and
accommodations that Mr. Eisenhower offers up as his
Weltanschauung.

Where the reader is rewarded, and the pickings are
exasperatingly slim, is by occasional factual revelations.
For instance, he and Dulles apparently discussed the
advisability of leaving the Geneva Summit Conference of
1955 in a huff, in open protest against the intransigence of
the Soviet delegation after the first three days. (Patience
prevailed.) I did not know, and am very interested to
know, that in 1951 he wrote a Shermanlike statement
disavowing any interest in the Presidency—and then tore
it up when an isolationist Senator (unidentified—and

* *Waging Peace, 1956-61*, Doubleday.

more anon about his exasperating refusal to give us the inside stuff) confided his opposition to the whole idea of a collective European defense plan (Eisenhower thereupon resolved to remain a "mysterious" political entity, the better to exert pressure on Congress). He tells us a nice anecdote the point of which is to reveal Stalin's lack of a sense of humor, though to be sure there are those who never ever suspected he had one. The nomination of Bohlen as ambassador to Russia turns out, interestingly enough, to have been Dulles' idea. I did not know, and am horrified to learn, that the great Arthur Vandenberg recommended William Brennan for the Supreme Court. Churchill was originally opposed to the European Defense Community. Attlee wanted to get rid of Chiang Kai-shek. Zhukov was a broken man at Geneva, after his humiliation toward the end of Stalin's career.

And that's about it. What Ike knows and won't, or at any rate doesn't, tell is infuriating to a reader who plunks down $6.95 seeking something more than a book-length verbalization of the President's press conferences. Little things and big things. Why did he slight Truman on Inauguration Day by declining to walk into the White House to escort him out? Why does he suppress his feelings about Taft during the months before the nominating convention? Why did he embrace Senator Jenner during the campaign of 1952? Why, in his defense of Bohlen, does he not discuss Bohlen's defense of Yalta, which was the principal criticism of him when his nomination was being debated? What did he really think of Nixon? How can he say that none of his confidants ever betrayed a confidence or spoke ill of him, when Emmet Hughes has even now a book on the best-seller list which does to Eisenhower roughly what Klaus Fuchs did to the Atomic Energy Commission?

And so on. So proper, so discreet is our ex-President, that he resists even the most human calls to political salacity. "In the whole sorry mess of thirty-six sessions [of

the McCarthy-Army hearings] the audience was absorbed
in such details as [a,] [b], [c], and finally a near fist fight
between Roy Cohn and the counsel for Democratic
members of the subcommittee." Now there are those of us
who remember who that was, but which of us would have
refrained from mentioning that the counsel for Democratic
members of the subcommittee was Robert Kennedy? One
can, having after all no alternative, forgive a bad President. But can one forgive a man with so deaf an ear
for political piquancy who hawks his memoirs?

And since Mr. Eisenhower's book submits to literary as
well as political evaluation, it should perhaps be said that
this is almost certainly his own book, *i.e.,* that there was
obviously no Emmet Hughes around when some of *these*
sentences were put together. For the most part it is good
plain prose, though there are lapses into what some people
have called West Point English (who, however, fail to
account for the fact that General Eisenhower and General
MacArthur presumably had the same English teachers).
"The year 1948 saw the institution of the West Berlin
blockade on the part of the Soviets" is a sentence which
actually sees its institution in this book on the part of
Eisenhower. He faces bravely the criticisms of his heroic
decision to permit his press conferences to be transcribed
exactly. "This decision," he writes in the understatement
of the era, "made a number of people nervous." It
must have made the Muses hysterical. "I soon
learned"—he explains—"that ungrammatical sentences in
the transcripts caused many to believe that I was incapable
of using good English; indeed several people who have
examined my private papers, many in my handwriting,
have expressed outright astonishment that in my writings,
syntax and grammatical structure were at least adequate"
(page 232). (Page 317: "This occasioned the sharpest
flareup I can recall between my staff and I.")

Indeed it is altogether conceivable that one of Mr.
Eisenhower's primary difficulties has to do with the

unmastered science, or art, of communication. In discussing the qualifications for a Chief Justice of the Supreme Court to succeed Mr. Vinson, for instance, he asserts that he excluded from consideration ". . . any candidates known to hold extreme legal or philosophic views." What on earth does that mean?—and never mind for the moment the irony of his having ended up with Warren. What is an "extreme legal view"? Or an "extreme philosophic view"? Does one hold an extreme legal view who relentlessly insists on the presumption of innocence in criminal proceedings? Does one hold an extreme philosophical view who holds adamantly to the idea of the separation of powers? Presumably the author means "extremist" where he says "extreme"; means "legalistic" where he uses "legal"; and means "ideological" where he uses (its noble antithesis) "philosophical." Even a President, when he writes, must, like other writers, *communicate*. Better, surely, to have charged $7.95 and paid a professional externalizer to wrench out of him what he meant to say; or even better, to force the author to reflect on the fact that he isn't really meaning anything at all.

I cavil? If so, let me put an end to it. It is my judgment that this book is, as history, unbelievably, perhaps even unforgivably, trivial. It is shot through with sheer travesty. His treatment of the McCarthy problem is, or ought to be, beyond even the patience of the most servile devotee of the McCarthy myth—I know of no one, save possibly Eleanor Roosevelt, who could have equaled it. As political philosophy it is pathetically, and even frighteningly, jejune (again, one thinks of Eleanor Roosevelt). There is one and only one passage of striking philosophical significance. It is one in which Mr. Eisenhower comes close to articulating a, yes, existentialist metaphysics for the middle of the road. "Frankly," he writes, "I think that the critical problem of our time is to find and stay on the path that marks the way of logic between conflicting arguments advanced by extremists on both sides of almost every economic, political and international problem that arises. Anything that affects or is proposed for masses of humans is wrong if the position it seeks is at either end of possible argument"! My exclamation point. How could any man who thinks that qualify, say, to sit as a member of a court? Let alone serve as commander-in-chief of the Western powers? The answer, of course, is that he was not qualified. He was elected. There is a difference.

Well, he served, and he bequeathed us a world every bit as troubled—in so many ways more far-gone in trouble—as the world Mr. Eisenhower took over when he began his long term of office. He harps, perhaps more often than on any other theme, on the necessity for a limited government and a balanced budget; but his budget was balanced only once during his eight years, and he was forever endorsing, in every field you ever heard of, an increase in the government's role—while solemnly fighting epiphenomenal government activity, e.g., in the field of public power. He left office well after the great gold lesion had been struck open; when Khrushchev, cynically exploiting the author's patience, was hard at work implementing his canny designs, in the cosy interstices between the Spirits of Geneva and Camp David. He did nothing, did not even try to do anything, about the monopoly labor unions, which continue, with effusive effrontery, to intimidate the nation, and the worker. He did nothing when the Soviet Union, eschewing an assault against Quemoy and Matsu—which Eisenhower courageously hung on to, but rather as an obsession than as a simple act of strategical consistency—settled instead for a salient into the Caribbean.

Is it any wonder that the politically active youth of today who lean to the right go months and years without giving a moment's thought to Eisenhower's name, or Eisenhower's program, as suggesting in any serious way a serious approach to the complex demands of our tortured age?

DWIGHT EISENHOWER

August 24, 1968

The accomplishments of Dwight Eisenhower will be copiously recorded now that he is gone, that being the tradition, and tradition being what one has come to associate with General Eisenhower, who comes to us even now as a memory out of the remote past. During his lifetime he had his detractors. There are those who opposed Dwight Eisenhower because he was the man who defeated Adlai Stevenson. In their judgment it was profanation for anyone to stand in the way of Adlai Stevenson. And so, when Eisenhower was inaugurated, they took up, and forever after maintained, a jeremiad on America the theme of which was: America is a horrible country because a banal and boring general with not an idea in his head gets to beat a scintillating intellectual who is in tune with the future. These gentry did President Eisenhower a certain amount of harm, and in later years they took to referring routinely to his tenure as "boring," "lacking in ideals," and "styleless."

Their criticisms never actually took hold. America wanted Eisenhower in preference to Stevenson; and however keenly we felt the death of Stevenson, it wasn't—speaking for the majority—because we had failed to confer the Presidency upon him. Stevenson was born to be defeated for the Presidency.

Among the critics of Mr. Eisenhower also from the liberal end of the world are a few who reckoned him as quite different from what it is generally supposed that he was. There are those—one thinks of the singularly acute

Mr. Murray Kempton, who all along has led that particular pack—who saw Mr. Eisenhower as perhaps the most highly efficient political animal ever born in the United States. They believe that his aspect of indifference to practical political matters was one of the most successful dissimulations in political history. He had, they maintain, the most accomplished sense of political danger that any man ever developed, and he always knew—they maintain—how to defend himself against the ravages of political decisiveness by (a) setting up another guy, who would easily fall victim; and (b) appearing to be innocently disinterested in the grinding of political gears.

The record is certainly there that over a period of a dozen years, it was, somehow, always somebody else who stood between him and the tough decisions: a Sherman Adams, a Richard Nixon, a CIA. General Eisenhower never really developed any mass opposition. His critics were either formalistic (the Democratic Party) or personal—men who held him responsible not for what he did but for what he failed to do.

It is, I think, this category of critics of the general which is the most interesting. Not the liberals, but the conservatives. It is hardly a surprise that liberals would have faulted Eisenhower's performance as President, they having so hotly desired the election of another man. But the conservatives, or at least many of them, were genuinely disappointed that he let the federal government grow at a rate no domesticated Democrat could reasonably have exceeded; disappointed by his failure to take decisive action against the Soviet Union notwithstanding unique historical opportunities as for instance in Hungary, Egypt, and Cuba; disappointed by his dismal unconcern with the philosophy of conservatism (of which he was a purely intuitive disciple) at a point in the evolution of America when a few conservative philosophers at his side might have accomplished more for the ends he sought to serve than the battery of sycophantic (and opportunistic) big businessmen with whom he loved to while away the hours.

The critique of General Eisenhower from the right will perhaps be the most interesting historical critique (to use the Army term); and one somehow feels that the general, retired from office, had an inkling of this. Never was he so adamantly and philosophically conservative as when he last addressed the nation, via the Republican Convention at Miami Beach.

Meanwhile we are left to mourn the passing of an extraordinary man, a genius of personal charm, a public servant manifestly infected with a lifetime case of patriotism. His country requited his services. No honor was unpaid to him. If he was, somehow at the margin, deficient, it was because the country did not rise to ask of him the performance of a thunderbolt. He gave what he was asked to give. And he leaves us if not exactly bereft, lonely; lonely for the quintessential American.

ALLEN DULLES

February 8, 1969

During the last years of his life Mr. Allen Dulles was under relentless attack as the symbol of James Bond diplomacy, so gruesomely inappropriate, it is held, to the realities of modern politics, to such higher sophistication as makes heroes out of traitors, gods out of Kim Philby and the Rosenbergs. *Ramparts* magazine—it would be heartening to refer to the late *Ramparts*, except that it will no doubt be succeeded by something worse, the human imagination being capable nowadays of even that—made such reputation as it fleetingly had from exposing that the

CIA under Mr. Dulles had done such outrageous things as subsidize *Encounter* magazine in London, the National Students Association in the United States, and a training program at a midwestern university for area specialists headed for service in the CIA. For all of this, obloquy for Mr. Dulles. I do believe that he'd have been better treated in his late years by some of the press if it had transpired that he had been in collusion with the Communists, in pursuit of détente.

All of this left Mr. Dulles on the defensive, and the general clamor subdued a criticism of his strategy which sounds faintly perverse, but which is naggingly relevant now that we have, once again, a Republican administration with critical decisions to make concerning such issues as faced Mr. Dulles. True, there were those who make the whole right-centered criticism of Mr. Dulles awkward by such surrealisms as that Mr. Dulles was a Communist agent (yes, that is among the contributions of Mr. Robert Welch). But the sane voices from the right wondered not that Mr. Dulles was involved in subsidizing social-political movements and journals around the globe, but that he selected for patronage the left-minded organizations, on the assumption that only people who occupy a position contiguous to that of the people you worry about are likely to be effective. Thus in Italy you deal with the Social Democrats in preference to the Christian Democrats. Or, if you deal with the latter, you deal with that branch within it which tends left. Ditto elsewhere.

The analogies abound. You deal with liberal Republicans in America, in order to try to satisfy Democrats. Rockefeller, yes, Goldwater, no. When time comes to send around subsidies, you send them around to journals of opinion like the *New Leader*, not those like the *National Review*. I know one person who did service in Mexico for the CIA who happens to believe profoundly that what would most benefit the Mexican people would be a stiff dose of capitalism, so as to free the poor from the sclerosis of years and years of supergovernment. He found himself a dozen years ago serving as a paymaster, with a wad of money in an envelope destined for an organization whose principal slogan was "Ni Comunismo, Ni Capitalismo," that is to say: neither Communism nor capitalism—leaving, well, leaving what Mexico has got.

The reasoning, as I say, is psychologically obvious. The mischief of it lay in the hesitation of Mr. Dulles and his superiors to adopt radical strategy, radical strategy being the defense of conservative institutions and ideas on the altogether reassuring assumption that they would result in radical relief for the wretched of this world. Shortly before he died, Henry Luce thought to formulate a similar position in addressing the National Council of Churches: Look (he intended to say), if you are genuinely concerned with the starving peoples of the world, which you no doubt are, are you not obliged to investigate the apparent corollary between agricultural plenty and the free marketplace, as also the corollary of agricultural privation and socialism? In other words, could you not, even in the name of Christianity, bring yourself to say a good word for capitalism?

During the Dulles years, conservatives starved to death; precisely those people who reasoned that you could not deal with the Soviet Union, that the politics of détente were doomed to suffer such deaths as Dubcek suffered last summer. It was a period during which the resoluteness of our anti-Communism was never in doubt, but a period during which the enemy gained vast continents, established himself in power, developed his hydrogen bombs and missiles, and continued to hold us at missile-point.

It seems mean to observe at this point that Mr. Dulles should have been spared the criticisms of the left, so as to expose himself to the criticisms of the right. Let it be recorded, at least, that he sought to maneuver within the realpolitik of the postwar era, and that although he may have made bad strategic miscalculations, he was made to suffer at the hands of the wrong people. Because even if he did not know how finally to cope with the enemy, he knew at least who the enemy was, and that, these days, is practically a virtuoso performance.

NORMAN THOMAS

January 4, 1969

The obituary notices on Norman Thomas stressed his early advocacy of "reforms" which have long since been institutionalized. Way back there, before the Democratic Party thought of it, Norman Thomas was campaigning for Social Security, minimum wage laws, Medicare, and the rest of it. Now we have these things, and they are very popular. Ergo, Norman Thomas was right. It all depends, of course, on the ergo.

Norman Thomas, it is said, had a passion for social justice, for individual rights, for the underdog. I think that that is true. And I think that Mr. Thomas was a hero. But I think that he was a hero not on account of his early advocacy of ideas that have proved popular.

What, after all, does it mean to have a passion for social justice and for the underdog—in a society so constructed as to make the dispensation of social justice impossible? Nehru had such passions, but India was worse off when he died than when he took power. And to the extent that modern India continues to fashion itself on the social principles of Norman Thomas, it will continue in its relative decline. Because, as John Kenneth Galbraith pointed out years ago in a studiously ignored book, it is only the affluent society that can afford such social goodies as Medicare and high minimum wages. I am not aware that Mr. Thomas ever contributed to making this country affluent or powerful. That was the work of other men. Men whom, consistently, Mr. Thomas disparaged.

I met the gentleman in public debate on perhaps a dozen occasions. I remember within the period of a year or two that we argued before different audiences on the perils of McCarthyism (Americans were losing their liberty under the lash of McCarthy's demogogy), the welfare state (we should have socialized medicine), and nuclear testing (America should unilaterally cease testing and developing a nuclear arsenal).

Now it can be said, surveying these positions, that Norman Thomas prophetically took the "right" side. But, in the calm of things, America can be shown not to have lost her liberty under McCarthy, or even to have come close to doing so; indeed, one day perhaps before the century is out, Americans may be free enough again to dare to say that McCarthy wasn't all that bad, that his enemies were the remarkable people who did and said the remarkable things.

We did not achieve socialized medicine, exactly, but, in Medicare, a form of compulsory medical insurance. It is very costly, but we can apparently afford it—because our country is very properous; and who made it so? Upton Sinclair?

We are not testing our weapons any longer, but we continued to test them right through the demands of Mr. Thomas that we should cease to do so: until in the judgment of the prevailing technicians, we had come close to the point of redundant development. If we had not done so, if, for instance, we had not, during the fifties, calmly proceeded—athwart the hysteria of the disarmament fetishists—to develop the hydrogen bomb and the delivery system, then just what use would have been our thirst for freedom? Freedom, to be quite concrete, for the West

Berliners, say, which freedom, when it was directly threatened by Krushchev, President Eisenhower promised to defend if necessary by the use of nuclear arms. . . .

That is the problem, surely; and that is one of the reasons why conservatives get so little credit in the march of time. They are doers: They discover the penicillin, learn how to merchandise it cheaply, develop laborsaving devices that increase productivity, generate the surplus that goes to help the poor, build the bombs which alone contain the enemy's appetite.

The heroism of Norman Thomas was an altogether individual thing: his dogged devotion to his ideals, even though they were ideals that could not have been served except by the political repudiation, again and again, of the man who espoused them so avidly. That idealism and the terrible physical rigors to which he exposed himself in behalf of others were the distinctions of this genial, talented, opinionated American.

EVERETT DIRKSEN

September 23, 1969

It is a sad fact that Everett Dirksen's death will not bring true national grief. On the left, they thought of him as a colorful politician who always maneuvered in such a way as to serve the Establishment, particularly the business establishment. On the right, they thought of him as a stabilizing force, on the whole; but so much the pragmatist that you couldn't really count on him in a pinch. Mr. Murray Kempton, the columnist, began a dispatch a few years ago by remarking that the Friends of

Katanga had "begun its career where most conservative organizations end them—with the desertion of Everett Dirksen."

The circumstances come to mind. A group of Americans who objected to the United Nations' declaration of war against Katanga formed a committee and invited the usual luminaries to join it. In came a telegram from Senator Dirksen consenting to the use of his name as a sponsor. That evening he was called to the White House by President Kennedy. On leaving, and being questioned by reporters about his support of the Katanga Committee, he replied that he had never authorized the use of his name. I sent him a Xeroxed copy of his telegram, to which he replied, with that sublime evasiveness which enraged and disarmed so many of his critics, that "as Lincoln said, the dogmas of the quiet past are inadequate to the stormy present."

I remember an occasion when I heard him deliver a speech and amused myself by doodling away at what the academicians call an "intellectual schematic," *i.e.*, a sentence by sentence paraphrase of the analytical narrative. I am telling you, that speech was utterly meaningless—empty of content—lacking in any development. He received a standing ovation. The audience had come to him on his own terms. They desired the resonant tones, the patriotic attitudinizations, the diapasonal rhetoric. I should have added that I, too, was enraptured.

The Chicago *Sun Times,* somewhere along the line, recorded about Senator Dirksen that in his seventeen years in the House of Representatives he changed his mind sixty-two times on foreign policy matters, thirty-one times on military affairs, and seventy times on agriculture. Upon reaching the Senate, as we all know, he achieved his stride, and greatly improved on that record.

And yet and yet . . . (1) he was a great democratic politician. By great, I mean that he was able upon shifting

positions to justify his new position in terms that satisfied
the moral conscience. If a politician changes his mind
merely because he has whiffed the Gallup poll, he can look
craven and, in doing so, can undermine the democratic
pride. Senator Dirksen always made his tergiversation
appear to have been the result of divine sunburst, so that
the silt of cynicism never came down to choke him.
Pleading for a nuclear test ban notwithstanding that the
proposed treaty failed to incorporate provisions Senator
Dirksen had a while before pronounced to be absolutely
essential, he opened his oration with words that would
have embarrassed Joyce Kilmer: "The whole bosom of
God's earth was ruptured by a man-made contrivance that
we call a nuclear weapon." A couple of those, and who
cares about what Dirksen said yesterday?

Add to this that Dirksen was a great Parliamentarian, to
be sharply distinguished from a great leader, but not for
that reason to be despised. He knew when movements
were developing into *forces majeures,* and knew
when therefore to yield. Great resistances never issue from
men like Dirksen, but then too, neither do civil wars. And
add, finally, his genius for accommodation to a variety of
interests, at which he was the supreme mosaicist. Such
men are very scarce, very valuable.

And then, (2) there was the theatrical Dirksen. I don't
care, I liked it. Politics is so much a fraud, it ought to
be entertaining, particularly in an affluent society.
Listening to Dirksen was a pleasure, as listening to
politicians goes. He sought to please, to cultivate the uses
of rhetoric, and bombast, and color. He was as sincere in
his cultivation of the art as he was in his related passion
for his garden, to which he returned lovingly day after
day, with the inescapable relief of someone who turns his
attention to creatures easier to bribe.

From time to time I have indulged the fantasy of
the hedonist's schedule—Columbus Day in Vermont,
Washington's Birthday in Switzerland, nightfall at

Kilimanjaro, that sort of thing. Always one staple has been: the Senate Gallery when Everett Dirksen delivers his annual testimonial to the marigold. Have you ever heard him on the marigold? What a splendid tribute it would be if the Congress voted to remember this memorable man by voting into law the only proposal he truly cared for, winter and summer, season after constant season, secure from the statistician of the Chicago *Sun Times:* naming the marigold as the national flower.

MOISE TSHOMBE

July 5, 1969

Shortly after Tshombe was kidnapped, a grimly humorous story got through the Algerian censors. The Algerians tortured and truth-drugged Tshombe, at the request of Joseph Mobutu. The idea was to get from Tshombe whatever information he had which would be useful to Mobutu in tracking down and liquidating potential enemies. But the questioners were over-diligent, and when they asked Tshombe who *actually* had given the order to murder Patrice Lumumba, he confided to them, in his truth-trance, that it had been Mobutu.

We do not know whether that piece of intelligence was communicated to Kingasha or Lumumbaville or Mobutuplats, or whatever they are calling Léopoldville nowadays. In fact, it is just possible that this particular revelation had something to do with Boumedienne's decision not, after all, to deliver Tshombe to the executioners in the Congo, though it isn't known, as it happens, whether he did Tshombe a favor.

Now Tshombe is dead, and Boumedienne called in eleven, count them, e-l-e-v-e-n Algerian professors to testify to his having died of natural causes. Myself, I would have insisted on fifteen Algerian professors, but then that's the way I was bought up—never trust less than fifteen Algerian professors, my mother warned me.

Really, it is astounding how the savages of this earth cling to bourgeois forms when they are troubled. First Boumedienne accepts custody of an alien who is delivered into his hands by professional bandits employed by a foreign government. Then he has him tortured. Then his court sycophantically "rules" that Tshombe may indeed by legally shipped to the Congo to be executed. Then something happens—something we are not privy to. The working of some mysterious pressures, probably American in source (the heroes of the Save Tshombe movement were a few Americans who labored privately to help him), that kept Boumedienne from handing Tshombe over to Mobutu.

But Boumedienne responded petulantly to those pressures. He did not send Tshombe off to be killed, but neither would he release him. Worse, he held him incommunicado. He could not be seen by his wife or by his lawyers. He was moved about from prison to prison, it was said. Rumors were rife, even as they were about Ben Bella, now forgotten. A few months ago it was reported that he would soon be released. Immediately after his death two lawyers reported that they had just completed ranson arrangements.

But it is not doubted that Tshombe is now dead. And it is not doubted that healthy men do not die of old age at forty-nine. In Latin America, in the revolutionary heyday, the practice of reporting that important prisoners had been "shot while trying to escape" became so routine that one general with a sardonic mind and a palpable contempt for public opinion reported that *his* prisoner had been poisoned while trying to escape. Boumedienne, on the contrary, seems to care about public opinion. That is why he brought in eleven Algerian professors who, of course, will report that Tshombe died of a latent heart defect.

There is a terrible sadness to it all. For the one-thousandth time we think of the awful resonance of Strausz-Hupé's remark that conservatives do not retrieve their wounded. Tshombe fought for the maintenance of certain standards of life in the Congo which were, and indeed are, threatened by totalist barbarism. He believed that whites and blacks should work together. He was plainspokenly Christian. He was a natural leader of men. A friend of the West.

And yet when Tshombe was kidnapped over Spanish soil, flying from one part of Spain to another, there was no protest from offical Spain. For months the friends of Tshombe endeavored to persuade the government of Spain to assert a quite natural legal claim against Algeria for husbanding someone kidnapped from Spanish soil. But Franco was apparently uninterested, like just about everyone else: Can anyone imagine the United Nations interrupting a session on the human rights of mankind in order to plead the human rights of one man, victimized by their beloved Third World?

Algérie Algérienne! Well, the "government" of Algeria, liberated from French colonialism, in the hands of a military dictator, has exercised its sovereignty. No doubt eleven Algerian professors can be got to write the history of Algeria's blamelessness in the handling of the final two years in the crowded life of Moise Tshombe.

HENRY HAZLITT

November 29, 1964

Mr. Hazlitt, Mrs. Hazlitt, Ladies and Gentlemen:

On this happy occasion I join with you in saluting an old friend and mentor, Mr. Henry Hazlitt, and his incomparable and gifted wife, Frances. I was greatly frightened, when our host, Mr. Larry Fertig, asked me to speak and after I saw the initial list of speakers, that this was designed as a *Festschrift,* to which I was expected to contribute an economic pearl, thereafter to be known as Buckley's Diminished Return. You can imagine with what relief I greeted the news that the great Rebecca West would also be speaking, since having read everything she has ever written publicly, and having felt the force of some of the things she has written privately to me, I suppose I can say that she probably knows even less about formal economics than I do. And I say this even knowing that she had read Barbara Ward. How do I know? Not because I have seen in any of her writings—talk about economic innocence!—any trace of the influence of Miss Ward, but because one time she wrote me and asked, "Is there anyone else in the world who writes worse English than Barbara Ward?" I was able to shoot back, "Yes, Walter Lippmann." She replied, with her usual generosity, "Let's call it a draw."

I knew it would be an awesome experience to speak on the same platform with the lady described quite accurately in this morning's New York *Times* as the greatest living woman writer. Now, exercising her female prerogative to do to the men what so often the men do to the ladies—she has not shown up. I am left with the difficult job to sound other than trivial and idiotic after the profundities of Professor von Mises, and in anticipation of those to come from the other speakers. I surrender. For those of you who, like myself, so often despair of following some of the cadenzas that these men play in the abstruse world of economic theory, I bring you this consolation: Only a fortnight ago Professor Milton Friedman confessed to me that he does not altogether understand the last work of Professor William Hutt. We must assume that this is not because Mr. Hutt is absolutely unintelligible, in the sense that Mr. Hazlitt proved that Lord Keynes so often was; but that in the spheres in which these men move, reciprocating wheels become a prerequisite to understanding each other's most elusive works. It is surely the genius of Henry Hazlitt that he is totally at home in the ether of the most abstruse economic theory and yet has never failed to communicate his analyses and his findings to the layman: for this contribution, perhaps above all others he has made, we are profoundly grateful. The force of his arguments and the special discipline he has imposed on himself to make those arguments public are a part of the patrimony of all of us who are concerned for the free society.

The free society. What's that? It is, let us face it, and notwithstanding the great labors of the men and women who are here tonight, a concept increasingly elusive. I think it would be interesting, Albert Jay Nock once wrote, to write an essay on the question, How do you go about discovering that you are living in a Dark Age? There is much ignorance of the meaning of a free society, and no one in the world, surely, who has done more than Henry Hazlitt to dispel whatever ignorance has, in fact, been dispelled about the rudimentary critical importance of economic freedom. What *is* a free economy? Christopher Hollis, the English Catholic journalist and historian, came to the United States just after the election in 1960 to do a piece on the first Catholic family and found himself interviewing one of the Kennedy ladies, to whom he put the question, "Have you found it very difficult as a wealthy person to find daily challenges of the kind that is said especially to commend the poor to God?" "Not at all," she said, "not at all." Mr. Hollis, making notes, murmured pleasantly, "Then you don't believe it's harder for a rich man to get to heaven than for a camel to pass through the needle's eye?" "What a quaint saying," said the lady. "Where did you pick that up?"

The sister of the first Catholic family apparently had not heard that; as, we warrant, the leader of the first country of the free West has probably not heard of the book *Economics in One Lesson*, although its worldwide circulation probably is the only rival to that of the Bible. Better, perhaps, *not* to have to read it than to have read it and disregarded it. Perhaps some people shouldn't read some books. "I approve of the Index," Evelyn Waugh once wrote. "I find it a convenient excuse for not reading Sartre." If the President of the United States should suddenly decide to read *Economics in One Lesson*, his reaction might be much like that of the Englishman who at church one day with his wife heard a sermon on the Ten Commandments. He walked away from church despondent, head bent; but suddenly he looked up, eyes shining, and exclaimed to his wife, "I've never made any graven images!" Close readers of Mr. Hazlitt's primer wll find there something, surely at least one commandment that Mr. Johnson has not violated.

But so dazzling are Mr. Hazlitt's accomplishments in economics that we tend to forget some of his other extraordinary feats. In the summer of 1960, for instance, during the period when the Russians had taken to announcing, several days after the event, spectacular feats of orbital acrobatics, Mr. Henry Hazlitt, the epistemological skeptic, felt the time had come to put aside his modesty, and so wrote a letter to the New York *Times:*

"Dear Sirs:

On August 17, two days before the Russians sent up the dogs, I was shot into orbit inside a twelve-ton spaceship. After seventeen revolutions around the earth I tilted by retro-rocket and landed safely within seven inches of a preselected target.

This means that I have scored a first, ahead even of the Russian claims. Reasons of military security prevent me from saying anything really informative about the mechanism of the satellite, or revealing the place from which I was shot into orbit or the place of landing, or any other such detail. Nor did I give out any advance notice of the intended time of the shot so that tracking stations could satisfy an idle curiosity. I may reveal, however, because of its extreme scientific interest, that my wife could distinctly see me through a television camera taking orange juice, toast, and coffee.

If either Russian or American scientists are malicious enough to ask for the evidence that this took place, they have my word, which is at least as good scientific evidence as an announcement by Tass. Besides, here is the clincher. I am alive and healthy, show no ill effects from my trip, and can be visited and photographed by skeptics. If I had not been recovered safely from the capsule, how would all this be possible?"

And now, at seventy, Mr. Hazlitt has turned to ethics—indeed what field, one wonders, could he not have mastered? One day years ago as editor of the *Freeman* magazine, the suggestion was made at an editorial conference that perhaps something appropriate should be said on the occasion of the death of King Carol's consort. Within moments Henry Hazlitt jotted down a proposed obituary. It read:

> *Said the beauteous Magda Lupescu*
> *As she rushed to Roumania's rescue*
> *It's a wonderful thing*
> *To be under a king*
> *Is democracy better, I esk you?*

No, he didn't publish it, though I understand he sent along a copy, for his private delight, to Mr. J. Howard Pew.

I know you will join me in wishing the very happiest birthday to an economist, philosopher, historian, poet, and astronaut, our friend Harry Hazlitt.

LEONARD READ

October 4, 1968

It is wise in this company to avoid any attempt to describe too closely the theory of freedom to which Mr. Leonard Read has devoted the first part of his life. The danger is in committing an economic or theoretical solecism: Can you imagine the result? I see the headline in tomorrow morning's *Daily News*:

> WORLD'S TOP ECONOMISTS/
> GAG AT BUCKLEY GAFFE/
> RUSHED BY AMBULANCE TO CITY HOS-
>   PITAL/
> HAYEK, HAZLITT AND FRIEDMAN DECLINE
>   "SOCIALIZED CARE"/
> READ, GUEST OF HONOR, URGES NO USE OF
>   FORCE
> EMERGES AS WORLD'S TOP ECONOMIST

My normal impulse to caution was heightened on reading this morning an account of a recently published book on Professors Ernest Lawrence and Robert Oppenheimer which records that on one occasion in the wartime secrecy of Los Alamos when Edward Teller was detailing on the blackboard to his fellow students the morphology of thermonuclear reactions, Mr. Teller turned white with shock when Mr. Oppenheimer gently interrupted—always assuming that such interruptions can be classified as "gentle"—to tell him that he had forgotten the square of the velocity of light in his equations, introducing a huge error in the results. One must mind one's exegesis in these quarters, surrounded as we are by these Geiger counters of economic heresy.

I remember adumbrating a plan for the salvation of Harlem back in 1965, before Mr. Lindsay disposed of the problem; which plan I was forced to disavow after receiving from Mr. Friedman a postcard, imagine, a postcard, illustrating the theoretical error in my proposal. No bull of excommunication, or notice by John L. Lewis of disaffiliation, was ever more direct, or more efficacious. Harlem was instantly spared salvation.

One must not conclude that these giants of knowledge and wisdom are themselves agreed on all matters of public policy. They are spirited in their own intramural discussions. John Kenneth Galbraith once wrote, referring to the present company and to others in their fraternity, that shortly after the end of the Second World War, the world's free-market economists met at a Swiss mountain peak in order to coordinate an effort to set the clock back, but that it is recorded that the discussion broke down over a disagreement on the question whether the British Navy should own their own ships or rent them from private entrepreneurs. That is an amusing, if Herblockean, construction of the differences between us, which not only animate us, but bind us together. A few months ago, the last time I saw Mr. Friedman, whom I revere as a scholar and worship as a man, he told me that he had espied yet another shortcoming in my campaign not to be elected as mayor. Like Mr. Teller, I paled. It is this, he said: your notion that drug addicts may be sequestered by the state on the grounds that "addiction is in metaphorical fact a communicable disease." "You see the trouble with that?" he said joyously, as though he were about to vouchsafe to me the emancipating formula in the search of which I had devoted my life. "No," I said ruefully. "Well," he replied—and he looked happier at that moment than Peter Pan—"suppose I said, 'We should sequester conservatives on the grounds that conservatism is a communicable disease!' " This one did not have on me quite the conclusive results that the postcard had, so I asked Mr. Friedman whether he thinks that the nonmetaphorically clinical diseases of a prostitute might legitimately be the concern of public health authorities in those communities that license prostitutes. And he said: "No. After all, there is legal recourse available to the victim against the tortfeasor: The syphilitic can sue the prostitute, can't he?" I tiptoed out of that discussion with the pure of heart, which was in any case interrupted by the arrival of the television producer, ordering us to proceed with our program to communicate our joint and several diseases to the viewing public.

But after that, I reflected, and continue to do so, on the relevance of near-absolutist libertarian theory, and my conclusion is that where it is practiced by those who do not feel the necessity to descend in ugly rages against those who demur on this or that application of the theory, it is altogether a good thing. Surely this distinguishes Leonard Read from some of his coadjutors, not to say supporters. So truly devoted is he to his beliefs that he goes so far as genuinely to tolerate even those in his own camp who disagree with him gently. Yet he has never corrupted that political and philosophical permissiveness into the ugly projection on the basis of which the epistemological relativists rule that what is true is determined by how many people decide that it is true. Mr. Read, unlike so many of us who have been so indebted to him for so many years, has always taken the high road. His invaluable friend and colleague, Dr. Edmund Opitz, once remarked in reviewing a volume by Frank Chodorov that there was not to be found in it an angry word. As much is true of Leonard Read, and yet that resolution has never made him bland or indecisive; he has always reserved for himself, also, the freedom to write as he thinks, and I understand the purpose of this evening to be to thank him precisely for that: Everyone is free to think as he likes, but to speak what one thinks is to engage such formidable realities, as, to name only one of them, the Internal Revenue Service, which, come to think of it, is younger by quite a few years than Mr. Read, and wouldn't it be absolutely splendid if *he* outlived *it?* That thought is so ennobling, so clearly educational, that I am resolved to deduct it from my taxable income.

But even if we fail to bring on the society we seek to achieve, which as Mr. Henry Hazlitt observed on *his* seventieth birthday, it seems increasingly unlikely that we shall be able to do; still, it is not cause—provided enough freedoms are left to us as, for instance, combined to bring about this single exuberant function—it is not cause for despair. We have hold of noble human intuitions, and we are resolved to serve them as we can, in our own way. We know as clearly as we know anything at all that the presumption is against the state's taking on social responsibilities. And then, apart from all of that, there is the community of us of which Leonard Read is a most venerable member. The community has gathered tonight to honor one of our own, who has greatly served us, genially and gravely. There is Larry Fertig, the organizer of this affair—what is the free-market value of his company? The sense of community means a great deal to a minority of the faithful. Because they exchange not only the tablets, but that sense of shared idealism which keeps idealism alive, which makes possible the sacrifices that are made in its behalf; which makes joyous the experience of fellowship in common purpose. Just for example, those of you who have not laughed together with Larry Fertig cannot imagine the pleasure of the experience. His kindness and thoughtfulness made this occasion possible, and his unerring sense of taste and justice made it the occasion for us all to honor the most honorable and inspiring and gentle and admirable Leonard Read.

XIII. SURCEASE

A WEEK ABOARD *CYRANO*[*]

May, 1970

Friday, December 19. We arrive at Antigua airport, and that is an achievement. J. K. Galbraith says you shouldn't use pull unless you need to. Well, I needed to get to Antigua inasmuch as I decided to go there for Christmas aboard *Cyrano*—that was two months ago —only to find all the airlines booked solid for December 19, and for a day or two bracketing that day. I tried everybody I knew—or almost everybody I knew. One terribly helpful passenger agent wondered whether I wouldn't just as soon go to Antigua on January 19. I retorted that perhaps his airline could arrange to reschedule Christmas for January 25. I then asked whether, since he could not get me directly to Antigua, he might get me there if I consented to go via, say, the Canary

---

[*] Reprinted by permission of *Rudder* magazine.

Islands. He very nearly concluded the itinerary before feeling the steel of my sarcasm, which was rather poorly tempered that day. But it does suggest an interesting form of prospective commercial exploitation, namely, bidding up a ticket to where you want to go, when the traffic is dense, by routing you via remote places and demanding the full fare. I *know* that if I had volunteered to go via Buenos Aires, Eastern Airlines would have got me to Antigua even if its president had to give me the copilot's seat.

When all else fails in life, I usually call Mrs. Julie Nicholson, who with her husband and family dominate Antigua more firmly than Horatio Nelson ever did. She is a yacht and charter broker, whose descriptions of any boat you are considering will make it sound like the boat Onassis could not afford to make available to Jackie. Her husband can get you a ticket from anywhere to anywhere, anytime. It was only ordained that we should make a stop at San Juan which is a bearable interruption. There, waiting for us, were the three Finucanes, who had come in from Los Angeles, joining three Buckleys and one Wagner, classmate of the younger Buckley, and the seven of us proceeded to Antigua. Without incident? Not quite. My son's .22 rifle caught the eye of Her Majesty's Customs. We explained that we keep the gun on board only for those occasions when it becomes necessary to talk back to sharks. Summit conference. An agent of H.M. Customs will accompany us to English Harbour, personally to deposit the rifle with the policeman there. Said policeman will turn over the rifle to us at the moment when we are actually ready to weigh anchor and head out. A satisfactory arrangement, and it is understood that I must pay the cost of the taxi to return the customs official to the airport, which is certainly reasonable: altogether a felicitous resolution of the occasional difficulty of traveling with a gun. At the dockside is our own Captain Killeen of the *Cyrano,* and a half-dozen partygoers, at the center of which is Mrs. Nicholson herself, who greets me warmly and, as I slip away in the tender, demands to know what comes after "Gaudeamus Igitur." My memory fails me, and I feel dreadful, after all the Nicholsons have done for me. However, I did not forget to bring her Barricini Chocolates and Ribbon Candy, which you must not forget to do if ever you find yourself coming from where you can get Barricini Chocolates and Ribbon Candy to Antigua at Christmastime. I have made a mental note to let Mrs. Nicholson know what comes after "Gaudeamus Igitur" as soon as I find out. Let us therefore rejoice. . . . What *would* follow naturally from that? At this point, I could only think: *Quam ad Antiguam pervenimus.*

Saturday, December 20. Cyrano is nowadays stationed in St. Thomas, and it was Ned Killeen's idea that it would make for a fun cruise if he "deadheaded" to Antigua, permitting us to cruise downwind back to St. Thomas. To deadhead, *v.i.*, means, I gather (I am afraid to ask Ned because that will once again remind him how much more he knows about sailing than I do and would make him positively unbearable)—to take a boat under power, without payload, against the wind. It took him two long nights, into midmorning, to deadhead from St. Thomas 220 miles to Antigua. Ned likes daytime landfalls. I like nighttime landfalls. Ned usually prevails. Ned always prevails when I am not aboard. Interesting thought. How much should we charge charterers to deliver them *Cyrano* in Antigua, should they so desire it? Ned suggests $200 for the two days, which is less than one half the $265 per day that we get for the use of *Cyrano*, but his point is that at $100 per day we are not actually losing money, and a little *noblesse oblige* on the high seas is always in order. I say something dour about how I wish the bankers would show a little *noblesse oblige* and acquiesce in the arrangement.

It is a beautiful morning, but I am feeling very blue. Because I learn, on arriving at dockside, that the Empress

Julie is not in her office today; that she will not be coming into the office today; and that there is no telephone in her house. How can I show her my beautiful *Cyrano*? So I walk, dejectedly, to the police department and ask for my rifle, which is handed over to me a little apprehensively so palpable is my gloom, and I return to the boat to begin the cruise.

My beautiful *Cyrano*. I have owned her for two and one-half years. I bought her through Ned Killeen, who brokered the transaction. We had become friends after he volunteered, qua broker, to skipper a weekend aboard another yacht I was interested in, which turned out to be a disaster—not only the weekend but the yacht, which under full sail in a brisk breeze could only manage about five knots.

Then he wrote me about *Pinocchio,* as she was then called. Built in Abaco, in the Bahamas, to an old fishing boat design. Sixty feet overall, 52 feet on the waterline, with an extraordinary 18 feet of bowsprit, 17 feet of beam, tapering back to about 13 feet at the transom where two stout davits hold up the tender. Acres and acres of deck space. And, below, an upright piano which the previous owner and skipper banged away at to the great delight of his passengers over the three years between the construction of the boat and my purchase of her.

What was needed, I thought on looking the boat over, was a great deal of impacted luxury plus complete equipment and instrumentation for ocean passages. The latter was obvious enough: running backstays, loran, radar, automatic pilot; that kind of thing. The former is I think less obvious. I had done a fair amount of chartering, not a great deal. But I had come to a few conclusions:

1. Sleeping quarters should be small and public quarters large. One needs only, in sleeping cabins, privacy and room to turn around in.

2. Every cabin should have a port, which should be situated at about eye level when your head is down on the

pillow. Why the hell not? I have been on boats all my life which require that in order to see through the port —presumably there for you to see through—you need to stand on tiptoe, which is hard to do while going to sleep. The naval architect gulped the presumptive gulp that all naval architects gulp when you go about tampering with their beloved Integrity of the Hull. But I had along a friend, a plastics consultant, graduate of MIT, who stared him down and calmly reminded the architect that he could put into the port a polysyllabic-ethylene-whatever, which is stronger than the original wood, etc. Anyway, I got my ports. Three of them on the starboard side, one for each of the cabins, and three of them on the port side in the saloon—all this in *addition* to the picture windows in the deckhouse.

3. Color, color, and more color. More boats are ruined by monochromatic dullness than by careless seamanship. So every room was decorated by my wife in a chintz of different color, of congruent patterns; so that we have the red cabin, the yellow cabin, and the green cabin, a green carpet, and a glazed cotton print for the settee and couches, a pattern taking off, in reds and blues, on an old Spanish sailing map.

4. Chairs, settees, and couches must be *comfortable*. I rebuilt the main settee three times, so as to make it finally slope back far enough and extend out far enough to make sitting in it truly comfortable for the slouchers of this world, who are my friends and clients. Opposite it, two club chairs, facing my three ports. Wall-to-wall carpeting, kerosene and electric torches. Then I persuaded my friend Richard Grosvenor, the excellent New England artist who teaches at St. George's School, to do three original oil paintings of boat scenes which exactly fit the principal exposed areas I had wired to receive them. So that every picture is lit as in an art gallery, the three little overhead lights providing plenty of illumination for the entire saloon, unless you want to read, at which point you snap

on one of the other lights. But the saloon now, with the oil paintings alone, lights up in color and comfort, a beautiful room of utter relaxation. When you are underway in a breeze, the seas sometimes rise up covering the ports completely, for whole seconds at a time. (Sometimes the moonlight comes in to you right through the water.) Aft of the piano is the bar and refrigerator which the former owner so thoughtfully installed to keep charterers from having to go back and back to the galley quarters which are a whole engine room away.

5. The deck area should be—well, perfect. There was no deckhouse. I had one designed and built, with two 6 1/2-foot-long cushions, usable as berths on either side. Between them, the companionway and then a well, where your feet can dangle while you navigate over an area larger than a standard card table and look into your radar, or your depth finder. Or at the compass, steering the ship electrically. That's when you want to come forward from the wheel to get out of the rain. Stepping aft, 6 or 7 feet, an enormous settee. Once again, the accent on comfort. In the Mediterranean many boats have main cockpit settees on which you can sprawl out in any direction. The trick was to accomplish this and also convert the new deckhouse into dining quarters for fair weather. Castro Convertible came to the rescue. The adaptation of his essential mechanism that permits the raising of a table. Then a custom-built tabletop which exactly fits the arc of the settee. So that when you are not eating, the table sinks down and three tailored cushions exactly cover the area, which now merges with the settee, giving you an enormous area of about 4 feet by 12 feet in which four or five people can stretch out and read, or merely meditate on the splendid achievements of the settee designer. At mealtimes, remove the three cushions, pull a lever and—hesto! a perfectly designed table rises elegantly into place, around which eight people can sit. At night, you can close off the

entire area with canvas, giving you something of the feel of a large Arabian tent.

6. The crew must have living space. Under existing arrangements it is almost never necessary to occupy the old dining quarters in the after section. There the crew has its privacy, adjacent to the captain's cabin, the main navigation table, the gallery, and the lazaret, etc.

7. Noise. Somebody, somewhere along the line, told me that the biggest most expensive generators make the least noise. I consulted Ned, who had volunteered to oversee the entire remodeling—which he was uniquely equipped to do, having at one point owned and operated a boat construction company—and he came up with an Onan so noiseless that you simply are unaware that it is turned on. It provides all the power you need, including 110-volt AC outlets. And finally,

8. Coolness. I do not care how much it costs, or how difficult it is to install. Air-condition, or die. I reason as follows: that if you live in the Caribbean the year round, perhaps you can get used to hot temperatures. But if you only *visit* the Caribbean, you plain get hot in the middle of the day—just as you can get hot in the middle of Long Island Sound. Turn on your air conditioner, and life changes for you; or it does for me, anyway. I shall never be without my air conditioner. If the bankers one day descend on me, I shall go on national teevee and deliver a Checkers speech about my air conditioner. They will never take it from me.

Now I also thought to dally with closed circuit teevee and did so. I bought one of those Sony jobs. The idea is that, at night in the islands, the children might get bored; or you might think it fun to show a movie. So why not stock an inventory of tapes of great movies pirated from the teevee channels, the commercials thoughtfully dubbed out. I do remember one night, 300 miles out toward Bermuda, lazy sailing conditions, a full moon, pleasant company, and I thought to ask my companions had they heard Horowitz's Carnegie Hall concert which had been televised that season as a CBS special. Well, no, they hadn't. Would they like to see it? The whole investment was worth that indelible memory of sipping brandy, smoking cigars, sailing at about eight knots out in the middle of the ocean, and viewing and listening to one hour of Horowitz doing Schubert, Chopin, and Liszt. There was another occasion—come to think of it—when an old friend, an official of the New York Yacht Club, arrived in full regalia late one evening in Padanaram in an advanced state of decomposition, to take (yet another) nightcap with us. He came upon us lounging around a television set. I solemnly informed him that I had requested the local television station to run the *Wizard of Oz* for us, and they had just begun. "I'll phone and tell them to start it again from the beginning for you," I said gravely. I disappeared below for a few seconds, turned a couple of knobs surreptitiously, and *Oz* quick-rewound and started again. I returned to see my friend clinging to the mast in amazement at my extraordinary powers over the local station. On the other hand, he'd have been clinging to the mast in any case.

But I gave up my Sony. It was too often not working, and the stuff and bother of getting it to New York to be fixed was too much. Also, stowage was a problem. And, somehow, charterers seldom get around to asking for a movie on board *Cyrano*. I like that. And Ned is delighted. Stringing the machine together required a certain electrical coordination which only he possessed; and that meant standing by late at night, which can be a bore. Especially if the impulse to see the *Wizard of Oz* comes to a charterer at, say, midnight.

I am staring at the chart as we cruise out of the tight little entrance to English Harbour. What do you say we go to Nevis? I suggest to Ned. Nevis is about 45 miles west, and it is already noon, what with the last-minute shopping one always has to do. The wind is as it should be, east northeast. Ned, so wise, so seasoned, suggests that perhaps we would be better off just going west along the coastline of Antigua, instead of striking out for so distant a goal so late in the day. I am glad I gave in.

Sunday, December 21. I said I was glad I gave in, and I imagine that I gave the impression that where we did spend the night, which was in Mosquito Bay in Antigua, was unique. Not really. It is a very beautiful cove (there are no mosquitoes on it, by the way), shallow, and if you want to know when the tide changes, it changes exactly when it changes in Galveston, Texas, for heaven's sake; and not even Ned knew instinctively how to figure *that* one out. I mean, if the Tide Book says: See Galveston, Texas, and you find that the tide begins to ebb at Galveston, Texas, at 1900, what time does it begin to ebb at Mosquito Bay, Antigua? You will immediately see that conflicting hypotheses are plausible. You may find yourself reasoning that when it is 7 P.M. at Galveston, the tide also begins to change at Mosquito Bay, which means you have to figure out the time zone for Galveston. Well, figure Galveston is two hours behind New York and we are one hour ahead of New York; ergo it changes at Mosquito Bay at 10 P.M. Right? Not necessarily. Maybe it means that just as when it is 7 P.M. local time at Galveston the tide changes, so when it is 7 P.M. local time at Mosquito Bay the tide changes—what's implausible about that?

The time has come to note a further complication, which is that when I sail *Cyrano* in the Caribbean, I go on what we call Buckley Watch Time, the only eponymous enterprise I have ever engaged in. What you do is tell everybody on board to move their clocks up one hour. The practical meaning of it all is that you can start the cocktail hour as the sun is setting, and eat dinner one hour later at eight o'clock, BWT. Otherwise, you start drinking at six o'clock and eat dinner at seven. The former offends the Calvinist streak in a Yankee, the latter the

Mediterranean streak in a yacht owner. Anyway, in order to avoid digging into the fine print of the Tide Book, we decide to fasten on the fact, that, after all, the tide is less than 1 foot anyway; so we throw out the hook at 150 yards from the beach rather than crawl up farther as we might have done if we had been absolutely sure that Galveston had another hour or so to go before the ebb began. No matter. The sunset was beautiful, we swam, ate—ate very well, thanks to Rawle who is a superb cook, a native of St. Vincent, and has the prestige of a real-life shipwreck under his belt. Then we played 21, and I won consistently. The tape player is the arena of a subtle contest between the generations. When one of *us* goes by it, we glide into the tape cavity something melodic. When one of the seventeen-year-olds goes by, unobstrusively he, or she, will slip in The Creams, or The Peanut Butters, or whomever. I acknowledge to myself that the war will be formally declared by about tomorrow, lunchtime. ("Will you please get those screaming banshees off the air, children?" "Mother, can we put on something that isn't Marie Antoinette?") I am right. We go to bed, and my wife and I can see, outside our port, the full moon and the speckly light it casts on the waters—our waters, because there is no one else in sight.

Monday, December 22. I must make myself plain. I am glad I took the advice that we make the shorter rather than the longer run to Nevis, because I know enough now about other people to know what suits the general taste in a cruise. I come from a rather Spartan tradition, which is not what cruising/chartering is about. I remember talking with Art Kadey, who owned *Pinocchio*, and the disbelief with which I heard him say that the typical charterer travels approximately four hours ever *other* day! I thought that (and still do) rather on the order of owning a Boeing 707 and operating it only every other day. It takes time to change your rhythm, if you have raced a boat in ocean races, getting accustomed to day-and-night running. Some come easily to the change and indeed find it easy to oscillate from furious implacable racing—day after day, week after week, in such as the Transatlantic or Transpac races—to strolling about for a few hours on the same boat you often race, going perhaps no farther than 10 or 15 or 20 miles in a single day.

I remember announcing to Ned last summer that I desired to bring *Cyrano* from New York to Bermuda to St. Thomas. He showed me an article that described the dangers of that passage in November, said article recommending instead that a boat should go warily down the coastline, in and out of the waterway to Morehead City in North Carolina, at which point you are south of the North Atlantic gale area; then shoot across the 1,200 miles or so to the Virgins. But going from Morehead City to St. Thomas simply isn't like going from Bermuda to St. Thomas; indeed, going from Morehead City to any place isn't like going from Bermuda to any place. And I had in mind bringing six classmates from Yale to share the trip with me. Ned begged me to let him and the crew take *Cyrano* on down to Miami, whence he would deadhead to St. Thomas, and let the lot of us meet him there, and simply cruise—we would have a much better time, he persisted. But I thought: How can you have a better time than to take a 1,000-mile ocean voyage in a tough comfortable schooner in absolute isolation, taking your chance with the weather and the seas? So, Ned and the crew having brought *Cyrano* down to Bermuda, the rest of us flew in and we took off at midnight—not because midnight is a melodramatic time to take off, but because the sixth friend came in from South America at eleven. The weather reports were discouraging. The strategy outlined by Ned, after accepting my resolution as an immovable object, was to head south (St. Thomas, by the way, is exactly south of Bermuda) as fast as possible for the 200 miles necessary to get into the trades and out of the formal limits of the North Atlantic gale area. However, a largish front was even then passing just north of Bermuda causing heavy seas, estimated at 12 to 16 feet, a datum that Ned gave me over the telephone with quite unseemly satisfaction, while I was still in New York, going on to suggest the advisability of postponing our departure until Thursday morning. I replied that unless there was every reason to suppose that everything would be pacific on Thursday morning, we might as well baptize the passengers into discomfort beginning at midnight, inasmuch as we had, but absolutely *had*, to get to St. Thomas by the following Wednesday at the latest. So there we were, excited, tucked away, the shifts assigned (four hours on, eight hours off), headed out of the little cut at St. Georges—through which, coming the other way, I had passed so often before, exhausted, elated, at the end of the Bermuda race—expecting the worst; and being most pleasantly surprised. Light winds from the northeast, quite moderate seas, and, darting in and out of the clouds, a moon that would be full in midpassage.

Cyrano is a shoal-draft boat, built for the Bahamas. It hasn't even a centerboard: merely a long keel stretching the entire length of the hull, 5 1/2 feet below the waterline. The result is a certain stodginess in coming about, as any boat has that isn't equipped with ballet shoes; but, with that great beam, and with whatever it is the designer did to those numinous lines, she achieves a glorious sea-kindliness that makes seagoing dry, fast, and stable. The storm front, unfortunately, kicked up most monstrous waves by the time it was several hundred miles northeast of Bermuda, and these rolled down on us the fourth and fifth days of our passage such as to give forty-eight hours of roller-coasting which severely taxed the equanimity of the passengers. As a matter of fact what I felt one night at dinnertime and after was either seasickness, which I hadn't experienced since I was twelve years old on one of the early voyages of the *Normandie* before they put the stabilizers on her; or some sort of a stomach virus. I felt dreadful, as did most of the rest of us. During the worst of it we put on a storm trysail and the forward staysail. I wanted to put up at least a part of the Genoa (we have it on a roller-reefing fitting). But the fitting on the halyard having slipped overboard while I was making an adjustment, the substitute swivel proved too weak, and the sail came tumbling down after a few hours. I went theatrically up to the masthead to bring down the halyard and put on yet another swivel, but this one, too, gave way after a half day, and now it was really too rough to go up again. The result was a heavy weather helm, which was unpleasant, and which also put too great a strain on the automatic pilot, reducing us to the humility of having to steer our own boat—imagine, with only ten people aboard. It was especially galling to lose the extra knot or two from the rudder's brake action—like driving a sports car in second gear mile after mile, day after day. We had the sun and a full moon, though, and I could bring down Polaris even at midnight, and Ned got perfect star sights, and our landfall was within a half hour of when it was anticipated. But the wind and seas were relentless, and it wasn't until we got right into the harbor at St. Thomas that we got a little relief, and my friends poured gratefully into Pan American, first class, minutes after arriving in St. Thomas, bruised and strained, my *Cyrano* rather weather-beaten. The twelve-year-old daughter of one of my friends wrote me a letter a week or so later on some vexing political question and added the P.S., "What *did* you do to my daddy?" The wife of another of my friends, who is a very nice man even though he did run for Congress against Shirley Temple, recounted a week or so later when we came upon them in California that three times, at three in the morning, her husband has suddenly risen stiff out of bed, stared straight ahead, and declared somnam-bulistically but firmly, "I have to go on deck!" whereupon he walks straight ahead into a closet, which sharply, but reassuringly, jolts him back into the knowledge that his nightmare is over. Ned would like that, and I'll tell him about it when I think of it.

It isn't easy for everybody to relax on a boat. I adore my boat: every boat I have ever had. But I feel, somehow, that I am always, in a sense, on duty; and that I must be going from here to there, and if there is a little weather or whatever, well, isn't that a part of the general idea? The point is, as Ned and others have patiently explained to me, there is the wholly other use for a boat, the use which is absolutely ideal for charterers, and that is the totally comfortable, totally unstrained cruise. So that if you decide this morning to go from Antigua to Nevis but the wind isn't right, why you simply go somewhere else, what the hell. You don't have any obligations to meet the New York Yacht Club Squadron at Nevis at 1700, and nobody will tell Dooley Roosevelt if, instead, you ease off to St. Kitts—I mean, some people come to total relaxation in boats more easily than others, and they do not feel any constraint to harness their boats to an instrumental objective, like getting from here to exactly there, and "there" had better be a good distance way from "here" in order to give you the feeling that you have accomplished a good run and earned the quiet hours of anchorage. All I say is: There are those of us who are driven, and if you are one of those, you will have to speak firmly to Ned. To say nothing of your wife.

St. Kitts is absolutely ravishing. We arrive latish and do not disembark, simply because we cannot be bothered to register the boat. Why, oh, why don't the islands issue a triptyque, or whatever the Euopeans called that document with all the coupons that they used to issue which facilitated car travel in postwar Europe? Hunting down the immigrations and customs officer, giving him (on one occasion, at Virgin Gorda, *six*) copies of the crew and passenger list. Why not a bond, that every boat owner could buy, the possession of which would grant free passage everywhere during a season, with a severe penalty if you are caught smuggling or whatever, guaranteed by the bonder? How easy everything would be if I were given plenipotentiary power over these matters.

The run to St. Bartholomew (St. Barts) is quite long—40 miles or so—and I suggest to Ned that we take off early at nine o'clock and sail under the great fort which they call the Gibraltar of the Caribbean. Surely you mean after the crew has breakfast? says Ned. What the hell, I say, why not get started under power, and *then* breakfast? We weigh anchor and proceed, and two days later I notice in the ship's log the stern entry, "Got underway before the crew had breakfast." A brilliant day, strong winds just abaft the beam, my poor son is seasick, the only time during the whole trip, but by two o'clock we have pulled in to the exemplary little harbor, so neat, so landlocked, so lackadaisical, where the rum is cheaper than the water, and the rhythm of life is such that the natives never go to work before breakfast, and not always after breakfast.

Tuesday, December 23. The proposal is to make a short run for St. Maartens, which my materialistic family favors sight unseen because the guidebook says that the prices there are even a little bit less than those at St. Barts. The sail is a mere 15 miles. We considered dropping by St. Maartens and then proceeding 4 or 5 miles west to Anguilla, perhaps to decolonize it, now that history has taught us how easy it is to do. But the iron schedule (we must relinquish the boat to charterers in four days) makes this imprudent. I feel very keenly the loss, inasmuch as during the few months of Anguilla's independence, when the rebel government took a full-page ad in the New York *Times* asking for contributions to revolutionary justice, I slipped the government a five-dollar bill in the mail and got back a hadwritten letter of profuse gratitude from the Prime Minister. Another day.

The idea is to spend a relaxed few hours at St. Maartens and then make the longish (100-mile) sail to the Virgins, touching in at Virgin Gorda. St. Maartens is half Dutch (the lower half) and half French (the other half). A very large harbor, almost the size of Provincetown, with beaches and calm and lots of picturesque boats. We swim, and water-ski, and then head out for dinner at the Little Bay Hotel, which is a Hilton type, with casino, triple-air-conditioned bar, so-so restaurant, and better than so-so prices. We did not get to gamble because the casino opened at 9 P.M. and we forgot that Buckley Watch Time wiped out the gambling hour we had counted on, so that we went back to *Cyrano* and started out.

I insisted on hoisting all sails, in anticipation of wind (it was just a whisper from the east), and by the time we had lost sight of the light off Anguilla two hours out, we pulled them down, as Ned predicted we would be doing, and settled for a long motor run in preternaturally calm seas which, I might add, the Caribbean owed us.

I took the watch until 0200, along with my sister-in-law, while my wife and her brother-in-law played gin rummy, and the boys and my niece lazed about on deck forward, discussing no doubt the depravities of their elders. I felt constrained (I am that way on a boat) to go forward every twenty minutes or so to make an aesthetic point—single out the moon, for instance, which was about as easy to miss at this point as the sun at dawn, and say casually, "Have you noticed the moon?" The Kids are so easy to ambush, because it never fails that they will look up from their conversation, stare about, focus eventually on the moon, and say, finally, "Uh."

It was a fine opportunity to write belletristically in the log. The man I admire most in the whole seafaring community is William Snaith, who lives a busy life as president of Raymond Loewy, and races his several Figaros strictly to win, which he usually does, although not often enough to satisfy his perfectionist appetites. In his enthralling book *Across the Western Ocean*, he writes, among other things, about the joys of entering the daily log. He takes a voluptuary delight from going on and on in his logbook with the most entertaining, descriptive, informative sea prose by anybody in memory, at once the businesslike Joshua Slocum explaining just how it was, and the reflective Hilaire Belloc, explaining just how it ought to be. I remember, after reading Mr. Snaith, resolving to expand on my anemic entries into the log, bearing in mind the diffuser graces of rhetoric. But I am face-to-face with the unfortunate difference between Mr. Snaith and myself, every one of them in his favor. Writing is what I go to sea to get away from. But I did *try*, and a year ago, taking *Cyrano* from Miami to New York, I got pretty talkative in the log the first two or three entries, but by the third watch I found myself writing, "Nothing new. Proceeding as above. Wind speed down, 2—5 knots." Then, remembering Snaith, I added, "Drank Coke." Six hours later, I observed that the intervening watch captain, who has sailed with me since he was twelve years old, had scrawled alongside my entry, "So why do you think we care if you drank a Coke?" He led with his chin, did my impudent colleague, because I was able to write down in headmasterish script to my beer-guzzling pal, "Go ye and do likewise." But of course that kind of thing really isn't what Mr. Snaith had in mind.

It was an uneventful overnight journey, except that at 3 A.M. I was roused from my cabin (Ned was still asleep, his watch scheduled for 4 A.M.) by my wife, who reported that my apprehensive brother-in-law desired me personally to confirm that the lights off at one o'clock were not (a) an uncharted reef; (b) an unscheduled island; or (c) a torpedo coming at us at full speed. I came on deck, peered out at the lights of what appeared to be a tanker going peacefully toward whatever it was going peacefully toward. A good chance, though, to show off my radar, which immediately picked him up at 6 1/2 miles away, heading toward, approximately, Dakar. I went back to sleep and awoke when Ned at the wheel was past the famous Anegada Passage, down which the Atlantic often sweeps bustily into the Caribbean, but which on this passage had acted like a wall-to-wall carpet; and now we were surrounded by tall, hilly islands, such that by contrast we felt almost as though we were going through a network of rivers, calm, warm, but breeze enough (finally) to sail. And we put in, at eleven, at Spanish Town, in order to regularize ourselves with the government of the British Virgins which, on Christmas Eve, was most awfully obliging, after Robert Mauer, the first mate, and I completed the six forms registering the names and affirming the nonsubversive intentions of the tired but happy crew and passengers of *Cyrano*.

Wednesday, December 24. We head now for a bay particularly favored by Ned, in Virgin Gorda. Getting there is a minor problem, requiring a certain concentration so as to avoid Colquhon Reef. In nonnavigational language, you proceed like up, over, down, back, and up so as to avoid the long reef. Look it up in any of the books or guides, and it is abundantly charted. The rewards are great because when you nestle down you see, along the reef a few hundred yards away from the anchorage, the beautiful blues and greens that you have been missing thus far, the water having been deep. It is strictly Bahamian here. They say, by the way, that the Virgins are vastly to be preferred to the Bahamas "from the water level up." This is shorthand to communicate the following: The islands are infinitely more interesting in the Antilles—the Virgins, the Windwards, and the Leewards. Every island is strikingly interesting and different, both topographically and culturally. St. Kitts, for instance, has Mount Misery, an enormous volcano rising to 4,300 feet. Nothing of the sort happens in the Bahamas, where the islands are almost uniformly low. But the Bahamian waters are uniquely splendid in coloration. The sand bars and reefs, which are so troublesome to the navigator, repay the bother to the swimmer, and to anyone who just wants to look. Anyway, Virgin Gorda is that way, and on shore is the Drake's Anchorage hostelry, which just that morning had changed hands. The previous owner of the little bar and inn has sold out to—would you believe—a professor at MIT. The bar and dining room is Somerset Maugham-tropical and was all dressed up for Christmas. The talk was of the necessity to persuade somebody to come down and take over the exciting underwater tours of the departing owner, who specializes in taking adventurous spirits for scuba diving in the Anegada Passage to poke about the wrecks at Horse Shoe Reef, not all of which by any means have reposed there since the eighteenth century. The flagpole at the hostelry is the corroded aluminum mast of the *Ondine* that foundered there just a few years ago, the navigator, or whoever, having been less lucky than we on the trip down from Bermuda.

Having reconnoitered, we went back to *Cyrano,* which at that point was almost alone in the anchorage, only just in time to see a smallish sloop come gliding toward us, brazenly avoiding the circumnavigatory imperatives of the guidebooks, treating the reef we had given such studied berth to as familiarly as if it were the skipper's bathroom. We watched in awe as a dignified lady with sunbonnet directed the tiller to conform with the directions given by the angular, robust old gentleman up forward handling the anchor. The landing was perfect, the motor never having been summoned to duty, and they edged down, 50 yards away from us. I discreetly manned the binoculars, peeked for a while, and said to my companions, "By God, I do believe that is Dr. Benjamin Spock."

I know the gentleman slightly, having sparred with him here and there in the ideological wars. I wondered what, under the circumstances, would be an appropriate way to greet him. I thought of sending Ned over to his sloop, instructed to say, "Dr. Spock, compliments of *Cyrano,* do

you happen to have anything aboard for bubonic plague?"
But the spirit of the season overcame me, and instead I
wrote out an invitation: "Compliments of the military-
industrial complex, Mr. and Mrs. William F. Buckley, Jr.,
would be honored to have the company of Dr. and Mrs.
Benjamin Spock and their friends for Christmas cheer at 6
P.M." The good doctor rowed over (I knew, I *knew* he
wouldn't use an outboard) to say thanks, how was I, Mrs.
Spock wasn't feeling very well, please forgive them, they
were pulling out anyway within the hour, come back soon,
once you've sailed the Virgins you can never sail
anywhere else, and rowed back. We struck out in the
glasshopper (all-glass dinghy) with the kids to explore the
reef, which they did for hours on end. I returned to
Cyrano (I enjoy skin diving, but a half hour of it is fine by
me), mounted the easel and acrylic paint set my sister-in-
law bought me for Christmas, and set about industriously
to document, yet again, my extraordinary lack of
talent—you would have to see it not to believe it; which,
come to think of it, makes my stuff pretty valuable. The
girls were working on the decorations, and by the time the
sun went down we had a twinkling Christmas tree on deck
and twinkling lights along the canvas of the dodger, and
the whole forward section was piled with Christmas gifts
and decorations; and when we sat down for dinner, with
three kerosene lights along my supper table, the moon's
beam, lambent, aimed at us as though we were the single
target of the heavens, Christmas music coming in from the
tape player, the wine and the champagne and the flambéed
pudding successfully passed around, my family there and
friends, I persuaded myself that nowhere, on that evening,
at that time of day, could anyone have asked for any
kinder circumstances for celebrating the anniversary of the
coming of the Lord.

Thursday, December 25. Intending to go to a church
service on Christmas Day at Road Town, the capital of
the British Virgins, we pull out earlyish, on the

assumption that there is a mass at noon. We arrive at
11:45 and come in, European-style, at the yacht basin.
European-style, by the way, involves dropping an anchor,
sometimes two, about thirty yards ahead of where you
intend finally to position your boat. Then you back up
toward the pier (usually stone or concrete) while someone
up forward, the anchor having kedged, is poised to arrest
your backward movement the moment you give the signal.
You back up the boat to about 10 feet from the landing.
At the right moment (Ned always knows just the right
moment) you toss out the port stern line diagonally, and
the starboard stern line ditto. Obliging passers-by secure
these lines on the pier, and you have—you can readily
see—a very neat situation. The stern lines are acting as, in
a way, spring lines, restricting the boat's sideward
movement, sideward being where other boats are lined up,
leaving, very often, no more than a foot or two of sea
room. Then, when you are safely harnessed, you motion
to the gentleman on the foredeck to ease the line to the
anchor, while the two gentlemen aft take up on their lines,
bringing the stern of *Cyrano* gently aft until the davits are
hanging quietly over the pier. You have now only to take
a step over the taffrail, touch down easily on the ground
and, without equilibratory gyration (something you
should practice), stroll on toward the nearest *tavèrna*. I
don't know why the custom isn't more widespread in
American harbors, the economy of space and motion being
so very obviously advantageous. Of course, you need to
have a sheer situation off the pier, which isn't always the
case, for instance, in many New England snuggeries. But
even when there is water, the habit is not practiced by
American yachtsmen. So much is it the drill in, for
instance, Greece that pleasure craft of any size carry
gangways that extend from the transom to the pier,
including stanchions and lifelines to serve as banisters for
milady to hang on to as she descends daintily to earth. I
remembered a year ago in the Aegean seeing a hedonistic

triumph called the *Blue Leopard*, an enormous yawl which, miraculously, ejected its gangway, it would appear electrically, from just beneath the deck level, where it is stowed—like a convair. Right down to the pier? No, dear. To six inches above the pier, contact with which it was protected from by two special halyards which quickly materialized and were quickly attached to the far corners. The purpose? Why, to spare the *Blue Leopard* the fetid possibility that a restive rat might amble up the companionway, it being a known fact that healthy rats crowd aboard a floating ship.

We linger only an hour or so. The gentleman who owns the bar, the Sir Francis Drake Pub, is moved by the spirit of the season and does not charge you, Merry Christmas, for your first drink, and we feel rather sneaky ordering only a single round, and then returning to *Cyrano* for lunch. Christmas lunch. Rawle, as I have said, is a splendid cook and would give us anything we asked for, beginning with lobster Newburg and ending with baked Alaska. We settle on a fish chowder, of which surely he is the supreme practitioner, and cheese and bacon sandwiches, grilled, with a most prickly Riesling picked up at St. Barts for peanuts or, more accurately, cashews. Then we wander off to the Fort Burt Gotel, which is built around the top of the old fort, providing a 300-degree view of the harbor and adjacent islands. There is another hotel there, dubbed the Judgment Day Hotel, which has not been completed, even though it has been abuilding lo these many years, and is therefore the butt of many local jokes, classic among them that it will finally open only on Judgment Day. The attitude toward progress in the Antilles is ambivalent. On the one hand, the natives recognize that "progress" is both ineluctable and commercially desirable. On the other hand the agents of progress are the presumptive disrupters of the natural order, and when bad fortune befalls them, as with the builder of the phantom hotel, they take pleasure in their fugitive alliance with adversity.

Off we go, to swim, and spend the night off Norman Island, which is reputedly the island that Robert Louis Stevenson described when he wrote *Treasure Island*. It is, needless to say, just like any other island (except that it lies adjacent to fascinating grottoes, complete with bats, into which you row, Disneylandlike). On the other hand, needless to say, like the other islands it, too, is captivating: a beach, a fine protected cove. I remembered when a few years ago my son, age fourteen, having done well at school, I took him with me cross country to San Francisco, where I was bound to record some television programs. My son is the prodigy of the McLuhanite dogma, but I was determined not to raise my voice in criticism. But finally, after four hours of flight during which, earphones glued on, Christopher stared at the ceiling while his overworked father fussed fetishistically with all his briefcases and papers, I lost control, turned to him, and said acidly, "Christopher, just out of curiosity, have you *ever* read a book?" He moved his right hand slowly, with that marvelous impudence the rhythm of which comes so naturally to the goddamn Kids, dislodging his right earphone just enough to permit him to speak undistracted, not so much as to cause him to lose the musical narrative of whatever rock-rolling fustian he was listening to, and replied, "Yeah. *Treasure Island*." Back went the earphone. The eyes did not need to revert to the ceiling of the plane. They had never left it.

It was our final night aboard *Cyrano,* and we felt, although we did not sentimentalize over it, the little pang one feels on approaching the end. The night was fine, calm, and peaceful. The moon made its appearance, although later, begrudgingly it seemed. I think that we all lingered, more than usual, before going below.

Friday, December 26. We stopped at Trunk Bay, St.

John, to skin-dive. St. John is the island most of which was given by the U.S. government to the Rockefellers, or vice versa, I forget which. In any case, you must drop your anchor well out in the cove, because the lifeguards do not permit you to come too close. In fact, when you come in to the beach with your dinghy you must, if you have an outboard motor, anchor it 50 yards from the beach, and off to the right, away from the swimmers. If you don't have an outboard, you may beach your dinghy. But if you do beach your dinghy, you may not attach its painter to the palm tree up from the beach, because you will be told that people might stumble over it, which indeed people might do, if they are stone-blind. Then you walk to the east side of the beach, put on your face mask and fins, and follow the buoys, ducking down to read underwater quite marvelously readable descriptions of flora, fauna, and fish, the reading matter engraved on stone tablets which tilt up at a convenient angle and describe the surrounding situation and the fishes you are likely to come across. The tablets I saw did not describe the barracuda which took a fancy to me, whose visage was fascinatingly undistinguishable from David Susskind's, but then my eye mask was imperfectly fitted. We got back to *Cyrano* and sailed on down past the Rockefeller Hotel at Caneel Bay, to Cruz Bay, where we officially reentered the United States of America. Embarrassing point. My wife thought, it being the day after Christmas and all, that it would be pleasant if I took to the lady who transacts these official matters a bottle of cheer. I went to her with Ned and found her wonderfully efficient and helpful. She completed the forms and then, rather like David Copperfield making time with the Beadle, I surfaced a bottle of Ron Ponche and, with a flourish or two, presented it to her. She smiled benignly and then explained that she could not, under The Rules, accept such gifts. I am crestfallen, embarrassed, shaken, and return feistily to my wife to say, "See, that's what you get trying to bribe American authorities," to which she replied, "Trying to bribe them to do what?" Which stumped me, and I took a swig of the rejected Ron Ponche, which tasted like Kaopectate, perhaps explaining the lady's rectitude.

We travel under power to St. Thomas, a mere couple of hours. Yacht Haven at St. Thomas might as well be Yacht Haven at Stamford, Connecticut, where *Cyrano* used to summer. Hundreds of boats, harried administrators, obliging officials, giving and taking messages, paging everybody over the loudspeaker, connecting pallid Northeasterners, with all their snowflaked baggage, with wizened boat captains. Only the bar, which opens at 8 A.M., made it obviously other than Yacht Haven, Stamford, and, of course, the weather. About 82 degrees, and sun, sun, sun: We had not been without it, except for an hour or two on either side of a squall, during the entire idyllic week. A charter was coming aboard the next afternoon, so the preparations were feverish. The adults obliged by taking a couple of rooms at the Yacht Haven Hotel. The boys stayed on board to help. We had yet to do a dinner cruise around the harbor, and our guests were my lawyer in New York, Mr. Charles Rembar, his wife, and son. They arrived (an hour late—a serious matter inasmuch as they had not been indoctrinated in Buckley Watch Time), and we slid out in the darkness (the moon would be very, very late) and cruised about, under power this time, bouncing off the lights of the five great cruise ships that lined the harbor and its entrance. St. Thomas is not unlike Hong Kong at night, except, of course, that it is less steep. But the lights are overwhelming, and the spirit of Christmas was everywhere, so that we cruised gently in the galaxy, putting down, finally, the anchor; had our dinner, pulled back into the slip, said our good-byes, and left my beautiful *Cyrano,* so firm and reliable, so strong and self-assured, so resourceful and copious, and made our way back, in stages, to New York, where for some reason—obscure after the passage of time—our ancestors left their boats, in order to settle down there, so that their children's children might dream, as I do, of reboarding a sailing boat, and cruising the voluptuous waters that Columbus hit upon in his crazy voyage, 500 years ago, because he did not have Ned aboard to tell him when enough was enough.

INDEX

498

503

504